365 DAYS

OF

CHARGING

UP

(A Devotional on Personal Revival)

TOYIN TAIWO

Revive Restore and Rebuild

Unless otherwise stated, all scripture quotation is from the New King James Version of the Bible

Although every precaution has been taken to verify the accuracy of the information contained herein, the author and publisher assume no responsibility for any errors or omissions. No liability is assumed for damages that may result from the use of information contained within.

Book may be purchased by contacting the Author and Publisher at:

publisher@exousiacreations.co.uk

Cover Design, Interior Design & Publishing Consultant: Hadar Creations

Publisher: Exousia Creations

ISBN: 978-1-7399917-2-2

DEDICATION

I dedicate this book to my Saviour, Redeemer, Author and the Finisher of my faith. He is the Bishop of my soul, Helper and the Lifter up of my head. My Love and my Life, who loves me enough to die for me, and has graciously called and anointed me despite who I am.

Your Majesty, I can only bow – I live to serve You

ACKNOWLEDGEMENT

I want to thank the Almighty God who saved me by His power and has sustained me till today. I thank God for making my life an epitome of grace; nothing deserved, nothing earned, nothing qualified for, yet he works daily in my life.

I thank God for the people He puts in my life over the last four (4) decades of my journey in the Lord

I want to thank my mentors:

- Pastor Sonny Wogu who has appeared at every important junction in my Christian walk and ministry
- Pastor Musa Bako, my father and guide in my UK ministry journey
- Pastor Funke Adeaga - my mentor in every aspect of ministry and family life.
- Rick Lewis whom the Lord has used to discover and activate the gifts and inner treasures deposited in me; and has been a great support system to me and the church I was graced to oversee
- Reverend Faith Okhuoya - God has used her as a pillar of intercessory prayer support for me and my ministry.
- Pastors Bioye and Biodun Segun for Your inspiring leadership in our RCCG Region

Also, I want to appreciate these amazing people in my life for the covenant relationship we share:

Pastors Mathias and Hilda Akhideno for Your belief in me and covenant partnership and friendship in the last 2 decades.

Pastor Bayo Olabisi for believing in me and graciously serving together with me both in Bible College and partnering with me on the Encounter Prayerline leadership team

Thank You, Vesta Thompson - my beloved friend and sister and cheerleader. I appreciate Your love, friendship, and prayer support for the past 10 years

I'm also grateful to the leaders and members of Grace Chapel (RCCG) Chesterfield. I am proud to be one of You and being Your Pastor has been inspiring and blissful –You are the best

Leaders and members of the Encounter Prayerline who took the journey of 365 Days Charging up with me – Your labour of love in these past years is highly appreciated

Shout out to my sisters and co-workers in the vineyard – Ebun Adenuga, Rosemary Mohammed, and Patrick and Dorothy Steve for recording, scribing, and transcribing the Charging Up sessions

A big thank You to my children and cheerleaders – we did it! Special thanks to my amiable and supportive husband, I enjoy the grace of doing life with You and I love You.

Toyin Taiwo

December 2021

FOREWORD

Over the last two years thereabout, a group of church leaders in Chesterfield have been meeting to pray. It's become something of a safe place where we can share the ups and downs of life and ministry together.

Sometimes there's only been a few of us present. Occasionally there have been periods where I haven't been able to make it due to the pressures and demands of my working life. Through it all however there has been one constant presence. The person who drew us all together and inspired us to pray.

That person is Pastor Toyin.

So when I say to you, "Pastor Toyin is person of prayer", please know that this isn't rhetoric because I was asked to write a forward.

I really mean it.

In fact, when my friend Toyin prays, I can tell she has sat in the presence of God for many hours. I feel the power of her Prayers and sense the deep closeness of her relationship with Jesus. I often feel moved, encouraged and blessed when we pray together.

This book will not only draw you closer to God I believe there is an anointing on the words that will stir you up and draw you closer to God. I say that because I know that these Prayers and thoughts have been shaped and fashioned in the presence of the Holy Spirit by a leader who truly lives what she preaches.

It's an honour and a privilege to commend this book to you all.

I pray you will feel as inspired and encouraged as I have been.

Carl Beech

CEO Edge Ministries & President of Christian Vision for Men (CVM).

carl.beech@edgeministries.net

ENDORSEMENTS

What do you do when you realise your spiritual batteries have run flat? It's a mistake to simply try harder, as if by our own power we can lift ourselves back to a place of spiritual vitality. The only remedy is to 'plug in' to God, our power source, through prayer. When we're at a place of low faith energy we need help to do that, and Pastor Toyin Taiwo has produced a wonderful resource that provides just the kind of support required. As you read and apply 365 Days of Charging Up you will be led through a carefully designed set of prayer practices that are rooted in Scripture. You can engage at a level you can manage. If you don't know what to pray, don't worry! Pastor Toyin has detailed points for prayer and extra scripture passages to use once you feel able to go further. Day by day, the themes for prayer open up pathways to receive God's power, charging us up and making us ready for a life of vibrant faith and effective service in God's kingdom.

Rev Dr Rick Lewis
Mentor, consultant and author of 'Mentoring Matters'

If you want an inspirational daily read, look no further than Pastor Toyin Taiwo's "365 days of Charging Up". A daily Prayer devotional from a leader with a rock-solid commitment to pastoral care

Bishop Mike Royal (Incoming General Secretary of Churches Together in England CTE)

Pastor Toyin has gifted God's people with a Biblical, practical, and powerful tool. I'm sure this will be an instrument for spiritual renewal to all who use it prayerfully. Read this book each day and get ready to be recharged!

Revive Restore and Rebuild

Simon Robinson, Lead Minister of Watnall Road Baptist Church, Nottingham and author

We are admonished by Paul the apostle in Ephesians 6:18 to Pray always with all prayer and supplication in the Spirit. Praying is an important and necessary aspect of the believer's walk with God. God gave us the gift of prayer so we can develop intimacy with Him and through the power of prayer we will be able to change things in our lives and impact the world around us. Praying is an important and necessary aspect of the believer's walk with GOD.

Praying shows that the believer recognises that he is helpless on his own and needs the help of God in life (John 15). The apostle Paul did not only admonish the believer to pray always but to pray always with all kinds of prayer (Ephesians 6:18). This is what makes '365 Days of Charging Up' a very powerful prayer book. This indeed is a fantastic piece of work by Toyin Taiwo. I pray every user will find it impactful and life transforming.

Prayer brings the believer closer to God. Prayer is a tool of spiritual warfare. I pray '365 Days of Charging Up' will help the user to develop deeper intimacy with God and enjoy many victories. Toyin Taiwo has carefully and intentionally put together a prayer guide to help the user pray in a personal and specific aspect of life, dealing with the everyday life challenges, helping the user to also pray in the different aspect of prayer effectively as in Ephesians 6:18.

I have known and worked very closely with Toyin Taiwo for many years; she is a praying woman, humble, passionate, effective and impactful Christian worker. '365 Days of Charging Up' is obviously born out of her personal experience of her prayer life and work with God. I unreservedly endorse this beautiful prayer book and recommend that you don't just read it through as a novel, and don't hang it on your bookshelf instead, use it as a prayer tool, it will help in transforming your prayer life, your relationship with the Lord and will bring you many victories.

Pastor Musa Bako
Senior pastor @RCCG Victory Assembly Sheffield
Assistant regional pastor @ RCCG UK

TESTIMONIES

Testimony 1

I am a preacher of the gospel whose prayer life and spirituality have been on the low for a few years. I was just going with the motion and still doing ministry though struggling.

I was in a desert place and had been there for a long time. I had seasons of spiritual highs that didn't last. I prayed in public but not in my closet. I faked it but I was desperate

I joined the Encounter Prayerline pioneered and run by Pastor Toyin the very month the 365 Days Charging up Challenge started. I wanted to go back to my first love and where I first met him which was a prayer I often prayed. I missed the intimacy with God and the fire I carried.

At charging up daily, I learnt to worship God in words more than in singing. I learnt to listen to the voice of God in the place of worship and prayer instead of just talking at God.

I began to understand how God speaks to me and interpret what he is saying.

One morning during charging up it felt like something broke in the spirit and that a cloud that was over me lifted and the Pastor began to say that "someone's tongue is being loosed to be the prayer warrior that you are"

From that moment till today, I can't pray enough. The heaven opened and my tongue was loosed.

Also, the word of Knowledge came that God was distributing gifts of the Spirit. That day I received the gift of word of knowledge and have since been operating in this gift and daily gaining understanding of how it operates with me.

I began to get from the word understandings and insight that I never got before even as a preacher.

My ministry has changed my prayer life changed, I am growing in leaps and bounds and it is obvious to all around me. Glory to God Almighty for His love for me and the work of the Holy Spirit in my life

Not only was I touched spiritually, many times there were word of knowledge about healing an many times diabetes was mentioned but it never occurred to me that it would be me until I went for my diabetic check and the nurse was so shocked that she asked me for what I did.

I becomes sensitised to it and started measuring at home and it has stayed normal even though I have gone back to eating the carbohydrates I was not eating before. I give praise to the name of the Lord our God for both spiritual and bodily healing.

Thank you God for the 365 Days of Charging up. I recommend this programme / book to anyone who is really serious about their walk with God and wants to stay connected to Him.

Take up the challenge and You will never regret it.

Grace T

Derby, UK

Revive Restore and Rebuild

Testimony 2

Thank God for the 365 Days of Charging up Programme. I joined Three months after it started

On Sunday 23rd May, Pastor Toyin said one morning that the Spirit of God had come that morning, with gifts, and her prophetic prayer was for us to receive the spiritual gifts we needed to fulfil purpose on earth and to fulfil our ministries, I remembered saying I receive, and I also typed a big Amen on the chatroom.

Since then, I have been experiencing the gift of word of Knowledge

One morning a word of knowledge came on forgiveness and to release those that have offended us. God shamed the devil whose plans was revealed through the word of knowledge given to God's glory the relationships are mended and closer knitted.

Praise the lord, I want to thank God for the FULLNESS OF HIS JOY & STRENGTH, He has continuously filled me with since His visitation during the Tuesday 20 July Charging Up, according to the prophesy that came.

Thursday 27May2021 to the glory of God, we had the presence of God Almighty in the platform during Charging Up, and He completely removed every suppression, oppression, and possession of the enemy off my dreams and life, granting me a full physical manifestation of His presence.

Our God who knows the end from the beginning and our need before we even realize a need for it, has gone ahead to bless my heart and life with this challenge

Now that it is been written in a book, I recommend it to every Christian.

Rosemary M
Ontario, Canada

Testimony 3

*Without a doubt my life has been tremendously enriched both physically and spiritually. I joined **Charging Up** 2 months after it started*

*From the Spiritual angle, aside my first year of conversion in 1990, I cannot remember a time I have read my bible so much! The increase in hunger for the word has been tremendous. I often read the bible while praying in tongues during **Charging Up***

An amazing thing I have discovered is how God allows my mind to engage with the word while at the same time my spirit prays in tongues. During these times I write a lot and the Lord gives me messages

The Charging Up Prayer Session passes so quickly I eventually understand how it is possible to be caught up in prayer for hours. I often easily read and pray for an additional hour after it ends at 7am. Generally, I have grown in desire, content, and length of prayer over the seven months of these sessions than at any other time in my Christian life

*I have also been promoted at work since coming on **Charging Up**. The miracle of this promotion was the one I wasn't even expecting. I had told myself I wasn't going to take on further responsibilities because I didn't want any more stress at work.*

But a job came up which I half-heartedly expressed an interest in. I applied and they wrote back to me that I had not met the criteria

*Few weeks later, declarations were made on **Charging Up** on 25 July 2021. God said his children would enter a season of prosperity. They would build houses and inhabit them. Three Days Prayers were made from Jeremiah 32:27 "I am* *the Lord, the God of all mankind, is anything too hard for me to do"*

We prayed against failure, barrenness, and lack of progress. On 9th August 2021, I received an offer for a Higher Executive Officer job, the same job I had been told I had not met the criteria! It has been a stress-free job working from home and likely to continue that way

I believe many things have "shifted" in the spiritual realm because of praying daily on **Charging Up**. There is a longing for the altar of prayer, power for holiness and exploring new frontiers of spirituality. I feel God's presence. It is a blessing.

M. Kay

Sheffield. UK

Testimony 4

The Charging Up experience has been a life-changing journey for me and my family. It has piqued my interest in God's manifold presence, leading in continual Koinonia with Him.

My Spirit-man has been rejuvenated, powered up, and revived as a result of my participation in this session.

Charging Up puts me in the right side of the day, like a two-edged sword, drawing God's daily benefits towards me and at the same time shielding me from the fiery dart of the enemy! Amen!

Charging up feels the same for our family's overall spiritual well-being, and it acts as a defence weaponry/ survival tactics against the ills of the day for us since it happens in the morning

Now, even when we are unable to make the meeting, there is this yearning to continually self-recharge!

This is the way to go for such times as we are, where the enemy plagues the world with depression, metal health and other psychometric disorder because it (the devil) knows that once the human mind is captured, victory is compromised! God forbid!

Indeed, as a man thinks in his heart, so is he!

Charging Up *-- tested & proven.... Highly Recommended!*

Patrick S

Abu Dhabi. UAE

PREFACE

The one challenge that the body of Christ face today is lukewarmness, lethargy, worldliness, compromise, backsliding and more

There is so much lawlessness in the world and Christians are fainting and losing heart. Our only adversary throws against us all manner of temptations, attacks, seductions, afflictions to bring discouragement, disappointments, guilt, pain and suffering in order to weaken our fellowship with God

Matthew 24:12(NKJV) says, "And because lawlessness will abound, the love of many will grow cold". We are seeing this scripture being fulfilled in our very eyes

Evil abounds in the world and a lot of Christians are getting weary and some are struggling to sustain a consistent prayer life and intimacy with God

Many have gone into spiritual slumber and have become preys to the enemy

We need personal and individual revivals!

In October 2020, the Lord drew my attention to this reawakening and instructed us to embark on a 365 day of speaking in tongues and listening to him. We ministered to the Lord daily and He built us up spiritually and dealt with other aspects of our lives as well

In the last 365 days, we have experienced the power of God in diverse ways. We have received more freedom in our souls, heaven has been opened, and there has been consistent divine visitation, baptism by the Holy Spirit and distribution of diverse gifts of the Spirit. Many have grown in leaps and bounds and "all other things have been added" *(Matthew 6:33b)* unto the lives of the partakers in this experience as you will read in the recorded testimonies at the end of this book.

Jude 1:20 **(NKJV)** says *But You, beloved, building Yourselves up on Your most holy faith, praying in the Holy Spirit*

As you speak in tongues and pray the word of God daily, power will be released upon you which would open channels of interaction between You and God. And as sweet fellowship with God evolves, growth will be kick-started and you will be built up daily.

Every battery needs charging or else it goes flat. This is the same with our spiritual lives. We need consistent charging up so that we are not deflated spiritually and only go through the motions.

This book is a manual and guide which will kick-start you on a journey of revival, renewal, and recharging

I pray that "Charging Up" will become a perpetual habit that will take you to greater depths in your relationship with Your Saviour and Redeemer

This book is a foretaste of the experience of the 365 days of "Charging up" in God's presence. I commend you to God and to the word of His grace, which is able to build you up. Amen.

HOW TO USE THIS BOOK FOR PERSONAL REVIVAL AND DEVOTION

- Speak in tongues for 30 minutes

- Listen to what God is saying to you.

- Read out scripture in the manual

- Pray the Prayers in the manual

- Read and Pray with other scripture in the manual and as led by the Spirit of God

- Study the scriptural bases for Prayers and meditate on them as You go about Your day

JAN 1

BOW WITH THANKSGIVING

Worship

Today's Scripture and Meditation

Psalm 95:1-3 *"Come, let us sing for joy to the Lord; let us shout aloud to the Rock of our salvation. Let us come before him with thanksgiving and extol him with music and song. For the Lord is the great God, the great King above all gods."*

PRAYERS:

- Thank You for Your compassion and Your unfailing love in the morning and Your faithfulness in the evening.
- Thank You for the privilege of a new beginning. Thank You for all You have done in my life including those I do not know about. I praise You for Your faithfulness and covenant loyalty to me. I praise You Jesus
- As I enter this new year, I come with thanksgiving in my heart glorifying Your name
- I give thanks for life, the freedom to enjoy it all, and all other blessings that pertain to life
- You are the Almighty God and there is none like You. Your glory fills the heavens! I will praise Your Name forever, for You have all wisdom and power.
- You are the self-existing God, the creator of all things. You are our help and our shield. Our hearts rejoice in You, for we trust in Your holy Name.
- The All-knowing God; all power belongs to You, to give wisdom to the wise, to give knowledge to those who have understanding.

- You are the only God, and You have no equal! If we were to recite all Your wonderful deeds, we would never come to an end
- I give thanks to You, LORD, with all my heart; I will tell of all Your wonderful deeds.
- Thank You for Your goodness and Your covenant loyalty over the years.
- Thank You for the privilege to be alive to see and partake in a new beginning.
- Thank You for all You have done in my life and for every good and perfect gift that You have given to me.
- I thank You Lord for You alone can do great wonders, You who made the heavens by understanding. You are the great God above other gods.
- I will praise You, O Lord, with my whole heart; I will tell of all Your marvellous works.
- I will be glad and rejoice in You; I will sing praise to Your name, O Most High. Amen! Praise, glory, wisdom and thanks and honour and power and strength be to our God for ever and ever. Amen!

Scriptures for further Prayers:

1 Chronicles 16:34, Psalm 103:1-2, Revelation 4:10-11.

JAN 2

THANKSGIVING FOR HIS WONDROUS WORKS

Worship

Today's Scripture and Meditation

Ps 75:1 *"We give thanks to You, O God, we give thanks! For Your wondrous works declare that Your name is near"*

PRAYERS:

- Heavenly Father, You are worthy of praise and thanks
- All Creation, the sun, the moon, the stars, every creature, every plant, every rock and grain of sand, the trees, proclaims the glory of its Creator, You are the God of wonders beyond the galaxies.
- You alone are genuinely great.
- By Your word the heavens were created; and all the host of them by the breath of Your mouth. Let all the earth fear the LORD: let all the inhabitants of the world stand in awe of the Almighty God. For You spoke, and it was done; You commanded, and it stood fast.
- I bless You Lord, whose dominion is an everlasting dominion, and whose kingdom is from generation to generation: You do according to Your will, and none can stay Your hand or question You because You are the creator and Owner of the Universe
- You made the earth by Your power, and established the world by Your wisdom, You have stretched out the heavens by Your discretion.

- I bless the Lord who being the brightness of God's glory, and the express image of His person, and upholding all things by the word of His power.
- I remember all the wondrous works that You have done; Your miracles, Your wonders and the judgements You have uttered.
- LORD You are good to all; and Your tender mercies are over all Your works. The eyes of all wait upon You, and You give them their meat in due season. You open Your hand and satisfy the desire of every living thing.
- Thank You for all Your wondrous works in my life. You are the Lord of the Heavens and the earth.
- Your majestic name fills the earth! Your glory is higher than the heavens! I will praise Your Name forever and ever.
- Thank You for Your amazing power and work in my life and for Your goodness and blessings over me.
- Thank You for life and breath within me and around me.
- Thank You for Your sustenance and Your light that surrounds me in times of storm.
- Let my life make evident the fragrance of the knowledge of God everywhere.
- I will proclaim Your wonders tirelessly, for You alone deserve the glory and honour.
- I love and need You, this day and every day.
- I give You praise and give You grateful thanks, for You alone are worthy! In Jesus' Name, I pray. Amen.

Scriptures for further Prayers

Ps 33:6; 8-9, Jeremiah 10:12, Hebrews 1:3

JAN 3

THANKSGIVING FOR HIS MERCY

Worship

Today's Scripture and Meditation

Psalm 118:29 *"Oh, give thanks to the Lord, for He is good! For His mercy endures forever."*

PRAYERS:

- Father, thank You for Your mercy that endures forever.
- It is of the Lord's mercies that we are not consumed, because his compassions fail not. They are new every morning: great is Your faithfulness.
- Thank You for being the God of our defence and the God of our mercy.
- You are long suffering and abundant in mercy. Lord God of heaven, O great and awesome God, You who keep Your covenant and mercy with those who love You and observe Your commandment.
- Father, thank You for Your sufficient grace and mercy over my life.
- Father, thank You for not withholding Your mercy over us because Your mercy endures forever.
- Father, thank You for not retaining my faults by Your mercy.
- Father, Thank You for showing me mercy and for giving me grace to help me in my time of need.
- I thank You for Jesus for being at my side, knowing my heart desires, my struggles, and pain. Thank You for

Your sustaining presence in my life. I acknowledge You as a merciful and gracious Lord, who is slow to anger and abounding in mercy.

- Thank You for Your blessings and gift of grace that covers all of my faults. I give thanks and praise to You Lord, for You are a great God and the Rock of our salvation

- I praise and bless You for all Your goodness and mercies over my life and family.

- O Lord, You are a God full of compassion, and gracious, longsuffering and abundant in mercy and truth, when and if my foot slips, Your mercy, O Lord, will hold me up.

- Father, thank You that You have never left me nor forsaken me, You fight my battles and have not given me as prey to the teeth of the enemy.

- Thank You for not allowing the rod of the wicked to fall on me. You restrained me for being a victim of the works of darkness.

- Thank You for frustrating all the plans of our adversaries. I'm grateful that You shield me, gives me victories and increase me on every side.

- Thank You for all the journey mercies and sustaining mercy that You have always granted us.

- Thank You for all the spiritual and physical enrichment in my life and for divine providence.

- Thank You for Your countless blessings and the challenges that draw me near to You.

- Thank You for not taking away Your mercy from me. Your great love that never fails in my life. You are a merciful God. Thank You, Lord, in Jesus name. Amen

Scriptures for further Prayers:

Lamentations. 3:22, Psalm. 59:17, Psalm 124:2-3 & 6

JAN 4

MERCY AND FORGIVENESS

Worship

Today's Scripture and Meditation

I John 1:8-10 *"If we say that we have no sin, we deceive ourselves, and the truth is not in us. If we confess our sins, He is faithful and just to forgive us our sins and to cleanse us from all unrighteousness. If we say that we have not sinned, we make Him a liar, and His word is not in us."*

PRAYERS:

- Father I thank You because You are full of mercy
- There is nothing I can do to deserve this mercy, but You are ever merciful and have given Your only begotten Son so that I need not perish in my sins
- Thank You for the blood of Jesus that is available to wash us whiter than snow, from all our sins
- I pray Lord, that You blot out my transgressions and forgive my sins, wash and purify me thoroughly and cleanse me from all sins
- Heavenly Father, have mercy on me. Grant me favour according to Your grace and truth. If You Lord should mark iniquities, who can stand? It is Your righteousness that makes me righteous and Your goodness is what declares me good
- Thank You for the atonement we receive through Christ. I am confident it is sufficient to cleanse me from my sin
- I confess all my sins before You... *(confess Your sins)* and repent of them

- Have mercy on me in any way I have failed to show compassion on the wounded and mercy to those around me
- Father, have mercy on me for my prayerlessness; lack of personal fellowship and devotion to You
- Father, have mercy on me for every sin committed with my tongue. You said in Your Word that, "a man that does not offend in word is a perfect man" – Father, I receive Your mercy for those times I have offended in words, deeds and speech
- Father, have mercy upon me for any time I have dwelled in criticism, murmuring, grumbling, unbelief, double-mindedness and doubting Your word
- Father, have mercy upon me for acts of unfaithfulness in the giving of my offerings, tithe, first fruits and vows. Or also in the payment of taxes and other lawful national obligations
- Father, have mercy upon me for acts of disobedience to Your word, my leaders, those in authority over me, traffic regulations on the highways and other governmental rules and regulations
- Father, have mercy upon me for acts of dishonesty in keeping to my words and lack of personal integrity
- Father, have mercy on me for the sins of hatred, jealousy, unforgiveness, vengeful acts. backbiting, backstabbing, discrimination in the Church, workplace and communities
- Father, have mercy upon me for carelessness, lackadaisical attitude, laziness, nonchalant attitude to Your word, the brethren and Your righteous causes
- Father, have mercy upon me for the sins of ingratitude; lack of appreciation for the free gifts of nature, and for not sharing testimonies
- Father, give me a heart of flesh to obey You in all things and to keep short accounts with You
- Your mercy is the rain on the desert of my soul, look upon me with mercy as You normally do to those who love Your name

- Father blot our every guilt in my mind and deliver me from timidity in coming before You and restore my joy again.
- Renew in my heart a deep sense of gratitude for the forgiveness I have in Christ
- Forgive me for all the times I withhold compassion and forgiveness from others. Would You work in my heart and make me more like You?
- Lord Your word promises that as far as the east is from the west, so have You cast my former sins away. Produce in me the fruit of the spirit that leads to a life of holiness and integrity
- Thank You for cleansing me from all unrighteousness according to Your word. Surely goodness and mercy shall follow me all the days of my life, and I will dwell in the house of the Lord forever

Scriptures for further Prayers:

Romans 9:15, Titus 3:2, Ps 51:1-3,7,9

Revive Restore and Rebuild

JAN 5

HE FIRST LOVED ME

Worship

Today's Scripture and Meditation

1 John 4:19. *"We love because God first loved us."*

PRAYERS:

- Thank You Lord for salvation and regeneration that produces love towards You.
- Thank You for the work of the Holy Spirit in my life that turned me from an enemy of God into a lover of God.
- I proclaim my love for You unashamedly and without any cowardly fear; Lord Jesus, I LOVE YOU!
- Looking through scriptures I see men of old cry out their love for You as expressed in the trust displayed
- Lord enable me to cry out my love for You by displaying my trust in You in all circumstances
- They loved You from the lion's den to the fiery furnace, from the dark dungeons to the fiery stakes; Father enable me to love You in dark times and good times, times of trials and times of strength, times of lack and times of plenty, times of sickness and times of health in all circumstances in Jesus' Name.
- While I was yet a sinner running away from You, You loved me and enable me to believe in God's love.
- Lord Jesus, I love You from the influence of Your own love, I

love You as gratitude for the finished work of the cross.

- I love You because You have shed Your love abroad in my heart and enabled me to love by Your Spirit.
- I thank You because You love me; chose me; redeemed me; called me; pardoned me; and took me into union with Yourself.

Scriptures for further Prayers:

Romans 5:5, John 16:27, Titus 3:4

JAN 6

HOLY SPIRIT BAPTISM

Worship

Today's Scripture and Meditation

Acts 2:1-4 *When the Day of Pentecost had fully come, they were all with one accord in one place. And suddenly there came a sound from heaven, as of a rushing mighty wind, and it filled the whole house where they were sitting. Then there appeared to them divided tongues, as of fire, and one sat upon each of them. And they were all filled with the Holy Spirit and began to speak with other tongues, as the Spirit gave them utterance.*

PRAYERS:

- I come before thirsting for you. I ask for the manifestation of Your presence and power in an unusual way and measure in my life today
- I open up my spirit to You alone; that Spirit that raised Jesus from the dead, not to any other spirit, but to the Almighty God, let there be a manifestation of the presence of Your Spirit; the power of the Living God in My life
- Demonstrate Your power in me to the unifying of Your people. Despite the diversity of education, spirituality, gifts, calling, family background, let Your Holy Spirit work in me to be in unity with the rest of the members of your body.
- Let Your fire and power fall upon me, let Your presence manifest in my spirit and soul.
- Let there be a shaking of the shakeable and unshakeable, let everything standing against the will and knowledge of God in my life

- Let everything that has hitherto resisted the manifestation of the Spirit and power of God in my life, be shaken to their roots and uprooted from my life.
- Let there be a spiritual earthquake to my foundations by the power of the Spirit of God according to the order of the day of Pentecost.
- I receive a fresh baptism of the Holy Spirit with the evidence of special utterances, diverse tongues etc.
- Let my tongue be untied and let boldness com upon me to preach the gospel.
- Let there be a public manifestation of what the Lord is doing right now in my life
- Let there be a public manifestation of the power of God in and through you says the Spirit of God.
- I receive that fresh infilling, by the Spirit of God is working in me, from here on I shall not be in obscurity, I am coming out, the Lord will yet manifest His power through me not in the secret but in public in the Name of Jesus.
- I receive unusual manifestations in my life and ministry, as a sign for the sceptics of my ministry, begin to receive it, they accept my ministry and be blessed by it
- Transform me the more that I will not be e fearful or timid, I have become bold as a lion
- Father showcase me in the city as a trophy of Your grace. Use me as a vessel of honour and an extension of your arms.
- From here on, I begin to grab attention with everyone in public space to the effect that they will begin to put their faith in You
- I am making an impact from here on, I am a source of impact, influence, with the power of the Lord Jesus Christ.
- Thank You, Lord, let Your Holy Spirit descend upon me to accomplish the will and purpose of Jehovah, fill me with fire, anointing, fresh fire and anointing. Spirit of God rest on my family, friends, acquittance and church. Let them move in the power of the Spirit of God, rest upon, and transform them.

Revive Restore and Rebuild

▪ Thank you, Father, thank You Lord, blessed be Your Name oh God, Alleluia!

Scriptures for further Prayers

Psalm 51:17, Acts 2:1-4

JAN 7

BE STEADFAST

Worship

Today's Scripture and Meditation

1 Corinthians 15:58 *Therefore, my beloved brethren, be steadfast, immovable, always abounding in the work of the Lord, knowing that your labour is not in vain in the Lord.*

PRAYERS:

- Lord, I ask for unusual grace to stand firm in You.
- Help me Lord that no matter what I see or hear, I will not to be moved.
- Father, please help me not to get weary in doing good and in my service to You.
- Father Lord, strengthen all your servants and ministers of the gospel, help them not to give up
- Almighty God I pray that You bless every of Your servants with courage and great faith
- Enable me to remain steadfast under trials, that I may receive the crown of life
- Enable me to stand the test that I will receive your promise of God to those who love him.
- Father give me grace to hold unto my original confidence in Christ firmly to the end.
- Thank you father, in Jesus name I Pray. Amen!

Scriptures for further Prayers:

James 1:12, Hebrews 3:1

JAN 8

A SWEET AROMA

Worship

Today's Scripture and Meditation

Esther 2:12 (ASV) Now when the turn of every maiden was come to go in to king Ahasuerus, after that it had been done to her according to the law for the women twelve months (for so were the days of their purifications accomplished, to wit, six months with oil of myrrh, and six months with sweet odours and with the things for the purifying of the women).

PRAYERS:

- Lord Jesus, I thank You that You are our bridegroom who is coming back for us.

- Father, we are in the days of our purification as we await Your coming, You have said no spots, no wrinkles and no blemish will enter into Your kingdom

- The Oil of Myrrh Signifies death and burial. My old man has been crucified, therefore, I pray, that the "body of sin" and tendency to sin be done away with in Jesus' Name.

- Sweet odours signify the removal of all ill scents and to beautify, Father I pray that my life would be a fragrance of good ointments and that my sacrifices be acceptable and pleasing unto You.

- A sweet aroma requires fire to be released, Father I pray that You will do all You need to do in my life, break me, melt me and mould me that I will be the fragrance of Christ among those who are being saved.

- Lead me in triumph in Christ, and through me diffuses the fragrance of His knowledge in every place.

- Fire purifies, Father purify me, refine me, cleanse me, purge me, make me ready to meet with You on the day of Your appearing.
- Purify my heart from all the *junk (e.g. Anger and Bitterness, Apathy, Disobedience mention what you need cleansing from).*
- Refine me as gold; Take away the dross (Physical and spiritual) Lord.
- Let my giving, offering and my sacrifices, praise, worship let my life be a sweet aroma unto You Lord.
- Bring out the genuineness of my faith, that I may be presentable to the king in Jesus name
- Thank you Father, in Jesus name. Amen!

Scriptures for further Prayers:

Romans 6:1-6, 2 Corinthians 2:14-15,

JAN 9

BE COURAGEOUS, DON'T QUIT

Worship

Today's Scripture and Meditation

1 Corinthians 16:13-14 *"Watch ye, stand fast in the faith, quit you like men, be strong. Let all your things be done with charity"*

PRAYERS:

- Father Lord, I thank You for Your counsel and for Your word
- Father Lord I pray that You enable me to be alert, to be vigilant, to be able to spot enemy attacks from a distance
- Let me not be distracted or left alone in the dark without defences
- Let me not be distracted by the world, fleshly needs and desires, or the schemes of the enemy
- Let my physical needs not overpower my desire to obey You
- Let me not be idle or sleep in the day of battle but that I will be alert and vigilant in Jesus name
- Father help me not to take my eyes off You, so that my values do not begin to shift, and my attention will not wander
- Enable me to be ready for Your coming, to continue bearing fruits for Your kingdom and to be ready to give account of my life here
- Give me grace to be steadfast in doctrine, not wavering or fainting but to be consistent in my faith and devoted to You
- Enable me to grow into maturity so I might fight the good fight of faith as a soldier of Christ

- Lord, let love be at the reason for all I do and that I will love actively and unconditionally. Enable me to do all things from the place of love

Scriptures for further Prayers

John 15:5, 2 Corinthians 2:11, 1 Timothy 6:18-19

JAN 10

EFFECTUAL DOOR

Worship

Today's Scripture and Meditation

1 Corinthians 16:9 *"For a great and effective door has opened to me, and there are many adversaries."*

1 Corinthians 16:13-14 *"Watch, stand fast in the faith, be brave, be strong. 14 Let all that you do be done with love."*

PRAYERS:

- Father Lord I thank You for the great and effective doors that You have opened before us. You are a faithful God who rewards those that diligently seek You
- I pray that You will open our eyes, that I may see, understand, recognize, the great and effective door that You have opened unto me
- That You will cause me according to the guidance of Your Spirit to walk through them in the name of Jesus, Amen
- Lord I ask that by Your Spirit, that You will strengthen me, that You will give me courage that will enable me to stand fast
- That You will show me the way to go, increase my faith, that You will help me to keep my eyes single
- That I will lean on You not on my own understanding, not on my own wisdom, not on any man, not anything that I have, not on anything that I am but trust in You more and more
- But I will trust in You, lean on You, and acknowledge You in all things and take instruction and guidance from You

- That my flesh will no longer be instructive in my life but that I will be instructed by the Spirit of God in all things in the name of Jesus, amen.
- I banish every, distraction, diversion, detour, I will not take a detour on the plans that the Almighty God has set for me
- I put before You, all my adversaries asking that You will deal with adversaries, fight my battles and give me victories as You normally do in the name of Jesus, amen.
- Let my faith be strengthened, and my focus be resolved as I continue to look unto You and hold unto You the author and finisher of our faith in of Jesus name, amen.
- Father, enable me to run this race acceptably that I will not quit but run it till the end, and fight a good fight of faith, finishing my course.
- Let me not occupy myself with fighting, chasing adversity and missing the plan and purpose of God for my life, My focus will not be dim or shifted in the name of our Lord Jesus Christ, amen
- Father Lord I give You praise, I worship, and I adore You, in Jesus mighty name I have prayed, amen.

Scriptures for further Prayers:

1 Peter 5:8, Deuteronomy 28:7

JAN 11

BUILD TO RECEIVE THE REWARD

Worship

Today's Scripture and Meditation

1 Corinthians 3: 10-15 *"According to the grace of God given to me, like a skilled master builder I laid a foundation, and someone else is building upon it. Let each one take care how he builds upon it. For no one can lay a foundation other than that which is laid, which is Jesus Christ. Now if anyone builds on the foundation with gold, silver, precious stones, wood, hay, straw— each one's work will become manifest, for the Day will disclose it, because it will be revealed by fire, and the fire will test what sort of work each one has done. If the work that anyone has built on the foundation survives, he will receive a reward. If anyone's work is burned up, he will suffer loss, though he himself will be saved, but only as through fire."*

PRAYERS:

- Lord Jesus, I thank You because You are our firm foundation.
- Thank You for the responsibility to build on the foundations.
- Enable me to pay attention to the Christiaan doctrines: The doctrines of salvation through faith alone, the doctrine of atonement of Christ, the necessity for holiness.
- Enable me to shun every fable, and endless genealogies, human traditions, human rights, ceremonies, information from my background with the truth of the word of God.

- That I will shun the wisdom of the philosophers, the ideologist and the speculative ideas makes one misinterpret the word of God.
- Enable me to build strong build quality, build capacity, build up myself in the most holy faith, speak in tongues daily, study the word daily.
- That I will build in obedience, in humility, in self-denial, in unity, in love.
- That I will not build on falsehood, disobedience, divisions in the body. That I will not build in pride, in haughtiness so that my work will not go up in flames.
- Thank You for the specific gifts to fulfil my calling, no matter the circumstance.
- Enable me to be responsible for my purpose, so You will find me faithful when my work is inspected
- Father let me be built up, precept upon precept, line upon line, a little patience here. Lord, be patient with me.
- Let me walk in step with You without being weary, knowing that this is a marathon, it is not a sprint.
- Lord let me know that You will continue to build me even when I may not see or sense You. Help me to continue to build in Jesus' Name
- That I will build according to Your will, enable me to build with incorruptible materials like gold, with silver, and to build with costly stones in the name of Jesus, Amen!
- That my work will not be burnt in the name of Jesus, that our work oh God will not be in vain
- Enable us to do things and Your work at the right time. Not at our own time, not at our own convenience. May we come out of our comfort zone and not do Your work half-heartedly, in the name of Jesus, Amen.
- That I will not do Your work oh God, according to my own terms, in the name of Jesus Amen. Oh Lord draw me closer to You; oh Lord draw me nearer to You.
- No one pleases You doing Your work according to their own terms or according to their own understanding. I will not do Your work according to the order of Saul the King in the Name of the Lord Jesus. Amen.

- That I will finish the course. I will fight good fights of faith, and I will finish the race.

Scriptures for further Prayers:

Isaiah 28: 10, 2 Timothy 2:20-21

JAN 12

ABUNDANT BLESSING

Worship

Today's Scripture and Meditation

1 Corinthians 3:6-7 *I planted, Apollos watered, but God gave the increase. So then neither he who plants is anything, nor he who waters, but God who gives the increase.*

PRAYERS:

- Thank You Lord because You are the God of increase.
- You reward efforts and hard work as You have commanded us to work.
- Father grant me the ability to be diligent in all areas of my life and in things committed into my hands.
- Give me the grace to continuously plant knowing that as Your word says "Cast your bread upon the waters, for you will find it after many days"
- Give me grace to nurture good seeds as they grow and to get rid of weeds for a maximum harvest.
- Grant me the grace to both work and pray for the increase, a good harvest and an abundance.
- Teach and enable me to honour You with my substances, so I can be able to benefit from the harvest I have laboured for.
- Enable me to put you first when I begin to prosper and when my harvest is ripe. That my efforts will not become fruitless.
- Father, please seal off every leaking pockets due to my disobedience in the area of giving to You and in areas

where I haven't made giving to You a priority and rebuke the devourer for my sake.

- Thank You for You are a gracious God.

Scriptures for further Prayers:

Haggai 1:4-6, Genesis 26:12-14, Ecclesiastes 11:1

JAN 13

LOVE YOUR BROTHER

Worship

Today's Scripture and Meditation

1 John 4:21 *"This commandment we have from him: Those who claim to love God ought to love their brother and sister also."*

PRAYERS:

- Father Lord, I thank You for grace to love you who are the almighty God, invisible and immortal God.
- Father help me to love the people I can see with unconditional love.
- Father as I strive to know the word, serve faithfully, pray fervently and demonstrate the fruit of the Spirit, let me not be a spiritual dwarf due to lack of love for the brethren.
- Father enable me to measure up on Your scale of discipleship as I love my brethren.
- I pray that no matter the outward appearance, behaviour or level of spirituality, I will love my brothers and sisters unconditionally.
- That my love for the brethren will not be for gain or out of pretence.
- Grant unto me to be gracious and to forgive unconditionally so that I can love unconditionally.
- Teach me to love You by loving Your children, whom I can see."
- Enable me to labour in love among the brethren, serving them and serving their gifts.

Revive Restore and Rebuild

- Grant me grace to forgive and not carry over offence against the brethren.
- Love covers a multitude of sins, let my love go beyond that of the Pharisees.
- Thank You Father in Jesus Name.

Scriptures for further Prayers:

Matthew 5:223-24, John 13:35

JAN 14

CAST OUT THE HORNS

Worship

Today's Scripture and Meditation

Zechariah 1:19 -21. 19 *And I said to the angel who talked with me, "What are these?" So, he answered me, "These are the [f]horns that have scattered Judah, Israel, and Jerusalem." 20 Then the Lord showed me four craftsmen. 21 And I said, "What are these coming to do?" So he said, "These are the horns that scattered Judah, so that no one could lift up his head; but [g]the craftsmen are coming to terrify them, to cast out the horns of the nations that lifted up their horn against the land of Judah to scatter it."*

PRAYERS:

- Father, I thank You for Your word and revelations from Your word.
- Horns speak of strength and authority, Father I pray that whatever has come against me or mine in any department of my life be scattered and destroyed
- Everything causing humiliation and shame in my life is be defeated.
- Whatever has terrified me, restricted my freedom or enslaved any department of my life, be destroyed.
- Father send your spiritual craftsmen to cast out the horns of destruction from my life.
- I pray that every lofty thing that raises its horns against me and God's people will be scattered, and their power destroyed.
- Let every satanic or collective power that wants to scatter what I have gathered, be destroyed

- ⦿ Association of evil gang-up to cause derailment in my life; be scattered
- ⦿ Any power put in place to supervise and actualise failure in my life, be destroyed
- ⦿ Anything in me contradicting the word of God to cause an error, be destroyed.
- ⦿ Any power making a decree to affect my standing in the Lord, be broken
- ⦿ Every counsel taken together will come to nothing
- ⦿ Evil decree or curse over my life, spiritually, physically, financially, matrimonially and educationally, be broken, in the Name of Jesus.
- ⦿ Anything in me, around me, within me, contesting with the presence of Holy Spirit in me be destroyed.
- ⦿ Spirit of the Living God, arise and take me to my place of blessing now, in Jesus' Name.
- ⦿ Father Lord, whatever weapon or tricks of the enemy to steal, kill and destroy, destroy them with their weapon forever, in Jesus Name.
- ⦿ Father Lord, connect, correct and direct my helpers to me anywhere, anywhere they may be, in the Name of Jesus.
- ⦿ Spirit of the Living God, arise and remove any evil veil covering my face so I can see clearly.
- ⦿ Thank you father for hearing my Prayers, in Jesus name. Amen!

Scriptures for further Prayers

Isaiah 8:9-10, Job 5:12

Revive Restore and Rebuild

JAN 15

ESCAPE THE POLLUTION

Worship

Today's Scripture and Meditation

2 Peter 2:20. *For if, after they have escaped the pollutions of the world through the knowledge of the Lord and Saviour Jesus Christ, they are again entangled in them and overcome, the latter end is worse for them than the beginning.*

PRAYERS:

- Father, I bless Your Name for Your amazing grace that has saved me from sin and death.
- Thank You, my Lord and Saviour, for redemption from all form of evil.
- Father I ask that You grant me the grace to remain in You till the end,
- Lord let me not go back to my vomit or backslide in my relationship with You
- Let my passion for You not be dowsed, but let me be zealous in my pursuit of You
- Enable me to escape the pollution of the world for good and not just in words.
- That I will no longer be entangled in the works of darkness but keep me in the way of righteousness.
- Almighty God uphold me with Your righteous right hand that I may not fall, do not allow us to go back to the things that held us bound in the past.
- That I will not be conformed to the former lusts, as in the days of my ignorance.

- I receive the power to remain free from the corruption of this world.
- I receive grace to stand and to be an overcomer in Jesus' Name.
- Thank you father, in Jesus name. Amen!

Scriptures for further Prayers:

Psalm 48:10, 1 Peter 1:14

JAN 16

BE IMMOVABLE

Worship:

Today's Scripture and Meditation

I Corinthians 15:58 *"Therefore, my beloved brethren, be steadfast, immovable, always abounding in the work of the Lord, knowing that your labour is not in vain in the Lord."*

PRAYERS:

- Father, Lord, I thank You for this morning; I worship and adore You. Thank You for Your encouragement to be steadfast, immovable and continue to serve knowing that the one I serve is a rewarder
- In this world where there is so much disappointment, distraction, personal agendas, so much activity of the work of the kingdom of darkness trying to derail us and trying to cause us to backslide, trying to cause us to think that our God is unfaithful - Lord enable me by the power of Your Spirit working in me and through me to be steadfast
- Enable me to be immovable, no matter what the devil is throwing at us; that no matter what I see or experience, that I will be immovable, that my eyes will be stayed on You
- Father enable me to work joyously in everything that has to do with working for the Lord NOW, because right now counts forever

- Father enable me to not only work, but to labour and put in all Your strength; under Your direction, and by Your influence; for without You I can do nothing
- Enable me to be rooted and built up in You and strengthened in the faith
- Give me the ability to satisfy You with my life. I plead for God's grace and mercy to comply with Your will
- I pray that You establishes my heart to be steadfast and not be moved by any storm of persecution or attack
- Thank You for the privilege of knowing You in Jesus name

Scriptures for further Prayers:

Colossians 2:7, Psalm 119:16, 24, 35. 47. 77

JAN 17

THE ESSENCE OF THE MEMORIAL

Worship

Today's Scripture and Meditation

1 Corinthians 11:23-26 *"For I received from the Lord that which I also delivered to you: that the Lord Jesus on the same night in which He was betrayed took bread; and when He had given thanks, He broke it and said, "Take, eat; this is My body which is broken for you; do this in remembrance of Me." In the same manner He also took the cup after supper, saying, "This cup is the new covenant in My blood. This do as often as you drink it, in remembrance of Me." For as often as you eat this bread and drink this cup, you proclaim the Lord's death till He comes."*

PRAYERS:

- Lord I commit my heart to You, I ask that You reign and rule in my heart today.
- Lord, I put in remembrance the events of the night before you were crucified. You were betrayed, crucified, died, buried and was resurrected
- I remember that You did this for my salvation and my redemption. Help me to always keep this fact I view in Jesus name
- Enable me to count it all joy in the days of suffering remembering that you took the same for me.
- Lord, I thank You for the new covenant that You made with Your blood
- I come to the table of communion to re-enact this covenant today
- By the cup of redemption, I am free from every form of slavery: to sin, Satan and his works

- ⬜ Thank You for the new relationship I have with God through the blood of the covenant
- ⬜ Thank You for the inner transformation and the law of God now written on my heart
- ⬜ I am now among Your people, and You are my God. Hallelujah!
- ⬜ Father let there be a manifestation of the covenant blessings in my life.
- ⬜ Let Your body and Your blood that we take at communion be life to my body, spirit and soul
- ⬜ Lord establish me such that I do not serve other gods irrespective of how they camouflage, help me to recognize You and serve You alone.
- ⬜ Help me not to break the edge thereby exposing myself to the enemy's attack.
- ⬜ Father, I know the weakness of this covenant lies with me, enable me to stand in the day of temptation.
- ⬜ I pray that the enemy despite devising means of taking me out of the place the Lord has planned for me, I will remain in the place of redemption.
- ⬜ Lord, I thank You for the communion elements made by human hands, I pray that You turn them to spiritual food in Jesus Name Amen.
- ⬜ Feed our body and soul as I partake tonight and re-enact your covenant with me.
- ⬜ Help me to always do this in remembrance of You in Jesus name. Amen!

Scriptures for further Prayers

John 6:53, Hebrew 13:2

JAN 18

O DEATH, WHERE IS YOUR STING

Worship

Today's Scripture and Meditation

1 Corinthians 15:54-57 *"So when this corruptible has put on incorruption, and this mortal has put on immortality, then shall be brought to pass the saying that is written: "Death is swallowed up in victory." "O Death, where is Your sting? O Hades, where is Your victory?" The sting of death is sin, and the strength of sin is the law. But thanks be to God, who gives us the victory through our Lord Jesus Christ"*

PRAYERS

- Father God I worship You, our Saviour I give You the highest praise, blessed be Your name
- I thank You that You raise Jesus from the dead; Death could not hold Him captive, even in the grave – JESUS IS LORD.
- Thank You, Lord, for the resurrection from the dead, it is because You resurrected that death was defeated
- By Your blood, I am washed clean, by Your nail-pierced hands, I am free; the power of sin is broken, Jesus You have won my freedom and I thank You Lord
- The sting of death is sin, and the strength of sin is the law.
- I thank You because I am not under the law, I am no longer subject to the penalty of the death, I am set free from sin. I have eternal life
- The sting of death is gone because I am a child of God, forgiven by grace and made righteous by Christ, I live through my Lord Jesus Christ

- Thank You, Lord, that through Christ, I have victory over death and will not fear death
- Father, enable me to walk in the understanding of this work of Calvary that I might live a victorious life in Christ
- The bishop of my soul, I worship You and I magnify Your holy name, I honour You for You have power over all things, over all men, over all circumstances, over all situations.
- There is no other person that loves like You, no other person that saves like You, no other person that cares about us like You.
- I look to You for the day of Your appearing and the day of eternal redemption without fear.
- I praise You Father in Jesus name

Scriptures for further Prayers:

Romans 6:23, Genesis 2:17, Romans 6:1-14

JAN 19

REST ON EVERY SIDE

Worship

Today's Scripture and Meditation

1 Chronicles 22:18 *"Is not the Lord your God with you? And has He not given you rest on every side?"*

PRAYERS:

- Father, I thank You because you have given me rest.
- My expectations shall not be cut off. Lord do great and mighty things in my life.
- And all that hear it shall know that I serve a living God who does not forget His people.
- I shall not be afraid; I shall not be put to shame because the Lord is the lifter of my head.
- Father I seek You with all my heart, please fight for me and give me victory and peace on every side.
- Lord, please reward my diligence. When I call You, Lord answer me. Lord show me Your righteous arm.
- Lord show mercy to me and my children and my generations as You have spoken in Your word.
- Lord give me rest from all my battles.
- Lord give me rest from every sickness, every depression, every suppression, every oppression, every bondage, every sorrow, every fear, every anxiety, every struggle, every pressure, every difficulty, every violence.
- Lord give me rest on all sides. Lord open doors on to me, that I do not expect. And Lord keep them open.
- Lord rewrite my story. Lord rewrite my history. "I am bringing pleasure out of this earthen clay."

- Lord pour Yourself into me. Lord beautify me, that I might be a blessing in the earth.
- Enable me to break grounds for you and to establish Your counsel in these last days.
- Lord contend with those who contend with me, and none shall be able to stand before me.
-

Scriptures for further Prayers

Isaiah 8:10, 2 Chronicles 32:8

JAN 20

THE ARK OF GOD

Worship

Today's Scripture and Meditation

1 Samuel 7:1-2 *"Then the men of Kirjath Jearim came and took the ark of the LORD and brought it into the house of Abinadab on the hill, and consecrated Eleazar his son to keep the ark of the LORD. So it was that the ark remained in Kirjath Jearim a long time; it was there twenty years. And all the house of Israel lamented after the Lord."*

2 Samuel 6:11 *"The ark of the LORD remained in the house of Obed-Edom the Gittite three months. And the LORD blessed Obed-Edom and all his household"*

PRAYERS:

- The ark represented God's presence, and I thank You Lord that I carry Your presence
- The Ark was in the house of Abinadab for 20 years and nothing tangible was recorded but the people lamented, meanwhile it was in the house of Obed Edom for 3 months and testimonies abound. Father, fill me with Your glorious presence so that my life will not be devoid of amazing testimonies
- Father I thank You that for the gift of salvation and for the gift of the Holy Spirt who dwells in me
- Father I thank You for the grace to be the temple for the Holy Spirit, teach me to keep Your temple hallowed

- I realise that I am not my own but I belong to You, so I surrender my vessel to You Lord to continually fill with Your presence and power
- I pray that I will not carry the ark of God in vain, like Abinadab, I will not bear the presence of God lamenting in Jesus name.
- Let the blessings of Your presence be seen in me; let me be an evidence of the fragrance of the knowledge of God everywhere
- According to the order of Obed-Edom, let the blessing of Your presence manifest in me, my family in all facets of life.
- Let me continue to be a God-Chaser, chasing after You continually.
- Thank You heavenly father. Amen

Scriptures for further Prayers:

1 Corinthians 6:19, 2 Corinthians 2:15,

JAN 21

THE SPIRIT FROM GOD

Worship

Today's Scripture and Meditation

1 Corinthian 2:10-1 *But God has revealed them to us through His Spirit. For the Spirit searches all things, yes, the deep things of God. For what man knows the things of a man except the spirit of the man which is in him? Even so no one knows the things of God except the Spirit of God. Now we have received, not the spirit of the world, but the Spirit who is from God, that we might know the things that have been freely given to us by God."*

PRAYERS:

- Thank You Father for the gift of the Holy Spirit in our lives. Thank You for the ministry of the Holy spirit, our Help, Comforter, Teacher, the One that reminds us and prompt us in all things.
- Without the Holy Spirit we can't engage You and it is He Who reveals the Father and the Son to us. Lord I am so grateful for a relationship with Him.
- Holy Spirit of the living God, I pray You come afresh on me.
- I want to know God more, I want to know the heart of God, to search all things.
- You know the deep things of God so I pray that You will help me as I search the deep things of God.
- You are from God, and You know the Father; please reveal the Father to me, reveal the Son to me; That I may know Him.

- Grant me unusual and deep revelation of God: reveal His person, reveal His will, plan. Purpose, Reveal His ways, reveal His acts.
- I have not received the spirit of the world, but the Spirit who is from God, that I might know the things that have been freely given to us by God, that I may walk the way of God.
- Give me wisdom that is beyond the wisdom of man; teach us wisdom to apply in all things.
- Wisdom for my life, family, work of my hands and ministry.
- Grant understanding, insight, and revelation of Your word, let the eyes of my mind be opened to receive understanding of the things of God, teach us to compare spiritual to spiritual.
- Grant me spiritual discernment, enable us to judge all things rightly, to know Your mind and Your heart and to have the mind of Christ.
- Enable me to be able to hear the truth, guide us into all truth.
- Reveal the Father's heart, reveal what He is saying, reveal what is to come to me in clear and tangible ways.
- Let there be light in our hearts and souls by the power of the Holy Spirit.
- I cast down every degree of spiritual blindness, rebellion, sin, oppression, suppression, demonic possessions, demonic attacks, sicknesses and diseases, lack, lack of direction, non-achievement, fruitless labour.
- I surrender to You spirit of God to do a work of transformation in every area of my life that is not yet transformed in Jesus' Name, Amen. Thank You Lord!

Scriptures for further Prayers:

Ephesians 1:18, Ephesians 3:5

JAN 22

I WILL SAVE MY FLOCK

Worship

Today's Scripture and Meditation

Ezekiel 34:22-24 *"Therefore, I will save My flock, and they shall no longer be a prey; and I will judge between sheep and sheep. I will establish one shepherd over them, and he shall feed them – My servant David. He shall feed them and be their shepherd. And I, the Lord, will be their God, and My servant David a prince among them; I, the Lord, have spoken."*

PRAYERS:

- Father Lord, I bless your name because I am Your sheep, and You are my Shepherd.
- Father enable me to be a sheep indeed who is meek, with the ability to take injury without murmuring or wanting to take revenge Father.
- The sheep listen to the Shepherd so enable me to listen to you always and to those you have put above me to care for me
- Let me be directed by You the shepherd as You know the way.
- Let me not be conceited and plotting my way and asking You to rubber-stamp it
- You are my Shepherd and the Defender of the defenceless, I look to You my Shepherd to defend me.
- I need Your help to get up, lift me up oh my shepherd. Restrain me from scheming and looking for other things to lift me up.
- Enable me to recognise Your voice that I may know when You are speaking to me.

- ☐ Sheep do not carry burdens, I put my burdens at the feet of Jesus.
- ☐ I am content and will not run after the cares of this world because a Sheep is always content.
- ☐ Thank You for the gifts you have given me. May I gain more and not bury my talents in a napkins
- ☐ I cannot care for my own wound and hurt so I take them to You my shepherd to care for. I carry all to the Lord. my wounds my hurt, my pain and challenges
- ☐ I submit my heart, soul, body, everything that concerns me, my family, career, ministry, children, everything I can and would ever be to You.
- ☐ That I will receive every form of nourishment from You.
- ☐ Carry me when I am weak, for your word says that "beneath me are your everlasting arms".
- ☐ Surely goodness and mercies shall follow us all the days of our lives and we shall dwell in the house of the Lord forever and ever in Jesus Name. Amen!

Scriptures for further Prayers

Psalm 23:1, John 10:11-14, Deuteronomy 33:27

JAN 23

NO CONFUSION

Worship

Today's Scripture and Meditation

1 Corinthians 14:33 *"For God is not the author of confusion but of peace, as in all the churches of the saints."*

PRAYERS:

- I praise you Lord because You are Holy and forever you are God, Your works and your ways are perfect
- You are not the author of confusion but the author of peace.
- Father in troubled times like this when some are confused about their personal lives, confused about their faith, Father let me be certain of my faith.
- Father enable me to be focused and not be discontent, disagreeable, and despair to the extent that I will go running helter-skelter.
- Father let me not become fearful, depressed, angry and violent, or turned to substance abuse.
- Let me not be a victim of the onslaught of the enemy against the emotions of the body of Christ.
- Enable me to constantly trust in You, look onto You, and set my mind on You so that I will be immoveable and will stand.
- Let me not be shaken by the activities of the enemy at this end time. Let me not make drastic changes not ordained by the Lord. I present the cross and the blood of Jesus against the battle, against   the attack and against the siege.
- I take refuge in You, I look to You and I trust in You, I know that for sure, the enemy cannot overcome You and evil cannot overcome good.

- Let my heart not fail because the earth is being shaken, the losses; loss of job, loss of family, loss of friends, and all manner of losses, the vicious diseases, failure and lack.
- Let my heart not fail because of the circumstances round about us
- May I not blame God for my problems, circumstances, or begin to ask God questions, querying, and challenging God.
- Lord step into my battles, take away every confusion.
- Even though we walk through the valley of the shadow of death we will fear no evil.
- Teach me the way to go, guide me to Your truth, guide me continually and make my brow strong.
- I shall be like the spring of waters that shall not fall. I shall rise up and build the foundations, I shall be called a repairer of bridge, restorer of street to dwell.
- Let my dry places be satisfied and make my bones strong oh Lord
- I will not be lacking in my spirit and grant unto me Your mind and purpose
- Guide me oh God, instruct me and give me knowledge and understanding. Reveal and speak to me in every circumstance of my life.
- I shall not be confused, I will be focused on You and receive instructions from You.
- We bind the spirit of confusion and command You out from my heart and mind in Jesus Name!
- I receive guidance and clarity from the Spirit of the Lord, receive excellence and accuracy!
- Let my feelings be fully controlled by the Spirit of God, I will not walk away from the place of my divine positioning in the   Name of Jesus!
- I receive the mind of Christ into manifestation in my live in all that I   do and of what You are doing.

Scriptures for further Prayers:

Isaiah 58:11, Isaiah 30:21

JAN 24

ASK FOR WISDOM

Worship
Today's Scripture and Meditation

1 Kings 3:11-13: *"God said to him, because you have asked this and have not asked for long life or for riches, nor for the lives of your enemies, but have asked for yourself understanding to recognize what is just and right,*

Behold, I have done as you asked. I have given you a wise, discerning mind, so that no one before you was your equal, nor shall any arise after you equal to you. I have also given you what you have not asked, both riches and honour, so that there shall not be any among the kings equal to you all your days."

PRAYERS:

- Father Lord I thank You because You are the God of wisdom, You are the God of understanding, counsel and might.
- Father let the thoughts and decision of my heart and my mindset and perspectives be pleasing unto You in Jesus Name.
- You said that whosoever lacks wisdom should ask You because You give liberally and without reproach and it will be given to him. Father I ask You for wisdom today.
- Wisdom to live my life in this world, wisdom in relationships, wisdom in the work of my hands, wisdom in ministry, all round wisdom.

- Father give me the Spirit of wisdom of knowledge, of understanding, of counsel, of might, of the fear of the Lord and a discerning mind that I will not ask amiss.
- Solomon had deep longing for communion with God and did not let riches come in between him and the Father! Give me deep longing for Your presence and fellowship with You that will not be affected by riches of this world in Jesus Name.
- Grant me the secret of the sweet companionship of the Lord and show and reveal to me the deep and inner meaning of Your covenant.
- Father give unto me exceedingly, abundantly above all that I ask like you did for Solomon in Jesus Name.
- Father cause me to excel in wisdom in all I do and among all people.
- Thank you, Father in Jesus Name.

Scriptures for further Prayers:

Ephesians 3:20, Galatians1:16, John16:13-14

JAN 25

REPENT

Worship

Today's Scripture and Meditation

2 Chronicles 7:14 *"If My people who are called by My name will humble themselves, and pray and seek My face, and turn from their wicked ways, then I will hear from heaven, and will forgive their sin and heal their land."*

PRAYERS:

- ⬚ I approach the throne of grace by the blood of Jesus, I come before You oh God with a humble heart.
- ⬚ I approach the throne of grace that I may obtain mercy. I come confessing my sins, committed in thoughts, words, actions, I confess every one of my sins of disobedience to your word, You, promptings, whispers, against my leaders, Pastors, to everyone that is ahead of me, to my bosses.
- ⬚ I confess the sin of disobedience because I know You require obedience. You said you prefer obedience to sacrifice.
- ⬚ Lord, I humble my heart, as I ask for mercy. Look upon me with mercy as You normally do to those who love Your name.
- ⬚ Be merciful to me, for every wrong behaviour, wrong words spoken, words not according to Your will that I give my lips to, wrong decisions made, wrong actions taken, wrong thoughts in my hearts, unholy thoughts, have mercy, thoughts that do not give glory to your

Name, thoughts that we will be ashamed of if replayed to others; Have mercy on me Lord.

- For every of my I confess every inconsistency, lack of discernment, and boastings
- All power belongs to You. I confess every time I have usurped authority; have mercy on me
- Where I have acted or thought wrongly against my brothers and sisters, mercy Lord, forgive me, cleanse me from all unrighteousness according to Your word.
- I stand before You by the finished work of Calvary, the Bible says You will not despise a contrite, broken heart, forgive and cleanse us this morning, forgive our cheerlessness.
- Forgive every self-deceit and forgive me for times when I have allowed the enemy to trick and lead me along, for when I have allowed the enemy to have his way or have an upper hand, and for when I have allowed the enemy to take a seat in my lives, families, churches.
- Have mercy for every carelessness, careless thoughts, and action.
- You are a merciful God, you said when we confess our sins, you are faithful and just to forgive us and cleanse us from all unrighteousness. I ask for forgiveness and cleansing Lord
- You said I should be holy for You are holy, I ask that You cleanse me by Your blood, that I may stand holy before You by the finished work of Calvary, that nothing will hinder me or stand between me and answers to my Prayers, look upon me with mercy as You do to those who love Your Name.
- Lord break up every covering of the enemy and deceit upon my heart, by Your power in the Name of Jesus,
- Expose every philosophy, culture, and tradition of men, that is affecting my relationship with You, break it up, tear it down, I cast it down in the name of Jesus.
- Every traditional and cultural belief, misinterpretation of scriptures and Your will, I cancel. Everything that hinders my relationship with You and Your presence in my life, flush it out, I give You praise and thanks.

- ▢ Father, hear my Prayers out of a contrite heart and heal our land in Jesus name.
- ▢ Glory to Your name, in Jesus Name I have prayed. Amen!

Scriptures for further Prayers

1 John 1:9-10, Proverbs 4:1-27

JAN 26

HONOUR

Worship

Today's Scripture and Meditation

Esther 6:1-3. *That night [a]the king could not sleep. So, one was commanded to bring the book of the records of the chronicles; and they were read before the king. 2 And it was found written that Mordecai had told of [b]Bigthana and Teresh, two of the king's eunuchs, the doorkeepers who had sought to lay hands on King Ahasuerus. 3 Then the king said, "What HONOUR or dignity has been bestowed on Mordecai for this?"*

PRAYERS:

- Father thank You for You are the God of wisdom and timing.
- I receive riches and wealth and honour, I receive double honour as my portion, I possess double honour and I rejoice in You.
- According to the order of king Ahasuerus, I pray the Lord will cause those who are to bring me honour to lose sleep until they honour me.
- They will lose their peace and sleep until I am honoured.
- My time of honour, dignity and reward is now.
- I pray that the book of records be opened, that I will be remembered this season for works I have done.
- I pray that my rewards will not elude me and my labour will not be in vain. I pray that my reward will not be given to another.
- That my case be open and reopened, that the gap in my reward be acknowledged and spotted.

- Father raise helpers to honour me.
- According to the order of Mordecai - I shall be rewarded when it matters the most
- When lives need to be saved, when the enemies plans need to be torpedoed.
- On my day of honour, the enemy will be engaged in the planning of my showcasing and celebration.
- May they be used to design my robe and regalia of honour because the Lord sets before me a table in the presence of my enemies.
- May the enemy be compelled to be my introducer, promoter, helper and enabler.
- It is the king's delight to honour me, therefore there will be glory in my present season and there will be glory in my future.
- Grant unto me the authority (ring), the mantle (robe) the vehicle to my destiny (Horse) that belongs to Jesus, that I might be your representative on earth.
- This season, the more the haters, competitors and those who strive with me, the more the glory that God will bestow upon me.
- I will not lack people during this season, when I call one, a multitude will answer. Thank You Father in Jesus Name.

Scriptures for further Prayers:

Esther 6:6, Provers 31:25, Isaiah 43:4

JAN 27

MOVE ON

Worship

Today's Scripture and Meditation

Deuteronomy 1:6-8. *"The Lord our God spoke to us in Horeb, saying: 'You have dwelt long enough at this mountain. Turn and take your journey, and go to the mountains of the Amorites, to all the neighbouring places in the plain, in the mountains and in the lowland, in the South and on the seacoast, to the land of the Canaanites and to Lebanon, as far as the great river, the River Euphrates. See, I have set the land before you; go in and possess the land which the Lord swore to your fathers – to Abraham, Isaac, and Jacob – to give to them and their descendants after them.'*

PRAYERS

- Father I thank You because You are a God of progress and You do not want anyone of Your children to be stagnant.
- I pray that You will move me on wherever I have been attached to locations and activities, such that I refuse to move on when I should.
- Father I pray that You jolt me out of and move me on from whatever I choose to continue doing what I have done repeatedly for years because I have gotten used to it and it is comfort zone for me, move me on in Jesus Name!
- Enable me to forget the former things and let me not miss the day when You are doing new things!
- Help me to deal with fear of the unknown so I can take risk of charting a new course.

- Father, wherever you lead me help me to follow; please help me to be receptive to changes in Jesus' Name. Amen

Scriptures for further Prayers:

Isa 43:17-18

JAN 28

THANKSGIVINGS FOR VICTORY

Worship

Today's Scripture and Meditation

1 Corinthians 15:57 (ESV) *"But thanks be to God, who gives us the victory through our Lord Jesus Christ."*

PRAYERS:

- Father Lord, I thank You for the gift of salvation.
- Lord Jesus, I thank You for all victory that You obtained and those that came to us by your works on the cross.
- Thank You that You conquered death. You have won the victory. It is by Your blood that I have been redeemed.
- I thank You that You are the light of my life, You are the light that shines in darkness, and darkness can never comprehend.
- You are the one that is seated at the right hand of the Father. Your kingdom is from everlasting to everlasting.
- There is no God besides You, there is none that can be compared with You.
- There is no other God but You. There is none that loves and cares for us like You.
- By Your grace, I have been healed. You are the one that has broken down the chains that bound us.
- You have set the captives free. You are the one that has put a new song in my mouth and in my heart
- You are the one that has called me by name, and I am Yours. I am grateful.

　　　　　　　　　　　Revive Restore and Rebuild

- I am excited, I am joyful, to know that I am Yours and that You are mine in the land of the living.
- I worship You faithful God, gracious God, merciful God. Hallelujah to Your name, in Jesus' Name I have prayed and worshipped, Amen.

Scriptures for further Prayers:

Deuteronomy 20:4, Psalm 20:6

JAN 29

THANKSGIVING FOR EVERYTHING

Worship:

Today's Scripture and Meditation

1 Thessalonians 5:18(AMPC) *"Thank God in everything no matter what the circumstances may be, be thankful and give thanks, for this is the will of God for You who are in Christ Jesus - the Revealer and Mediator of that will."*

PRAYERS:

- Father I thank You for saving my soul from the eternal judgement that is to come to those who reject You
- Father, thank You that You have never left me nor forsaken me; You fight my battles and have not given me as prey to the teeth of the enemy
- Thank You for not allowing the rod of the wicked to fall on me. You restrained me from being a victim of the works of darkness
- Thank You, Lord, for being my refuge from the storm and shelter from the heat, my shield, my fortress, my strong tower and my hiding place.
- Thank You for frustrating all the plans of my adversaries, shielding me and giving me victories and increase on every side.
- If it had not been the Lord who was on our side, When men rose up against us, then they would have swallowed us alive, When their wrath was kindled against us. Lord, I am grateful for Your presence in my life and making me evidence of this testimonies

- I bless You LORD, for You have not given me as prey to their teeth
- Lord You are my strength and my shield; My heart trusted in You, and I am helped; Therefore, my heart greatly rejoices in You Lord, and with my song I will praise You
- Almighty God, I thank You for Your goodness, faithfulness and truth that endures throughout all generations in Jesus name
- Father, I thank You for granting my request and meeting my demands.
- Thank You, Lord, for all the spiritual resources given to me, filling me with Your Holy Spirit for life and calling, protecting me under Your blood, and for giving us Your name as a backing authority
- Thank You for You surround me with favour as with a shield
- Thank You for all Your benefits bestowed on me. The benefit of Your covenant and all the covenant blessings; health and healing, provisions and supply, victories in battles, grace and mercy, life and safety, security and peace
- Thank You for the strength You gave me for the hard moments and the strength to weather the storm, for the hope You bring through the toughest of times and the good times as You make all things works together for my good
- Thank You for the time when I had little or nothing and for when I had abundance
- Thank You for Your joy and peace in the days of success, progress and prosperity Thank You for drawing me close this season and for renewing my spirit, reviving my soul and filling me daily with Your peace and joy

Scriptures for further Prayers:

Psalm 124:2-3 & 6, Job 5: 12, Psalm 28:7

JAN 30

PRAYING FOR CHILDREN

Worship

Today's Scripture and Meditation

1 Kings 1:5-6 *(Here we see the story of Adonijah who all of a sudden decided he will be king, got horses and chariots and men, got a priest for himself to come and anoint him)*

PRAYERS:

(If you do not have children in your family, please pray for children in your church or in the world)

- Father, thank you for the gift of children in my family, our church, the world.
- I pray that our children will not be in error or presumptuous.
- Enable them to follow God's order so they do not self-destruct themselves.
- That my children will not aspire to be whom God has not called them to be in the Name of Jesus
- That they will not take over the calling of another man in the Name of Jesus.
- They will not enter the assignment of another man, they will not be presumptuous, they will not be derailed in their career, education, marriage, finance, ministry.
- They will not follow the path that is not good for them, they will not miss their destinies they will not call themselves; they will not work or live in the counsel of the ungodly.
- Send godly influencers to our children that the people that gather unto them will not be sycophants.

- ▢ Let them not follow the advice of the ungodly or path of sinners by the way of the Lord. Teach them to wait for You and to follow You.
- ▢ Lord raise a "Nathan" for our children, who will teach me how to save the children in every circumstance they find themselves.
- ▢ Lord save the children who have stepped out of God's order, we call them back to God's order in the Name of Jesus.
- ▢ I cast down every ideology and philosophy keeping all the children from encountering God.
- ▢ It was by the word of God that the world was created, may the word of God establish my children, that they will be for signs and wonders and serve the Lord God with all their mind and soul in the Name of Jesus.
- ▢ Father break down the walls of our children and invade their lives, emotions, I speak order in the Name of Jesus.
- ▢ I speak peace be still to every stormy emotion in the Name of Jesus.
- ▢ My seed shall be blessed my generation shall be blessed.
- ▢ Work out your original plan in the lives of the children, disgrace the work and agenda of the devil in their lives.
- ▢ I receive the confidence of the Lord in the raising of my children.
- ▢

Scriptures for further Prayers

Psalm 1:1, 1Kings 1:5-6; 11-14, Proverbs 11:21.

JAN 31

NO ONE CAN HARM YOU

Worship

Today's Scripture and Meditation

1 Peter 3:13. *And who is he that will harm you, if ye be followers of that which is good?*

PRAYERS:

- Father I pray that You will enable me to dwell in Your presence that I may be guaranteed the banishment of fear.
- Father hide me in Your inner room until the battle is over.
- That I will become impregnable and be above all enemies.
- Enable me to live a holy life so that I will be kept from all harm.
- Enable me to obey You in all things so that I can wear the Lord as a garment to be able to face the devil and his wiles.
- Enable me to be able to use the word of God which is the sword of the Spirit to win in spiritual warfare.
- Enable me to follow only that which is good that no harm will come to me in Jesus' Name.
- Enable me to stand for You in the days of opposition and persecution.
- Enable me to deny myself. Pick up my cross and follow You all the days of my life.

Scriptures for further Prayers:

Psalm 91:1, Psalm 118:6, James 1:22 & 25

FEB 1

ANXIOUS FOR NOTHING

Worship

Today's scripture and Meditation

Matthew 6:28-34. 28

"So why do you worry about clothing? Consider the lilies of the field, how they grow: they neither toil nor spin; and yet I say to you that even Solomon in all his glory was not arrayed like one of these. Now if God so clothes the grass of the field, which today is, and tomorrow is thrown into the oven, will He not much more clothe you, O you of little faith? "Therefore, do not worry, saying, 'What shall I eat?' or 'What shall I drink?' or 'What shall I wear?' For after all these things the Gentiles seek. For Your heavenly Father knows that you need all these things."

PRAYERS:

- ▢ Father Lord, I thank You for Your word that You have sent to me today words of peace and encouragement. I depend on every word You speak about our future, day and tomorrow
- ▢ I receive grace to trust You in a way that does not make sense to humans
- ▢ Lord, You turn up, sometimes at the last minute, and I discover whenever You turned up, You were never late - when there was a deadline and an expiry date, You came through on time

- ☐ Grant me grace o trust You in the face of negative evidence, unusual grace to trust You even when the circumstance seems bad
- ☐ You have the ability and capacity to provide everything I need and worry about
- ☐ You have apportioned to me to seek Your kingdom; Lord I seek Your kingdom; teach and reveal me to seek Your kingdom first
- ☐ Grant me the enablement, strength, ability, wisdom to stay on track in Jesus name. Amen
- ☐ Lord because of Your faithfulness, as I seek You, everything I seek as human, let it be added in Jesus name
- ☐ Let me not chase after the same things the world is chasing after or imbibe the values of the world in Jesus name
- ☐ And I do all this with all our heart, all our strength with all that I am and all that I have and all that I will ever be

Scriptures for further Prayers:

Philippians 4:6-7, 2 Corinthians 9:8

FEB 2

LIFT UP YOUR FACE TO GOD

Worship

Today's scripture and Meditation

Job 22 :26-28 *"For then you will have your delight in the Almighty and lift up your face to God. You will make your prayer to Him, He will hear you, and you will pay your vows. You will also declare a thing, and it will be established for you; So, light will shine on your ways."*

PRAYERS:

- Father I thank You for Your love for me, I come to You today and thank You for the privilege of prayer, I delight in You
- Lord I am lacking in energy and motivation. And I am so in need of You. I need Your strength and Your fresh touch to get back on track again.
- You have chosen to dwell with us because You delighted in us. You brought me out into a spacious place; You rescued me because You delight in me
- Lord, help me not to quit. Help me to keep running the race faithfully, and to find strength in that safe, secret place of Yours, under the shadow of the Almighty
- I will lift up my eyes to the hill, knowing fully well that my help comes from You. Lord render help to me out of Zion
- I lift up my face and make my Prayers to You. Thank You for You hear me always.

- Enable me to pay all vows I have made and never to make foolish vows
- You said to declare a thing, and it will be established for me; so, I make my prayer to You… *(begin to declare what You want the Lord to do)*
- Father let Your light shine on me and on my way in Jesus name
- Let every darkness vanish, let my life be all about You in Jesus name

Scriptures for further Prayers:

Psalm 18:19, Job 22:26, Numbers 6:25

FEB 3

GOD IS LOVE

Worship

Today's Scripture and Meditation

1 John 4:7-11(AMPC) *"Beloved, let us love one another, for love is (springs) from God; and he who loves [his fellowmen] is begotten (born) of God and coming [progressively] to know and understand God [to perceive and recognize and get a better and clearer knowledge of Him]"*

He who does not love has not become acquainted with God [does not and never did know Him], for God is love. In this the love of God was made manifest (displayed) where we are concerned: in that God sent His Son, the only begotten or [a]unique [Son], into the world so that we might live through Him. In this is love: not that we loved God, but that He loved us and sent His Son to be the propitiation (the atoning sacrifice) for our sins. Beloved, if God loved us so [very much], we also ought to love one another."

PRAYERS:

- Father Lord, I thank You because You are love, You are life and I praise You
- It is because You are love that You gave up Your only son, Your only begotten son, Your only unique son.
- It is because of Love that Jesus, You went to calvary, and You took the pain that I should have taken.
- Thank You for Your unfailing, unconditional, and sacrificial love, I give You praise.

- You are our example in love, as You are our example in all things.
- I repent before You for not loving enough, and for being self-centred.
- Forgive me for all the things I do that work against love, every striving, hatred, and jealousy.
- I seek to know Your love in my hearts, I submit myself to You.
- Flush out every self-centeredness, selfishness, unforgiveness, hatred, strife, jealousy, haughtiness, and pride.
- Fill my mind and heart with unconditional love which is a fruit of the Spirit
- Enable me to bear the fruit of love, without love the fruit of the Spirit will not manifest.
- Lord manifest Your love through me, enable me to love others.
- Enable me to meet Your standard of love, enable me to love openly and secretly so men know I am Your disciple.
- Enable me to lay my life down for the brethren and help me to increase and overflow in love.
- Help your children to respect one another, to show love to my brothers and sisters as no one has shown.
- Enable me to be able to put aside my own need for my brother's need.
- Give me unfailing love for the people of God that covers multitude of sins. Enable us to love for one another so we do not walk in pride, enable us to avoid offences.
- I pull down every stronghold and tradition of men preventing people from loving properly.
- Let me not use the liberty that we have as an opportunity for the flesh but that I will love and serve the brethren with a pure heart and pure motives.
- Every evil that has come into the hearts to perverse the unconditional love of God, I rebuke you. I will not be a stumbling block to or grieve my brother in Christ through my personal preferences.

- That I will not judge my brother or cause one who Christ died for to stumble but that I will do only that which is expedient and will be enabling to the brethren.
- Thank You Lord in Jesus Name.

Scriptures for further Prayers:

1 Corinthians 13:4-8, Romans 13:8, Galatians 5:13

FEB 4

FOLLOWING PROTOCOL

Worship

Today's Scripture and Meditation

1 Samuel 13:11-12 *"And Samuel said, "What have you done?" Saul said, "When I saw that the people were scattered from me, and that you did not come within the days appointed, and that the Philistines gathered together at Michmash, then I said, 'The Philistines will now come down on me at Gilgal, and I have not made supplication to the Lord.' Therefore I felt compelled and offered a burnt offering."*

PRAYERS:

- Faithful God, I worship You and honour You, I bow before Your throne, blessed be Your Name.
- Thank You because You are a God of principles and a God of order.
- I pray that You teach me Your principles and Your order.
- I pray that You will give me the grace to be patient and not break your principles.
- That I will not usurp authority, that I will not take up another man's assignment in the kingdom
- That I will not cave under any pressure to the point of disobeying You or going against divine order.
- That the fear of being left alone or deserted will not make me compromise or offer a strange sacrifice unto You
- That I will run the race lawfully and on Your terms that I might win the price
- That the fear of being deserted will not make me compromise or take matters into my hands.

- That I will never feel compelled to do anything that will not please You in Jesus Name.
- Father, please set a watch at my heart and guide me in all I do.
- Thank You Father in Jesus Name.

Scriptures for further Prayers

2 Timothy 2:5, Act 5:29

FEB 5

THE DAY OF THE LORD

Worship

Today's Scripture and Meditation

1 Thessalonians 5:1-2

"But as to the suitable times and the precise seasons and dates, brethren, you have no necessity for anything being written to you. For you yourselves know perfectly well that the day of the [return of the] Lord will come [as unexpectedly and suddenly] as a thief in the night"

PRAYERS

- Dear Lord, I am grateful that I am not lost in this evil world forever that You are coming back for me in order to take me to Your Kingdom.
- I thank You for the hope of eternal life and the mansions You have gone to prepare for me in Your Kingdom.
- I know that the day of the Lord will come as a thief in the night. A thief does not announce the exact time of his arrival. Therefore Lord, I ask that the day will not catch me unawares.
- That I will not be caught sleeping (spiritual indifference), being unfaithful, or without oil in my lamp.
- Lord, You said we should walk circumspectly as the day approaches, being sober, watchful and on guard.
- Holy Spirt, I submit to You, enable me to prepare me for the coming of the Lord.
- Enable me to continually look away from all distractions unto You the Author and the Finisher of my faith to safely take me to shore on this pilgrimage.

Revive Restore and Rebuild

- That I may be able to endure all the temptations and sufferings of this world, that I might not be ashamed on the day of your appearing in Jesus Name.
- Help me to lay aside every unnecessary weight of which will prevent me from going with You on the day You appear. Let me be caught up with You in the air.
- Help me to overcome the sin that so readily entangles me, and enable me to run with patience, endurance, steady and active persistence, the course You have appointed to me in the race that is set before me.,
- I lay aside every manifestation and gratification of the flesh, everything that does not please God and anything that the enemy can accuse me of, every property of the kingdom of darkness.
- Enable me to continue to deny myself, carry my cross and follow You.
- Holy Spirit of the living God, teach me to fear You oh God, to fear You more than I have ever done, give me a deeper understanding of the fear of the Lord, that I may fear You the more
- Holy Spirit, help me not to miss it   because of little things, let Your Name be glorified in my life
- Thank You Heavenly Father, I give You praise, worship and adore You Lord, I magnify Your holy Name.
- Thank You, heavenly Father, in Jesus Name I have prayed. Amen!

Scriptures for further Prayers

1 Thessalonians 4:17, Mathew 25:1-13, Hebrews 12:1-2

FEB 6

BE AN EXAMPLE

Worship

Today's Scripture and Meditation

1 Timothy 4:12b-14 *"But be an example to the believers in word, in conduct, in love, in spirit, in faith, in purity. Till I come, give attention to reading, to exhortation, to doctrine. Do not neglect the gift that is in You, which was given to You by prophecy with the laying on of the hands of the eldership."*

PRAYERS:

- Father Lord, I thank You for choosing me to be Your child and to serve before You.
- I pray that You will work in me to make me an example to the brethren and to those who do not believe or those who are yet to believe.
- Enable me to be an example in word. Let my word be with grace seasoned with salt.
- Let my words bring life and peace to anyone I come across, let my words be accurate and not offensive.
- Let me be an example in conduct. Let my life reflect Your character, that all I meet will see Christ likeness and the image of Christ in me.
- That I will live a holy life and according to Your word.
- That I will be an example in love. That I will be a dispenser of unconditional love. That my love would be to all men without discrimination. That my love will be sacrificial, the kind of love that You have towards us.

- I cast down bitterness, unforgiveness, we cast down pride, enable us to love, enable me to serve others in love.
- Let my love increase, let me excel in love, give me overflowing love for others. I receive grace to love the natural way like You love.
- Father let me be an example in faith in faithfulness. That I will not let people down or be a source of discouragement and disappointments.
- Faith to save, to heal, to deliver, and miracle moving and saving faith.
- Father let me be an example in spirit i.e., in my attitude. That my motives will be right, and my attitude will not be of pride or haughtiness
- Father let me be an example in purity that I will not compromise or be conformed to the world. That I will not be in the church and live like the world.
- Enable me to stay in the word, to pay attention to exhortation and sound doctrine.
- Let Your gifts begin to manifest in my life and ministry to edify the body of Christ and for a sign to those who do not believe.
- Thank You, heavenly Father in Jesus Name, Amen!

Scriptures for further Prayers:

Romans 12:2, 1 Timothy 1:16

FEB 7

GRACE TO CULTIVATE THE CHRISTIAN DUTIES

Worship

Today's Scripture and Meditation

1 Timothy 4:15. *Practice and cultivate and meditate upon these duties; throw yourself wholly into them [as your ministry], so that your progress may be evident to everybody.*

PRAYERS:

- Father Lord I thank and praise You for You have not left me without instruction.
- Thank You because You have given us adequate instruction and directions for our lives here on earth.
- Father I pray that You give me the grace to practice all the duties as enumerated in Your word.
- That I will nourish my own self on the truths of the faith and of the good [Christian] instructions.
- That I will constantly refuse and disapprove irreverent legends, profane and impure, godless fictions, and silly myths.
- Lord train me towards godliness, keeping myself spiritually fit.
- That I will value godliness and pursue it and strive to attain it in hope of eternal life.
- That I will devote myself to readying, studying, exhortation, teaching and instilling doctrine.
- Give me grace to stir up the gift of the Spirit given to me.

- I pray for grace to cultivate all these, meditate on them and give myself wholly to them so that I may grow and advance in You.
- Thank You Father in Jesus' Name.

Scriptures for further Prayers:

1 Timothy 4:6-15, 1 Timothy 6:3, 2 Peter 1:3, 5-6

FEB 8

BE BLAMELESS

Worship

Today's Scripture and Meditation

1 Timothy 5:7(AMPC) *"Charge [the people] thus, so that they may be without reproach and blameless"*

PRAYERS:

- Father, search my heart as I come before You Lord, to know where I have brought reproach and blame upon myself."
- I come before the throne of grace to obtain mercy, let the blood of Jesus cleanse me.
- I ask that You would take away every one of those blames that I might become blameless before You
- Father I ask for the grace to pay attention to my life; my relationship with different categories of people, my thoughts, my actions, my words.
- Help me pay attention to my service to You, that it would be with pure motive and will be done with all faithfulness and zeal that I might remain blameless.
- Help me to focus Lord, on pleasing the audience of one and not on man's opinion, but let me take Your as the priority of my life
- Help me to maintain integrity in the secret when no one is looking as I do in the open, that I may not bring reproach to your Name,
- Holy Spirit, enable me to know how to possess my body, and to know how to possess and be in control of my emotions.

- Let me not look to people for acknowledgement or elicit support from man but that I will seek approval from you alone.
- Let me not insist on carrying out my own plans but that I will carry out Your own plan and agenda, that I will be blameless on the day of Your appearing.
- Enable me to take my prayer life seriously, making solid decision and commitment to the Lord.
- I pray that I will not deal in offence, bitterness, anger, jealousy or envy.
- Let me walk away from worldliness, chasing fame and popularity.
- Father Lord, thank You for making me a ready vessel for You, blameless, that can be used as conduits for You in this world.
- Enable me to discipline myself, to mortify my carnal body, and me to be faultless before You
- Enable me to be true and to become a worthy witness for You.
- Deliver me from deceiving and arguing tongue that lies, and enable me to tame my tongue
- May I be spotless, untainted, without blemish before You in Jesus Name.
- Be glorified in my life and circumstance O God
- I praise You Lord because you are able to keep me from falling and present me blameless to Yourself
- Glory and honour be unto You forever and ever in Jesus. Amen!

Scriptures for further Prayers

Deuteronomy 18:13, Acts 24:16, Revelation 14:5

FEB 9

BELIEVE GOD AND HIS PROPHET

Worship

Today's Scripture and Meditation

2 Chronicles 20:20 *"Hear me oh Judah and you inhabitants of Jerusalem believe in the Lord your God and you shall be established believe in his prophet and you shall prosper"*

PRAYERS:

- Father, I bless You for You are a faithful and dependable God.
- You are the Lord my God, give me continuous grace to believe in You and in Your word so that I will be established in faith, in Your kingdom and every area of my life.
- Lord help me to put my trust and my faith in You because I know that nothing is impossible with You.
- Let my faith in You rest on the fact that You will never leave nor forsake me; You will never let me down because my life today is a testimony of Your greatness.
- God give me the grace to believe in Your prophets so that I can prosper in all things.
- Lord, I remember David, who refused to touch the anointed of God, he refused to kill Saul, he said he will not stretch out his hand against Saul because Saul was the anointed of God even though at this very time Saul had been rejected by God and an evil spirit was living within him. Father grant me the grace to look at Your anointing upon the lives of my leaders and not on the packaging in Jesus Name.

- Our God of Heaven according to the order of David, please fill me with fear of Your grace and anointing upon my leaders, show me the way that I will relate to my leaders that I will not cut the robe of our leaders, that we will not touch the anointed of God in the days of their weakness in Jesus Name.
- David restrained himself by the Spirit, Father restrain me that I will not be claiming rights and go into error.
- Have mercy on me for every time I have despised my leaders that the enemy will not rob me of my prosperity.
- I will not follow the multitude or culture of men to despise leaders.
- Oh God give me the grace to submit to them, the grace of God to believe in them in the Name of Jesus.
- Every problem that was incurred due to ill-treatment of leaders or not believing in your prophets, Father remove from me in Jesus Name.
- Everything stagnant, we command you to move, everything that is not working well, begin to work well.
- Every valuable that has been carted away in the Name of the Lord Jesus be restored in the Name of Jesus.
- From today, Lord, we choose to believe in You, we choose to believe in Your prophets in the Name of Jesus.
- Spiritual prosperity is my portion, physical prosperity is my portion, financial prosperity is my portion in the Name of Jesus.
- Blessed be Your Name oh Lord Hallelujah in Jesus mighty Name we pray. Amen!

Scriptures for further Prayers

1 Chronicles 16:22, Genesis 16:4 & 9, Hebrews 13:17.

FEB 10

SEED TO THE SOWER

Worship

Today's Scripture and Meditation

2 Corinthians 9:10 (GNT) *And God, who supplies seed for the sower and bread to eat, will also supply you with all the seed you need and will make it grow and produce a rich harvest from your generosity.*

PRAYERS:

- ⬚ Father, I thank You because You supply all my needs according to Your riches in glory.

- ⬚ You give me seed to sow and cause it to germinate, grow and give me a great harvest
- ⬚ Father increase the fruits that grow from my giving and that I will be enriched in everything for all generous giving
- ⬚ You are a generous God and I worship You
- ⬚ You give bread to the eater father I ask for divine provision that I will never beg for bread
- ⬚ You said not to care about what to eat, drink, wear, etc. Lord, I cast all my cares on you that you will provide all my needs
- ⬚ Father let my life be to the glory of God, and the good of others, especially those that belong to the household of faith
- ⬚ Give me good gifts that I may be a blessing to others and the glory be directed to You
- ⬚ Father, let my supply be according to Your riches in glory by Christ Jesus

- ☐ Father cause there to be an increase, Father, increase my seed and enlarge my territory.
- ☐ Father as I go out today, let every seed I sow find good soil to grow.
- ☐ Let the seed of the gospel I sow, bring forth fruits in Jesus Name.
- ☐ Thank You Father in Jesus' Name.

Scriptures for further Prayers

Matthew 13:1-9, Matthew 18-23

FEB 11

HOLINESS

Worship

Today's Scripture and Meditation

1 *Peter 1:16* *"Because it is written, "Be holy, for I am holy."*

PRAYERS:

- Thank You Lord Jesus, we praise You Lord, I adore You, Holy God Holy! Holy!
- Lord I come before You by the blood of Jesus, the blood of cleansing, that I may obtain mercy before the throne of grace.
- I confess of all sins wilful and against one another, against the body of Christ, and anything, against organization thinking no one will know, every sin against one another is against You, against our spouses, children, parents, families, acquaintances etc.
- Lord I ask that You help me to do that which You are asking of us this morning. I receive grace to live a holy life, blameless and without blemish in the Name of Jesus!
- Help me to be holy in conduct and in all godliness.
- I put down the old man and put my body under subjection. I silence the flesh in our lives in the Name of Jesus, Amen!
- Sanctify me oh God uproot the Adamic nature from our hearts.
- I pour out myself for cleansing by the blood of Jesus that I will be a holy vessel that is usable by You and be a useful vessel in Your Kingdom in the Name of the Lord Jesus!
- I receive the ability to be holy, let Your presence flood my life, that no darkness will remain.

- Let me live a holy life that I might be free of every oppression and be filled with fullness of joy.
- I ask oh God, the grace to be holy so that we will be permanent carriers of Your presence.
- Let Your presence be with me, enable me to live a holy life so that I can make it to Your kingdom at last in Jesus Name, I pray, Amen.
- Thank You Heavenly Father, blessed be Your Name oh God. Amen.

Scriptures for further Prayers:

Isaiah 6:3, Habakkuk 1:13 - Peter 3:11

FEB 12

NO CONDEMNATION

Worship

Today's Scripture and Meditation

Romans 8:1 *"There is therefore now no condemnation to those who are in Christ Jesus, who do not walk according to the flesh, but according to the Spirit."*

PRAYERS:

- Lord, I thank You that You took my place to go to Calvary
- I thank You that You paid all that we owed in full, on the cross when You said, "it is finished!"
- I thank You that what the law was powerless to do because of the weakness of our flesh, God did by sending his own Son, to be a sin offering for us
- Help me to rest in the truth that there is no condemnation for me because I am in You
- I thank You for adopting me as a member of Your family. I am accepted and not rejected, I am justified and not condemned. I am redeemed and not in bondage
- Heavenly Father, thank You, that I am Your child, accepted in Christ and called to be fruitful. I ask that today I would live every moment of my life as unto You, bringing forth spiritual fruits that is pleasing in Your sight
- By the law of the Spirit of life, I ask to be set free from the law of sin and death. I pray that the Spirit of God will live in me and that I will be controlled by Him

- ▢ Help us to live according to the Spirit rather than the flesh so that we will submit to Your will and ways every time
- ▢ Though my body is dead because of sin, may my spirit be alive because of Your righteousness
- ▢ In You I have redemption, that is, I have deliverance and salvation through Your blood, which paid the penalty for my sins and resulted in the forgiveness and complete pardon of my sins, according to the riches of Your grace that You lavished on me. Hallelujah!
- ▢ My old self - my human nature was nailed to the cross with Christ, in order that my body of sin might be done away with, so that I am no longer a slave to sin
- ▢ I cast out every guilt and rejection. I recognise God as my Father and cry "Abba, Father," I rejoice in my status as heirs of God and co-heirs with Christ
- ▢ I thank You that You will not condemn those who are in Jesus. I am not condemned, I will not be condemned, and I cannot be condemned
- ▢ I pray that the Spirit of God that raised Jesus from the dead will live in me and that God will give life to our mortal bodies through that same Spirit
- ▢ I surrender to be led by the Spirit, to put to death the misdeeds of the body through the Spirit and find life as sons of God

Scriptures for further Prayers

Romans 6:1-7, Romans 8:11, Ephesians 1:7-8

FEB 13

BE SPIRITUALLY MINDED

Worship

Today's Scripture and Meditation

Romans 8:6: For to be carnally minded is death, but to be spiritually minded is life and peace.

PRAYERS:

- Lord I come to You asking that You show me mercy and take away every carnal mindset from me.
- Father Lord please deliver me from every form of carnality.
- Father Lord, thank You for making me ready for You, blameless vessels that can be used as conduits for You.
- Enable me to be able to discipline myself, to mortify my carnal body.
- Enable me to be faultless before You in this world.
- That my mind be rid of fleshly passions and appetites, sensual and carnal pleasures. merely human; temporal, secular, carnal leanings.
- That I will not slip from spiritual mind-set to carnal mind-set.
- That I will move away from me, I and myself attitude but let my love for others grow and that I might change to a selfless attitude.
- That I will not be obsessed with getting more or seek pleasure without boundaries but that I will be content with what You have given me.
- That I will not slip into worshipping people or ideas instead of worshipping God.

- Enable me to be true and to become a worthy- witnesses for You.
- Lord I ask that Your spirit takes charge of, transforms, and renew my mind.
- Sprit of God help me to constantly fellowship with You so that I may have life in Christ.
- Lord I receive the life which You alone can give by Your Spirit.
- Thank You Lord in Jesus' Name.

Scriptures for further Prayers:

2 Timothy 3:1-5, 1 John 4:20

FEB 14

THE SPIRIT OF THE LORD

Worship

Today's Scripture and Meditation

Isaiah 11:1 *"And the Spirit of the Lord shall rest upon him, the spirit of wisdom and understanding, the spirit of counsel and might, the spirit of knowledge and of the fear of the Lord"*

PRAYERS:

- Lord, I thank You for Your Holy Spirit without Whom, I am empty, and have no life.
- Without the Holy Spirit, I cannot know You or have a relationship with You.
- It is with the Holy Spirit that I have been sealed unto the day of redemption, Lord without Your Holy Spirit there is no anointing, no unction, wisdom, understanding, counsel, fear of the Lord.
- Lord, I need Your presence so that my life will not be as lost as the people of the world, without direction or instruction, wisdom, understanding, knowledge, might and counsel of God.
- Lord, Holy Spirit, I ask that You will rest on me afresh.
- I know that the anointing of yesterday is not sufficient for today, the infilling of yesterday is not sufficient for today, unction and utterances of yesterday are not sufficient for today, and so I come before You for a fresh infilling,
- Pour into me Lord, let me receive freshness from Your presence Holy Spirit rest on us afresh.

- ⬚ Fill me up, fire me up so that I will go out there to do signs and wonders and be worthy representatives of God.
- ⬚ I cannot get enough of you Lord, as David said as the deer pants for the water brooks so does my soul pant after You, I pant after You Lord, I thirsty for You, Lord come and quench my thirst.
- ⬚ You are the One that quenches the thirst of those that seek You, I seek you for a fresh infilling, a fresh fire I pray, fresh fire I pray, a rain of fresh fire from heaven.
- ⬚ I do not want to walk by experience, but by Your Spirit; refresh me Lord.
- ⬚ When the fire is dying, dimmed, or being doused, Father ignite Your fire in me.
- ⬚ Lord grant me the Spirit of wisdom as You normally give liberally and without reproach to all, that I might be wise.
- ⬚ Let the Spirit of understanding rest upon me that I might have the capacity to judge rightly in matters relating to life and conduct, to be able to make right and righteous judgement.
- ⬚ Let the Spirit of counsel rest upon me that I might receive the roadmap of life and execute what the Lord has given me already. The might, that the Lord has already spoken to me, grant me the grace to execute that which the Lord has already given to me in the Name of the Lord Jesus Christ.
- ⬚ I cast down the spirit of fear, I arise and begin to do what the Spirit of the Lord says to me with courage
- ⬚ Thank You heavenly Father I give You praise and honor, I magnify Your holy Name in Jesus Name I have prayed. Amen!

Scriptures for further Prayers

Isaiah 30:21, Ps 42:1

FEB 15

CONTENTMENT

Worship

Today's Scripture and Meditation

1 Timothy 6:6-7 *"Now godliness with contentment is great gain. For we brought nothing into this world, [a]and it is certain we can carry nothing out."*

PRAYERS:

- Father Lord I thank you that you have reminded me that You are sufficient, that You are enough for me.
- You are sufficient and all I need to do is to remain in You and remain godly.
- When the people of the world and the children of God are not content, I will not chase after the unnecessary things of the world, so I am not led away and deceived.
- Holy spirit I surrender my life, heart, mind circumstances, situation, aspirations, and desires So in all things I can remain godly, please do the work of ultimate salvation in us.
- Help me to remain godly and be contented with You, Your ways, instruction and the things You have given, and not given to us.
- Help us to be content with the things of God, instructions of God and grant us inner sufficiency.
- I came naked and brought nothing into this world, So, let me be satisfied with food and raiment that I will not crave the foolish desires if the world. Let me not be overtaken by the love of money. As I will not take anything out.

- Let no evil take root in my life, so I am not led astray by our desire from the flesh but to flee from   every appearance of evil.
- Grant us the reverent fear of God, to become more Christ like. Grant me faith so we will not chase after what to eat, drink, wear, and where to live.
- These are Your responsibilities. Let us seek Your kingdom as first priority in our lives. So that in turn You will add unto us every other thing we need.
- You clothe the grass. And feed the birds who neither sow nor reap nor gather into barns, Our great provider. Grant us to live You with contentment in my heart in Jesus' Name.
- Enable me to love the brethren with all my heart. Grant unto us gentleness of heart   as we walk the work of faith.
- Let our lives mirror our confession of faith so we will not chase after   what the world chases after.
- Let the world see contentment in us and be drawn to You I bind and cast any unsatiable Spirit in me in Jesus Name.
- Lord, I give You praise, I give You honor and magnify Your holy Name, I pray, Amen.

Scriptures for further Prayers:

1 Timothy 6:7, Job 1:21, 1 Thessalonians 5:22

FEB 16

ESTABLISHED AND GROUNDED SECURELY

Worship

Today's Scripture and Meditation

1Peter 5:10. (AMPC) *And after you have suffered a little while, the God of all grace [Who imparts all blessing and favor], Who has called you to His [own] eternal glory in Christ Jesus, will Himself complete and make you what you ought to be, establish and ground you securely, and strengthen, and settle you.*

PRAYERS:

- Father Lord, I thank You because You are the God that sees, and You are always thinking of me.
- I thank You that nothing I am going through is hidden from You and You have allowed it for a purpose.
- Lord, I thank You that You also chastise me as Your child out of love that I may grow in my knowledge and understanding of You, and that I might grow in character.
- I thank You because everything is for a purpose and for a reason, and everything will work together for my good because I love you and I am called according to your purpose.
- Father enable me to be well balanced and sober of mind, to be vigilant and cautious at all times; for that enemy, the devil, roams around like a lion roaring seeking someone to seize upon and devour.
- Father enable me to withstand him; to be firm in faith against the enemy's onslaught.

- Enable me to be rooted, established, strong, immovable, and determined,
- that I will always know and remember that the same identical, sufferings are experienced by all Christians from all over the world and that I am not alone.
- Let my light momentary affliction produce God's richest blessing and glory in me.
- Strengthen me in the day of adversity and suffering, that I may not lose faith or integrity
- I thank You that You bring a message out of every mess of our lives.
- Father help me to understand what I am to learn from all situations that may be a point of learning and a solution for others.
- Thank You Lord in Jesus Name, I pray. Amen!

Scriptures for further Prayers

2 Corinthians 4:17, 1 Peter 5:8, Romans 8:28

FEB 17

MERCIFUL AND FORGIVING

Worship

Today's Scripture and Meditation

Daniel 9:9 *The Lord our God is merciful and forgiving, even though we have rebelled against him.*

PRAYERS:

- Thank You oh Lord for You are a merciful and a forgiving God.

- Thank You for Your grace to reason with You and negotiate with the Almighty God.

- Thank You, Almighty God, for Your love always bring us back to You.

- Mighty God I come back to You and acknowledging the times I have missed it asking Lord that please cleanse me, wash me clean by Your blood.

- Heavenly Father, have mercy on me. Grant me favour according to Your grace and truth. If You Lord should mark iniquities, who can stand? It is Your righteousness that makes me righteous and Your goodness is what declares me good

- Thank You for the atonement we receive through Christ. I am confident it is sufficient to cleanse me from my sin

- I confess all my sins before You... *(confess Your sins)* and repent of them

- Show me Your mercy Lord and wash me whitter than snow of every stain that sin may have left on me.

- Father, have mercy upon me for the sins of ingratitude; lack of appreciation for the free gifts of nature, and for not sharing testimonies
- Father, give me a heart of flesh to obey You in all things and to keep short accounts with You
- Thank You Lord, for throwing our sins into the sea of forgetfulness, Lord, I bless You.

Scriptures for further Prayers:

Isaiah 1:18, Hebrews 10:7

FEB 18

NOT MY OWN

Worship

Today's Scripture and Meditation

1 Corinthians 6:19-20 *What? know ye not that your body is the temple of the Holy Ghost which is in you, which ye have of God, and ye are not your own? For ye are bought with a price: therefore, glorify God in your body, and in your spirit, which are God's"*

PRAYERS:

- Thank You that You left Your throne on high to walk the streets of this earth and then went to the cross. Now you have made my earthly vessel of clay your temple and I am grateful.
- I am humbled that you fill me with your Spirit to make me a sacred place where You dwell. This truth makes me to stand in awe of You.
- Father teach me to possess my body and that I will not be involved in anything that will defile your temple in Jesus Name.
- I know that my body belongs to You because You dwell in me, I have been bought with a price therefore I am not my own.
- Give me grace not to pollute and abuse my body which is Your property.
- Give me grace not to leave it idle and sluggish when it comes to Your work or lie waste due to my appetites and preferences in Jesus Name.

- You in me means that I have power over sin, Father strengthen me to resist all temptations and take Your provided way of escape in Jesus Name.
- You in me means that I can do all things
- Father glorify yourself in my body and in my spirit always in Jesus Name.
- Thank You Father in Jesus Name.

Scriptures for further Prayers:

1 Thessalonians 4:4, 1 Corinthians 6:19-20

FEB 19

JOY DESPITE PERSECUTION

Worship

Today's Scripture and Meditation

Act 13:50-5 *"But the Jews stirred up the devout and prominent women and the chief men of the city, raised up persecution against Paul and Barnabas, and expelled them from their region. 51 But they shook off the dust from their feet against them and came to Iconium. 52 And the disciples were filled with joy and with the Holy Spirit"*

PRAYERS:

- Lord, I thank You for the gift of salvation. Thank You for taking the suffering, shame and death that I deserved.
- I count it joy that I can be a partaker in the suffering of Christ in rejection, persecution, false accusations, despise, verbal abuse, etc. because of the gospel and my life in Christ.
- Teach me to shake off the dust and to advance in the course of the gospel.
- Every time the disciples were persecuted, You filled them with joy and with the Spirit again and again and manifested Your power in them. I pray Lord that I will experience Your deep inner joy come what may.
- I ask Lord that You will baptize me afresh by Your spirit, fresh fire, I pray, fresh infilling, I pray!
- Fill me afresh, to overflowing that out of my belly shall flow rivers of living water.
- Let me be filled again and again!

- Lord the infilling/anointing of yesterday is not sufficient for today. I need to be continually filled throughout my life father fill me by Your Spirit again in Jesus Name.
- Let my soul be filled with the Spirit of God and with joy. I cast down every one of my worries, anxiety, sorrow in Jesus Name.
- Nothing will happen to me, that is against the will of the Father. And today, I just want to desire the Lord, breathe on me Lord!
- I desire to be filled, again, by the Spirit of the living God. You are, all I want. I want more of You. I'm desperate for You.
- Spirit of God, penetrate my life, infiltrate my life, invade my life, break down my walls
- When the fire is dying, when the anointing is stale, fresh anointing; I pray for fresh fire, fresh grace, fresh baptism, fresh fire, in Jesus Name.
- Let the fire fall, fall upon me, I receive the fire. Fill my life with your presence, fresh unction!
- I receive greater grace, greater heights, greater levels, greater assignments, a greater calling, greater works.
- I cancel every limitation and decision of darkness and pray that only the will, counsel and plan of God will prosper in my life in Jesus Name.

Scriptures for further Prayers

John 7:38, John 20:22, Joel 2:28-29

FEB 20

DOUBLE PORTION

Worship

Today's Scripture and Meditation

2 Kings 2:9 *"And so it was, when they had crossed over, that Elijah said to Elisha, "Ask! What may I do for you, before I am taken away from you?" Elisha said, "Please let a double portion of your spirit be upon me"*

PRAYERS:

- Father I thank You because You give gifts to Your body, Thank You for those that You have given for oversight over our lives.
- Thank You that the number of our days are before You, I ask that You enable me to walk into Your plan for my life…
- Give me grace to submit to mentoring, listening, taking counsel, and following my leaders with unwavering resolution.
- Elijah walked in the steps of Moses and Joshua to part the water and walked on dry lane. Father enable me to walk in the steps of my leaders whose hearts are before You. Give me double portion of the grace and anointing than I have experienced in the ministry of my leaders in Jesus' Name, Amen.
- Father may I not seek after wealth, or position, or worldly power; or a share in those advantages as my first my choice in life but to seek Your kingdom first.
- Enable me to seek for the first-born portion (double portion), for the spiritual power to fulfil the calling I have already received.

- Father enable me to be devotedly watchful and persistent in the day of my spiritual endowment by Your Spirit in Jesus Name, Amen!
- Father let me not stumble in words or be distracted on the journey of life and walk with God.
- Enlighten my eyes to see You high and lifted, shining in the light of Your glory.
- Thank You Father in Jesus' Name, Amen!

Scriptures for further Prayers:

Isaiah 6:5-7, Exodus 14:21, Joshua 3:15-17.

FEB 21

THE LORD'S ANOINTED

Worship

Today's Scripture and Meditation

1 Samuel 24:4-6 (AMP) *"David's men said to him, "Behold, this is the day of which the Lord said to you, 'Behold, I will hand over your enemy to you, and you shall do to him as seems good to you.'" Then David arose [in the darkness] and stealthily cut off the hem (edge) of Saul's robe. Afterward, David's conscience bothered him because he had cut off the hem of Saul's robe. He said to his men, "The Lord forbid that I should do this thing to my master, the Lord's anointed, to put out my hand against him, since he is the anointed of the Lord."*

PRAYERS:

- Father, I thank You because You always speak to Your children.
- Thank You because You always fight for us and give us victories.
- Help me not to make mistakes under pressure and sin against You.
- Let my conscience be alive to guide me when I fail You.
- Oh Lord, let me hear Your Voice when You call in Jesus' Name, Amen!
- Oh Lord, deliver my enemies into my hand in Jesus' Name, Amen!
- Oh Lord, grant to me divine insight to abstain from every compromise and action that invalidates Your word

- ⟐ Oh Lord, I repent from every presumption sin, the sin of omission, the sin of commission, and ignorance of Your word.
- ⟐ Enable me not to be conformed to the word or its principle and way of Life
- ⟐ Help me to restrain myself and not to claim rights or revenge against my leaders so that I will not touch the anointed of God
- ⟐ Give me the grace to obey and submit to my leaders as you have commanded that I might prosper
- ⟐ Thank You Father Lord, in Jesus name. Amen!

Scriptures for further Prayers

Romans 12:2, 2 Chronicles 20:20

FEB 22

FIRE IN OUR MIDST

Worship

Today's Scripture and Meditation

Zechariah 2:4-5(GNT) *"The first one said to the other, "Run and tell that young man with the measuring line that there are going to be so many people and so much livestock in Jerusalem that it will be too big to have walls. 5 The Lord has promised that he himself will be a wall of fire around the city to protect it and that he will live there in all his glory."*

PRAYERS:

- Father, I thank You because You are the glory in the midst of us, Thank You for restoration and return.
- I pray that lines will fall for me in pleasant places.
- You said there will be no walls, so I break forth to the left and right, I lengthen the chords and spread out.
- I receive the extension and enlargement freely by the power God.
- According to Your word, be the wall of fire round about me for protection round about me.
- By the fire that surrounds us, I walk in the light.
- By Your fire, consume the enemy and keep out every intruder and prey.
- Let there be no plunder or destruction of goods in my life by the enemy

- By the fire of God, no works of darkness can survive; I am free from oppression.
- No matter how fierce the battle is, the fire of the Lord is there to protect me and consume my enemies.
- The Lord will be the glory in our midst and appear glorious to me and through me.
- The glory of the Lord is upon me; I will arise, shine, and do nothing by struggles.
- As others are being covered by darkness, let the brightness of Your presence be with me.
- I pass from shame to glory from death to life physically and spiritually.
- Let nations gather unto me and kings be drawn to my brightness.
- It is a new dawn of glory I receive it; I obtain glory through Your works in my life so the ears of all who hear it will tingle.
- According to Your word, Lord, build the wall of fire and glory in the midst of us.
- From here on it will be glory and no more shame in Jesus Name! Amen!

Scriptures for further Prayers

Psalm 125:2, Psalm 97:3, Exodus 13:21, Isaiah 54:17

FEB 23

SECRET BACKSLIDING

Worship

Today's Scripture and Meditations

2 Samuel 12:1-7a & 12 *"Then the Lord sent Nathan to David. And he came to him and said to him: "There were two men in one city, one rich and the other poor. The rich man had exceedingly many flocks and herds. But the poor man had nothing, except one little ewe lamb which he had bought and nourished; and it grew up together with him and with his children. It ate of his own food and drank from his own cup and lay in his bosom; and it was like a daughter to him.*

And a traveler came to the rich man, who refused to take from his own flock and from his own herd to prepare one for the wayfaring man who had come to him; but he took the poor man's lamb and prepared it for the man who had come to him."

So David's anger was greatly aroused against the man, and he said to Nathan, "As the Lord lives, the man who has done this shall surely die! And he shall restore fourfold for the lamb, because he did this thing and because he had no pity."

Then Nathan said to David, "You are the man! .... For you did it secretly, but I will do this thing before all Israel, before the sun.'"

PRAYERS:

- Father, I thank You that Christ was sacrificed once and for all to take away my sins, I pray that I will continue to grow in grace and not backslide in Jesus name
- Father, I repent of every secret sin and further sins to cover sins. I cannot cover or hide sin from You, and I

cannot persist in deceiving myself. If I hide any sins in my heart it prevents me from prospering spiritually, physically and in every way. So, I repent of all my sins - Lord cleanse me from all sins in Jesus name

- Father, I pray that my heart will not be dulled and let me not be insensitive to the Holy Spirit. I choose to hear His promptings and know when I have offended Him. I will not be used to a lifestyle of sin
- Let my heart be tendered before the Almighty God
- I pray that sin will no longer have dominion over me, and that sin will not separate me from God or cause Him to hide His face from me
- Father forgive my iniquities and let me continue to grow spiritually until I attain the height of living without sin
- Enable me to keep short accounts with You like David did in Jesus name
- Let no work of darkness thrive in my life Lord. I reject every form of hypocrisy in Jesus name
- Help me to keep living in the consciousness of Your love for me and let that love begin to flow from me to others
- Thank You Father, in Jesus name

Scriptures for further Prayers

Romans 6:14, Jeremiah 31:31-34. Isaiah 59:1-2

FEB 24

DON'T BREAK THE HEDGE

Worship

Today's Scripture and Meditation

Ecclesiastes 10:8b *"And whoso breaks an hedge, a serpent shall bite him"*

PRAYERS:

- Thank you, Lord because you are a forgiving Father.
- I thank you for the hedge of protection that you have put around each one of your children; hedge of protection that repels the enemy.
- The enemy could not touch Job because of your hedge around him, let your hedge be sure around me.
- I repent for every time I have transgressed your commands and your ways that have resulted in the breaking of the hedge.
- I repent of very time I have transgressed against my neighbour's boundaries, properties or involved in any wrong doing against my neighbour that have resulted in the breaking of the hedge.
- I take refuge in you that I will not be bitten by the serpent in Jesus Name.
- That I will not be bitten by the serpent of mishaps, losses, ill health conditions, broken relationships, ruined reputations, vanished ambitions, wasted lives, poverty, shame, and enfeebled will, death, etc in Jesus' Name.
- Let the blood of Jesus seal off every crack in the wall.
- Father restore me back into full fellowship with You, let the angel of the Lord encamp around me, because I fear You reverently Lord.

- Let me have the assurance of Your covering and protection. Thank You heavenly father, in Jesus Name.

Scriptures for further Prayers:

Psalm34:7,Psalm27:5

FEB 25

THE BLESSING OF HEALING

Worship

Today's scripture

Deuteronomy 7:14-15 *You shall be blessed above all peoples; there shall not be a male or female barren among you or among your livestock. And the Lord will take away from you all sickness and will afflict you with none of the terrible diseases of Egypt which you have known but will lay them on all those who hate you.*

PRAYERS:

- ▢ Father God, I thank You that I am blessed above all people because I am Your child and I belong to You
- ▢ Father God, I thank You for taking away barrenness from among us Your children, I pray to enforce termination of barrenness in any area of my life and family. I refute barrenness and unfruitfulness in the work of my hands, in family and in ministry and in every area of life in Jesus name
- ▢ Father God, I thank You that You have taken away every form of sickness and affliction from our midst, I pray to enforce complete healing and deliverance from all manner of sicknesses in the body and mind in Jesus name
- ▢ I submit under the power of the Holy Spirit as I resist and rebuke every sickness, every disease, every health condition, physical, emotional, spiritual in my life
- ▢ I bind every spirit of infirmity, I cast you out of the lives of the people this morning into the abyss in the name of Jesus

Revive Restore and Rebuild

- I declare the word of God over my life that by the stripes of Jesus I am healed from every sickness. I am healed from every disease, I am healed from every infirmity from today, in the name of Jesus
- Holy Spirit of the living God overshadow me: overshadow me in my body, in my spirit and in my soul
- Quicken my body, quicken my mind by Your power in Jesus name
- I plead the blood of Jesus against every demonic induced sickness, every disease, every infirmity, every health condition that is against the will and counsel of God
- I command, that everything that has been planted into my body and mind that is not planted by the Almighty God be uprooted by the power of God in Jesus name
- I speak all round recovery into my life in Jesus name.

Scriptures for further Prayers:

Exodus 23:26, 1 Peter 2:24, Luke 1:74

FEB 26

MERCIFUL AND FORGIVING

Worship

Today's Scripture and Meditation

Daniel 9:9 *The Lord our God is merciful and forgiving, even though we have rebelled against him.*

PRAYERS:

- Thank You oh Lord for You are a merciful and a forgiving God.
- Thank You for Your grace to reason with You and negotiate with the Almighty God.

- Thank You, Almighty God, for Your love always bring us back to You.

- Mighty God I come back to You and acknowledging the times I have missed it asking Lord that please cleanse me, wash me clean by Your blood.

- Heavenly Father, have mercy on me. Grant me favour according to Your grace and truth. If You Lord should mark iniquities, who can stand? It is Your righteousness that makes me righteous and Your goodness is what declares me good
- Thank You for the atonement we receive through Christ. I am confident it is sufficient to cleanse me from my sin
- I confess all my sins before You… *(confess Your sins)* and repent of them
- Show me Your mercy Lord and wash me whitter than snow of every stain that sin may have left on me.

Revive Restore and Rebuild

- Father, have mercy upon me for the sins of ingratitude; lack of appreciation for the free gifts of nature, and for not sharing testimonies
- Father, give me a heart of flesh to obey You in all things and to keep short accounts with You
- Thank You Lord, for throwing our sins into the sea of forgetfulness, Lord, I bless You.

Scriptures for further Prayers:

Isaiah 1:18, Hebrews 10:7

FEB 27

THANKSGIVING FOR SALVATION

Worship

Today's Scripture and Meditation

2 Corinthians 9:15 *"Thanks be to God for His indescribable gift!"*

PRAYERS:

- Father God, I give You thanks and praise for Your amazing gift of salvation and for keeping me in the faith thus far
- Father, we thank You for sending Your only begotten son Jesus Christ to this world to die for me for the forgiveness of my sins
- Thank You for enlightening my heart to say "yes" to You when You called me to be Your child
- Thank You for revealing Yourself to me as The Way, The Truth and The Life; the one who has the name through which all will be saved.
- Thank You for the incredible sacrifice You made that I might have freedom and life. Thank You for Your mercy and grace
- Thank You for the forgiveness of my sins, You are the Rock of our salvation.
- Thank You for peace and grace to be part of the body of Christ, a son in Your family and a citizen in Your kingdom
- Thank You for healing all my diseases, for the redemption of my soul from the pit.

- Thank You for crowning me with steadfast love and mercy
- You have the name above all names; at Your name every knee bow, and every tongue confess that Jesus is Lord to the glory of God the Father
- Thank You for all the things that have bowed and left my life because of Your name
- Thank You for translating me from the kingdom of darkness to the kingdom of Your dear Son: the kingdom of light
- Thank You for Your deliverance from the hand of the enemy that I may serve You without fear, being set apart and made righteous before You all our days
- Thank You for receiving Your kingdom with an unshakable firm foundation
- I surrender all to You, take my life and let it be as You have ordained it to be, from the foundation of the world
- Enable me to share Your gospel at every opportunity that others may benefit from the mercy and saving grace that I have obtained
- Thank You, my Saviour, my Master and my Lord in Jesus name

Scriptures for further Prayers:

Philippians 2:9-10, John 3:16, Psalms 107:1-2

FEB 28

IN THE NAME OF THE LORD

Worship

Today's Scripture and Meditation

1Samuel 17:45-47 Then David said to the Philistine, "You come to me with a sword, with a spear, and with a javelin. But I come to you in the Name of the LORD of hosts, the God of the armies of Israel, whom you have defied. This day the LORD will deliver you into my hand, and I will strike you and take your head from you. And this day I will give the carcasses of the camp of the Philistines to the birds of the air and the wild beasts of the earth, that all the earth may know that there is a God in Israel. Then all this assembly shall know that the LORD does not save with sword and spear; for the battle is the LORD's, and He will give you into our hands."

PRAYERS:

- Father I thank You because You are the victorious Lord.
- No matter the threats of the enemy, grant me grace to stand and not fear but to continue to put my faith in You.
- I pray that all defiling the church of God and His people be silenced.
- You use the foolish things to confound the wise, Father pour out Your Spirit on me and use me to defeat the enemy in the lives of men.
- Father deliver the enemy into my hands, some trust in chariots and others in their horses but I trust only in Your Name.
- By the power of the Spirit of God I command every giant in my life, family and church to fall.
- I receive victory over everything which torments me and

the people of God.
- Today in the mighty Name of Jesus, Let the head of any giants in my life and church that it may not come back, and the entire earth shall know that I have the Almighty God as my God.
- Thank You, Lord, because I know the battle belongs to You and You have triumphed gloriously.
- Father, do what only can do and cause men to know that You have the power to save.
- Thank you father, in Jesus name I pray. Amen

Scriptures for further Prayers:

Isaiah 49:24-25, 1 Corinthians 1:27.

MARCH 1

MOUNTAINS MELT LIKE WAX

Worship

Today's Scripture and Meditation

Psalm 97:1-6(NKJV) *"The Lord reigns; Let the earth rejoice; Let the multitude of isles be glad! Clouds and darkness surround Him; Righteousness and justice are the foundation of His throne. A fire goes before Him, And burns up His enemies round about*

His lightnings light the world; The earth sees and trembles. The mountains melt like wax at the presence of the Lord, At the presence of the Lord of the whole earth. The heavens declare His righteousness, And all the peoples see His glory."

PRAYERS:

- Lord You reign on high over all the earth, and You reign in heaven. You reign over thrones and dominions, over principalities and power, rulers and spiritual hosts. You are in control of everything
- You reign in majesty, in righteousness and justice
- Father let the enemy tremble like water boiling over a hot fire. Come and reveal your power to your enemies and make them tremble at your presence!
- Lord come down and make Your name known to Your adversaries in my life in the name of the Lord Jesus Christ, Amen
- My enemies are nothing, standing in the way of God's will and purpose in my life; I pray that You will deliver me from the hand of my enemies that I might serve You without fear, in holiness and righteousness before You all the days of my life

- Let every mountain in any department of my life melt at Your presence
- Let every sickness, disease, satanic bondage, lack, failure, stagnancy (if applicable) be destroyed in the name of Jesus name
- Every oppression, suppression ad possession of the enemy in my life be broken in Jesus name. Amen
- At Your presence let the enemy turn their backs and take to flight in my life
- Lord begin to do wonderful, mighty and awesome things in the life that none shall be able to stand before me because of Your presence in my life Let the world know that indeed God is with me
- I pray commanding everything that stands like a mountain in my life to melt like wax at Your presence
- Thank You Father for Your righteousness and justice, for Your miracles and deliverances in Jesus name, Amen

Scriptures for further Prayers

Isaiah 64:2, Luke 1:74-75, Exodus 23:27

MARCH 2

A TABLE BEFORE ME

Worship

Today's Scripture and Meditation

Psalm 23:5(NKJV) *"You prepare a table before me in the presence of my enemies; You anoint my head with oil; My cup runs over"*

PRAYERS:

- Father I thank You for Your provision and Your goodness as You invite me to a rich table prepared for me
- I am grateful for Your power to protect me and the confidence I have to sit at the table to feast even in the midst of enemies
- Thank You for the preparation You have made for me with foresight and care and for the personal connection I have with You
- I thank You that even in the presence of my enemies I can experience God's goodness and bounty
- In Your presence there is no confusion, no disturbance, no pandemonium, with You Lord, everything is in perfect peace."
- Father I pray for grace to be at peace instead of worry and anxiety, that my mind will stay on You
- Anoint my head with the oil of gladness by the Spirit of the Lord. Let Your graces that teaches all things and fill with spiritual joy and comfort rest upon me
- Let Your anointing that breaks the yoke rest upon me to break every yoke in my life in the name of Jesus Christ, Amen

- Let me not be overcome by the torment of fear but let my heart be overwhelmed by Your faith and love
- Set me free from every entanglement with the enemy and everything that has plagued us in generations past
- Let my whole life be full till it overflows with Your blessedness and abundance

Scriptures for further Prayers

Philippians 4:7, Isa 61:3, Isaiah 10:27

MARCH 3

GROW SPIRITUALLY

Worship

Today's Scripture and Meditation

2 *Peter* 3:18 (AMP) *"But grow [spiritually mature] in the grace and knowledge of our Lord and Saviour Jesus Christ. To Him be glory (honor, majesty, splendor), both now and to the day of eternity. Amen."*

PRAYERS:

- Thank You Lord for the Holy Spirit given to me, to teach me and lead me into all truth.
- Holy Spirit I pray that You will reveal the Father and the Son to me.
- Work in me to change me from glory to glory to the image of Christ.
- Help me to grow the knowledge of your word that the word may dwell richly in me
- Help me to know how to apply God's grace in my life
- Enable me to break free of the sinful nature and follow You wholeheartedly
- Enable me to grow in our appreciation of the never-ending grace we have been given.
- Enable me to grow in You that I will not be stagnant or backslide
- Reveal to me Your secrets and deep things that I do not know.
- Father, enable me to grow in grace and knowledge of our Lord and Saviour Jesus Christ!
- Reveal Your manifold presence in my life, let me experience the warmth of Your love.

       Revive Restore and Rebuild

- Lord Jesus, help me to know and love You more.
- Thank You Father in Jesus Name, Amen!

Scriptures for further Prayers

2 Corinthians 3:18, Ephesians 4:2, Colossians 3:16

MARCH 4

DIVINE INTERRUPTION

Worship

Today's Scripture and Meditation

Act 9:3-6 (NIV) *"As he neared Damascus on his journey, suddenly a light from heaven flashed around him. 4 He fell to the ground and heard a voice say to him, "Saul, Saul, why do you persecute me?" 5 "Who are you, Lord?" Saul asked. "I am Jesus, whom you are persecuting," he replied. 6 "Now get up and go into the city, and you will be told what you must do."*

PRAYERS:

- Thank You Lord for You foreknew and predestined me from the foundations of the world.
- Thank You because You called me and enabled me to answer the call to be Your child and to serve you
- I thank You that from the beginning when I did not know You until now, You have guided my paths and caused me to walk as ordained.
- Father, please interrupt me if I am going about my purpose in the wrong way.
- Lord interrupt me when I am going outside Your will, plan and purpose for my life.
- Deliver me from zeal without knowledge in Jesus' Name.
- Lord shine Your light in my path and Your light to my feet
- I ask that Your light shine into every aspect of my life that may need illumination
- Let me not be serving You outside Your will or for my own glory.

- Lord, I need You to speak into every area of my life today and set it straight.
- Oh Lord help me to turn back to You at any point where we are about to miss it.
- Father, I pray that You keep instructing me daily.
- Thank You, heavenly father, in Jesus name

Scriptures for further Prayers

Psalm 119:105, Jeremiah 1:5

MARCH 5

BE RELIABLE

Worship

Today's Scripture and Meditation

Acts 15:37-41 "Now Barnabas wanted to take with them John called Mark [his near relative]. But Paul did not think it best to have along with them the one who had quit and deserted them in Pamphylia and had not gone on with them to the work.

And there followed a sharp disagreement between them, so that they separated from each other, and Barnabas took Mark with him and sailed away to Cyprus. But Paul selected Silas and set out, being commended by the brethren to the grace (the favor and mercy) of the Lord. And he passed through Syria and Cilicia, establishing, and strengthening the churches"

PRAYERS:

- Father I thank You for the privilege of knowing You and of serving You.
- Father forgive me for the time I have fallen short in the area of faithfulness, integrity and dependability.
- Enable me to be able to follow through with whatever I do and do all things with sincerity and excellence.
- I pray that You will transform me that I will grow in reliability.
- That I will not quit or desert in the middle of an assignment in Jesus Name, Amen!
- That I will not be the source for disagreements or separation within the body.
- Father let me never lose sight of Your blessing not matter what trials await me tomorrow,

- Father let me never lose sight of the eternal glory that awaits me, not matter what trials await me tomorrow,
- May I never forget the blessings You have shown to me. Help me remember Your steadfast love and faithfulness to me in all things. That I may remain faithful also.
- May I observe to do as the Lord God has commanded me: that I shall not turn aside to the right hand or to the left.
- Enable me to endure till the end denying myself that I might reign with You.

Scriptures for further Prayers:

Deuteronomy 5:32, Proverbs 28:20.

MARCH 6

HOLY SPIRIT ENDUEMENT

Worship

Today's Scripture and Meditation

Acts 2:1-4 *"When the Day of Pentecost had fully come, they were all with one accord in one place. And suddenly there came a sound from heaven, as of a rushing mighty wind, and it filled the whole house where they were sitting. And there appeared unto them cloven tongues like as of fire, and it sat upon each of them. And they were all filled with the Holy Ghost and began to speak with other tongues, as the Spirit gave them utterance."*

PRAYERS:

- Father God, I come to You today in the name of Your Son Jesus, asking that You baptise and fill me afresh with the Holy Ghost as in the day of Pentecost
- Lord, release Your presence over my life afresh and ignite Your fire in me
- Holy Spirit come upon me, break my walls down, infiltrate, penetrate, invade and rule my life
- Let the power of the Highest overshadow me so that Christ can be fully formed in me
- Father, incubate me with the fire of the Holy Spirit, in Jesus' name
- Let there be the manifestation of the Spirit transforming power in my life
- Fill me up with fresh fire, fresh grace, fresh anointing that I may impact the world around me for You

- Let the Spirit of God quicken my mortal body in a supernatural manner
- As You transformed the timid and fearful disciples, Lord transform me to be a bold and fearless witness for You
- Ignite Your fire within me
- Let there be a spiritual disruption by the power of the Spirit in my life and through me
- Father, let me not receive Your Spirit and power and be mute, Let there be and unusual manifestation that will cause the non-Christian community to pay attention
- Enable me under the unction of Your Spirit, let me grab the attention of everyone in my proximity for Christ
- Transform me into spaces that ignite conviction and change people's lives and direction.
- Let me be continually filled with joy of the Holy Spirit in Jesus name

Scriptures for further Prayers

1 Corinthians 4:7a, Luke 1:35, Joel 2:28, Acts 13:52

MARCH 7

WALK WORTHY

Worship

Today's Scripture and Meditation

Colossians 1:10 *"That you may walk worthy of the Lord, fully pleasing Him, being fruitful in every good work and increasing in the knowledge of God."*

PRAYERS:

- ⬚ Lord I thank You for Your love for me

- ⬚ Thank You for longsuffering towards me, Thank You for Your patience with me, thank You for the work of the Holy Spirit in my life-changing me and enabling me daily

- ⬚ It is the desire of my heart to walk worthy of You, Father enable me to walk in the grace of those who have been redeemed from darkness; never involved in any work of darkness

- ⬚ Father, enable me to be fully acquainted with You and reveal to me Your glorious purpose, that I might walk worthy of You and of the gospel

- ⬚ Let my life be pleasing unto You. Let the words of my mouth, the meditations of my heart and my actions please You.

- ⬚ Let my lifestyle and character please You in the way I relate to people. Father let my love be unconditional, enable me to be please You always

- ⬚ Let me be fruitful in good works, that I will not be used for division or break ranks, but I will endeavour to keep the unity in the body through peace

▢ Use me to teach all the manifold wisdom of God, and show forth His praises

Scriptures for further Prayers:

1 Corinthians 12:25, Colossians 1:10, 2 Timothy 3:16-17

MARCH 8

REBUKE THE DEVOURER

Worship

Today's Scripture and Meditation

Malachi 3:11 *"And I will rebuke the devourer for your sakes, So that he will not destroy the fruit of your ground, Nor shall the vine fail to bear fruit for you in the field," Says the* LORD *of hosts; "*

PRAYERS:

- Father, I thank You for You defend me and everything that You have given to me.
- Thank You because You have blessed me with all I need and all that pertains to life and godliness.
- Thank You for the work of my hands and Your blessings; enable me to be faithful in my giving to You and for Your righteous causes.
- According to Your word, Father rebuke the devourer for my sake.
- Let the fruit of my hands not be plundered or destroyed by the enemy.
- Let every legal ground the enemy has to destroy or steal from me be dealt with as I obey you.
- Let the work of my hands bear fruit and prosper.
- Let me not work in vain in ministry. Let there be fruits in souls and life transformation.
- Let me not work in vain in my career but let there be progress and results.
- Let my work in the family not be in vain but let there be fruit in love and character.
- Lord fight for me in every facet of life and give me all round victory, peace and success in Jesus' Name.

- Let everything being devoured the enemy be delivered, that I will not labour in vain.
- Thank You Father in Jesus Name. Amen!

Scriptures for further Prayers

Jeremiah 30:16

MARCH 9

I AM A GIFT

Worship

Today's Scripture and Meditation

Ephesians 4:11- 12 *"And He Himself gave some to be apostles, some prophets, some evangelists, and some pastors and teachers, for the equipping of the saints for the work of ministry, for the edifying of the body of Christ"*

PRAYERS:

- Thank You, Lord Your life, death, and resurrection through which You have purchased men, for God
- Thank You for the gift of men that You gave for the perfecting of the saints, the work of the ministry and the edification of the body of Christ
- Thank You for the gift of the Holy Spirit to me and that I am a gift by the power of the Holy Spirit
- Thank You for giving us Apostles who pioneer the work of the kingdom, Prophets who speak words from You, Evangelists who preach the good news, Pastors and teachers who shepherd and teach the word that the church may attain unity of faith and full maturity in Christ
- Lord, break my walls down, pour out Your Spirit upon me that I might manifest the gifts of the Spirit in Jesus name
- Lord I pray for a fresh fire, fresh in filling by the Spirit of God to launch me to the miraculous
- Grant unto me the Spirit of humility, enable me to cast down every form of pride as I serve with others in the body and make room for each other's gifts

- I receive spiritual gifts needed for me to fulfil my calling and edify the body of Christ. I receive the gift of *(ask for any gift as desired - the gift of word of wisdom; word of knowledge; faith; working of miracles; prophecy; discerning of spirits; divers kinds of tongues; interpretation of tongues)*
- I believe, I will not hold back or strive with You, I will serve You with all my heart and strength and soul in love in Jesus name
- That You will be central and supreme in all of my life's activities and that I will be filled with deep genuine revelation of Christ
- That I will grow in humility, gentleness, patience, forbearance, love, unity
- I pray that I will be blameless in my relationship with the saints and how I dispense my duties within the body
- Thank You Heavenly Father for Your gifts in Jesus name

Scriptures for further Prayers

1 Corinthians12:4-7, Joel 2:8, Rev 22:12

MARCH 10

GROW AND BE BUILT UP

Worship

Today's Scripture and Meditation

Ephesians 4:13-16 *Until we all attain to the unity of the faith and of the knowledge of the Son of God, to mature manhood, to the measure of the stature of the fullness of Christ, so that we may no longer be children, tossed to and fro by the waves and carried about by every wind of doctrine, by human cunning, by craftiness in deceitful schemes. Rather, speaking the truth in love, we are to grow up in every way into him who is the head, into Christ, from whom the whole body, joined and held together by every joint with which it is equipped, when each part is working properly, makes the body grow so that it builds itself up in love.*

PRAYERS:

- Father I thank You for Your love for me and for saving me.

- You called me, gave me gifts and gave me as a gift to the body of Christ and our world.

- Enable me to be used of You to edify the body of Christ that we may all grow in understanding of You and of Your word.

- That I might grow to attain the unity of the faith and grow in the knowledge of God.

- Enable me to continue to mature towards the measure of the fullness of Christ.

- Father, enable me to stay grounded in Your word, in You and in love.

- That I will not be tossed to and fro by every wind of doctrine, by human cunningness, by craftiness in deceitful schemes.

- Enable be to continue to grow in every way into Him who is the Head, into Christ.

- Enable me to stay connected to You and to stay in the place of divine positioning where You have ordained me to supply my bit so that all may be equipped for the body to work properly.

- Enable me to be in unity with all Christians across the world that we may grow and be built in love.

- Thank You Father in Jesus' Name.

Scriptures for further Prayers

Colossians 2:8, Ephesians 2:21

MARCH 11

SPIRITUAL VIOLENCE

Worship

Today's Scripture and Meditation and Meditation

Matthew 11:13 *"And from the days of John the Baptist until now the kingdom of heaven suffers violence, and the violent take it by force."*

PRAYERS:

- Lord, I thank You for the grace given to me to be Your child and to be called a soldier of Christ
- I come before You to draw strength, grace, capacity and to be enlarged and sharpened in the Spirit in order that You will make me robust in the spirit
- I understand that this race is not for the swift and it is by Your mercy. Neither can I take the enemy by my strength, so I receive daily strength to take the kingdom of God by force
- I receive the spirit of holy "violence", to fight the good fight of faith, overcome the oppression, suppression of the enemy
- I break free from the oppression, suppression and bondage of the enemy
- I take hold of eternal salvation; I take hold of my deliverance. I take hold of my freedom, I take hold of all my possessions that the enemy has stolen, killed or destroyed
- I reject lukewarmness but I receive grace and courage to forcefully take hold of the kingdom of God, to grow and to advance in it
- I take hold of the kingdom of God, and I magnificently push back the frontiers of darkness

Revive Restore and Rebuild

- Let my heart be inflamed with a desire after the knowledge and obtaining of heaven and heavenly things
- Let Your power work in me to produce a response that I will not be deceived by lazy wishes and cold endeavours but be a candidate for heaven
- Let the Holy Spirit and power quicken me, enlighten me, open my ears, melt and soften my heart
- Let every numbness in my heart and mind be uprooted by force
- Let the zeal of the Lord consume me and compel me to run with Your righteous cause
- Enable me to always be on my knees in the agony of prayer having intensity towards heaven in taking glorious inheritances it by force
- I receive grace not to fall away in times of tribulation and trouble but to remain steadfast, immovable, always abounding in the work of the Lord
- I continue to hold on to You and continually look forward to the day of Your appearing and reward in the name of Jesus

Scriptures for further Prayers

1 Timothy 6:12, Luke 3:15-16, I Corinthians 15:58

MARCH 12

NO NOISE

Worship

Today's Scripture and Meditation

1 Kings 6:7 *And the temple, when it was being built, was built with stone finished at the quarry, so that no hammer or chisel or any iron tool was heard in the temple while it was being built.*

PRAYERS:

- Father I thank You that I am not without a purpose. You have had a plan and a purpose, and You are working out Your plan in my life.
- Thank You for choosing to build me up for such a time as this; I have been called to offer, to offer up spiritual sacrifices that are acceptable and are pleasing through Jesus Christ!
- Father I know that You are preparing me to fit into the spiritual house being built by You so I can be fit for purpose.
- You said that there was no chiselling or hammer or iron tool in the temple because all that was done in the quarry so that there would not be noise in Your house.
- Father I submit to Your preparation in the quarry; through Your hammer to break me, Your axe to cut off everything I have been entangled with and with all manner of tools of iron by Your word in Jesus Name, Amen!
- Have Your way in cutting off my excesses, shaping me as You will.
- I repent from the noise I have brought into Your house through grumbling and murmuring, strife, competition,

claiming rights, clamouring for popularity or publicity….

- I submit to Your training and chastening, break me, and shape me into a usable vessel as You desire that I might be used of You in Jesus name, Amen!
- I submit and surrender all to You Lord, oh that we may decrease, oh that You may increase in our lives!
- Take over body, spirit, and soul, take me over, everything I own, everything I am and could ever be.
- Take us over completely oh God, fill us oh God, use us oh God, separate us oh God!
- Separate me unto Yourself, I surrender, separate me, and consecrate me that I may offer spiritual sacrifices unto You
- That we may offer acceptable sacrifices that we may not offer strange fire.
- That we will not be shapeless before You in the name of the Lord Jesus Christ, that we will not be a misfit oh God in the kingdom, that we will not be unusable in the kingdom, that we will not be useless in the kingdom!
- Father let my body and mind continually be whole that we may be able to serve You oh God, without fear in holiness and righteousness before You all the days of our lives.
- Thank You heavenly Father in Jesus name, Amen!

Scriptures for further Prayers:

1 Peter 2:5, Luke 1:74-75, 1 Corinthians 3:9

MARCH 13

SAVED FROM DISTRESS

Worship

Today's Scripture and Meditation

Psalm 107:13-16 *"Then they cried out to the Lord in their trouble, And He saved them out of their distresses. He brought them out of darkness and the shadow of death, And broke their chains in pieces. Oh, that men would give thanks to the Lord for His goodness, And for His wonderful works to the children of men! For He has broken the gates of bronze, And cut the bars of iron in two."*

PRAYERS:

- Lord I give You praise because You are the great deliverer
- You are the Mighty God, You are the one that descended into hell and You took the keys of hell and hades from the hands of the enemy, to bruise his head
- You are the one who rose from the dead, who has all power in heaven on earth and under the earth
- It is in Your power to bring deliverance from every oppression, suppression, depression, possession, Father please break out in Your power in the name of the Lord Jesus Christ.
- In the days of trouble and distress, darkness and shadow of death, Father break the chains in pieces
- Let every form of bondage in my life known and unknown, whether I am conscious or unconscious of, be broken in Jesus name
- The Lord says, "I will break his yoke bar from upon you and will tear off your shackles." I command for every

curse or bondage to break, every form of cords of bondage be broken in the name of the Lord Jesus

- I will not continue to go round in circles; I command progress, advancements, an upward movement, next levels. In the name of the Lord Jesus Christ
- Every ancestral chain be broken, In the name of the Lord Jesus Christ.
- Whatever the enemy has put in my life, to deprive me of joy, to steal my joy, to destroy my joy to kill my joy, be removed by the power of the Holy Spirit in the name of Jesus

Scriptures for further Prayers:

Psalm 23:4, Nahum 1:13, Isaiah 42:7

MARCH 14

ENSLAVED TO RIGHTEOUSNESS

Worship

Today's Scripture and Meditation

Romans 6:16 *"Do you not know that to whom you present yourselves slaves to obey, you are that one's slaves whom you obey, whether of sin leading to death, or of obedience leading to righteousness?"*

PRAYERS:

- Father Lord, I thank You for saving my soul. Thank You for the daily work of the Holy Spirit to transform me
- I pray You enable me not to live according to the flesh, that my mind will not be set on the things of the flesh but the things of the Spirit.
- I submit my members to You alone as my God and will not submit my members to any other; It is only You I will serve and obey all the days of my life
- Search me Lord, and examine my heart and my attitudes, and may I keep my old fleshly self and the old sinful nature nailed to the cross of Christ, and learn to walk in spirit and truth more and more.
- Deliver me from this fleshly mindset   , worldly thoughts, actions, reactions, behaviour and lifestyle
- Thank You for setting me free from slavery to sin, and having become slaves of God, enable me to bear fruit in holiness and righteousness.
- I yield my members to You in obedience to You, to Your word, to the whisperings and the promptings of the Holy Spirit that will lead me to righteousness

- I submit my body, spirit and soul unto You. Let the flesh be silenced and not gratified in my life but let the Spirit take rulership of my life
- I submit my will and my every plan, my agenda, my dreams, my aspirations, and ambitions; let them be overtaken by Your will, plan and purpose
- Let my mind be set on the things of God and not the things of the flesh. Let me not be carnally minded but rather   be spiritually minded that I may have life and peace.
- Lord transform my heart, ideas and perspectives; let my heart be malleable, changeable, transformable and instructible by Your Spirit.
- Enable me to sow to the Spirit and not to the flesh so I do not reap corruption.
- Let me not be taken over by temptation, enable me to always see and take the way of escape that You provide for me in Jesus name
- Enable me to walk in the Spirit and live by the Spirit; that I will not be a people-led or led by the flesh but rather, Spirit led. Holy Spirit have Your way in my life. Thank You Lord, in Jesus name. Amen

Scriptures for further Prayers:

Romans 8:5, Romans 6:22, Galatians 6:8, 1 Corinthians 10:13

MARCH 15

PERFECT PEACE

Worship

Today's Scripture and Meditation

Isaiah 26:3 *"You will keep in perfect peace those whose minds are steadfast (are stayed You), because they trust in You"*

PRAYERS:

- Father, You have been faithful from generation to generation. You do what You say, and You are committed to us Your children.
- Lord help me to trust in You, every moment of the day and every moment of my life as my rock and help me to stay with You.
- Father Lord help me to trust You even when things are not working out the way I expect them to, help me trust that You have a better plan and to stick to You
- Let every distraction of the enemy in my life lose its influence over me. I will look to You for Your own perfect will
- I will give myself fully to the work of the Lord to serve Him in the way possible because He who has called me is faithful and will also do it.
- Father let me experience the peace that surpasses all understanding as I keep my focus on You and garrison my heart with thanksgiving
- Let every distraction or despair be stripped away that I might see only Jesus, His power and glory in my life.
- Holy Spirit of the living God, You are the encourager, the enabler, the comforter, the helper, the teacher, help my mind to be steadfast because I trust in You

- Father, I thank You for the directions and instructions You give me, please continue to guide me so that Your name may be glorified in me and through me.
- Thank You heavenly Father, in Jesus name, I pray, Amen!

Scriptures for further Prayers:

Philippians 4:6-7, John 16:33, John 14:27

MARCH 16

HE ANSWERS

Worship

Today's Scripture and Meditation

Hosea 2:21-23 *"It shall come to pass in that day, that I will hear and that I will answer, says the Lord, I will answer the heavens, and they shall answer the earth. The earth shall answer with grain with new wine and with oil.*

They shall answer, Jezreel, then I was sow her for myself in the earth. And I will have mercy on her, who had not obtained mercy. Then I will say to those who are not my people, you're my people, and they shall say, You are my God"

PRAYERS:

- Thank You, Lord that You are not like the gods of this world that have eyes but cannot see, have ears but cannot hear, You hear, You see and You answer when we call.
- You are the living God, so I ask that as I ask today, hear me. and answer my call, You answer me when I inquire, open to me when I knock and let me find You when I seek.
- Lord grant me the great blessing of real, vibrant relationship with You. That my heart will beat in rhythm to Yours, and so that what I want will be what You want, and I will never ask amiss.

- Father enable me to constantly abide in You and Your words abide in me so that what I ask will be done for me in Jesus' name, Amen!
- I know that when my relationship with You is real and where it is supposed to be, You will abundantly provide. So today I chose to seek Your Kingdom first that You might add every other thing unto me in Jesus Name.
- Father Lord I pray that You restore me unto abundant blessing and sow my life into the world as a seed of righteousness.
- Lord let me experience Your mercy afresh, grace and total restoration to my life.
- Let every department of my life, receive complete restoration.
- Let mercy override judgments, that we may override every works, attacks, and agenda of the darkness in our lives.
- Let mercy make a way, grant my desires, lift me up because of mercy, that I will be able to say, You do great things, do mighty things, in my life.
- Let me experience the warmth of Your love once more that I may relate to You as my God on Your own terms.
- Let me see the manifestation of Your love and power in my life for all to see and testify in the Name of the Lord Jesus Christ.
- Reveal Yourself as my God. Thank You father in Jesus' Name, Amen!

Scriptures for further Prayers:

Jn 15:7, James 2:13

MARCH 17

FOR MY GOOD

Worship

Today's Scripture and Meditation

I Peter 5:1 *"But may the God of all grace, who called us to His eternal glory by Christ Jesus, after you have suffered a while, perfect, establish, strengthen, and settle you"*

PRAYERS:

- Lord, I thank You because You are the way maker and the miracle worker, the promise keeper
- Thank You because no matter my experience and even when weeping may endure for a night, I believe joy comes in the morning. Everything is for a season and a reason and the end will come.
- Lord I commit my ways to You and continue to trust You, I wait for Your reward
- Father crown this year with goodness let my path will drip with abundance in the path of restoration
- I receive grace to sustain and not to give up
- Father, all power belongs You let You power manifest in my pain and sufferings for You to make an end of it and please perfect, establish, strengthen, and settle me in Jesus name
- I take my eyes off the things that surround me; bringing distraction and fear and I look unto You, Jesus, the author and finisher of my faith
- I have overcome the world because I obtain peace in Jesus because He has overcome the world
- Let heavenly treasures be unto us and let vindications break out in our favour as the midday sun.

- Let me stand again as the light lit in the midst of darkness. Let me stand out as the top of the hill where others will flow to
- Father use my brokenness and let the Prayers of a contrite heart that has made me shed tears be heard by the Lord.
- Let me be perfect and established, strengthen and settled by the sufferings I experience
- Thank You because everything works together for my good in Jesus name.

Scriptures for further Prayers:

Psalm 30:5, Joel 2:25, Psalm 37:5 Hebrews 2:24

MARCH 18

WELL OF SALVATION

Worship

Today's Scripture and Meditation

Isaiah 12:3 With Joy shall you draw out of the well of Salvation.

PRAYERS:

- Father, I thank You for salvation that came by the way of the cross.
- I come to the well of salvation today to draw water Lord for the journey of life.
- Without water I will faint so, I have come to the well to drink.
- You said if any man thirst let him come on to You and drink. I am here that You might quench my thirst.
- I delight in You and my soul rejoices in You, You are my Saviour, I thirst for You, I long for You.
- I have come to You to drink, You said, "He that believes in You out of his belly shall flow rivers of living water."
- I pray that You fill me afresh, I have come to the well of Salvation to drink water, only You can satisfy my soul.
- Living God, I pray for fresh fire, I pray for a fresh baptism of the Holy Spirit, fresh fire I pray.
- Father let me be like a watered garden and like a spring of water, whose water does not fail.
- With joy shall I draw from the well of salvation in the Name of Jesus I receive a fresh filling this morning.
- When light shines in darkness, darkness cannot comprehend it. I command every darkness to go.

- It is my morning of joy the night has ended, I receive favour.
- Today I draw joy, I draw mercy, I draw hope, I draw deliverance this morning in the Name of Jesus.
- I draw open doors, I draw liftings, I draw progress, I draw advancements this morning in the Name of Jesus.
- I draw faithfulness from the well of salvation in the Name of Jesus.
- Thank You Lord! Blessed be Your Name! There is divine correction of the past, the past is erased.
- Divine connection of destiny, direction is corrected, and I am brought back to divine destination.
- I draw out from the well of salvation and let it be that from my bellies shall flow rivers of living water.
- Thank You Lord Jesus in Jesus mighty Name I pray. Amen.

Scriptures for further Prayers

John 7:37-38, Isaiah 58:11, John 1:5.

MARCH 19

HOLY GHOST ANOINTING

Worship

Today's Scripture and Meditation

Acts 10:38 "*How God anointed Jesus of Nazareth with the Holy Ghost and with power: who went about doing good and healing all that were oppressed of the devil; for God was with him.*"

PRAYERS:

- Father, I thank you that You anointed Jesus by the power of the Holy Spirit to do good and to heal all those who are oppressed.
- For this reason, the works of darkness were destroyed in the lives of men.
- I thank You because I am free from every entanglement, oppression and influence of the enemy because of Your work here on earth.
- Father, I thank You that You gave me and all Your children the authority to trample on serpents and scorpions, and overall the power of the enemy and nothing shall by any means hurt us.
- I receive the anointing with power from Your Spirit today, that, nothing shall be impossible to me.
- I receive the power by the Holy Ghost, the ability to manifest in the authority of God in the Name of Jesus.
- Holy Spirit of the living God, come upon me afresh the power of the Highest overshadow me.
- I lift my voice to speak the word of God with authority let there be the manifestation of the power of God!
- I lift my voice to speak the word of God, let the ways and doors be open before me!

▢ I cast down everything that I have planned and surrender to You, and I pick up Your agenda this morning!

▢ I receive the power to fulfil destiny and purpose, the Holy Ghost is here!

▢ I receive the power, my labour shall not be in vain, my service to the Lord shall not be in vain.

▢ I receive the power to demonstrate the Spirit of God in our world, to build and tear down, to worship and to serve our God!

▢ I receive power to perform signs and wonder, the power will manifest wherever I go.

▢ I receive the fire of the Holy Ghost to fulfil my purpose, to be witnesses and live above sin.

▢ Thank You, Jesus, I praise and worship You Lord in Jesus name. Amen!

Scriptures for further Prayers

Luke 10:19, Luke 1:35

MARCH 20

GOD AS DEFENDER

Worship

Today's Scripture and Meditation

Psalm 124:6-8

Blessed be the Lord, Who has not given us as prey to their teeth! We are like a bird escaped from the snare of the fowlers; the snare is broken, and we have escaped! Our help is in the Name of the Lord, Who made heaven and earth.

PRAYERS:

- Father God, I bless You for Your mighty acts. I thank You for Your awesome power, I praise You for Your power to save and to deliver. You are the Lord that fights for me, and You never lose. Thank You for defending me.
- Thank You for not giving me as a prey to the enemy, I am not consumed because You are my hiding place.
- I pray to enforce the word of God in my life today, that "the snare is broken"
- I cannot be captured, I cannot be limited. I cannot be stagnant. I will not go round in circles, I am advancing and making progress.
- I have escaped the snare of the enemy, totally escaped. Totally set free. Whosoever the Son of man set free is free indeed. I am free indeed.
- I am free from every unknown or unacknowledged bondages, I am free from them all in the Name of Jesus and I praise You Lord

Revive Restore and Rebuild

- The snare is broken. I have escaped in the name of the Lord Jesus Christ.
- You break the gates of brass and bars of Iron, the "prison" doors are opened in the Name of Jesus.
- I arise quickly in the Name of Jesus. Let the chains fall. Let the iron gates opened of their own accord and I have escaped in the Name of our Lord Jesus Christ
- I have escaped from bondage, sickness and diseases, failure, stagnancy, backwardness and from everything holding me down. I have escaped from oppression and suppression and all physical and spiritual restraints and conspiracies.
- I am free indeed and set at liberty by the Spirit of God to serve the Almighty God, Thank you father in Jesus' name, Amen!

Scriptures for further Prayers:

Deuteronomy 20:4, Psalms 107:16, 2 Corinthians 3:17

MARCH 21

SPIRITUAL TIMELINES

Worship

Today's Scripture and Meditation

Ecclesiastes 3:1 *"To everything there is a season a time for every purpose under heaven."*

PRAYERS:

- Father I understand that under heaven there is a timeline but that above heaven time is irrelevant in the spiritual realm time is not relevant.
- I understand that timelines are crossed hence scripture says that the Lamb of God who was slain from the foundation to earth.
- Father, I pray that You will go into my eternity past and divinely correct all things that are impacting my present and eternity future.
- I pray that all things that are generational but impacting my life today be addressed.
- Father, just like in the case of king Ahasuerus and Mordecai, orchestrate that everyone who has the power to change things in my present will lose sleep until they locate their role in my story and perform it in Jesus Name.
- God is not unjust to forget my work and labour of love I receive the reward for my labour in Jesus Name.
- Let the records of Chronicles be brought and the books that there will be a time correction for my rewards in Jesus Name.
- Let dignity be awarded to me in place of oppression and shame.

- Let every decree received against me in the physical and spiritual be overturned.
- How God turn things around and that night when there was a timely update.
- Let the table be overturned that the destroyer becomes the destroyed.
- I will not bow to any principalities or power because I carry the Most High God within my very being. I am the temple that the Spirit of God dwells in.
- It is my morning of joy all my hardships were triggered by the update of my timeline.
- Today I receive access to the spiritual realm and step in by grace and mercy for the purpose of re-writing my history
- By the blood of Jesus, let there be a divine correction of my past in the Name of Jesus.
- I raise the banner of the blood of Jesus and decree that only the covenant in the blood of Jesus speaks in my life.
- By the authority and decree of the King according to the very work of destiny, my rewards are downloaded today.
- Every private and public shame ends today in the Name of Jesus.
- I enter the season of public dignity, and manifestations I become the king's delight. I receive honour from the kings.
- Thank You Jesus for Jesus mighty Name I pray. Amen!

Scriptures for further Prayers

Esther 6:1-11, 1 Corinthians 3:16, Hebrews 6:10

MARCH 22

GUARD YOUR STEPS

Worship

Today's Scripture and Meditation

Ecclesiastes 5:1 *"Guard your steps and focus on what you are doing as you go to the house of God and draw near to listen rather than to offer the [careless or irreverent] sacrifice of fools; for they are too ignorant to know they are doing evil."*

PRAYERS:

- Father Lord I thank you for your love for me.
- You are my light and my guide, I will not be misled or misguided.
- Draw near to Me and I will draw near to you, draw near that I might hear You, draw near that I might sense You.
- I choose to obey you and because to obey is better than to give the sacrifice of fools.
- Father restrain me from being careless, irreverent, ignorant, conceited.
- I want to come with you wherever you lead; guide and lead me in every aspect of my life and enable me to come with you.
- I want to go deeper with you Lord please draw me to a deeper place that you might reveal more of yourself to me.
- Lord draw me into your secret place that You will reveal more of Yourself and things that I have never known to me.

- Lord break out in my life, do unusual things and turn me into Your fragrance to the world.
- I let go of the flesh, as it is only robbing me of Your presence, Your will, Your purpose for me, my growth in You and deeper knowledge of You.
- That I might decrease and that the Almighty God might increase in me.
- Lord guard my steps that I will not slip away. That I will not fall, falter or fail You.
- Father enable me to focus on what I am doing in the house of God; that I will not be slothful, lazy or give You substandard, unacceptable service.
- Enable me to do all things as unto you and not for the audiences of any other man but for You alone.
- Grant unto me divine instruction for my journey from point of salvation to maturity in Christ.
- That we may come to the knowledge of Your overflowing and outflowing power.
- We want to know You from the knowledge of the power outflowing from Your resurrection.
- Let Your power be exerted over my life so that I will know You experientially and share in everything that You are   and that You stand for i.e. sharing in Your divine nature and presence.
- There is nothing more precious than to know You. Reveal Yourself to us afresh, anew and in a deeper way. Reveal the deeper things of Your person to us.
- Oh Lord have Your way in our thoughts and every department of our   lives, open our eyes to see You, open our ears and draw us closer.
- We want to lay our hearts on Your chest so we may hear Your heartbeat and know You intimately not far away.
- Reveal Your intimate self. Draw us to You as we draw ourselves and enable us to live the new life, so we do not gratify the flesh.
- I separate myself unto You and refuse to yield to the flesh. I surrender to Your way; Change my perspectives and ideology to align with Yours.

Revive Restore and Rebuild

Scriptures for further Prayers:

Galatians 5:16, Philippians 3:10

MARCH 23

REJECTED BY THE ENEMY

Worship

Today's Scripture and Meditation

Exodus 12:31-36 *Then he called for Moses and Aaron by night, and said, "Rise, go out from among my people, both you and the children of Israel. And go, serve the LORD as you have said. Also take your flocks and your herds, as you have said, and be gone; and bless me also."*

And the Egyptians urged the people, that they might send them out of the land in haste. For they said, "We shall all be dead." So the people took their dough before it was leavened, having their kneading bowls bound up in their clothes on their shoulders. Now the children of Israel had done according to the word of Moses, and they had asked from the Egyptians articles of silver, articles of gold, and clothing. And the LORD had given the people favor in the sight of the Egyptians, so that they granted them what they requested. Thus they plundered the Egyptians.

PRAYERS:

- Father I thank you because you are mighty in battle; the Lord of Host is Your name.
- Just as you did to Egypt Lord Shoe Your mighty arm to everything that has help me in bondage
- Father, please put fear and dread on the enemy that they may take to flight, they turn their backs
- I pray that whatever has held me bound will release me in a hurry due to the manifest power of my God

- I pray that whatever has held down my prayer life and my intimacy with God will release me now
- Whatever has oppressed my understanding and wisdom be lifted in Jesus name
- I pray that you will enable me to grow into the fullness of Christ
- I pray that my love for God be not impacted in a negative way by any distractions, problems or affliction.
- Enable me to love the brethren unconditionally
- Renew my zeal for God, anoint and energize me to carry out and fulfil my purpose
- I pray for healing and restoration in every area of my life that has hitherto be under oppression
- Let the enemy reject me and release me without delay, in every facet of life in Jesus name
- Thank you Father, in Jesus name.

Scriptures for further Prayers:

Exodus 23:27

MARCH 24

REDEMPTION THROUGH HIS BLOOD

Worship

Today's Scripture and Meditation

Ephesians 1: 6-8 *"To the praise of the glory of His praise wherein He has made us accepted in the blood. In Him we have redemption through His blood, the forgiveness of sins according to the riches of His praise wherein He had abounded towards us in all wisdom and projects"*

PRAYERS:

- Father Lord, I thank You and praise You for Your redemptive power.
- I thank You and praise You for the forgiveness of sins. and for redeeming me from the curse of the law and also from every curse.
- I pray for mercy, I ask that every manifestation of a curse be broken, every curse that came upon my life because of my actions, be broken in the Name of Jesus.
- Through the blood of Jesus, I have been brought near and I am accepted, in the Name of Jesus.
- By the blood of Jesus, I have boldness to enter the holiest,
- Any spiritual indebtedness, standing against me is blotted out by the blood of Jesus.
- Every wall erected in my life due to my refusal to serve other gods is broken now.

- That bold arrest warrant of the enemy is cancelled by the blood of Jesus,
- Every spiritual tyrant working against me is destroyed in Jesus Name.
- Every strip of authority over my life, family, my calling, and ministry are made impotent.
- I am redeemed from every work of darkness, every spiritual slavery and the power of the grave.
- I am redeemed from the power of the grave, that I may live a life in Christ in Jesus name.
- The blood of Jesus paid the price for my soul and it speaks better things for me.
- I am no longer an enemy of God but I am a child of God.
- I walk in the light that I may have fellowship with God and be cleansed by the blood of Jesus
- Thank You Father in Jesus name. Amen

Scriptures for further Prayers

Colossians 2:14, 1 John 1:7, Ephesians 2:13.

MARCH 25

DEAL WITH YOUR ANGER

Worship

Today's Scripture and Meditation:

Ephesians 4:26

Be angry, and do not sin: do not let the sun go down on Your wrath

PRAYERS

- Father, I give You praise, honour and adoration. I magnify Your Holy Name for You are the Almighty God.
- I submit my body, spirit, and soul unto You. Let the flesh be silenced and not gratified in my life but let the Spirit take full authority over my life
- I pray that You enable me not to live according to the flesh so that my mind will not be set on the things of the flesh but only on the things of the Spirit.
- Heavenly Father, let me not be estranged from You who created me and saved me by dying on the cross to pay the price for my sins.
- Give me grace to put my body under the influence and authority of the Holy Spirit every day and refusing the reign of the flesh.
- Let me not be taken over by temptation, enable me to always see and take the way of escape that You have provided for me in Jesus name, Amen!

- I cast down every pride in me that causes reactions when my ego is touched!
- Father I pray that I will not plan evil, speak evil, execute evil, be vindictive or lose integrity because of anger.
- Lord transform my heart, ideas, and perspectives; let my heart be malleable, changeable, transformable and instructible by Your Spirit.
- Refrain me from destructive behaviour when I am angry, that I will not go tearing down or causing division in my family or in Your body due to anger in the name of Jesus, Amen!
- Let every seed of anger be destroyed in me, that I will not be led into sin through anger.
- By Your grace give the control of my emotions to the Spirit of God as I submit to You
- I pray that you enable me to bear fruit of the Spirit in Jesus Name, Amen. Thank You Lord!

Scriptures for further Prayers

1 Corinthians 9:27, Galatians 5:22-23

MARCH 26

YOU SHALL LIVE

Worship

Today's Scripture and Meditation:

Ezekiel 37: 1-3; 12-14 *"The hand of the Lord was on me, and he brought me out in the Spirit of the Lord and set me down in the middle of a valley; it was full of bones. And he led me around among them, and behold, there were very many on the surface of the valley, and behold, they were very dry. And He said to me, "Son of man, can these bones live?" So I answered, "O Lord GOD, You know."*

Therefore prophesy, and say to them, Thus says the Lord God: Behold, I will open your graves and raise you from your graves, O my people. And I will bring you into the land of Israel. 13 And you shall know that I am the Lord, when I open your graves, and raise you from your graves, O my people. 14 And I will put my Spirit within you, and you shall live, and I will place you in your own land. Then you shall know that I am the Lord; I have spoken, and I will do it, declares the Lord."

PRAYERS:

- Father I thank You because You are the God of the Living.
- I pray the Spirit of the Living God will breath the breathe of life upon every circumstance that is dead, against You will or plan, and the course of the Almighty God in my life.
- Spirit of the living God, Spirit of life, that Spirit that raised Jesus from dead, bring resurrection this day and unto those dead bones in my life!
- Let there be a resurrection of everything that stands as dead bones in my life, let them come back to life

- I receive hope in every situation, whatever has been cut off against the will and counsel of God from my life, be restored
- I command by the Spirit of the Lord, that every one of my graves be open in the Name of the Lord Jesus Christ
- Those graves that have buried my fortunes, my progress, my success, my talents, my finances, my health, sound health, my star, my jobs - be opened in Jesus name!
- Those graves that have buried my peace, so I do not experience peace in my ministry, my calling, in my life - I command it to open.
- I command all deadness against God's counsel to come alive and out of the grave in the name of Lord Jesus Christ. Amen.
- I command my talents, my gifts, my ministry, my calling, my progress, my success, my advancement, my lifting - come out of the grave
- I command my family, my children, my marriage, my sound mind, my sound health, *(mention whatever applies to you)* to come out from under every oppression and suppression of the enemy in Jesus Name, Amen!
- Whatever the enemy stole, killed, destroyed, and buried, come out of the grave
- By the resurrection power of the Spirit that raised Jesus from the grave, everything that God has not buried physically and spiritually are coming out
- My peace, my joy, my talent, *(mention whatever applies to You)* are coming out,
- I praise You Lord, for You shall yet shine in my life and Your glory shall be revealed in me in Jesus name. Amen!
- Spirit of the Living God fall upon me afresh, let there be a refreshing from Your presence!
- Let the anointing from Your presence completely set me free in Jesus' name. Amen. Thank You Father!

Scriptures for further Prayers:

Isaiah 49:24-25, Romans 8:11

MARCH 27

YOUR GRAVES OPEN

Worship

Today's scripture and Meditation

Ezekiel 37:12-14 *"Therefore prophesy and say to them, 'Thus says the Lord God: "Behold, O My people, I will open your graves and cause you to come up from your graves and bring you into the land of Israel. Then you shall know that I am the Lord, when I have opened your graves, O My people, and brought you up from your graves. I will put My Spirit in you, and you shall live, and I will place you in your own land. Then you shall know that I, the Lord, have spoken it and performed it," says the Lord"*

PRAYERS:

- I thank God because You are the restorer
- Father, I ask oh Lord, that everything the enemy took from my life and has put in the grave against Your will and counsel for my life: be resurrected in the name of Jesus. Amen
- I thank God because You are opening the graves and they are resurrecting by the power that raised Jesus from dead
- Every lost opportunity, every lost gift and talent, loss of virtue, loss of spirituality and every dormant talent, everything the enemy has put in the grave, every lost career, lost children lost marriages and lost relationships .... **(pray as applicable)**, every lost or dead ministries, I command you to come out of the grave
- Everything the enemy has stolen, destroyed and killed and put in the grave or I have put in the grave by myself, I retrieve it in the powerful name of Jesus

- I receive the resurrection of my purpose, destiny, gifts, my talents, my prayer life and all that the Lord have purposed for me in Jesus name. Amen
- Manifest Your power in my life as regards my purpose, destiny, ministry and calling
- Manifest Yourself in my family in the name of Jesus. Amen
- Let Your resurrected power be manifested in me in the name of Jesus
- Everything that is said to be a foregone conclusion, impossible or buried, let them all resurrect and be fulfilled in Jesus name. Amen
- I shall accomplish my purpose and redeem my destiny in the name of Jesus. Amen
- Every dry bone will arise, and every buried bone will rise
- Thank You for the resurrection power, blessed be Your holy name, in Jesus mighty name I have prayed. Amen.

Scriptures for further Prayers:

Romans 12:6, 1 Peter 4:10

MARCH 28

THANKSGIVING & WORSHIP

Worship

Today's Scripture and Meditation

2 Samuel 7:22-28. Therefore, You are great, O Lord God. For there is none like You, nor is there any God besides You, according to all that we have heard with our ears. And who is like Your people, like Israel, the one nation on the earth whom God went to redeem for Himself as a people, to make for Himself a name — and to do for Yourself great and awesome deeds for Your land — before Your people whom You redeemed for Yourself from Egypt, the nations, and their gods?

For You have made Your people Israel Your very own people forever; and You, Lord, have become their God. "Now, O Lord God, the word which You have spoken concerning Your servant and concerning his house, establish it forever and do as You have said. So let Your name be magnified forever, saying, 'The Lord of hosts is the God over Israel.' And let the house of Your servant David be established before You.

For You, O Lord of hosts, God of Israel, have revealed this to Your servant, saying, 'I will build you a house.' Therefore, Your servant has found it in his heart to pray this prayer to You. "And now, O Lord God, You are God, and Your words are true, and You have promised this goodness to Your servant.

PRAYERS:

- I worship You Lord because You are great, You are King, You are gracious and You are merciful.
- There is none like You, nor is there any God besides You. You are more than what people say because no one can fully fathom You.

- Who is like unto You in all the earth and who is like Your people whom You redeemed with Your own blood and called friends.
- You have been given a Name that is above every name, a dominion that is above all.
- Great and awesome deeds! You are great among other gods.
- When You say a thing, You bring it to pass because You are not a liar or the son of man that you would repent. You are not a deceiver and I am grateful.
- Therefore, let me find favour in Your eyes today o God of heaven and earth in Jesus' Name.
- Let me bask in Your awe, show Yourself great in my every situation in Jesus' Name Amen!
- Lord hasten to establish Your word in my life and make me an epitome of Your goodness in Jesus' Name.
- Lord God, You are God, and Your words are true
- Lord of hosts, God of Israel
- **You are great, O Lord God. For there is none like You, nor is there any God besides You**
- Who is like you, O LORD, among the gods? Who is like you, majestic in holiness, awesome in glorious deeds, doing wonders?
- I bless Your holy name in Jesus name

Scriptures for further Prayers:

Isaiah 44:6, Exodus 15:11.

MARCH 29

THANKSGIVING FOR SPIRITUAL RESOURCES

Worship

Today's Scripture and Meditation

2 Thessalonians 1:3 *"We are bound to thank God always for you, brethren, as it is fitting, because your faith grows exceedingly, and the love of every one of you all abounds toward each other"*

PRAYERS:

- Almighty God, I thank You for Your goodness, faithfulness and truth in our lives that endures through all generations
- Thank You for Your strength and empowerment through the years
- Father, I thank You for granting my request and meeting my demands.
- Thank You, Lord, for all the spiritual resources given to me; filling me with Your Holy Spirit for the assignment, protecting me under Your blood and for giving us Your name as a backing authority.
- Thank You for enabling my faith to grow exceedingly, and my love has grown in leaps and bounds
- Thank You for Your peace that surpasses all understanding.

- Thank You for all Your benefits that You load us with daily.
- Thank You for Your word, which is a lamp unto my feet and light unto my path; for guidance and direction
- Thank You for the numerous things that Your word transform, effectively works and accomplishes in my life
- Father, I thank You for all the signs, wonders and miracles that You have worked in my life. You are the Lord of heaven and earth. You are the God of wonders beyond the galaxies.
- Thank You for Your strength and empowerment through the years and for the awesome privilege of being the expression of Christ to a world that desperately needs him
- Thank You for Your powerful name, thank You for healing in my body when I needed it. Thank You for destroying the power of the enemy and preventing any deadly thing to harm me. I thank You for all Your miracles in my life. I will proclaim Your wonders tirelessly, for You alone deserve the glory and honour.
- Father, we thank You because You are the God of possibilities.
- Thank You Father, for the blood of Jesus that is available to wash us whiter than snow, from all our sins.
- Thank You for the blood of Jesus that speaks better things over my life.
- Thank You Father for the blood of Jesus that purges our conscience from dead works to serve the living God.
- Thank You for counting me worthy to put me in ministry
- Thank You for victories that came by the way of the cross and all that pertains   to life and godliness which You have already given,
- I thank You and praise You, for You are a great God

Scriptures for further Prayers:

1 Thessalonians 2:13, Hebrews 9:14-15, 1 Timothy 1:12

MARCH 30

NO ESCAPE

Worship

Today's Scripture and Meditation

2Chronicles 20:17 *"You need not fight in this battle; take your positions, stand and witness the salvation of the Lord who is with you, O Judah and Jerusalem. Do not fear or be dismayed; tomorrow go out against them, for the Lord is with you"*

PRAYERS:

- Father Lord, I thank You because You are a Great and Powerful God, great in battle, the Battle Fighter, Grace in Glory. Let the earth shake. Great, are you, Lord, in Zion, greatly to the praised. The Lord breaks in pieces, the cedars of Lebanon, He makes Lebanon leap like a calf. We stand in awe of Your majesty; we stand in awe of Your power. Great in favour, great in battle, great in wonder, great in Zion.
- As I worship You come and fill my heart and my life with your presence so that no enemy will remain in my life.
- Set an ambushment and let there be confusion in the camp of the enemy that there will be inner fighting and an imploding within the enemies camp that it will not fulfil its enterprise.
- Whatever my enemy may stand for this season: be it sickness, disease, demonic oppression, failure or stagnancy, marital problems, career issues, let there be deliverance in Jesus Name.
- Let every sickness and diseases in my body or that of family members, implode until they are no longer

existing, and their potency is totally destroyed in the Name of the Lord Jesus Christ.

- I hand over all my struggles and battles to You because You never loose battles because Your salvation is with me.
- Today I take spoil because You O Lord have dealt with the enemies by Your power. I take the spoil of happiness, the spoil of joy, the spoil of harmony, the spoil of togetherness, the spoil of unity, the spoil of peace, the spoil of healing.
- I claim a restoration of all that the enemy has stolen, killed or destroy from me and take delivery of my portion and miracles and the promises of God for my life in Jesus' Name.
- I take the spoil of salvation for my children (where applicable), I take the spoil of deliverance! I take the spoil of promotion for my children, take the spoil of upliftment for my children, take the spoil of a career for my children, take the spoil of education for my children.
- I receive a fresh infilling of the Holy Spirit, an overflowing measure of the presence of God in my life, I receive divine guidance, instruction, and counsel.
- I receive an upgraded prayer life, and fellowship with God. Thank You Lord in Jesus Name.

Scriptures for further Prayers:

Deuteronomy 3:22, Isaiah 42:21-22

MARCH 31

HEALING FOR THE MIND

Worship

Today's Scripture and Meditation

2 Corinthians 10:4-5 *"For the weapons of our warfare are not carnal but mighty in God for pulling down strongholds, casting down arguments and every high thing that exalts itself against the knowledge of God, bringing every thought into captivity to the obedience of Christ."*

PRAYERS:

- Father God, I thank You because You are my God in whom I trust. You are my help, my refuge, strong tower and my hiding place.
- You have the name that is above every other name and according to Your word, at Your name, every knee shall bow, and every tongue must confess that Jesus Christ is Lord to the glory of God the Father
- Lord, I bow the knee to Your lordship and majesty and command every knee that stands against Your will and counsel in my life to bow in the name of Jesus
- I command everything that does not bring glory to Your name in my life to bow in the name of Jesus
- Let every stronghold in my life be pulled down in the name of Jesus. Every stronghold of pride, fear, control, criticism, independence, resistance, sexual perversion, unbelief, quenching the Spirit, anger, competition, contention, cruelty, division, envy, hate, jealousy, cruelty, murder, rage, fighting, quarrelling, restlessness, revenge, selfishness, spite, suspicion, wrath, conceited provoking, controlled by own desires, strife, divisions,

bitterness, sensual devilish, lying, selfish ambition, covetousness, carnality, etc. *(please mention the ones that apply to you)*

- Lord, free me from the mindset of the flesh, which is hostile to You, and which does not and cannot submit to You
- I refute and cast down every argument, theories, reasoning, philosophies and ideologies, traditions and culture, every proud and lofty thing that sets itself up against the true knowledge of God in my life in Jesus name
- I bring into captivity every one of my thoughts to the obedience of Christ. Let every unhelpful, unwholesome, unholy and wandering thought *(add yours)* be taken captive to the obedience of Christ in Jesus name
- I have not received the spirit of fear but of love, of power and of a sound mind. I pray for a sound mind and complete healing for my mind in Jesus name
- Father let there be total freedom in my mind from every form of torment
- I pray for healing for   every weariness, hurt, pain, stress, heartbreak, disappointment, rejection, anxiety, depression, panic attacks, confusion, lack of concentration, memory loss negativity, overthinking, torment, etc. *(please mention and/or add the ones that apply to you)*
- Grant me peace of mind and calm me when my heart is troubled. I declare that I have the mind of Christ
- Father, build me up when I am broken hearted; I receive the garment of praise for the spirit of heaviness, I receive joy in place of sadness, I receive peace in place of torment
- Give me the strength and clarity of mind to find my purpose and walk the path You've laid out for me
- Thank You Father for answering my Prayers in Jesus name

Scriptures for further Prayers

2 Timothy 1:7, Isaiah 61:1-3, Isaiah 53:5b

Revive Restore and Rebuild

APRIL 1

MADE ALIVE IN CHRIST

Worship

Today's Scripture and Meditation

Ephesians 2:5-6 *Even when we were dead in trespasses, You made us alive together with Christ (by grace you have been saved), and raised us up together, and made us sit together in the heavenly places in Christ Jesus*

PRAYERS:

- Father, I thank You for Your unconditional love for me. You started loving me, when I was dead in trespasses and unlovable
- You died for me when I was dead in sin and could not justify myself by any means
- You enabled me by the workings and convictions of Your Holy Spirit to pass from death to life in salvation
- Thank You for raising me up together with Christ, and for making me sit together in the heavenly places in Christ Jesus as a demonstration of Your surpassing grace
- You have eternally positioned me to be complete in Christ therefore I cannot be oppressed, suppressed and possessed of the enemy
- Thank You for Your great love for me, You are rich in mercy, I pray that I will not be moved away from You by the flesh, satanic deception and worldliness.
- I pray that I will not gratify the cravings of our sinful nature or follow its desires
- Thank You Lord that You rose from   the dead and You are immortal and imperishable. Because I have passed from death   to life, then I am dead to sin, I am

alive to God, sin cannot reign in my mortal body, I am separated to God and my members are solely for God's use.

- Let the Holy Spirit working in my life give me power over pressures and temptations that could take me away from God and let me be drawn closer to Your love
- I am God's handiwork, created in Christ Jesus to do good works, which God prepared in advance for me to do. Therefore, I pray that You will use me for good works in our world in Jesus name
- Father enable me to continue to grow in grace and in the knowledge of the Lord Jesus, for the rest of my life
- Thank You Heavenly Father, in Jesus mighty name I have prayed, Amen

Scriptures for further Prayers:

Romans 6:8-14, 1 Corinthians 15:3-6, Ephesians 2:10

APRIL 2

ENSLAVED TO RIGHTEOUSNESS

Worship

Today's Scripture and Meditation

Romans 6:16 *Do you not know that to whom you present yourselves slaves to obey, you are that one's slaves whom you obey, whether of sin leading to death, or of obedience leading to righteousness?*

PRAYERS:

- Father Lord, I thank You for saving my soul. Thank You for the daily work of the Holy Spirit to transform me
- I pray You enable me not to live according to the flesh, that my mind will not be set on the things of the flesh but the things of the Spirit.
- I submit my members to You alone as my God and will not submit my members to any other; It is only You I will serve and obey all the days of my life
- Search me Lord, and examine my heart and my attitudes, and may I keep my old fleshly self and the old sinful nature nailed to the cross of Christ and learn to walk in spirit and truth more and more.
- Deliver me from this fleshly mindset   , worldly thoughts, actions, reactions, behaviour and lifestyle
- Thank You for setting me free from slavery to sin, and having become slaves of God, enable me to bear fruit in holiness and righteousness.
- I yield my members to You in obedience to You, to Your word, to the whisperings and the promptings of the Holy Spirit that will lead me to righteousness

- I submit my body, spirit and soul unto You. Let the flesh be silenced and not gratified in my life but let the Spirit take rulership of my life
- I submit my will and my every plan, my agenda, my dreams, my aspirations, and ambitions; let them be overtaken by Your will, plan and purpose
- Let my mind be set on the things of God and not the things of the flesh. Let me not be carnally minded but rather   be spiritually minded that I may have life and peace.
- Lord transform my heart, ideas and perspectives; let my heart be malleable, changeable, transformable and instructible by Your Spirit.
- Enable me to sow to the Spirit and not to the flesh so I do not reap corruption.
- Let me not be taken over by temptation, enable me to always see and take the way of escape that You provide for me in Jesus name
- Enable me to walk in the Spirit and live by the Spirit; that I will not be a people-led or led by the flesh but rather, Spirit led. Holy Spirit have Your way in my life. Thank You Lord, in Jesus name. Amen

Scriptures for further Prayers:

Romans 8:5, Romans 6:22, Galatians 6:8, 1 Corinthians 10:13

APRIL 3

HIDDEN FROM THE SCOURGE OF THE TONGUE

Worship

Today's Scripture and Meditation

Job 5:21 *You shall be hidden from the scourge of the tongue, and you shall not be afraid of destruction when it comes.*

PRAYERS:

- Lord, I thank for Your word to me and pray I will not be a victim of the scourge of the tongue in Jesus name
- Every tongue that will rise against me in judgment is condemned and every word spoken against me for physical or spiritual impact will not stand in Jesus name
- I receive grace to address every word spoken against my life physically or spiritual today in Jesus name
- I pray that every mouth speaking against me be silenced. Only the will of God will be spoken about me or into my life
- No curse speaking against God's purpose for my life will prosper
- I shall not be a victim of the scourge of the tongue
- Every impact of words spoken about or into my life that has impacted my self-worth, self-esteem or identity shall be destroyed - My identity is from my maker, My identity is informed by the finished work on the cross of Calvary
- I reject every low self-esteem, unhealthy self-portrait and reduced self-worth resulting from words spoken into my life in the past in Jesus name. Amen.

- I am adopted into the family of God, I am a child of the Almighty God
- I am grafted into the vine, I am accepted in the beloved
- My identity is in Christ Jesus.

Scriptures for further Prayers

John 15:5, Isaiah 8:10, John 6:63

APRIL 4

VIRTUE TO VIRTUE

Worship

Today's Scripture and Meditation

2 Peter 1:5-9 *For this very reason, make every effort to supplement Your faith with virtue, and virtue with knowledge, and knowledge with self-control, and self-control with steadfastness, and steadfastness with godliness, and godliness with brotherly affection, and brotherly affection with love.*

For if these qualities are yours and are increasing, they keep you from being ineffective or unfruitful in the knowledge of our Lord Jesus Christ. For whoever lacks these qualities is so near sighted that he is blind, having forgotten that he was cleansed from his former sins.

PRAYERS:

- Father I thank You for the gift of salvation. Thank You for revealing to us by Your Spirit how we should build on this foundation.
- I thank You that You want to partner with me to cause spiritual growth to happen in my life.
- Enable me to give all diligence to my walk in the lord as a partaker in Your divine nature.
- Father let my faith progress into virtue, knowledge, self-control, perseverance, godliness, brotherly kindness, and love. That I may have a well-rounded Christian life, complete in every fashion in Jesus' name, Amen!
- Let me not be unfruitful in the knowledge of God.
- Father let me not be an ineffective and unfruitful Christian due to lack of or little knowledge of You or

not knowing You relationally. Let me know You increasingly in a fuller and deeper sense in Jesus Name, Amen!

- Let me abound in good and godly qualities so that I will not be spiritually short-sighted or blind. That I will not lose sight of the finished works of the cross and the cleaning power of the blood.
- Enable me to pay good attention to my growth in the Lord in Jesus name, Amen!

Scriptures for further Prayers:

2 Peter 3:18, Hebrews 5:14

APRIL 5

GROW IN GRACE

Worship

Today's Scripture and Meditation

2 Peter 3:18 But grow in the grace and knowledge of our Lord and Saviour Jesus Christ. To Him be the glory both now and to the day of eternity. Amen.

PRAYERS:

- Thank You Lord for the grace that appeared to us and brought us salvation.
- Thank You that grace goes beyond salvation into the way we stay steadfast in You.
- Father I ask for a deeper revelation of grace and that You will cause me to grow in grace.
- Your grace is infinite, everlasting; bottomless and shoreless. Enable me to grow in Your grace and not be stagnant in it.
- Enable me to grow in the knowledge of Jesus Christ that my growth will not be stunted.
- Enable me to know You more, in the face of the danger of false prophets and scoffers draw me close to You.
- Enable my life to reflect Yours that I will not be carnal in the way I live, remaining a babe in the Lord.
- Let me feel the warmth of Your embrace, You are all I need.
- You are my desire, no other one matter to me.
- I am resolute about my faith in You, my trust and dependence on You.

Scriptures for further Prayers:

Ephesians 1:17, 1 Corinthians 3:1

APRIL 6

HERE OR THERE?

Worship

Today's Scripture and Meditation

Exodus 6:6-8 *Accordingly, say to the Israelites, I am the Lord, and I will bring you out from under the burdens of the Egyptians, and I will free you from their bondage, and I will rescue you with an outstretched arm with special and vigorous action and by mighty acts of judgment.*

And I will take you to Me for a people, and I will be to you a God; and you shall know that it is I, the Lord Your God, Who brings You out from under the burdens of the Egyptians. And I will bring You into the land concerning which I lifted up My hand and swore that I would give it to Abraham, Isaac, and Jacob; and I will give it to you for a heritage. I am the Lord. You have the pledge of My changeless omnipotence and faithfulness.

PRAYERS:

- Father I thank You for You are a covenant keeping God.
- Thank You because You are always working and making things happen for me, even when I can't feel it, even when it's not evident. When You are silent, You are working in my life and situation.
- You transform us progressively, You transform sand into pearls and coal into diamonds by using time and pressure. Father work in me to transform me.
- I believe that all things are possible with You, help me when my faith is weak, Help my unbelief!
- Father I know that before every situation You prepared the solution to save me out of all these troubles. Enable me to use all my pains for growth.

- Bring me out completely from under the burdens of Egypt that I will not be slave to any other thing in this world but You
- Release me from ever bondage and anything that limits me, limits my potentials, limits my prosperity, reaps the fruit of my labour, lives in houses built for me in Jesu name
- Work out Your will in me work out humility in me, work out kindness, mercy, long-suffering, and much more.
- Let everything work together for my good because I love You Lord.
- Let the light and momentary troubles achieve for me an eternal glory that far outweighs them all.
- I fix my eyes on You and choose not to work by sight.
- Father work it out in me, both to will and to work for Your good pleasure.
- I am set free from everything that symbolizes Egyptian's bondage in my life.
- I put my trust in you Lord, take me to the promise land of my life in Jesus Name.
- Let me not be weary in doing good so that I will not lose my reward in Jesus' Name, Amen!

Scriptures for further Prayers

Philippians 2:13, Isaiah 10:27

APRIL 7

DECLARING NEW THINGS

Worship

Today's Scripture and Meditation

Isaiah 42:8-9 *I am the Lord, that is My name; And My glory I will not give to another, Nor My praise to carved images. Behold, the former things have come to pass, And new things I declare; Before they spring forth, I tell you of them. Behold, the former things are come to pass, and new things do I declare: before they spring forth I tell you of them.*

PRAYERS:

- I worship You the King of our kingdom, the King of kings, the King of Glory, the King eternal, the King upon the throne, the King over the nations, the King over the whole universe
- I ascribe greatness to You Lord; I ascribe glory and strength unto Your name
- You are faithful all the time, You are constant, You are consistent, You are dependent in all Your ways
- You are not a God in need of anything we can give. You are God all by Yourself
- The self-existing God. You are God alone from before time began.
- You are God who sits upon Your throne, reigning in majesty. The only true God
- Father Lord, I thank You that You are He who created the heavens and stretched them out, who spread forth the earth and that which comes from it, who gives breath to the people on it
- Father Lord, I thank You for the privilege of salvation, won for us by Jesus Christ

- Thank You that You called me to righteousness so I submit my members to You as instruments of righteousness and not of unrighteousness that the calling upon my life may be fulfilled
- Father hold my hand and never let me go, let me not be left behind or get lost but let Your purpose which You have called me into, be fulfilled
- Father, I submit myself to You for Your use; use me throughout the world to do miraculous works of freedom, restoration and healing, both physically and spiritually in the lives of people
- Use me to open eyes that are blind, to free captives from prison, and to release from the dungeons those who sit in darkness both physically and spiritually
- It is the dawn of new things; the former things will not threaten my present or diminish my future; I set my focus on Jesus, who makes all things new
- You are the master of both the former things and the new things, Father establish new things in my life today, let them spring forth in Jesus name
- You declare the end from the beginning, and I praise You Lord in Jesus name. Amen

Scriptures for further Prayers:

2 Peter 1:19, Isaiah 43:18-19, Isaiah 46:9-10

APRIL 8

I COME QUICKLY

Worship

Today's Scripture and Meditation

Matt 25: 11-13. *He who is unjust, let him be unjust still; he who is filthy, let him be filthy still; he who is righteous, let him be righteous still; he who is holy, let him be holy still."*

"And behold, I am coming quickly, and My reward is with Me, to give to everyone according to his work. I am the Alpha and the Omega, the Beginning and the End, the First and the Last."

PRAYERS:

- Father, I thank You because You are a gracious God.
- I come today repenting of any injustice I may have been involved in knowingly and unknowingly.
- I reject anything that catches my attention more than God and has become an idol to me, whatever takes more time from me than the time I give You, I cast down and put in the background from today.
- I repent of every time I have caused pain or divisions because of what I have said or done.
- I repent of every form of pollution caused through gossiping, backstabbing, slandering, I may have partaken in, I ask that You will be merciful unto me and cleanse me from all unrighteousness.
- Lord help me to set my affection on things above and not lose out on Your coming like the five foolish virgins.
- Holy Spirit, help me not to be deceived, enable me to put to death everything that causes my members to sin, I put to death the flesh that causes me to sin, let there be a

manifestation of the death of my flesh to the world in Jesus name

- I dethrone the flesh and refuse its promptings, desires, reactions and works.
- I cast down pride, arrogance, that I may not live in bitterness, I cast down every activity and power of the flesh.
- The flesh no longer has an influence on me. Today I am delivered from the rule of flesh, I will no longer be ruled by the flesh or by the quest for popularity, I belong to Jesus and I'm dead to them, from today I set my affection on Jesus.
- Give me the zeal to serve you till the end out of a pure heart and not to lose my reward.
- Enable me to continue to be righteous and to be Holy that I might receive Your reward.
- Thank you father in Jesus name I pray. Amen.

Scriptures for further Prayers

Ephesians 4:31, Colossians 3:2

APRIL 9

THE GOD THAT SEES

Worship

Today's Scripture and Meditation

Genesis 21:17-20 (MSG) *Meanwhile, God heard the boy crying. The angel of God called from Heaven to Hagar, "What's wrong, Hagar? Don't be afraid. God has heard the boy and knows the fix he's in. Up now, go get the boy. Hold him tight. I'm going to make of him a great nation." Just then God opened her eyes. She looked. She saw a well of water. She went to it and filled her canteen and gave the boy a long, cool drink. God was on the boy's side as he grew up. He lived out in the desert and became a skilled archer.*

PRAYERS:

- Father, I thank you because you always hear my out-cry!
- Oh Lord God, let the host of heaven and Your angel of grace single me out for a response from heaven, for a solution and for a blessing.
- Lord Jesus, open my eyes to see the resources You have already provided for me
- Father, encapsulate me in Your grace that I may not struggle in the journey of life
- Father send the helpers of my destiny my way.
- Let my heart be changed, renewed, flowing from the grace
- My father, hold me close and be jealous over me.
- Oh Lord, make me an exceedingly great nation after the order of Father Abraham.
- Oh Lord God, open my eyes of understanding that I might drink from You.

- Father, satisfy me early! Stand by me and monitor my progress!
- Father, cause me to soar like an eagle o'er every circumstance of life.
- Oh Lord Jesus, cause my dread to be upon my enemies.
- Father, make me a skilled archer in the face of life's battle.
- Thank You Father in Jesus Name.

Scriptures for further Prayers

Daniel 6:22, Psalm 33:18-19

APRIL 10

REAPING A HUNDREDFOLD

Worship

Today's Scripture and Meditation:

Genesis 26: 12 *And Isaac sowed in that land and reaped in the same year a hundredfold. The Lord blessed him*

PRAYERS:

- Father Lord, I thank You for good times and bad times. For the time of plenty and the time of famine. The times of high and the low times because You are God all the same.
- No matter my season Lord, I chose You and I chose to follow You.
- I chose to obey Your instructions even when I don't understand the reason.
- I pray that You will reward every of my effort with reaping a hundred-fold, that I will build and inhabit it, plant a vineyard and eat the fruit of it.
- That no matter the season, I will enjoy the works of my hands and not labour in vain.
- I pray that I shall not bear children for calamity, in the Name of the Lord Jesus Christ, Amen.
- Father cause me to be fruitful spiritually, be fruitful in the work of my hands, and be fruitful in my body in the name of Jesus, Amen.
- Blessed be Your name Oh Lord, in Jesus mighty name, Amen.

Scriptures for further Prayers:

Psalm 127:1, Isaiah 65:23

APRIL 11

MY HIDING PLACE

Worship

Today's Scripture and Meditation

Psalms 32:6-8: *For this cause everyone who is godly shall pray to You, In a time when You may be found; Surely in a flood of great waters, They shall not come near him. You are my hiding place; You shall preserve me from trouble; You shall surround me with songs of deliverance. Selah. I will instruct you and teach you in the way you should go; I will guide you with My eye.*

PRAYERS:

- I thank You Lord that You care for me and care about me. I thank You that You are responsible for my life and the reason why I live
- Thank You that You are my protector, my cover, my refuge, my fortress, my hiding place and dwelling place.
- My God, my rock, in whom I take refuge, my shield, and the horn of my salvation, my stronghold and my refuge, my saviour; I worship You
- Thank You that You answer when I call and pray to You. I'm glad I found You and continually find You when I call. You said when I set my love on You, You will deliver me and set me on high because I have known Your name
- Indeed, You have been true to Your word and fulfilled Your promise, Thank You Lord
- You are my hiding place, and under Your wings I can always find refuge. Protect me from trouble wherever I go, and keep evil far from me

- I pray for Your emotional, physical, and spiritual protection. Keep evil far from me, and help me to trust You as my refuge and strength.
- I pray that no weapon that is fashioned against me shall succeed, and the Lord shall confuse every tongue that rises against me in judgment
- Father, strengthen me, help me, uphold me with Your righteous right hand
- I pray that You will guard my mind from harmful instruction and grant me discernment to recognize the truth. I pray You will make me strong and courageous in the presence of danger
- Protect me from the onslaught of the enemy and surround me with songs of victory
- Show and teach me the way that I should go, guide me with Your eye
- Let me experience Your protection. Let me experience that I am under the shadow of Your wings. Father Lord, be with me, be within me, be behind me, be before me, be beside me, be with me to comfort and restore me, be beneath me, be above me. Be with me in quiet, be with me in danger
- Keep me safe, hidden, and secured in You

Scriptures for further Prayers:

Psalm 121:7, Isaiah 54:17, 2 Samuel 22:3-4

APRL 12

THERE SHALL BE DELIVERANCE

Worship

Today's Scripture and Meditation

Obadiah 1:17 (AMPC): But on Mount Zion [in Jerusalem] there shall be deliverance [for those who escape], and it shall be holy; and the house of Jacob shall possess its [own former] possessions.

Prayers:

- Lord, I thank You because You are a faithful God that fulfils His promises.
- Today, I have come boldly into Your presence where there are innumerable company of angels, I have come to that place of love and mercy by the almighty God. Father I pray that I will experience the warmth of Your love in tangible ways today in Jesus' Name, Amen
- I thank You for the invitation to draw near to You I ask that You draw near to me today Lord!
- I thank You for the work that Jesus did on the cross which satisfies the justice of God, made the spirits of just men perfect.
- I have come to Jesus and to no other who is the mediator of the new covenant, I pray the covenant be re-enacted in my life today that I may enjoy the blessings of the covenant.
- I have come to the blood of sprinkling, and I ask for the sprinkling of the blood on my life that I might obtain victory from the hand of the enemy and his cohorts.
- I ask that the blood would speak better things into my life than the speaking of the blood of Abel.

- Let the superior covenant that I have serve destroy every other covenant in my life.
- I will never reject or undermine the finished work of Jesus and the New Covenant through Him.
- Father, the trials and burdens in my life are only temporary; let there be deliverance upon this mount Zion
- I pray for deliverance from every entanglement, oppression, and suppression by the enemy.
- Let whatever devours me or any department of my life be devoured
- I am delivered body, spirit and soul, in my family, in my work/business place, in ministry, I receive all round deliverance in Jesus' Name. Amen!
- I call upon the name of the Lord for my salvation and deliverance from the enemy and his works
- Let me possess all that is mine; my health, prosperity in all things, everything that the enemy has stolen.
- Let me possess the rich heritage of every spiritual blessing in the heavenly places in Christ.
- Thank You Father in Jesus Name, Amen!

Scriptures for further Prayers:

Hebrews 12:22-24, Joel 2:32., Ephesians 1:3

APRIL 13

THERE SHALL BE DELIVERANCE

Worship

Today's Scripture and Meditation

Obadiah 1:17 (AMPC): *But on Mount Zion [in Jerusalem] there shall be deliverance [for those who escape], and it shall be holy; and the house of Jacob shall possess its [own former] possessions.*

PRAYERS:

- Lord, I thank You because You are a faithful God that fulfils His promises.
- Today, I have come boldly into Your presence where there are innumerable company of angels, I have come to that place of love and mercy by the almighty God. Father I pray that I will experience the warmth of Your love in tangible ways today in Jesus' Name, Amen
- I thank You for the invitation to draw near to You I ask that You draw near to me today Lord!
- I thank You for the work that Jesus did on the cross which satisfies the justice of God, made the spirits of just men perfect.
- I have come to Jesus and to no other who is the mediator of the new covenant, I pray the covenant be re-enacted in my life today that I may enjoy the blessings of the covenant.
- I have come to the blood of sprinkling, and I ask for the sprinkling of the blood on my life that I might obtain victory from the hand of the enemy and his cohorts.
- I ask that the blood would speak better things into my life than the speaking of the blood of Abel.

- Let the superior covenant that I have serve destroy every other covenant in my life.
- I will never reject or undermine the finished work of Jesus and the New Covenant through Him.
- Father, the trials and burdens in my life are only temporary; let there be deliverance upon this mount Zion
- I pray for deliverance from every entanglement, oppression, and suppression by the enemy.
- Let whatever devours me or any department of my life be devoured
- I am delivered body, spirit and soul, in my family, in my work/business place, in ministry, I receive all round deliverance in Jesus' Name.
- I call upon the name of the Lord for my salvation and deliverance from the enemy and his works
- Let me possess all that is mine; my health, prosperity in all things, everything that the enemy has stolen.
- Let me possess the rich heritage of every spiritual blessing in the heavenly places in Christ.
- Thank You Father in Jesus Name, Amen!

Scriptures for further Prayers:

Hebrews 12:22-24, Joel 2:32., Ephesians 1:3

APRIL 14

SURROUNDED BY GOD

Worship

Today's Scripture and Meditation

Psalm 125:1-2 *Those who trust in the Lord. are like Mount Zion, which cannot be moved, but abides forever. As the mountains surround Jerusalem, So the Lord surrounds His people from this time forth and forever.*

PRAYERS:

- I honor You our King, You are encamped in Zion, You are our captain, and You deserve great praise, great worship, and great adoration.
- Because You are great in deliverance, governance and great upon the throne
- No one is higher than You, nor greater than You, in You there is great safety, You are our refuge.
- Lord you are my refuge and strength my present help I will not be moved by circumstances in my life.
- You are our fortress, You are our stronghold, You are our strong tower, I bless You oh Lord.
- I worship and honour You oh Lord; the enemy are terrified of me because of You
- I thank You oh God, I am a terror to the kingdom of darkness.
- As the mountains are round about Jerusalem, so the Lord is round about   His people from this time forth and forever.
- The enemy will take to flight, marvel, be surprised, and lose their peace at the presence of the Lord.

- There is deliverance from the enemy in Zion, deliverance form sickness, failure, unfruitfulness, bareness, sicknesses, diseases and death
- Fetters, chains are broken off my life, from my children, my   business, and my ministry.
- I love you Lord my shield, defender, rock of salvation and strong tower. In you I have my security no one shall make me afraid.
- It is my set time to be blessed. Therefore, I will prosper in every area of my life
- The plans of the enemy are thwarted, the assault of the enemy against me, my family, against the work of my hands is destroyed in the Name of Jesus.
- Wherefore God also hath highly exalted Him and given him a name   which is above every name, that at the name of Jesus every knee should bow, of things in heaven, and things in earth, and things under the earth, and that every tongue should confess that Jesus Christ is Lord, to the glory of God the Father.
- Therefore, I proclaim You as Lord over my life and circumstances and command every form of sickness to bow (arthritis, hypertension, etc.) in the Name of Jesus.
- The Lord strengthens me in Zion and I become impenetrable fortress in the Name of Jesus, my ministry, our   churches, our families, our body, spirit, and soul.
- The strength of the Lord is upon me, for this God is my guide forever and ever till the end.
- I will call upon the Lord, who is worthy to be praised; Blessed be Your name forever in Jesus name.

Scriptures for further Prayers:

Psalm 46:1, Psalm 20:2

APRIL 15

DECLARING NEW THINGS

Worship

Today's Scripture and Meditation

Isaiah 42:8-9: *I am the Lord, that is My name; And My glory I will not give to another, Nor My praise to carved images. Behold, the former things have come to pass, And new things I declare; Before they spring forth, I tell you of them. Behold, the former things are come to pass, and new things do I declare: before they spring forth I tell you of them.*

PRAYERS:

- I worship You the King of our kingdom, the King of kings, the King of Glory, the King eternal, the King upon the throne, the King over the nations, the King over the whole universe
- I ascribe greatness to You Lord; I ascribe glory and strength unto Your name
- You are faithful all the time, You are constant, You are consistent, You are dependent in all Your ways
- You are not a God in need of anything we can give. You are God all by Yourself
- The self-existing God. You are God alone from before time began.
- You are God who sits upon Your throne, reigning in majesty. The only true God
- Father Lord, I thank You that You are He who created the heavens and stretched them out, who spread forth the earth and that which comes from it, who gives breath to the people on it

- Father Lord, I thank You for the privilege of salvation, won for us by Jesus Christ
- Thank You that You called me to righteousness so I submit my members to You as instruments of righteousness and not of unrighteousness that the calling upon my life may be fulfilled
- Father hold my hand and never let me go, let me not be left behind or get lost but let Your purpose which You have called me into, be fulfilled
- Father, I submit myself to You for Your use; use me throughout the world to do miraculous works of freedom, restoration and healing, both physically and spiritually in the lives of people
- Use me to open eyes that are blind, to free captives from prison, and to release from the dungeons those who sit in darkness both physically and spiritually
- It is the dawn of new things; the former things will not threaten my present or diminish my future; I set my focus on Jesus, who makes all things new
- You are the master of both the former things and the new things, Father establish new things in my life today, let them spring forth in Jesus name
- You declare the end from the beginning, and I praise You Lord in Jesus name. Amen

Scriptures for further Prayers:

2 Peter 1:19, Isaiah 43:18-19, Isaiah 46:9-10

APRIL 16

REST FROM SORROW

Worship

Today's Scripture and Meditation

Isaiah 14:3 In that wonderful day when the LORD gives his people rest from sorrow and fear, from slavery and chains.

PRAYERS:

- Thank You, Lord, for this is the day You have made.
- Thank You, Lord, for You have chosen to give us rest this very day, rest on all sides.
- I pray that You would grant me victory in every battle, and quench all struggles.
- Father Lord, I pray that from this day I shall not experience any form of fear.
- I come against the spirit of fear, I receive boldness and sound mind today in Jesus' name.
- I declare that sorrow is far from me, from this day no more sorrow in Jesus' name.
- Lord I receive the liberty You have given to Your people, at Your presence today, chains are broken I am set free, thank You Jesus'.
- I come to you will all my labour and burdens, father give me rest
- Let your presence go with me that I might enter Your rest
- Enable me to be still before You and to wait patiently for You
- I enter the place of rest that You have prepared for those

who love You',

- Thank You Father in Jesus' name.

Scriptures for further Prayers:

Matthew 11:28-30, Psalm 37:7

APRIL 17

SAY TO THE RIGHTEOUS

Worship

Today's Scripture and Meditation

Isaiah 3:10 (AMP) *Say to the righteous that it will go well with them, for they will eat the fruit of their [righteous] actions.*

PRAYERS:

- ☐ Thank You Lord because You declared me righteous.
- ☐ Thank You because it is well with me.
- ☐ My father, cause me to stay positive.
- ☐ Lord Jesus, fill my heart with Your word.
- ☐ Let my heart's desire be made manifest.
- ☐ Lord Jesus, because I am made in Your image after Your likeness, cause my every declaration to come to pass, let me say "it is well"
- ☐ My Father, let me eat the fruit of my labour and actions.
- ☐ I renounce every fruit sown in ignorance that does not glorify You.
- ☐ Lord Jesus, I cut short every harvest of evil in my life sown (known, unknown) by me or on my behalf
- ☐ My Father every tree that You have not planted in my life let them wither by fire in Jesus Name.

  - • It is well with me
  - • It is well with my family
  - • It is well with my work
  - • It is well with my calling
  - • It is well with my ministry
  - • It is well with our church
  - • It is well with my city

- ▪ It is well with me all round
- ▪ It is well with me by day in by night

- No matter what I face, it is well with me in Jesus name
- Thank You Father in Jesus Name.

Scriptures for further Prayers

Romans 4:22-25, Psalm 46:1-3.

APRIL 18

MY HELPER

Worship

Today's Scripture and Meditation

Isaiah 50:7 *"For the Lord GOD will help Me; Therefore, I will not be disgraced; Therefore, I have set my face like a flint, And I know that I will not be ashamed.*

PRAYERS:

- Thank You Lord Jesus, we praise You Lord.
- I worship You Lord, we honour You Lord, we magnify Your holy Name.
- There is none like You oh God, in heaven and on earth there is none like You.
- Father, I thank You because You will help me.
- The very reason why I come into Your presence is that You are my helper.
- Without You, I can do nothing; I am helpless.
- You observe the troubled, the grieved, the helpless and hopeless and You help them.
- You are my helper; I will not fear. What can man do to me?"
- Father. you sent David as a helper for Mephibosheth; send when I have been forgotten and in my time of need.
- I receive help from heaven, I receive help in my life, I receive help for my situation, I receive help for my health, I receive help for my job, I receive help for my family.
- Holy Spirit, You are our helper that is why I need Your guidance and direction.

- Teach me all things, how to live my life, teach me ministry, teach me how to live and be in my family.
- Lord remind me of things I have been taught, give me an accurate recollection of all things I have been taught or have read.
- Bring Your word to my remembrance when I need to speak it, prevent/ heal every memory loss and command restoration of good memory.
- I pray that You will help and bless me with the blessing of the dew of heaven, and of the fatness of the earth, and plenty of grain and new wine in the Name of Jesus.
- Lord will send me help out of Zion, send helpers of my destiny, my faith, my family, my work, and my ministry.
- I receive all manners of help in all facets of my life in Jesus name. Amen!

Scriptures for further Prayers

Psalm 54:4-5, John 14:26, Hebrews 13:6

APRIL 19

IN HIM

Worship

Today's Scripture and Meditation

Acts 17:28: For in Him we live and move and exist [that is, in Him we actually have our being], as even some of Your own poets have said, 'For we also are His children.'

PRAYERS:

- My Creator God, I praise You. I praise You because You made me in Your image and likeness.
- My life comes from You and I know that it does not belong to me, my life in in Your hands.
- I thank You for purchasing my freedom on the cross, I owe everything to You.
- Lord I am acutely aware that without You, I can do nothing, be nobody and become nothing.
- I am completely dependent on You for my life because my life belongs to You.
- In You, I have salvation, I am reconciled back to the father, In You I have faith, I am righteous, I am alive in Christ, I have grace in Christ I am wise, I am free, I have hope I am victorious, I am strengthened, I have peace and security because You are everywhere and You control all events, In You I have joy and confidence and my identity is clarified.
- Outside You my life would decay and be extinguished as a flame deprived of its sustaining element. Father let

Revive, Restore and Rebuild

me remain in You, that I will not stray away from You in Jesus Name.

- I receive the Zoe life of God, I receive it life from the Spirit of God in Jesus Name, sleeping spirit, every spirit that is slumbering, receive life, receive revival, receive an awakening in the Name of the Lord Jesus Christ
- Let my soul wake up to Christ and be awakened to a ŧin Christ, in the Name of Jesus Christ.
- In You I move because You give strength not to the weary, and You increase the power of the weak. Even Youths grow tired and weary, and young men stumble and fall; but he who waits on the Lord will renew their strength.
- May every of my move be carried out under your supervision and for Your glory.
- I will not detach from you lest I, wither, or die, I will not come out of Your shadow, I will stay in Your secret place.
- In You we exist oh Lord, without You we do not exist, we are not alive, we are not existing.
- I am attached to You my existence depends solely on You; my existence is sustained by You.
- In Him I live, in Him I move, and in Him I have my being in the Name of Jesus!
- Make it impossible to move out of You, make it impossible to move life You, without You or after You.
- Thank You heavenly Father, I give You praise Lord, I give You honor and adoration.

Scriptures for further Prayers:

John 15:5 Isaiah 40:29-31a, Proverbs 21:1

Revive, Restore and Rebuild

APRIL 20

GIFTS OF THE SPIRIT

Worship

Today's Scripture and Meditation

1 Corinthians 12:31: *But covet earnestly the best gifts: and yet show I unto you a more excellent way.*

PRAYERS:

- Father, I worship and I adore You, I magnify Your Holy name, blessed be Your name forever
- Thank You Jesus for the gift Of the Holy Spirit in me
- Father, please cleanse my heart and renew my mind, as I pour out my soul unto You. Bless me with spiritual gifts, Lord, so I can use them to edify Your body here on earth
- Thank You that my body is a temple of the Holy Spirit, and that You have sent Him to indwell my heart and to lead and guide me into all truth
- Thank You for Your mercies that qualifies me for the gifts of the Holy Spirit
- Take my life and let it be fully consecrated to You, use every part of me for Your glory
- You are a good father that gives good gifts to His children, I ask for the gifts of the Spirit to manifest in my life.
- I ask for and receive that gift that will enable You to manifest and fulfil Your purpose and calling in God on this earth
- I desire the manifestations of these gifts, and I give You full control to manifest these gifts through me at anytime
- I pray, Oh Lord, that You manifest Yourself in me with revelational gifts

Revive, Restore and Rebuild

- Lord, manifest Your power gifts through me I pray
- Lord manifest Your inspirational gifts through me I pray in the name of Jesus
- Help me to fan to flame, the gifts that You already gave me in Jesus name
- Give me the courage to use these gifts for Your glory and the grace and humility to not use them for my glory and fame
- Thank You Lord for Your love which is the excellent way

Scriptures for further Prayers:

James 1:17, 2 Timothy 1:6, Romans 11:29

APRIL 21

WHO HINDERED YOU?

Worship

Today's Scripture and Meditation

Galatians 5:7-9 *You ran well. Who hindered you from obeying the truth? This persuasion does not come from Him who calls you. A little leaven leavens the whole lump.*

PRAYERS:

- Father I pray that I will not be hindered from following the truth but that I will run well.
- Father I pray oh Lord that I will not be entangled and persuaded by evil.
- Help me oh God to be able to discern when You are the one persuading me to do something and when it is not You Lord so that I do not miss it.
- Father I pray that You grant me the grace not to yield to the persuasion of man to do wrong.
- Grant unto me to have understanding of the things which are proper for sound doctrine.
- Enable me to be an example to the believers in word, conduct, in love, in spirit, in purity and in faith.
- Let Your word be hidden in my heart, that I will not sin against You
- Enable me to be conformable to Your word and not to the world
- Lord strengthen me with Your might in my inner man through Your Spirit.
- That I will not compromises in any aspect of my life and

Revive, Restore and Rebuild

faith.

- Father Lord please help me to hear and recognize Your voice as my shepherd and not to hear the voice of the hireling.
- Help me to know and understand every of Your instructions Lord.

Scriptures for further Prayers:

1 Timothy 4:12

APRIL 22

OPEN MY EYES

Worship

Today's Scripture and Meditation

Ephesians 1:18-19 *May the eyes of [your] hearts be enlightened, that you may know what is the hope that belongs to his call, what are the riches of glory in his inheritance among the holy ones, and what is the surpassing greatness of his power for us who believe, in accord with the exercise of his great might.*

PRAYERS:

- Father I thank You that You took me from my blind state and now I see.
- Thank You for the gift of salvation that came to me by the way of the cross.
- Thank You for calling me to be Your child and a member of Your kingdom.
- Lord I wish to have deep understanding of the faith I have received and the hope of this call so I pray that you will enlighten the eyes of my heart to understand that I may gain real knowledge and understanding.
- Lord show me the immeasurable greatness of Your power and Your strength towards me according to the working of Your mighty Power n Jesus Name.
- Lord give me the understanding that as You have called me, You have a specific calling for me to fulfil.
- Let me receive a more secure and enduring hope in life by simply knowing Your call for my life.

Revive, Restore and Rebuild

- Lord let me know the hope that belongs to this call as regards the world to come.
- Father invest in me Your riches of love, wisdom, suffering and glory that they may accrue to riches of inheritance in me in Jesus Name.
- Father let me know the greatness of Your resurrection power. That power that raised Jesus from the dead will manifest in me and through me to bring life.

Scriptures for further Prayers:

Hebrew 6:19, Ephesians 1:19

APRIL 23

PRAISE THE GOD OF WISDOM

Worship

Today's Scripture and Meditation

Romans 11:33. *O the depth of the riches both of the wisdom and knowledge of God! How unsearchable are his judgements, and his ways past finding out!*

PRAYERS:

- Father I bless You for You are the only wise God. Your wisdom is past finding out.
- Lord grant me a deeper revelation of the depth of Your riches, both of the wisdom and knowledge.
- The greatest minds among the scientists of this world are incompetent to discern Your wisdom.
- The philosophers of the world cannot assess or comprehend the knowledge and wisdom of God.
- You use the foolishness of preaching the message of the Gospel to save men.
- You are the all-knowing God who also created the world. Halleluyah!
- Human logic, intelligence, science, and philosophy are grossly inadequate to bring man to Your saving knowledge.
- Thank You for the power and privilege of salvation that brought intimacy with the almighty God.
- I reject the wisdom of the world and chose the fear of the Lord that I might gain wisdom.
- Father, please open my spiritual eyes to behold wondrous things according to the riches of Your wisdom and knowledge, in Jesus' Name.

Revive, Restore and Rebuild

- Thank You Father in Jesus' Name.

Scriptures for further Prayers

Psalm 139:6, 2 Corinthians 1:12

APRIL 24

PERFECTION IN THE FLESH?

Worship

Today's Scripture and Meditation

Galatians 3:3 *Are you so foolish? Having begun by the Spirit, are you now being perfected by the flesh?*

PRAYERS:

- Father I bless Your Name for giving me Your spirit Who is at work in me.
- Father, please have mercy and forgive me for giving room to the flesh to dictate to me, please have mercy.
- Lord help me find my way back to You and make all things right, take away every fleshly desire from me.
- Deliver me from every entanglement of the world and set me free from every be-setting sin.
- I renounce every activity of the flesh that has hindered the flow of Your Holy Spirit in my life.
- Help me to constantly walk in the Spirit that I might not be perfected in the flesh.
- I pray that You destroy every perfection of the flesh in me as I know that there is nothing impossible with You Lord.
- Father take away every spiritual foolishness from me and help me to be wise and remain in the Spirit.
- Spirit of God, take the whole of me and encapsulate my entirety that I may be dead in this world but alive to You all of my days.
- Thank You heavenly Father in Jesus' Name! Amen!

Scriptures for further Prayers:

Galatians 5:1, 2 Timothy 2:24

APRIL 25

FLESH VS SPIRIT

Worship

Today's Scripture and Meditation

Galatians 5:17 *For the flesh lusts against the Spirit, and the Spirit against the flesh; and these are contrary to one another, so that you do not do the things that you wish.*

PRAYERS:

- Thank You Father for Your Holy Spirit given to us who bears fruit in us.
- Almighty God, I ask for help from You that the flesh should not take over me.
- Father Lord, please help me to always be in the Spirit, let Your sweet Spirit always possess me Lord.
- I cast down every lust of the eyes, lust of the flesh and pride of life
- Help us Lord to always do Your will and not to yield to our fleshly desires.
- Almighty God, please help me kill every desire of the flesh that may draw me away from You.
- Strengthen me in my inner man to stand against the flesh
- Give me grace to sow to please the Spirit, so that I will reap eternal life from the Spirit
- That I will not sows to please their flesh that I will not reap destruction from the flesh
- Enable me to sew righteousness that I may reap true reward
- Thank you father, in Jesus name.

Revive, Restore and Rebuild

Scriptures for further Prayers:

Galatians 6:8, Proverbs 11:18b

APRIL 26

AUTHOR AND FINISHER

Worship

Today's Scripture and Meditation

Hebrews 12:2 Looking unto Jesus, the author and finisher of our faith, who for the joy that was set before Him endured the cross, despising the shame, and has sat down at the right hand of the throne of God.

PRAYERS:

- Oh Lord, I worship You, Lord I magnify Your Holy Name.
- Father, enable me to look away from all that will distract me and to look unto Jesus, Who is the Leader and the Source of my faith.
- Lord let me behold You as I look to You to bring me to maturity and perfection that I might obtain the prize of my high calling.
- Father, enable me to deny myself, take up my cross, despise and ignore the shame to follow You.
- Lord come and do Your bidding, Lord come and do Your will, Lord come and do Your pleasure, come, and establish Your counsel in my life in the Name of Jesus, Amen!
- Father Lord I ask for a refreshing when I am weary in the name of Jesus Amen.
- Hold my hands and take me to that place of rest, of refreshing, of promise and of prosperity that You have apportioned to me in the name of the Lord Jesus Christ Amen.

Revive, Restore and Rebuild

- Give me strength in my inner man to stand even in the place of oppression, in the place of persecution, in the place where I am being despised, in the place of conspiracy.
- Give me strength and grace to stand, that I will continue the race, and that I will not fall behind.
- That I will not fall by the wayside in the Name of the Lord Jesus Christ Amen.
- I look to You for strength oh God, I look to You for courage oh God, I look to You oh God in the Name of Jesus Amen.
- I look to You always, I will not be afraid because You are with me always, I will not be dismayed in the Name of the Lord Jesus Christ Amen.
- Father Lord You are the Owner of my life, I come before You for an outpouring and infilling of Your spirit, a fresh fire, fresh baptism, fresh grace.
- Lord I cannot have enough of You, I cannot be too full for Your Spirit, fill me to overflowing. Let the living water flow over my soul, that out of my belly shall flow, rivers, not drops, of living water.
- Grant me a fresh Pentecost experience.

Scriptures for further Prayers

Ephesians 3:16, James 1:2-4

APRIL 27

LEAD ME IN THE WAY I SHOULD GO

Worship

Today's Scripture and Meditation

Exodus 13:17-20 *Then it came to pass, when Pharaoh had let the people go, that God did not lead them by way of the land of the Philistines, although that was near; for God said, "Lest perhaps the people change their minds when they see war, and return to Egypt." So God led the people around by way of the wilderness of the Red Sea. And the children of Israel went up in orderly ranks out of the land of Egypt. And Moses took the bones of Joseph with him, for he had placed the children of Israel under solemn oath, saying, "God will surely [e]visit you, and you shall carry up my bones from here with you."*

So they took their journey from Succoth and camped in Etham at the edge of the wilderness. And the Lord went before them by day in a pillar of cloud to lead the way, and by night in a pillar of fire to give them light, so as to go by day and night. He did not take away the pillar of cloud by day or the pillar of fire by night from before the people.

PRAYERS:

- Father Lord, I thank you for Salvation. Thank You because You delivered me form the hand of the enemy.

- Thank You Lord, that you have not let me by the difficult way

- Thank You because I have not come out of one bondage to enter another.

Revive, Restore and Rebuild

- I thank You because You will not allow me to be tempted with more than I can bear.

- Thank you for taking away every discouragement and for a new season of rest

- Thank you for making sure by Your Spirit that I don't give up, or enter into another battle so that I don't walk

- away from the faith
- Help me to follow the way that You lead me and not follow the shortcut

- Enable me to pay the price of building up myself; to study, pray and serve others

- Help me to take the long route of character building: of obedience, of faithfulness, of commitment, of following, honoring and serving my leader

- Grant me grace to wait for You in order to renew my strength; that I may not be weary or faint.

- Let me constantly focus on the exceeding and eternal weight of glory, rather than the light afflictions

- Father let Your presence go with me on life's journey. Protect and show me the way in Jesus name.

Scriptures for further Prayers:

Romans 8:15, 1 Corinthians 10:13, 2 Corinthians 4:17

Revive, Restore and Rebuild

APRIL 28

REDEEMED FROM THE CURSE

Worship

Today's Scripture and Meditation

Galatians 3:13-14 *Christ has redeemed us from the curse of the law, having become a curse for us (for it is written, "Cursed is everyone who hangs on a tree"), that the blessing of Abraham might come upon the Gentiles in Christ Jesus, that we might receive the promise of the Spirit through faith.*

PRAYERS:

- Thank You Lord for redemption, paying the price to purchase and rescue me back from bondage.
- Thank You that I am no longer under a curse because You bought me.
- Thank You Jesus that bought me out of defeat, out of slavery, and out of a death sentence to reign as kings and priests with You forever.
- Thank You Lord Jesus You took the curse, which I deserved, and You did it, so that I could receive the blessings of Abraham.
- In You every legal ground to hold me in captivity by the enemy is destroyed and I am free by the blood of Jesus.
- I speak in the Name of Jesus against principalities, powers, every spirit that rule the present darkness and spiritual wickedness in heavenly places that you have no right to operate against me or afflict me
- I am redeemed from the empty way of life handed down to you from your ancestors with the blood of Jesus
- Through the blood of Jesus Christ, I am free. Thank You, Jesus, for setting me free.

Revive, Restore and Rebuild

- All bondages are disarmed and dismantled from my life now, through the power in the blood of Jesus Christ, and in his name.
- I am the purchased treasure of Almighty God, and I give the devil no place in my life. Because I dwell in the secret place of the Most High God and under His shadow and I am loved by God.
- Father make me abound in all good work and to be fruitful that You may rejoice over me for good.
- Thank You Father, Thank You Jesus!

Scriptures for further Prayers:

1 Peter 1:18-19, 1 Corinthians 6:20

APRIL 29

THANKSGIVING FOR FAITH

Worship

Today's Scripture and Meditation

Jeremiah 30:19 *Then out of them shall proceed thanksgiving. And the voice of those who make merry, I will multiply them, and they shall not diminish. I will also glorify them, and they shall not be small.*

PRAYERS:

- Father Lord, thank You for mercy, grace and for the salvation of our souls today.
- Father Lord, I worship You, I adore You, I say, blessed be Your holy Name.
- I thank You oh God for Your everlasting mercies in my life.
- I thank You that according to Your mercy You saved me, through the washing of regeneration and renewal by the Holy Spirit.
- I thank You God because You came to this earth, while we were yet sinners, You died for us.
- We did not know that we needed You, yet You went to the cross and died.
- You rose again for my sake. I thank You oh God for the forgiveness of my sins.
- I thank You for the covenant I have with the Father through the blood that was shed for me.
- I thank You for I am born of God and I have overcome the world.
- I thank You that I do not need sacrifices or a token in the flesh but just as Abraham "believed God, and it was

accounted to him for righteousness, I am righteous in You.

- I thank You that I am justified by faith and therefore have peace with God through my Lord Jesus Christ.
- Thank You Lord Jesus because through You I have access by faith into this grace in which I stand, and rejoice in hope of the glory of God.
- Thank You Lord because I am a new man created according to God, in true righteousness and holiness.
- Thank You God for Your right hand is exalted; You right hand oh LORD does valiantly.
  Thank you. Oh God, for my faith even though I have passed through difficult times, Your Spirit has strengthened me and I have not lost my faith.
- I will continue to stay on this path of salvation and thanksgiving where You have set my feet in Your grace.
- I will rejoice Lord, because You will cause multiplication in my life and I shall not diminish
- Thank You because You will also glorify me, and I shall not be small.
- I give You praise, in Jesus mighty name, I have prayed. Amen.

Scriptures for further Prayers

Romans 5:1-11, Titus 2:11-12, Luke 1:75, 77

Revive, Restore and Rebuild

APRIL 30

NOTHING IS IMPOSSIBLE

Worship

Today's Scripture and Meditation

Luke 1:37 *"For with God nothing will be impossible."*

PRAYERS:

- Thank You Lord, thank You Lord for all You have done, thank You Lord for all You are doing and all that You have in Your heart to do; The ones I can see and the ones that I cannot see.
- Thank You for all the healings, for the ones we know about and the ones that we do not even know about.
- I come before You with a grateful heart for doors that You open, the ones I know about, and the ones we don't worry about.
- Thank You, Lord, for Your peace that surpasses all understanding. Thank You for the storms that You calm. Thank You for the battles that You fight for the victories that were delivered to us Your children.
- Thank You for the salvation of souls. Thank You for those that You have moved from religion into a relationship with You.
- Thank You for destroying the works of darkness, for clearing my channels that I may hear you and for dislodging satanic deposits, deposits of the world and world system.
- Thank You for every disease uprooted, every bondage broken, every chain broken, every prison door opened, every iron gate opened. Oh, I worship, You Lord.

Revive, Restore and Rebuild

- Thank You, Lord, because You took my darkness, and You gave me light and You continue to increase the intensity of Your light, in my soul.
- By Yourself, You led me into prayer, by Yourself, You answered the prayer and brought about manifestation of the answers, You healed, You saved, You helped, You delivered.
- And I have seen the manifestation of Your word that says, with You, nothing shall be impossible.
- What the doctors, finance houses, marriage counsellors, organizations and parastatals thought impossible. They did not have real hope. They did not expect a real solution; You surpassed their expectations. You surpassed our expectations. You did more than we ever hoped for.
- You gave life, in place of death, healing, in place of sickness and diseases.
- I bow before Your throne. Almighty God, I worship before You. From the depths of my heart, and the depth of my frame.
- I give You all the honour possible I give You all adoration, that's possible.
- I give You all worship, that is possible for any human being to give.
- I have seen that manifestation of Your grace and mercy.
- I have experienced Your ability, that is un-matchless.
- You tore down the darkness. How You kicked down the doors. How You tore down deceit and the lies of the enemy.
- What You cannot do, does not exist, Nothing is impossible with You
- I praise You Lord in Jesus name. Amen

Scriptures for further Prayers

Philippians 4:7, Hebrews 11:6

Revive, Restore and Rebuild

MAY 1

THE BLESSED MAN

Worship

Today's Scripture and Meditation

Psalm 1: 1-3

Blessed is the man, who walks not in the counsel of the ungodly, nor stands in the path of sinners, nor sits in the seat of the scornful; But his delight is in the law of the Lord, And in His law, he meditates day and night. He shall be like a tree, planted by the rivers of water, that brings forth its fruit in its season, whose leaf also shall not wither; And whatever he does shall prosper.

PRAYERS:

- Thank You Lord because You are righteous.
- Father I thank You, that in You I am blessed, let me walk upright before You.
- Father, enable me to be content in my life as I stand right or "straight" with God.
- Lord, enable me to be discerning enough to stay away from the counsel of the ungodly.
- Lord, enable me to be different in how I think, behave and know to whom I belong.
- Let me not listen to or act in bad counsel so that I will not do evil.
- I will not walk in the counsel of the ungodly, let me be counselled by the Spirit of God Who knows all things including the mind of God.
- Let Your testimonies be my delight and my counsel.

- Lord I pray that I will be able to take the narrow gate because it will lead me to blessings, happiness, joy and eternal life.
- Lord show me the path of life, which is in Your presence that I might have fullness of joy.
- When others are criticizing Christians and our faith, let me not partake in it or sit in the seat of the scornful.
- Father, enable me to be proud to follow Jesus, never hiding.
- Enable me to delight in and meditate in Your word day and night.
- Father let me be like a tree planted by the rivers; connected to constant source of water; that I may bring forth fruits and that I will not partake in a season of dryness and death.
- I pray that I will prosper in all I do in Jesus name. Amen!

Scriptures for further Prayers

Psalm 119:24, Romans 7:22.

MAY 2

CHOSEN BY GOD

Worship

Today's Scripture **and Meditation**

John 15:16 *You did not choose me, but I chose You and appointed you that You should go and bear fruit and that your fruit should abide.*

PRAYERS:

- Father I thank You for the great privilege of being chosen by You.
- Thank You for the privilege of friendship with the Master, answered Prayers, bearing much fruit, knowing things from the Father.
- Thank You that I am in Christ because Christ holds me and not because I hold Him.
- Father, You are the Vine and I am a branch. Help me day by day to abide in You and to be fruitful in all I say and do. I know that without You I can do nothing.
- Father enable my fruit to remain so that my Prayers will be answered to Your glory.
- Lord Give me a heart that is open to the work of the Holy Spirit and a vision that will outlast me.
- Thank You for choosing me out of the crowd... I want to serve You with all my heart I pray You will obtain an inheritance in my life.
- You've not chosen me, you are on this altar, because you're one of my chosen ones. You're not here, by mistake, says the Lord.
- The purpose of being chosen by You is to bear fruit. Father enable me to bear fruit, fruit of repentance, fruit

of righteousness, fruit of souls into Your Kingdom and fruit of the Spirit.

- Father take away every unfruitful thing in my life in Jesus' name, Amen!
- Lord cleanse me by Your word and repeatedly prune me that I might continue to bear more, richer and excellent fruits.
- Jesus You are the True Vine. We must be rooted in Him.
- Enable me to dwell in You to get nourishment and to bear fruit.
- Let me not be broken off or wither away in Jesus' name, Amen!
- Thank You, heavenly father in Jesus' name. Amen!

Scriptures for further Prayers:

Ephesians 5:26, Galatians 5:22-23

MAY 3

GATE OF HEAVEN

Worship

Today's Scripture and Meditation

Genesis 28:12-17(NKJV) *And he dreamed, and behold, there was a ladder set up on the earth, and the top of it reached to heaven. And behold, the angels of God are ascending and descending on it! And behold, the Lord stood above it and said, "I am the Lord, the God of Abraham your father and the God of Isaac. The land on which you lie I will give to you and to your offspring.*

Your offspring shall be like the dust of the earth, and you shall spread abroad to the west and to the east and to the north and to the south, and in you and your offspring shall all the families of the earth be blessed. Behold, I am with you and will keep you wherever you go and will bring you back to this land. For I will not leave you until I have done what I have promised you."

Then Jacob awoke from his sleep and said, "Surely the Lord is in this place, and I did not know it." And he was afraid and said, "How awesome is this place! This is none other than the house of God, and this is the gate of heaven."

PRAYERS:

- Father I thank You for a revelation of divine visitation. May I receive divine visitation today in the name of Jesus
- I ask that heaven touch earth on my behalf, let there be angelic visitation in my life and let me receive angelic assistance today

Revive, Restore and Rebuild

- Let the heavens above me open for the voice of God in affirmation, in promise and for divine visitation
- Let heaven open to empower me by Your Spirit Oh God
- Father give me an inheritance in the land where I reside, make Your good inheritance to come unto me
- Let me sow in this land and reap a hundred-fold in the same year
- Let me be blessed to be a blessing in the land
- Father do not leave me until You have done what You have spoken concerning me and fulfilled Your promises in my life
- Let every promise made to me in the secret in the open be made good in my life in the name of the Lord Jesus Christ, amen
- Every physical promise, every spiritual promise, every ministry promise, every career promise, every family promise, father make them good in the name of the Lord Jesus Christ. Amen
- Father, rend the heavens and come down, that the mountains may shake at Your presence, that the mountains will melt at Your presence, in the name of Jesus
- Therefore, I stand at the gate of heaven. The place of God's presence
- Everywhere I go or reside becomes the gates of heavens (a place of divine presence, divine visitation and divine transaction) in the name of the Lord Jesus Christ

Scriptures for further Prayers:

Exodus 3:5, Matthew 3:16, Acts 2:4

MAY 4

THE LORD'S ANOINTED

Worship

Today's Scripture and Meditation

1 Samuel 24:4-6 (AMP) *David's men said to him, "Behold, this is the day of which the Lord said to you, 'Behold, I will hand over your enemy to you, and you shall do to him as seems good to you.'" Then David arose [in the darkness] and stealthily cut off the hem (edge) of Saul's robe. Afterward, David's conscience bothered him because he had cut off the hem of Saul's robe. He said to his men, "The Lord forbid that I should do this thing to my master, the Lord's anointed, to put out my hand against him, since he is the anointed of the Lord."*

PRAYERS:

- Father, I thank You because You always speak to Your children.
- Thank You because You always fight for us and give us victories.
- Help me not to make mistakes under pressure and sin against You.
- Let my conscience be alive to guide me when I fail You.
- Oh Lord, let me hear Your Voice when You call in Jesus' Name, Amen!
- Oh Lord, deliver my enemies into my hand in Jesus' Name, Amen!
- Oh Lord, grant to me divine insight to abstain from every compromise and action that invalidates Your word
- Oh Lord, I repent from every presumption sin, the sin of omission, the sin of commission, and ignorance of Your word.

Revive, Restore and Rebuild

- Enable me not to be conformed to the word or its principle and way of Life
- Help me to restrain myself and not to claim rights or revenge against my leaders so that I will not touch the anointed of God
- Give me the grace to obey and submit to my leaders as you have commanded that I might prosper
- Thank you Father Lord, in Jesus name. Amen!

Scriptures for further Prayers

Romans 12:2, 2 Chronicles 20:20

MAY 5

GO ON TO MATURITY

Worship

Today's Scripture and Meditation

Hebrews 6:1. Therefore, let us leave the elementary doctrine of Christ and go on to maturity, not laying again a foundation of repentance from dead works and of faith toward God.

PRAYERS:

- Father, I thank You because You are a not a stagnant God, You desire progress and growth.
- Thank You for the privilege of knowing you and the people you put in my life to teach me the foundational principles of Christ
- Father, Your desire is that I grow into perfection, so, I surrender my mind, intellect, heart and soul to You that You will work in me by Your Spirit.
- Enable me to move into maturity, beyond just the rudiments and beyond religion.
- Enable me to study, meditate on and dwell in Your word that I may grow thereby.
- Enable me to take Your word as the nourishment for my Spirit and not neglect it.
- That I will not just be feeding on milk and as such remain unskilled in the word of righteousness.
- Enable me to put down every dead works and live the life apportioned to me by God.
- Give me grace to take solid food of the word and be able to exercise my senses discerning good from evil.
- Enable me to move from immaturity to maturity knowing that being and living like You disciple includes

Revive, Restore and Rebuild

hardship and suffering.
- That I may know You more in the power of resurrection and in the fellowship of Your sufferings. Amen!

Scriptures for further Prayers

Hebrews 5:14. Philippians 3:10

MAY 6

I WILL ANSWER

Worship

Today's scripture and Meditation

Hosea 2:19-23 *"I will betroth you to Me forever; Yes, I will betroth you to Me In righteousness and justice, In lovingkindness and mercy; I will betroth you to Me in faithfulness, And you shall know the Lord. It shall come to pass in that day that I will answer, says the Lord; "I will answer the heavens, and they shall answer the earth. The earth shall answer with grain, with new wine, and with oil; They shall answer Jezreel. Then I will sow her for Myself in the earth, and I will have mercy on her who had not obtained mercy; Then I will say to those who were not My people, you are My people!' And they shall say, 'You are my God!'*

PRAYERS:

- Father I thank You that You are my husband, let me obtain mercy before You. May Your favour always surround me
- Thank You for Your faithfulness and commitment to me
- Thank You that You hear me, and all things will hear You to respond to me, accordingly, thank You that it is my season of harvest
- When the world is saying recession, lack, hunger and loses, You will sow for me in the time of famine, recession, and my portion will be abundance and a great harvest in the name of Jesus Christ. Amen
- I pray that You will hear the heavens and that the earth and all within it, will respond to me
- I praise You Lord and receive this harvest into manifestation in every department of our lives, physical,

Revive, Restore and Rebuild

spiritual, emotional, work of our hands, business, ministry, churches I represent, in the name of the Lord Jesus
- Let there be the flow of abundance of grace and anointing

Scriptures for further Prayers

Psalm 119:132, Genesis 39:21, Exodus 20:6

MAY 7

RUN TO WIN

Worship

Today's Scripture and Meditation:

I Corinthians 9:24-27

Do You not know that in a race the runners all compete, but only one receives the prize? Run in such a way that You may win it. Athletes exercise self-control in all things; they do it to receive a perishable garland, but I am imperishable one. So I do not run aimlessly, nor do I box as though beating the air; but I punish my body and enslave it, so that after proclaiming to others I myself should not be disqualified.

PRAYERS:

- Father I give You praise, honour and adoration. I magnify Your holy name.
- Father I thank You for You are the one Who called me to this race, I want to run according to Your own rules, running the race circumspectly, I refuse to run the race aimlessly or according to my own rules but according to Your own rules.
- Let my focus be on You as my rewarder expecting no reward or acknowledgement from anyone for the work I do in the kingdom.
- Lord, enable me to run for Your approval and not for the praises of men, let me be self-controlled in all things.
- I choose to control my temper unlike Moses who lost the promise land due to lack of self-control.
- I choose to control my appetites unlike Noah who cursed his children.
- I choose to control my desires unlike Samson who lost his power and his life.

- I choose to be submitted to Your instructions unlike King Saul who lost his kingdom and ministry.
- I choose to control my quest for power and importance unlike Haman who ended up at the gallows.
- I choose not to be controlled by money like Ananias and Saphira, who were killed by the love of money.
- Father restrain me by Your spirit and that I will not destroy my own destiny in Jesus name, Amen!
- Lord, enable me to be meek, and control my appetites that I might be Christ-like in all things.
- Lord, enable me to run this race, and finish well.
- I run according to the order of Joseph who had the opportunity with Potiphar's wife, and he refused it.
- I need self-control so that Christ and my love for Christ, will rule over my desires.
- Father enable me to run for the price, there is a price of our calling that I shall get on the day of His appearing
- Lord, give me grace to put my body under the influence and authority of the Holy Spirit every day and refuse our flesh to reign! So that having preached, having taught, having sang in the choir, having been an usher, in the house of the Lord, I will not be disqualified.
- Thank You, heavenly father in Jesus' Name, Amen

Scriptures for further Prayers

Numbers   *20:11,*   *Genesis*   *39:7-9*

MAY 8

DESTINY HELPER

Worship

Today's Scripture and Meditation

I Kings 1:11-14. *Then Nathan asked Bathsheba, Solomon's mother, "Have you not heard that Adonijah, the son of Haggith, has become king, and our lord David knows nothing about it? Now then, let me advise you how you can save your own life and the life of your son Solomon. Go in to King David and say to him, 'My lord the king, did you not swear to me your servant: "Surely Solomon your son shall be king after me, and he will sit on my throne"? Why then has Adonijah become king?' While you are still there talking to the king, I will come in and add my word to what you have said."*

PRAYERS:

- Father, I thank you because you are Counsellor and mighty God
- I ask for counsel from Your Spirit every time it is needed that I may not go into error or make mistakes in the journey of salvation and life
- Help me not to get wrong counsel from mere men and the wisdom of men that will always fail.
- I shut every evil and human counsel concerning my family.
- Father Lord, I ask that only Your counsel for my children's lives will stand.
- I pray Lord that my life and that of my children shall be saved by Your hands.
- I ask oh Lord that I will not be ignorant of the enemies plans, or devices

Revive, Restore and Rebuild

- Helps me Lord to keep watch and to always be on guard.
- I pray that you send destiny helpers to me and loved ones
- Lord bless me with those that will guide us at every step
- Lord hasten to perform your word and promises in our lives and that of our children.
- May the children in my family not miss their place in destiny or be replaced.
- Thank you, father, in Jesus Name. Amen!

Scriptures for further Prayers

Esther 2:15-18, Acts 18:26

MAY 9

SOUND OF ABUNDANCE

Worship

Today's Scripture and Meditation

I Kings 18:41: *Then Elijah said to Ahab, "Go up, eat and drink; for there is the sound of abundance of rain."*

PRAYERS:
- Father, I thank You for the manifestation of Your power in our lives and in our world, nothing happens behind You
- Israel had drought because they worshipped idols, Father I pray that anything that has caught my attention more than You, that has taken the place of a higher priority than You please take it away in Jesus name
- Whatever clashes with You or Your kingdom in my life, whatever has become a god to me, I put them down that nothing will be a god to me in Jesu name
- Father I pray all gods in my life be defeated, that days of physical and spiritual drought may come to an end
- Enable me to be persistent and wait in the place of prayer when evidence are slow, in order to enable the furtherance of the will of God
- Father make an end to any drought in my life in Jesus name – let the rain fall
- I receive divine nourishment for my body, spirit and soul
- Lord enable me to enter a season of abundance physically and spiritually in Jesus name that I may yield much fruit

Revive, Restore and Rebuild

- Enable me to be mighty in the secret place like Elijah, to pray Prayers of faith that are founded on the word and promises of God and not on my senses
- Guide me into a place of prayer marked by deep reverence, intense and earnest fervency and that are to the point
- Give me a word, an insight and a revelation always from the place of prayer
- Grant me to reap the fruit of my labour in Jesus name

Scriptures for further Prayers:

Colossians 4:2, 1 Peter 5:5-6, James 5:16-18

Revive, Restore and Rebuild

MAY 10

SOBERNESS

Worship

Today's Scripture and Meditation

I Peter 5:8. Be sober, be vigilant; because your adversary the devil walks about like a roaring lion, seeking whom he may devour.

Prayers

- Father Lord I thank You because of Your love for me.
- Even though I live in this flesh, I am not in the flesh, I will not walk in the flesh but choose to walk in the Spirit
- Enable me to keep watch, to stand guard, to be sober, and to be vigilant, not to be controlled by our feelings or our emotions
- That I will walk continually in the Spirit so that I will not fulfil the desire of the flesh
- Help me to watch what I do with my body, my soul, and in the spirit
- Enable me not to fall into the trap of the enemy, not to be meats for the roaring lion
- Lord, enable me to be able to stand guard, enable us to be able to put on Your whole armour
- Enable me to be guarded, while I work, while I build, while I worship and serve You; and to also have held in the other hand, the weapons of our warfare
- Enable me to live our lives circumspectly, that I will not be engaged or be entangled with affairs of civilians because I am soldiers in Your army
- Enable me to watch and pray as You have said so I will not fall into temptation

Revive, Restore and Rebuild

- That I will not be a victim of destiny manipulation, that God's plan for my life will not be destroyed, that my purpose and destiny in God will not be derailed
- Lord, I surrender my emotions to You that it may be controlled by the Spirit of God
- Enable me to stand the wiles of the enemy by putting on the whole armour of God
- Let me not be careless, slothful or conceited but enable me to be careful, zealous, sober and watchful
- Grant me the grace to endure and to look unto You continually no matter what I face
- Blessed be Your name God, in Jesus name, amen.

Scriptures for further Prayers:

Nehemiah 4:17-18, Mark 14:28, 2 Timothy 2:4

MAY 11

PREPARE YOUR HEART

Worship

Today's Scripture and Meditation

I Samuel 7:3. Then Samuel spoke to all the house of Israel, saying, "If you return to the LORD with all your hearts, then put away the foreign gods and the Ashtoreths from among you, and prepare your hearts for the LORD, and serve Him only; and He will deliver you from the hand of the Philistines."

PRAYERS*:*

- Father, I pray that anything that has caught my attention more than You, that is of a higher priority than You please take away in Jesus name
- Whatever clashes with You or Your kingdom in my life, whatever has become a god to me, I put them down in Jesus name
- Father, enable my eye to be single, that I be fully devoted to You. Let my heart not be distracted from You. Let my thoughts continually be of You,
- Father, I adore You above all. Jesus, You are most precious to me. Holy Spirit I rely upon You alone. My Lord,
- I want to always be thinking of You with affection so that, whether I speak or I am silent, love for You pours forth. I pray in the name of the Father, Son, and Spirit. Amen.
- I turn my hearts to me, I do not want to be hypocrites, who speak alone God, who show the world that they know God, who recites scriptures, who knows scriptures, but whose hearts are far away from the Lord
- Who only go about the law, who quote the law, but do not understand grace and do not dispense grace

Revive, Restore and Rebuild

- Lord, I turn my heart to You today and ask that You take the things that are hindering my spirit
- Enable me to strengthen my relationship with You, to go deeper, to serve You with sincerity, honesty and transparency
- I desire unhindered flow, unhindered connection, unhindered relationship with You
- Thank You because You are clearing the threshing floor for a new beginning

Scriptures for further Prayers:

Matthew 6:22, Luke 16:13

MAY 12

FEAR OF MAN

Worship

Today's Scripture and Meditation

Matthew 10:27-28. 27: *"Whatever I tell You in the dark, speak in the light; and what You hear in the ear, preach on the housetops. And do not fear those who kill the body but cannot kill the soul. But rather fear Him who is able to destroy both soul and body in hell.*

Prayers

- Father we thank You for the gift of salvation. You word says that the fear of the Lord is the beginning of wisdom; Give us wisdom to fear You in all things and everywhere in Jesus' Name, Amen.
- I come before You, confessing my failings in the fear of men over You. I repent and confess that I have compromised in certain situations through fear of bosses, fear of parents, fear of pastors, fear of those in authority, fear of losing friendships, Father please forgive me.
- Through fear I have watered down Your word and instructions for eyeservice and men pleasing.
- I have been quiet when I should have spoken and have spoken in error when I should have been quiet.
- I have borne false witness and have been an unwilling part of conspiracies at work and in the family, in church and in the city/ town.
- Father, forgive me and cleanse me from all unrighteousness according to Your word.
- Let the effect of all these compromises be wiped out of my soul and conscience that I may serve You without guilt and timidity in Jesus name, Amen.

Revive, Restore and Rebuild

- Let every foot hold of the enemy in my life be removed and doors open unto him in my life be shut.
- Let the peace of God that surpasses all understanding keep my heart and mind.
- By the power in the blood of Jesus, remove them, by the power in the blood of Jesus we uproot them from our lives (every foothold of the enemy) in the Name of Jesus.
- In some ways, we have given the enemy a foothold, because of compromise.
- I pull down the stronghold of fear and I command a stop to the activities of the spirit of fear against my salvation and spiritual wellbeing in Jesus' Name, Amen!
- The scripture says that the righteous are as bold as the lion; father fill me afresh with Your spirit and grant me boldness to take the kingdom of God by spiritual violence.
- I stand and will not fall or falter in in the name of Jesus Christ,
- I receive grace to speak Your word in the light and to tell of Your salvation and mighty acts.
- I receive grace to treasure Your word within me and to proclaim Your word and my faith on the roof tops.
- I praise You Lord. Blessed be Your name Amen!

Scriptures for further Prayers:

1 John 1:9, Psalm 111:10, Ephesians 6:5-6

MAY 13

PALM OF HIS HANDS

Worship

Today's Scripture and Meditation

Isaiah 49:16. *Behold, I have graven You upon the palms of my hands; Your walls are continually before me.*

Prayers:

- Father, I thank You because You cannot and will not forget me, leave me or abandon me.
- I am grateful that I am engraved on the palms of Your hands.
- I thank You because You took the pain of being forsaken on the cross when you shouted "Eli Eli, lama sabachthani"
- Lord help me to remember that You are with me when I am being forgotten by friends, relatives, family members, and those I have really counted on.
- Lord, please take away the fear of being alone, forgotten, abandoned and separated from loved ones.
- Let me know that You are near that I will not feel empty or that You are distant.
- Enable me to stay closer to Your word for constant reminders that You care and that You are the present help in times of trouble.
- Help me to always remember that You will never abandon e me.
- I pray that whenever I call upon You Lord in times of trouble, You will answer in Jesus' Name.
- No matter what I am going through, I will hold on to You, the Author and the Finisher of my faith knowing that You will see me through.

Revive, Restore and Rebuild

- ☐ I am confident that You will not forget me. I rest on Your word of promise because You are dependable.
- ☐ Thank You for engraving me on the palm of Your hand. Thank You for having me in constant remembrance.
- ☐ Engravings are permanent inscriptions, therefore it symbolizes I know You love me and You want me to constantly remember.

Scriptures for further Prayers

Isaiah 49:15b, Psalm 46:1

MAY 14

COVENANT OF PEACE

Worship

Today's Scripture and Meditation

Isaiah 54: 10: *For the mountains may depart and the hills be removed, but my steadfast love shall not depart from You, and my covenant of peace shall not be removed," says the Lord, who has compassion on You*

Prayers:

- Thank You for Your steadfast love, unfailing love, unconditional love, unwavering love that You said will never depart from us.
- Father I thank You for Your kind of Love: Love that does not depend on anyone, that does not depend on any circumstance, the kind that does not depend on anything; it does not even depend on me, nor does it depend on our mistakes or behaviours
- Thank You for your steadfast love. I am persuaded that even in the midst of the unexpected, Your love will not depart from me, and Your covenant of peace will not be removed.
- I praise You Lord for peace, I ask for the activation of the covenant of peace in my life when I am troubled, and in the lives of those that are struggling emotionally, in my company.
- For those suffering mentally, I activate the covenant of peace, oh God!
- Peace be still in the name of the Lord Jesus Christ, for troubles in the families, for trouble at the workplaces, and financial struggles and challenges.

Revive, Restore and Rebuild

- No matter what the trouble is, I speak peace this morning and I speak resolution of those circumstances, in the Name of Jesus. Amen!
- I ask for a manifestation of Your love.
- Let each one of us experience the warmth of Your love in our lives today in the Name of Jesus.
- Thank You for Your love, Thank You for Your love, Thank You for Your immeasurable love, I acknowledge that no one loves like You.
- I am grateful that the Almighty God, the one that has powers in heaven, on earth and under the earth, the one that seats upon the throne and upon the circles of the whole earth will grant me peace on all sides.
- The only creator, the only true God, He loves me, and I am grateful for Your love.
- All I am praying for is, the days when I am searching for You and cannot sense You that you might grant me Your tangible peace and love.
- I pray that I may know that Your love is always constant and whether I can sense You or not, You are right there with me.
- Thank you, Heavenly Father in Jesus name

Scriptures for further Prayers:

Ezekiel 37:26. Ephesians 2:14, Numbers 25:11-12

Revive, Restore and Rebuild

MAY 15

NO SHAME

Worship

Today's Scripture and Meditation

Isaiah 54:4-6a. *"Do not fear, for you will not be ashamed; Neither be disgraced, for you will not be put to shame; For you will forget the shame of your youth, and will not remember the reproach of your widowhood anymore. For your Maker is your husband, The LORD of hosts is His name; And your Redeemer is the Holy One of Israel; He is called the God of the whole earth. For the LORD has called you...*

Prayers:

- I worship and adore my Maker, my husband, the Lord of my life, my Redeemer.
- I will not fear because You are my God and are in control in the affairs of men.
- I will not be put to shame because I am on the Lord's side and the Lord is on my side; I am not forsaken.
- Father supply and meet my emotional needs and rescue me from any form of disgrace.
- Father, let my hope not be disappointed, I will not be put to shame.
- Thank You that You prove to be such a good and gracious God, for your great goodness.
- Thank You for the long-suffering and mercy, You showed mercy to Your people Israel despite their errant ways, which You are showing to me today.
- You Who started a good work in me will continue it until the day of Christ Jesus.

Revive, Restore and Rebuild

- Enable me to dwell safely in Your glory, establish me in righteousness and in all things and do not withhold anything good from me, and restore my loses.
- Let every reproach, shame, and dishonour be turned to glory, let every adversary see and acknowledge the hand of God in my life.
- Enable me to listen to Your word, sow honour and not to keep the company of fools who are not doers of Your word.
- Father make me like the mighty men, who tread down Your enemies and are victorious in Your battlefields.
- Enable me to remain humble and not sit with the proud and angry, that I will not walk in the counsel of the ungodly or sit in the seat of the scornful or walk in the path of sinners, so I will not suffer shame. Enable me to delight in Your word and walk circumspectly in Jesus name.
- The Lord has taken my captivity captive, he has set me free, I am set at liberty to worship Him all the days of your life.
- I shall not need to fight any of my battles because the Lord will fight for me and strengthen me.
- Lord establish me and withhold no good thing from me
- Father restore the years that I because I favour Your righteous cause and cause me to prosper
- I will prosper in all things that His name may be glorified.
- My adversaries will see the hand of the Lord, they will acknowledge the hand of God in your life, no more shame in the Name of Jesus.
- My head is lifted, I stand up tall no matter what the circumstances are saying right now.
- Lord, I give You praise, there is indeed none like You. Thank You heavenly Father, in Jesus name. Amen.

Scriptures for further Prayers

Isaiah 54:4-6, Zephaniah 3:18-20, Romans 10:11,

MAY 16

I KNOW YOU

Worship

Today's Scripture and Meditation:

Jeremiah 1:5 *"Before I formed you in the womb, I knew you; Before you were born I sanctified you; I ordained you a prophet to the nations.*

PRAYERS:

- Father Lord, I thank You because You are my Maker, before I was formed You knew me and created me for specific purpose.
- Thank You that I am loved by You and I'm important in the scheme of things; I cannot be despised, abused or relegated to the background or looked down upon.
- Thank You because I have a calling and an inheritance in You, I pray that You will help me align my will to Yours as You daily unfold and reveal it to me.
- You chose me for Yourself so please reveal the details of my assignment to me in Jesus Name, Amen!
- Lord, enable me do Your work, showcase Yourself through me.
- Lord, bring me into a good land, a land of brooks of water, of fountains and springs that flow out of valleys and hills.
- Those who have despised me because of my background, because of my past because of my story, because of my current situations, because of my (current) status, they will come back to me for help.
- Father give me strength and good courage; I will not fear nor be dismayed because You are with me wherever I go.
- Truly, You have chosen the foolish things to confound the wise; I refuse to see my incapabilities and weaknesses in

fulfilling my calling, Father please equip me for the assignment You have given to me.

- Father save those who are conspiring against your work in my hands, according to the order of Joseph.
- Lord, use me to fulfil your mission here on earth in Jesus Name.

Scriptures for further Prayers

Joshua 1:9, Deuteronomy 8:7-I0,

MAY 17

LOOKING UNTO JESUS

Worship

Today's Scripture and Meditation

Hebrews 12:2. *"Looking unto Jesus, the Author and Finisher of our faith, who for the joy that was set before Him endured the cross, despising the shame, and has sat down at the right hand of the throne of God"*

Prayers:

- Father I am grateful to know and be reminded that You are the Author and Finisher of our faith who has eternal life.
- That no man is the author or the determiner of my faith, the One who never sleeps or slumbers and never goes on holiday.
- I am grateful to look onto You as the Author and Finisher of our faith; You suffered for me so that I might be saved and reconciled to the Father.
- Your time does not end but is eternal; I look onto You whose times are eternal.
- I look onto You for spiritual and physical battles.
- I look unto You for ultimate salvation to the end so when You appearwe will be caught up with You.
- I look unto You for our salvation, for this race, which is not easy, that You will grant us increased faith no matter the attacks we face.
- I look onto You for healing of sicknesses and diseases for I cannot serve You well when there is illness in our bodies, I look onto You for deliverance, to overcome weariness and heavy burden, for rest.

Revive, Restore and Rebuild

- I look to you to take off the heavy burdens.
- The beginning and ending of our faith who never fails or disappoints like man, for every man can disappoint.
- Enable me to endure our cross and despise the shame and enable me to look onto You and focus not look away for a second likePeter did and started to fall.
- I look onto You for healing of our land and nations, for effectual doors to open to me, for fruitfulness , transformation of our lands, for healing, to bringlife out of death, for lifting, resurrection, resolution, peace, promotion, reveal more of Yourself to me, for prosperity, for deeper relationship with You, for life and godliness for the salvation, character, promotion, covering, protection of my children and ,for grace, mercy, anointing, touch our lives, everything (*Delete as applicable*)
- My eyes are fixed on You, and I look unto You for yoke breaking, for You will always bring solution.
- Help me to continually look onto You for this race, joy and manifold blessing, I receive these in my life in Jesus Name.
- Lord I chose to deny myself take up my cross and follow you come what may I will follow you and I will not turn back in Jesus Name.

   Scriptures for further Prayers:

   Matthew 11:28, Matthew 16:24-26. Hebrews 12:1

Revive, Restore and Rebuild

MAY 18

PLEASE SPEAK

Worship

Today's Scripture and Meditation

Daniel 10:19 (ESV), *And he said, "O man greatly loved fear not, peace be with you; be strong and of good courage." And as he spoke to me, I was strengthened and said, "Let my Lord speak, for you have strengthened me." At this, I regained my strength and replied, "Please speak! You have already made me feel much better."*

PRAYERS:

- My Father, cause my feet to perpetually walk into the beauty of Your embrace.
- Oh Lord, cause me to be a carrier of good tidings.
- My Father, give me strength and courage for my assignment.
- Please speak to me Lord and I will be strengthened to do Your biding.
- Oh Lord, May I receive Your peace that surpasses all understanding, let me draw strength from Your peace.
- Lord Speak that I might be strengthened by Your word
- Father teach me to completely trust Your every word that You speak or that I study.
- My father, let my right hand be a carrier of Your riches and honour
- Above all Lord, cause my ways to be pleasant to You and let Your Holy Spirit continue the great work He started in me.
- Father, make me resourceful, that I will be a life-giver by the power of Your Spirit to everyone that comes in

Revive, Rebuild and Restore

contact with me and everyone that I come in contact with.
- Father make me an ambassador of Your Peace, and glory
- Thank You father in Jesus name, Amen!

Scriptures for further Prayers:

Isaiah 52:7 Isaiah 53:5, Proverbs 3:16-18

MAY 19

HIS COUNSEL SHALL STAND

Worship

Today's Scripture and Meditation

Isaiah 46:10-13 *Declaring the end from the beginning and from ancient times things not yet done, saying, 'My counsel shall stand, and I will accomplish all my purpose,*

' Calling a bird of prey from the east, the man of my counsel from a far country. I have spoken, and I will bring it to pass; I have purposed, and I will do it. "Listen to me, you stubborn of heart, you who are far from righteousness: I bring near my righteousness; it is not far off, and my salvation will not delay; I will put salvation in Zion, for Israel my glory."

PRAYERS:

- Father I thank You because You are omniscient, You know the end of a matter and of every course or circumstances, just as clearly as anyone else can see the beginning of it.
- So, I turn to You for counsel on all matters because You see the full picture already. Father lead me *(mention the area of life where You need guidance)* for I delight in You.
- Father I pray that only Your will be done, only Your counsel shall stand and only You purpose shall be established in my life for You have the final say.
- I pray that Your works and plans will never fail in my life, that You will do all Your pleasure and direct the affairs of my life.

- I pray that Your purpose will be accomplished in my life, that the will of the enemy or the will of man will not stand in my life in the name of the Lord Jesus Christ.
- Father I realise that Your timing is always precise and wise. Help me to obey and not be stubborn-hearted when You speak as You never delay, and You are never late.
- Send Your help into my life at the exact time to bring Your deliverance that You might obtain all glory and my faith be built.
- Lord remove the ability to resist your will from me let Your counsel be my guide always.

Thank You Father in Jesus Name, Amen

Scriptures for further Prayers

Psalm 31:15, Psalm 37,

MAY 20

FOLLOW PEACE AND HOLINESS

Worship

Today's Scripture and Meditation

Hebrews 12:14. *Pursue peace with all people, and holiness, without which no one will see the Lord:*

PRAYERS:

- Oh Lord my God, How excellent is your name. You are the God of love, You are our peace who has broken down every wall of partition, therefore, there is no longer any distinction in race, in gender and in status.
- Father strip away pride, arrogance, suspicion, prejudices, racism, fear so that we may seek peace and justice in our families, churches and communities.
- Father enable be to love beyond any human classification as love breaks all barriers and never fails. Kindle true love and peace in my heart Oh God
- Lord, help me to strive for peace with everyone and to live holy lives that will grant unto us access before Your presence
- Flood our lives with Your light so we can humbly walk peace and unity
- Father enable me/us by the power of Your Holy Spirit to be drawn together by one baptism into one faith, serving one Lord and Saviour.
- Father restrain us that we do not tear away from one another through division or hard arguments or different doctrinal expressions. Help us to embrace our

differences in peace thereby, preserving us in unity, as one body of Jesus Christ our Lord.

- Father set me apart unto Yourself to live my life in a manner that is worthy of You and pleasing to You.
- Purify my heart, cleanse my inner thoughts and examine every motive behind my acts and attitudes, for I desire to live in the holiness of heart that I might see You and be with You
- If there is any sin lurking in my heart or anything that is displeasing to You in my life, I ask that You root it out in Your mercy, so that I may live a holy and righteous life in Christ. Lord, I do not want to be separated from You but unto You
- Thank You, Father, in Jesus name. Amen.

Scriptures for further Prayers:

Ephesians 4:3, 1John 3:8

MAY 21

I WILL GO BEFORE YOU

Worship

Today's Scripture and Meditation

Isaiah 45:2-3. '*I will go before you and make the [c]crooked places straight; I will break in pieces the gates of bronze and cut the bars of iron. 3 I will give you the treasures of darkness and hidden riches of secret places, That you may know that I, the Lord, Who call you by your name, Am the God of Israel.*

PRAYERS:

- Father I thank You because You are my guide, I commit my ways into Your hands Lord that I will not miss my way.
- I ask that You will go before me as You did for Israel on the way to the promise land, showing them the way and protecting them.
- Lord do not let me go anywhere, if You will not go with me, I acknowledge You in all my ways.
- I do not want to go on my own; father take the take the driver's seat of my life,
- Father I pray that You will go before me and make the crooked place straight.
- Father, break every gate in my life preventing me from manifesting Your glory.

- Lord, every bar that has hindered me from entering or remaining in Your presence, Father, break it in Jesus' Name.
- Let the gates be continually open that men may bring to me the wealth of the heathen.
- Let me stand before kings and let kings minister to me by Your grace.
- Father keep me in Your secret place and under Your shadow that I may access the treasures of darkness and the hidden riches of the secret places.
- Jesus, reveal to me the deep secrets and hidden treasures of the nations and of Your kingdom.
- That I may know that You are God and there is none like You.
- Thank you father for hearing me in Jesus name I have prayed. Amen!

Scriptures for further Prayers:

Isaiah 60:11, Psalm 107:16

MAY 22

A NEW THING

Worship

Today's Scripture and Meditation

Isaiah 43:19. *Behold, I will do a new thing, Now it shall spring forth; Shall You not know it? I will even make a road in the wilderness and rivers in the desert.*

PRAYERS:

- Father Lord, I give You praise, because You always do new things; Your mercies are new every morning and great is Your faithfulness
- Thank You for new opportunities, new levels, new graces, new grounds to cover
- Lord, help me every moment to recognize the new things
- Give me wisdom, discernment, and revelation in this new day. I pray for You to give me the words and actions to help others draw closer to You. Please make this new life journey to help me have a closer relationship with You. Help me to put You first, not myself
- Lord, You make all things new in my life, You are the Creator, please create new realities in my life, continually nurture, renew, develop and strengthen me in Your will
- Take all I am, all I care for, and all I love and bring newness in knowledge and understanding

- Father give me the grace to recognise what You are doing at any point in time that I might align myself with Your will
- Give me the courage to step out into the new things that You are doing, knowing that the pages of my life were written of You.
- Guide my every step and enable me to continually look to Jesus, the author and finisher of my faith.
- Father make a way in the wilderness where there is no way. Chart my course as You do new things in my life
- Bring freshness, new life and fruitfulness in my dry places, do something new in me and cause me to be fruitful in You.
- I receive grace to do what I was not able to do before, may this new season usher in new levels of grace, anointing, excellence success in Jesus name
- Thank You Heavenly Father in Jesus name.

Scriptures for further Prayers:

Isaiah 42:9, John 15:2

MAY 23

WORST CASE SCENERIO

Worship

Today's Scripture and Meditation

Matthew 12:43-45: *"When an unclean spirit goes out of a man, he goes through dry places, seeking rest, and finds none. 44 Then he says, 'I will return to my house from which I came.' And when he comes, he finds it empty, swept, and put in order. 45 Then he goes and takes with him seven other spirits more wicked than himself, and they enter and dwell there; and the last state of that man is worse than the first. So shall it also be with this wicked generation."*

PRAYERS:

- Father Lord, please uproot everything that is not of You in my life,
- Spirit of God I release myself to You, please fill my life, fill my home and all that concerns me.
- Oh Lord, I pray that Your Spirit takes charge of this generation.
- Please deliver this generation Lord from every evil spirit that wants to take over this generation and trying to destroy it.
- Father Lord, we trust You oh Lord to have Your way and not allow our life and that of our children's be destroyed by evil.
- We pray that every plan of the evil spirit to cause havoc on this generation shall fail Name

Revive, Rebuild and Restore

- Let my life not be a dwelling place for any other spirit but the Spirit of God.
- Fill me with Your Awesome presence and let it be evident that "greater is He that is in me that he that is in the world"
- Let there not be a relapse, of any issues that You have already dealt with in my life and let no affliction rise a second time.
- Thank You for Your power to save heal and deliver.
- I praise You Lord, in Jesus name. Amen!

Scriptures for further Prayers:

Nahum 1:9, 1 John 4:4

MAY 24

RESTORATION OF HEALTH

Worship

Today's Scripture and Meditation

Jeremiah 30:17-19: *For I will restore you to health and I will heal you of your wounds,' declares the LORD, 'Because they have called you an outcast, saying: "It is Zion; no one cares for her."*

"Thus says the LORD, 'Behold, I will restore the fortunes of the tents of Jacob and have compassion on his dwelling places; And the city will be rebuilt on its ruin, And the palace will stand on its rightful place. 'From them will proceed thanksgiving, And the voice of those who celebrate; And I will multiply them and they will not be diminished; I will also honour them and they will not be insignificant.

PRAYERS:

- Thank You Lord that you are the God that heals us – Jehovah Rapha!
- Your word says, "by His stripes you were healed."
- You have said I will restore health and I will heal your wounds; I pray for healing in my body, and mind in the Name of Jesus.
- I pray that Your life-giving spirit will give life to my mortal body to make me strong and whole bodily in the Name of Jesus.

- I receive life in my body, receive the Zoe life of God and quickening in my body and for my wounds in the Name of Jss
- I receive the restoration of health and healing for my physical wounds.
- I pray for reversal and renewal of the negative effect of age, weather, hard work and abuse of my body in Jesus Name.
- I pray for healing for my emotions, mind, negative memories due to rejection, isolation, etc in Jesus Name.
- I am well favoured and well sought after and cannot be set aside and rejected.
- Father restore every fortune I have lost and have compassion on my dwelling places; Be compassionate on my household.
- Lord rebuild me, build my family build the city and nation where I belong and reside.
- I pray for a release from every captivity in the name of the Lord Jesus Christ.
- I receive mercy for my family, work, ministry, receive mercy and obtain grace to help this morning in the Name of Jesus.
- There is restoration back to where I was, restoration back to that erde and beautiful and excellent and perfect place.
- I receive a restoration of that which the cankerworm, and the caterpillar, and the palmerworm has eaten. I receive restoration and deliverance for my ministry and every department of my life.
- Father, honour me everywhere, so that I shall be no longer contemptible.
- Grant me more with joy in You and bring multiplication my way.

Scriptures for further Prayers:

1 Peter 2:24, Joel 2: 28

Revive, Rebuild and Restore

MAY 25

RETURN AND GIVE THANKS

Worship

Today's Scripture and Meditation

Luke 17:15-19

> *15 And one of them, when he saw that he was healed,*
> *returned, and with a loud voice glorified God, 16 and fell*
> *down on his face at His feet, giving Him thanks. And he*
> *was a Samaritan. 17 So, Jesus answered and said, "Were*
> *there not ten cleansed? But where are the nine? 18 Were*
> *there not any found who returned to give glory to God*
> *except this foreigner?" 19 And He said to him, "Arise, go*
> *your way. Your faith has made you well."*

PRAYERS:

- Father Lord, You are good indeed and Your mercy is from everlasting to everlasting.
- I bless and honour You from the depths of my being.
- I am grateful for the abundance of benefits, not trickles that You (daily) bless me with.
- Thank You for forgiving my sins; in Your covenant of mercy, You do not hold grudges against me.
- I am grateful that You healed me of (please mention if applicable).
- I am grateful that You redeemed my life from destruction and the pit, from the hand of the enemy, from all curses with Your own blood, You paid the price I was supposed to pay.
- You took the punishment that I was supposed to take, and today I am redeemed.

- Oh thank You for the divine exchange for my soul, I worship You God because you are my Saviour.
- I am grateful that You beautify my life. You dignify and crown me with your loving-kindness.
- Thank You because You set my feet upon the solid rock.
- Thank You for You delivered me from the hand of the enemy, for translating me from the Kingdom of darkness to the kingdom of light.
- Thank You, that I am not alien to You or to Your Commonwealth, I was an enemy of God, but You adopted me and called me friend and You made us men citizens of Your kingdom. I am grateful that You are my Father and I love the way
- You Father me.
- Hallelujah to Your Name, Our Father, You satisfy my mouth with good things, that my Youth is renewed like the eagles, I am strong, t I am an overcomer.
- I am grateful because You are working in me and through me.
- I am grateful for the peace that You gave me in place of worry, joy in place of sorrow, heaviness and mourning, for healing that You gave to us in place of sickness, provision, in place of lack, for the clothes on my back, sanity in my head. You are our shepherd and we will not want.
- I am grateful that You nurture me all round, You will never leave me or forsake me.
- I am grateful that You are the one that leads us beside the green pastures and still waters.
- I am grateful for Your love, compassion, and pity. We have a high priest who knows us as we are.
- I am grateful for my family, my friends, and acquaintances, for my colleagues, for all in my circle,
- I am grateful for the jobs and the businesses, the ministry You have given me,
- Thank You for your care, for keeping all that concerns me in perfect peace. That peace that surpasses all understanding.
- Thank You for Your mercy. Thank You for Your loving kindness and Your covenants with us.

Revive, Rebuild and Restore

▢   Your throne oh God, is forever; Your sceptre is the right
    sceptre.
▢   Accept our thanksgiving this day. Accept my
    praises from the heart and establish Your
    counsel in my life and family
▢   Thank you Father in Jesus mighty Name I have prayed.
    Amen

Scriptures for further Prayers

Psalms 23, Psalm 45:6

MAY 26

NAME ABOVE EVERY NAME

Worship

Today's Scripture and Meditation

Philippians 2:9-11: *Therefore God also has highly exalted Him and given Him the name which is above every name, that at the name of Jesus every knee should bow, of those in heaven, and of those on earth, and of those under the earth, and that every tongue should confess that Jesus Christ is Lord, to the glory of God the Father.*

PRAYERS:

- Lord with heart bowed and my voices lifted I worship You.
- I declare that You are Lord. I proclaim You as Lord. I worship You as Lord.
- I magnify You as the Lord. You are the Lord over our lives
- You are the Lord over every circumstance; You are the Lord over families
- You are the Lord over our towns and cities. You are the Lord over nation. Because You are the Lord, every knee shall bow before You
- Every knee shall bow. Every power bow. Every principality bow to the name of above all names. The name of Jesus
- Spiritual wickedness in high and low places bow to Your name because You are Lord
- You are the Lord of lords. You are the Lord of host; The one that has never lost a battle before. You fight to win.

Revive, Rebuild and Restore

- You are the victorious Lord, I bow before You Lord in worship of You.
- In honour of You our King. I bless Your holy name
- All the kings of the earth must bow at Your feet, because You are our Lord Jesus Christ
- Lord I pray that every argument and every lofty opinion raised against the knowledge of God in my life be destroyed
- You are our Lord Jesus Christ, You are the Lord, Jesus Christ, You are Lord
- I gave You the highest praise. Hallelujah to the reigning King.
- Blessed be Your name oh Lord, in Jesus name I have prayed, amen.

Scriptures for further Prayers:

Luke 10:19, Luke 9:1, Mark 6:13

MAY 27

IT IS ENOUGH

Worship

Today's Scripture and Meditation

> *2 Samuel 24:16: And when the angel stretched out His hand over Jerusalem to destroy it, the* LORD *relented from the destruction, and said to the angel who was destroying the people, "It is enough; now restrain your hand." And the angel of the* LORD *was by the threshing floor of Araunah the Jebusite.*

PRAYERS:

- Father Lord, we thank you because you have all power in heaven, on earth and under the earth.
- I pray for forgiveness for every door we have opened to the enemy due to my own fault and ask for forgiveness in Jesus Name.
- Every handwriting of ordinances that was against me and contrary to me has been nailed to the cross and I have a clean slate in Jesus Name.
- I command a stop to every plague, calamity, attacks and every destruction, every evil in Jesus Name.
- Have mercy on me Lord as You normally do to those who love your name
- Father let the enemy relent of all evil against me in Jesus Name.
- I pray for the mark of the blood to be activated upon my life such that when any angel of destruction

passes, he shall see the blood and shall pass over me in Jesus Name.
- I command that the hand of the enemy be stayed as I proclaim "It is enough! It is enough!! It is enough!!!" in Jesus Name.
- Thank You Father in Jesus Name.

Scriptures for further Prayers:

Colossians 2:14, Psalm 119:132

MAY 28

ANGELIC ASSISTANCE

Worship

Today's Scripture and Meditation

Acts 12: 6-10: *And when Herod would have brought him forth, the same night Peter was sleeping between two soldiers, bound with two chains: and the keepers before the door kept the prison. And, behold, the angel of the Lord came upon him, and a light shined in the prison: and he smote Peter on the side, and raised him up, saying, Arise up quickly. And his chains fell off from his hands. And the angel said unto him, Gird thyself, and bind on thy sandals. And so, he did. And he saith unto him, Cast thy garment about thee, and follow me.*

And he went out and followed him; and wist not that it was true which was done by the angel; but thought he saw a vision. When they were past the first and the second ward, they came unto the iron gate that leadeth unto the city; which opened to them of his own accord: and they went out and passed on through one street; and forthwith the angel departed from him.

PRAYERS:

- Father raise prayer warriors to take up my battle and fight in the place of intercessory prayer for me in Jesus name

- Father Lord, I thank You because You give Your beloved sleep. Peter slept in the face of looming danger of execution. Lord give me Your peace that surpasses all understanding
- Let the light of God shine for my sake that the powers of darkness will be confounded
- Lord, I thank You because nothing can stop Your work in the lives of Your children: not chains, or guards, nor prison doors nor iron gates. You are the only powerful God
- Lord confound those doing the bidding of Satan and seeking to fulfil his mission to steal, kill and destroy in my life in Jesus name
- Even when I do not fully understand or cannot trace You, Lord help me to obey You, Let me not be stuck with the explanations and reasons
- Father let the iron gates in my life begin to open of their own accord that I might experience total freedom in every area of my life. Only Your will and purpose will be fully fulfilled in my life in Jesus name
- You are a rescuer, when the enemy pursues, saying; I will overtake, I will divide the spoil; my lust shall be satisfied upon them; I will draw my sword, my hand shall destroy them. You blew with Your wind, the sea covered them: they sank as lead in the mighty waters.
- When the stocks were locked and guards were placed and the gates were shut, You sent Your angel and made a way of escape, Father send Your angelic assistance to me in Jesus name
- When enemies say "aha" we have got him, Lord arise for me and discomfit Your enemies in Jesus name
- Let the light of God shine upon my situation and let every chain be broken in Jesus name
- Take over my life, Lord, send Your angelic assistance and set me completely free in Jesus name

Scriptures for further Prayers:

Exo 15:9-10, John 10:10, 1 Corinthians 10:13, Psalm 70:3

MAY 29

SINS CONNECTED TO SICKNESSES

Worship

Today's Scripture and Meditation

Mark 2:3-12: *Then they came to Him, bringing a paralytic who was carried by four men. And when they could not come near Him because of the crowd, they uncovered the roof where He was. So, when they had broken through, they let down the bed on which the paralytic was lying.*

When Jesus saw their faith, He said to the paralytic, "Son, your sins are forgiven you." And some of the scribes were sitting there and reasoning in their hearts, "Why does this Man speak blasphemies like this? Who can forgive sins but God alone?" But immediately, when Jesus perceived in His spirit that they reasoned thus within themselves, He said to them, "Why do You reason about these things in Your hearts? Which is easier, to say to the paralytic, 'Your sins are forgiven you,' or to say, 'Arise, take up your bed and walk'?

But that you may know that the Son of Man has [a]power on earth to forgive sins" – He said to the paralytic, "I say to you, arise, take up your bed, and go to your house." Immediately he arose, took up the bed, and went out in the presence of them all, so that all were amazed and glorified God, saying, "We never saw anything like this!"

PRAYERS:

- I thank You Lord because You are a God Who forgives, and of Your own accord died for sinners on the cross.

- I come before You today asking forgiveness in every way I could have sinned and come short of Your standard; sin paralyzes so I pray that nothing in my life be paralyzed due to sin.
- Lord destroy the power and effect of the law of sin and death in my life in Jesus Name.
- Let every foot hold of the enemy in my life be destroyed in Jesus Name.
- Father, send helpers to me on the day of my need that would go the extra mile for my salvation, deliverance and healing.
- I enter the arena of healing today, father, touch my body my soul and spirit and make me whole.
- I declare over my body, "by the stripes of Jesus you are healed."
- Confirm my healing and let it manifest tangibly in Jesus' Name, Amen!
- Lord single me out of the multitudes and put your finger on my life and let it be evident that I have touched of You.
- Open my ears so I can hear You clearly and release my tongue so I can speak of You.
- Ephphatha! Be opened! I command everything that closed against the will of God in my life to be opened
- I pray that You will give me a burden for the lost no matter their lifestyle or level of blasphemy in Jesus Name, Amen.
- Give me the spirit of collaboration and the ability to go extra mile for the salvation of souls.
- Let me not be ashamed of the Gospel of Christ that has power to save but to declare it always till You come.
- Thank You heavenly father in Jesus name, Amen!

Scriptures for further Prayers:

Romans 1:16, Mark 7:33,

MAY 30

DIVINE PROVIDENCE

Worship

Today's Scripture and Meditation

2 Kings 7:3-8:

*Now four men who were lepers were at the entrance of the
city's gate; and they said to one another, Why do we sit
here until we die? If we say, we will enter the city – then
the famine is in the city, and we shall die there; and if we
sit still here, we die also. So now come, let us go over to
the army of the Syrians. If they spare us alive, we shall
live; and if they kill us, we shall but die.*

*So, they arose in the twilight and went to the Syrian camp.
But when they came to the edge of the camp, no man was
there. For the Lord had made the Syrian army hear a noise
of chariots and horses, the noise of a great army. They had
said to one another, The king of Israel has hired the Hittite
and Egyptian kings to come upon us.*

*So, the Syrians arose and fled in the twilight and left their
tents, horses, donkeys, even the camp as it was, and fled
for their lives. And when these lepers came to the edge of
the camp, they went into one tent and ate and drank, and
carried away silver, gold, and clothing, and went and hid
them [in the darkness]. Then they entered another tent
and carried from there also and went and hid it.*

PRAYERS:

- Father I praise You because You are a merciful God. The Help of the helpless.
- I come to you with a repentant heart for every way I have sinned against you please forgive me and cleanse me from all unrighteousness in Jesus Name.
- The lepers could not go in because they were outcasts, Father I pray that because I am redeemed by the blood of Jesus, everywhere I have been rejected or regarded as an untouchable, Father let me be accepted in Jesus Name!
- I thank You because in the time of famine, You will make both physical and spiritual provision.
- Thank You for divine direction to places of Your providence and that I may walk into it.
- I pray for Your wisdom and guidance when I am at the place of indecision that I may make decisions according to Your will, plan, and purpose.
- Where I sowed Father let me reap a hundred-fold and like Isaac prospered let me prosper, continue to prosper until I am prosperous in all areas of my life.
- Help me to move forward in faith, letting go of the past and even the present circumstances believing in Your ability to carry me through to a brighter, better and victorious tomorrow.
- Lord when I face things that I am so powerless against reveal Yourself as the powerful God in Jesus Name
- Where the enemy stopped any of my God ordained efforts, Father give me grace to contend for lost ground until I possess my possession.
- I pray that You will unseat the enemy that is sitting on my blessing and inheritance in God.
- I pray that You will put fear and dread on the enemy so much that they will take to flight and that the matter be ended.
- I pray that in the day of freedom and victory, You will enable me to take the spoil and possess all that You have given to me.
- I pray for grace to share Your divine provision with others in Jesus' name, Amen!

- Thank You Father in Jesus name. Amen

Scriptures for further Prayers:

Genesis 26:12, -23, Exodus 23:27

MAY 31

THE TONGUE IS A FIRE

Worship:

Today's Scripture and Meditation:

James 3:6 (AMP)

And the tongue is [in a sense] a fire, the very world of injustice and unrighteousness; the tongue is set among our members as that which contaminates the entire body and sets on fire the course of our life.

PRAYERS:

- Thank You Lord for this beautiful day that You gave me the privilege to see.
- I see the power of the tongue in Your word today and I give my tongue over to You.
- David said set a watch at my mouth, Father I pray that You restrain my tongue by the power of the Holy spirit that unwholesome words will not come out of it in Jesus Name, Amen!
- Lord set a watch at my mouth when I am emotional: when I am hurt, pained, angry, anxious, unwell, disappointed, discouraged, etc
- Father help me to bridle my tongue, that the words coming out of my mouth will be controlled by Your Spirit in the Name of Jesus, Amen.
- As You did in the time of Isaiah, touch my tongue and mouth with the coal of fire to deliver me from the unrighteous works of the lips, mouth, and tongue. Amen!

Revive, Rebuild and Restore

- I will not be involved in gossiping, back biting, slander, grumbling and murmuring, cursing, and other evil committed with the tongue.
- Lord give me grace to marshal and direct every of my word, effort, energy, strength, ability, towards establishing Your kingdom in my patch, serving You and towards serving God's people.
- Lord help me to do all these towards growing my faith, so that the works of the flesh will diminish in my live.
- Holy Spirit fill me afresh and manifest Your power in and through me; that men may look at the level of control that You are manifesting through me, desire same and return to You.
- I pray that on the day of Your appearing when every word I have spoken will be judged, I will not be found wanting. I put my body under, punishing and enslaving it to the Lord Jesus!
- Thank You heavenly Father, I give You the highest praise in Jesus name, Amen!

Scriptures for further Prayers

1 Corinthians 6:12, Psalm 15:1-3, Proverbs, 16:28

JUNE 1

PERFORM YOUR WORD, LORD!

Worship

Today's Scripture and Meditation

Jeremiah 1:12. *Then the Lord said to me, "You have seen well, for I am ready to perform My word."*

PRAYERS:

- Father I praise You for You are a Holy God. You never lie, You never disappoint, and You can be trusted.
- You are Dependable, Reliable, Unquestionable, Indefatigable God
- You are the promise keeper, and You never fail, I pray that You will increase my faith and grant me grace to wait on You for Your promises.
- I call upon You because I want to know You more, I lose my peace, have phobias, and am tormented because I am not trusting Your word and ability
- I'm weary of waiting; Lord help me keep my eyes to stayed on You and to be strong in You.
- Lord enable me to trust You implicitly so that I can be anxious for nothing.
- You the Almighty God, and You watch over Your word to perform it. You are a faithful God, and You will answer my Prayers. I put everything in Your care.
- Enable me to be diligent in building up my faith and in the things of the kingdom more than ever before to build me up.
- Let me trust You when You are doing new things or consolidating old ones. When I am in abundance or when I

am in lack, in sickness and in health, when there is peace and when I am facing opposition or persecution, when I have deep encounters with You and when I cannot trace You.

- Enable me to seek Your kingdom and Your righteousness first so that no matter what may come I will continue to follow You.
- Enable me to continue to hold on and continue to follow You no matter the overwhelming negative evidence in our fallen world.
- You are the Lord who sits upon the throne the giver of good gifts, I trust You to give to me the desires of my heart in righteousness.
- When You open, no man can shut. When You shut, no man can open. You make decisions in the affairs of men, I handover the rulership of my life to You. Let no man have authority to determine my fate.
- Father perform Your word already spoken and written about me in Jesus name, Amen
- Enable me to fix my eyes on You, for You do not fail, I turn my eyes to the mountain the only place where I will find help.
- My help is not in man because man will fail and disappoint me., but You do not fail so I renew my trust in You.
- You have the heart of kings and princes, in Your hands and can turn it in whichever direction that pleases You Lord, I trust You to grant me unusual favour in the eyes of all I connect with
- You are the bridegroom of the church, and I know You love me and are not careless concerning me. Lord, I trust You to perform Your will in my life.
- I fix my eyes on The Author and the Finisher of my faith. The Owner of the church, and I fix my eyes on the One who can do all things.
- Thank You, Heavenly Father, for You are faithful and I need not worry, or be fretful, for You watch over Your word to perform it.
- Thank You, Heavenly Father, blessed be Your name oh God. Hallelujah!

Scriptures for further Prayers:

Philippians 4:6, Isaiah 46:11b, Psalm 37:5

JUNE 2

REPAIRER OF BREACHES

Worship

Today's Scripture and Meditation

Isaiah 58:11-12 (TLB):

The LORD will always guide you and provide good things to eat when you are in the desert.
He will make you healthy. You will be like a garden that has plenty of water or like a stream that never runs dry.
¹² You will rebuild those houses left in ruins for years; you will be known as a builder and repairer of city walls and streets.

PRAYER:

- Oh I seek You with a sincere heart, I want more than the religious acts, but a deep relationship with You.
- As You enable me to continue to serve, Father let me accomplish great things for You in Your Kingdom.
- Let my walk with You not just be superficial but that I will be used to build and called the Repairer of the Breach, the Restorer of Streets to Dwell in.
- Enable me to be used to bind broken hearts, build broken relationships, and lives of men through the gospel.
- Oh Lord satisfy me with divine health.
- Oh Lord, water the garden of my life.
- Lord Jesus, may I never run dry in my Spiritual life, and every aspect of my life.

Revive, Rebuild and Restore

- Oh Lord, empower me to rebuild and recover every lost grounds.
- Lord Jesus, let me not be called the name that You have not given me.
- Oh Lord, let heaven know my name, and give me a name that reflects Your will for my life.
- Oh Lord, in this dispensation cause me to be relevant and through me let men be drawn to You in Jesus' name, Amen!
- Thank You Father, in Jesus name I pray. Amen

Scriptures for further Prayers:

Jeremiah 17:8, Psalm 1:3

JUNE 3

SOVEREIGN GOD

Worship

Today's Scripture and Meditation

Jeremiah 27:5 "It is I who by my great power and my outstretched arm have made the earth, with the men and animals that are on the earth, and I give it to whomever it seems right to me.

PRAYERS:

- Father Lord, I thank You because You are the creator God. You made the heavens, even the highest heavens, and all their starry host, the earth and all that is on it, the seas and all that is in them. You give life to everything, and the multitudes of heaven worship You
- By Your outstretched arm, You have made the earth and that is it.
- You are the giver of every good gift and I trust that You will supply all my needs according to Your riches in glory by Christ Jesus.
- Let me find favour before You and before all men that I may have an inheritance on the earth.
- Father let me not be led into captivity but into freedom because You, the defender of Israel, shall defend me, Lord!
- I know that nothing can remain safe except God exercises His power from heaven, so I ask for divine intervention from heaven, Father I ask for Your safety always.

- Let me not labour in vain, sow in vain or build in vain but let me reap the fruit of my labour, reap a harvest of my seeds and inhabit that which I build.
- You are the creator of all things and you give it to whom you will; Father bless me and give me an inheritance on the earth.
- Give me my own city/town as an inheritance in Jesus Name, let it please You to give to me and to bless me in Jesus Name, Amen.

Scriptures for further Prayers

Philippians 4:19, Psalm 127:1

JUNE 4

GOD'S THOUGHTS

Worship

Today' Scripture and Meditation

Jeremiah 29:11(AMPC): *For I know the thoughts and plans that I have for you, says the Lord, thoughts and plans for welfare and peace and not for evil, to give you hope in your final outcome.*

PRAYERS:

- Lord I thank You that I am not a product of the pleasure or mistake of man
- Thank You that I did not come to make up the number or complete the statistics but I'm significant and important
- I thank You because You know me by name and know the number of my hairs on my head and they are named, You see my reins and my heart
- Thank You that You are thinking of me, and for Your good (not evil) thoughts towards me
- Your thoughts toward me cannot be recounted to You in order; if I would declare and speak of them, they are more than can be numbered
- You think of me as a father think towards His children and as a father that pities His children, for this I am grateful
- Though Your thoughts are higher and deeper than I can comprehend, yet You know them.
- Your thoughts towards me are of peace and not of evil. No matter where I am or find myself at any point, I am assured that Your thoughts are favourable to me

Revive, Rebuild and Restore

▢   Thank You for creating me with a plan and a purpose in mind, You have thought and planned my welfare and peace

▢   Thank You for Your thoughts and plan to give me hope in my final outcome. That I will not perish on the journey but will reach my eternal destiny

▢   Father let me be content with Your thoughts and plans for my life, let me accept Your will for my life and not chase shadows

▢   I pray for Your counsel every time, even at night, to instructs me. Let my eyes always be upon You

▢   Father show me Your ways, teach me Your paths, guide me in Your truth and teach me, for all my hope is in You all day long

▢   Enable me to fulfil my God-ordained purpose in Jesus name. Amen

Scriptures for further Prayers:

Psalm 25:4-5, Psalm 16:7-8, James 1:5

JUNE 5

GRACE TO WAIT

Worship

Today's Scripture and Meditation

Job 14:14. If a man dies, shall he live again? All the days of my appointed time will I wait, till my change come.

PRAYERS:

- Father, I thank You because You always fulfil the expectations of Your children.
- Lord teach me to wait on You as I know that a waiting period always precedes the manifestation of great expectations.
- Let my expectations be very great that my manifestations be great.
- Father grant the grace and determination to wait for my own appointed time as designed by God.
- Father come to my aid, and may You find me still waiting for and on you in Jesus Name.
- As I await Your second coming, I pray that You will find faith in me and find me faithful.
- Help me to be patient in the place suffering and tribulation, knowing that You will intervene and fix it for me.
- Enable me to wait for Your time; trusting in Your love for me, Your faithfulness to Your promises and Your unlimited power to do anything You want to do.
- As I wait, I know it shall be well with me because You said so.

- ▢ You may not be privileged to know the times and the seasons when He will manifest His power in Your life; Father, I surrender to Your will work in my life at Your own time.
- ▢ Give me the grace to wait in tears, knowing that joy will come in the morning.
- ▢ Help me to wait for the day of my blessing and get my expectations.
- ▢ Father, teach me patience in the place of waiting and deliver my expectations from failure.
- ▢ Thank You Father in Jesus Name.

Scriptures for further Prayers

Luke 18:8, Isaiah 40:31

JUNE 6

POUR OUT YOUR SPIRIT LORD!

Worship

Today's Scripture and Meditation

Joel 2:28-29: "*And it shall come to pass afterward, That I will pour out My Spirit on all flesh; your sons and your daughters shall prophesy, your old men shall dream dreams, your young men shall see visions. And also on My menservants and on My maidservants, I will pour out My Spirit in those days.*"

PRAYERS:

- Father I thank You for the gift of the Spirit and His anointing is poured upon us.
- I pray for an outpouring of Your Spirit upon my life today.
- I pray for the children in my family and in our church that they receive the gifts of the Spirit, that they will prophesy and manifest in other gifts in Jesus Name, Amen!
- I pray for the men in my family and in our church that they receive the gift of the Spirit, that they see vision and manifest in other gifts in Jesus Name, Amen!
- I receive the gift of the word of knowledge and the gift of the word of wisdom, the gift of faith, the gift of healing and working of miracles.
- The gifts of speaking in tongues and the interpretation of tongues.
- I receive the gift of the Apostle, Evangelist, Prophet, Pastors and Teachers (delete as applicable).
- Thank You Lord for making me a gift and giving us gifts to serve before You and to manifest Your glory in this world.

- Lord I am grateful, and I do not take this honour to myself or take it for granted.
- I will not take my gifts in vain. You say, 'I have given You as gifts and I have given You gifts, do not be idle'
- I receive every gift I need for ministry and to fulfil my assignment by faith in the Name of Jesus. amen.
- I will not be diverted, distracted, or miss my calling, but I will finish well in the name of Jesus, amen
- I receive fresh infilling of the Holy Spirit, this very moment in Jesus Name, Amen!
- I receive fresh fire from above in Jesus's Name!
- I receive boldness and fresh anointing to be able to step out and do what You have allocated for me to do!
- As Your fire falls on me burn out anything in me that is not worthy of You in Jesus Name!
- Touch my lips, anoint my lips and use me to your own glory in Jesus Name!
- Thank You Heavenly Father, blessed be Your Name oh God, in Jesus mighty Name I have prayed, Amen!

Scriptures for further Prayers:

John   7:38,   Acts   2:1-4

JUNE 7

GRACE FOR GRACE

Worship

Today's Scripture and Meditation

John 1:16. *And of His fullness we have all received, and grace for grace.*

PRAYERS:

- ☐ Lord, I thank you for the grace that appeared to us and showed us the way of salvation and taught me to live lives worthy of You.
- ☐ Thank You for it is by grace I am saved through faith. I am grateful that You know me by grace.
- ☐ Grace has qualified me who was unqualified, I receive grace in Your sight O Lord.
- ☐ I receive grace to pursue God honestly, Grace to achieve, receive grace to overcome, grace to recover. grace to win the battles, grace to be victorious, grace to be the head, grace to be an inventor, grace to help. Grace for every unqualified moment in my life.
- ☐ I receive divine grace, divine empowerment, grace that breaks down mountains, grace that solves impossible problems, grace that opens closed doors, grace that breaks down every barrier and obstacle in the Name of Jesus.
- ☐ Lord show me grace, give me a portion in your holy place, enlighten my eyes and grant revival to my soul.
- ☐ I pray that grace will manifest for me, pour grace upon my lips in Jesus Name.

- ☐ I ask You Lord that You teach me Your ways, show me Your face, show me the right path and cause me to know You always.
- ☐ Lord will give grace and glory; No good thing will He withhold.
- ☐ I know I require grace to receive, so Lord grant me the grace to receive in the Name of Jesus.
- ☐ Father place an ornament of grace on me and a crown of glory for all to see and praise your Name.
- ☐ A crown of glory she will deliver to you.
- ☐ I receive grace for grace in Jesus' Name.
- ☐ Thank You heavenly Father I praise You oh God of heaven in Jesus mighty Name I have prayed. Amen.

Scriptures for further Prayers

Proverbs 3:34, Exodus 33:17, Titus 2:11-12, Ezra 9:8

Revive, Rebuild and Restore

JUNE 8

I AM THE DOOR

Worship

Today's Scripture and Meditation

John 10: 7-10. So, Jesus said again, I assure you, most solemnly I tell you, that I Myself am the Door [a]for the sheep. All others who came [as such] before Me are thieves and robbers, but the [true] sheep did not listen to and obey them. I am the Door; anyone who enters in through Me will be saved (will live). He will come in and he will go out [freely], and will find pasture. The thief comes only in order to steal and kill and destroy. I came that they may have and enjoy life, and have it in abundance (to the full, till it [b]overflows).

PRAYERS:

⬚   Dear Heavenly Father, I am grateful that I am associated with You the Almighty God, Most High God, the Creator God who has all power, Omniscient, in heaven and earth and under the earth.

⬚   I approach the throne of grace by the blood of sprinkling, for a cleansing and purging

⬚   You are the Door and I thank You that I have gained admittance to fellowship with God and all the people of God, through You.

⬚   I pray that I will not be lured away by deception and trickery, robbers, violence and destruction or by conmen and muggers of the spiritual world.

⬚   That my life in Christ not be taken away from You who gives abundantly.

⬚

- ⬚ Let me not follow hirelings or blind leaders but that I will follow the good shepherd who is also the Door to the sheep.
- ⬚ Grant me the liberty to come in and go out [freely] and find pasture in and through You.
- ⬚ The thief comes to kill, steal and destroy but You came that we may have life and have it more abundantly, to the fullest till it overflows. Father, I receive life to the fullest.
- ⬚ Let me not fall victim to the devil who only comes to steal, kill and destroy.
- ⬚ I submit to You and thereby resist every one of His works in my life
- ⬚ I command a reversal of the works of the enemy and pray for a restoration of joy and peace.
- ⬚ Restoration of all virtue that the enemy has stolen from me: spiritual gifts, my prayer life, my study of the word of God, my service of the Almighty *God... (mention anything that needs to be restored in your life)* in Jesus Name.
- ⬚ Restoration of all things killed and destroyed in my life aspirations, visions, missions, calling, ministry, assignments, members of my body, let them resurrect in the Name of the Lord Jesus Christ.
- ⬚ I shut the door of every department of my life to any invasion of the devil.
- ⬚ I receive life by the Spirit of God in my body, soul and spirit, and family.
- ⬚ Father put Your Spirit upon me that I shall live.
- ⬚ Let me enjoy life and have it in abundance to the fullest and till it overflows.
- ⬚ Every door through which the enemy has stolen, killed and destroyed in the past, I command them to be shut.
- ⬚ Every door that the enemy opened or that I opened for the enemy, I command such doors to be shut.
- ⬚ Through God, I shall do valiantly, for it is He Who shall tread down my adversaries today and forevermore.
- ⬚ I give you the highest praise, blessed be your Name, in Jesus Name I have prayed Amen!

Scriptures for further Prayers

Ezekiel 37, Psalm 60:12

JUNE 9

SERVE HIM WITHOUT FEAR

Worship

Today's Scripture and Meditation

Luke 1:74-75: *To grant us that we, Being delivered from the hand of our enemies, Might serve Him without fear, In holiness and righteousness before Him all the days of our life.*

Prayers:

- According to the word of the Lord, The Lord will deliver me from every enemy. Whatever is preventing me and distracting from fulfilling the purpose of God for my life, from bringing glory to the name of Jesus is an enemy; I rebuke them in the name of the Lord
- Everything that may bring distress into my life, everything that may bring shames into my life is destroyed
- Every chain, every fetter around my life, or any departments of my life be broken in the name of the Lord Jesus Christ
- Every distress be removed and be uprooted from my life, in the name of Jesus, Amen
- I command that even every of our enemies will turn against each other according to the word of God
- And whosoever digs a pit, let them fall into it in the name of the Lord Jesus Christ, that the world around us, may know that we serve a Living God
- Our God has saved us in the name of Jesus Christ, Amen
- Every form of darkness in our lives, Lord let Your light shine in the name of Jesus Christ

- In the name of Jesus, where there is a hint of death. Let there be life in the name of Jesus
- Every gate of brass, everything that has put me in stock, everything that has devoured me, every bar of iron, every illegal checkpoints in the name of Jesus be broken into pieces
- Whatever is preventing me from moving forward, whatsoever is causing stagnancy, be broken in pieces, to become the thoroughfare to greatness in the name of Jesus
- Thoroughfare to those businesses, career, spiritual growth where the gates has been shut in the name of Jesus, Amen
- Whatever prevents the will and the purpose of God, from prospering in my life, be destroyed in Jesus name
- Whosoever the Son of God sets free is free indeed. I declare my freedom from every entanglement with the enemy
- You will "grant me to be delivered from the hands of my enemy, so that I might serve You without fear but in holiness and righteousness before You all the days of my life"
- I ask for grace to serve before You without fear, grace to serve before You in holiness, Grace to serve before You in righteousness, all the days of my life.
- Father Lord I give You praise, I worship You, I magnify Your Holy name, blessed be Your name oh God. Hallelujah

Scriptures for further Prayers:

Psalm 124:7, Acts 12:6-10

JUNE 10

I WILL SPARE YOU

Worship

Today's Scripture and Meditation

Malachi 3:16-18(NIV)

Then those who feared and loved the Lord spoke often of Him to each other. And he had a Book of remembrance drawn up in which he recorded the names of those who feared him and loved to think about him. 17 "They shall be mine," says the Lord Almighty, "in that day when I make up my jewels. And I will spare them as a man spares an obedient and dutiful son. 18 Then You will see the difference between God's treatment of good men and bad, between those who serve him and those who don't.

PRAYERS:

- Thank You that You are the Father that shows compassion to His children. Thank You for Your compassion revealed in my life.
- Thank You for the privilege of knowing and loving You. I pray that I will not be discouraged in my faith in Jesus Name. Amen!
- Thank You for Your ownership of my life. That I am Your jewel, Your treasured possession.
- Thank You for exemption from evil that You have promised to those that fear and serve You.
- Thank You for the difference You make between those that serve You and those that do not. Let that difference be seen

in me, in my life, in the things that happen to me and through me.

- You commanded the angel not to do anything to the land or seas or grass until You have sealed the forehead of the servants of GOD. I pray that no evil will come to where I am until I have received the mark of exemption from You, that will preserve me and my household from evil.
- Father, let the blood of Jesus, the blood of sprinkling, blot out every mark the enemy may have put on me, every distortion from normal, or disfavour.
- By the blood of Jesus, I receive a mark of exemption from the Lord!
- Let my name be recorded in the book of remembrance.
- Father spare me and all mine as a man spares his obedient and dutiful son in Jesus Name. Amen!

Scriptures for further Prayers

Psalm 103:13, Revelation 7:3, Colossians 2:14

JUNE 11

ESTABLISHED IN RIGHTEOUSNESS

Worship

Today's Scripture and Meditation

> **Isaiah 54:14:** *In righteousness you shall be established; you shall be far from oppression, for you shall not fear; And from terror, for it shall not come near you.*

PRAYERS:

- ☐ Father thank You because I am justified by Christ's righteousness
- ☐ Thank You for the ability to stand in Your presence without the sense of guilt or inferiority or condemnation
- ☐ Thank You for my identity in Christ which has enabled my relationship with God
- ☐ Thank You for grace to exercise righteousness, purity of manners, doing justice and judgment and holiness
- ☐ I pray that I will be solidly built and grounded in righteousness and that through righteousness I shall be established
- ☐ Lord Jesus, You established me in a good position which made us sit together in heavenly places, give me the grace to continually acknowledge You as the Lord of my life
- ☐ Through righteousness I am fortified, and I am far from every form of oppression - either from within or from without; from false teachers that oppress the mind with legal doctrine; or from persecutors that oppress to injure from without

- ▢ Through righteousness, I shall not be far from oppression, I shall not be tormented by fear I shall be free from terror. The enemy has no window to come through to afflict me
- ▢ Through righteousness, I am positioned in the place of constant fellowship with God. Unwholesome thoughts of oppression or destruction, fear and terror are far away from me
- ▢ Through righteousness, I am positioned to do exploits in all of my endeavours. Righteousness will bring the prosperity of the Lord to my lift me high above those who oppose me
- ▢ Through righteousness, I am under the covering of the Almighty and none can stand against me Lord, victory belongs to You, and I trust in You
- ▢ You are the controller of all human activity in the world who will grant victory in every battle of life in Jesus name. Amen

Scriptures for further Prayers:

Romans 5:19, 2 Corinthians 5:21

JUNE 12

NOTHING IS TOO HARD

Worship

Today's Scripture and Meditation:

Jeremiah 32:27. *"Behold, I am the Lord, the God of all flesh. Is there anything too hard for Me?*

PRAYERS:

- Thank You because You are the Lord, and the God of all flesh.
- What mighty and awesome things You do in the congregation of men! What mighty things You do in the Earth!
- Awesome things happen in Your presence, I lift You high oh God!
- I acknowledge that there's nothing too hard or too difficult for You.
- Indeed, You're the God of all flesh. The creator of the whole universe.
- I ask that every hard situation and every difficulty situation, no matter the level of impact that it may be having in my life. I ask oh God that You will step in.
- You are powerful to save, Lord save me!
- You have power to heal, Lord heal me physically and spiritually!
- You have power to deliver, break every bond and set me free form all forms of captivity!
- I ask that You intervene. I ask that You Lord do something new.

- Make a way for me where there is no way and spring forth rivers in the desert!
- I ask God that You will resolve every of my problem in the name of the Lord Jesus Christ, Amen!
- You sent a raven to feed the prophet and changed laws to set your children free, Lord break protocols for my sake
- I depend on you because You have all powers, nothing is ever too hard for you and all things are possible in You

(Spend a minute to tell Him something you need Him to do for you)

- Lord reveal Yourself as the God of all flesh. Blessed be Your name oh God! Hallelujah to Your name!
- Thank You Lord Jesus, in Jesus name we have prayed. Amen.

Scriptures for further Prayers

Isaiah 43:19, Jeremiah 32:17

JUNE 13

LET GOD ARISE

Worship

Today's Scripture and Meditation

Psalm 68:1. Let God arise, Let His enemies be scattered; Let those also who hate Him flee before Him.

PRAYERS:

- Father, I worship You today as the battle fighter, the Lord of host; Jehovah Sabaoth, You have never lost any battle.
- I bring myself under the covering of the blood of Jesus and confess every sin that may bring offence.
- Lord, I proclaim Your triumph over all Your enemies, when You go forth no enemy can stand.
- Lord, I pray like Moses and David prayed, "Rise Up Oh Lord and let those who hate You flee before You."
- Father, go before me in this journey of life take care of the enemies of my purpose and wellbeing
- Lord Jesus, when You rose up in glory and in strength all Your enemies scattered; none dared to oppose You. Therefore, Lord since I am in You, all enemies will scatter before me, because all my victory is found in You resurrected glory.
- Enforce Your deliverance from the mighty and the captor, and contend with those that contend with me, till all know that You are the mighty One.
- Father release me from satanic bondages and captivity, every inherited bondage and collective captivity is destroyed

- ▢ I receive the keys to the Kingdom, to spiritual power, and bind every enemy of my soul
- ▢ I send the fire of the Lord against every evil implantation. Let the fire of God consume everything not planted by the Father in my life
- ▢ I command total liberation for my spirit and soul from every spiritual bondage hindering my life.
- ▢ I rebuke every spiritual blindness and dumbness.
- ▢ Every spirit of confusion and every unwanted stranger, we command you to come out of closed places. Every oppression and suppression be broken.
- ▢ Every fountain of sorrow dry up, we bind the spirit of heaviness and cast it out.
- ▢ I command everyone on this altar, be released from spiritual altars including myself. Be broken and consumed by the fire of the Holy Ghost.
- ▢ Let every load the enemy has placed upon my life be it, sickness, trouble in marriage, business, ministry, or problems with children be removed. Every burden is lifted. Every evil altar is broken, we command the activity of the evil altar to be disgraced.
- ▢ Every evil anointing in my life, be removed.
- ▢ Every arrester of our lives, children, ministry, walk with God, we command you to be arrested by the power of the Holy Ghost. I command release from sicknesses, diseases and bondage.
- ▢ The yoke of sickness, diseases, cancer, mental sickness, be broken. By the anointing of God, begin to rise, be outstanding and become fruitful.
- ▢ Every stronghold is released from the enemy. By the power of the Spirit of God, I cast down every imagination, I bind the spirit of pride and cast you out!
- ▢ Every door you have opened to the enemy knowingly and unknowingly, we command such doors to be shut!
- ▢ Let there be complete restoration in every facet of my life

Scriptures for further Prayers

Numbers 10:35, Matthew 16:19

JUNE 14

ROOTS BY THE RIVER

Worship

Today's Scripture and Meditation

Jeremiah 17:7-8. Blessed is the man who trusts in the LORD, and whose hope is the LORD. For he shall be like a tree planted by the waters, which spreads out its roots by the river, and will not fear when heat comes; But its leaf will be green, and will not be anxious in the year of drought, nor will cease from yielding fruit.

PRAYERS:

- Lord I thank You because You saved me and imputed Your righteousness for me that I might be the planting of the Lord.
- I trust You Lord and my hope is in You. I thank You because I am blessed by You.
- I ask for grace to live a life that pleases You and is worthy of You.
- That I will not walks in the counsel of the ungodly, I will not stand in the path of sinners, I will not seat in the seat of the scornful.
- I am planted by the waters with my root by the river, I will never lack both spiritual and physical nourishment.
- Lord I decree that the heat of this life and the world shall not get to me or my household in Jesus' Name.
- Father, let me experience Your peace that surpasses

Revive, Rebuild and Restore

all understanding. Cause me to enjoy peace and flourishing in Jesus' Name.

- Lord, help me to stay connected to Your Holy Spirit. That I continually may bear fruit
- Father cause me to be totally sold out to You
- By Your grace I shall stay green in every area of my life in Jesus' Name
- Lord God, I declare that anxiety, depression, and others in the spectrum are not my portion in Jesus Name.
- Father I reject spiritual and physical malnutrition in Jesus Name.
- Lord, I declare that my life shall not be like that of the fig tree that was fruitless but that I will be fruitful in Jesus' Name.
- I decree that I shall be perpetually fruitful in every area of my life, enable me to flourish in the courts of my God.
- Thank you father for hearing my Prayers in Jesus name I have prayed. Amen!

Scriptures for further Prayers:

Psalm 92:13, Psalm 104:16a

JUNE 15

I SEE THE LORD

Worship

Today's Scripture and Meditation

Isaiah 6:5: So I said: "Woe is me, for I am undone! Because I am a man of unclean lips, and I dwell in the midst of a people of unclean lips; For my eyes have seen the King, The Lord of hosts."

PRAYERS:

- Father Lord, I thank You for the gift of salvation and for the righteousness of Jesus imputed on me
- Thank You for the access given to us to come boldly before the throne of grace to obtain mercy and find grace to help in the times of need
- Father let me experience the reality of Your presence, Let me see You sitting upon the throne that I might be compelled to a life of unhindered worship unto You
- Help me keep my eyes fixed on heaven and spend time in true worship of You, let me be empowered to rise above the circumstances of lives. Let me be changed and transformed
- Let me see myself in the light of Your awesome holiness that I might align my life with Your will in Jesus name. That I will not only be righteous outwardly but that You will be enthroned upon my heart in Jesus name
- Take me deeper in my prayer life and in intimacy with You. Help me to walk in Your light and holiness. I want to know You more; Oh Lord

- Give me joy in Your presence and help me to bring joy into the lives of others
- I want to dwell in Your house and gaze on Your beauty. I want to seek Your face daily; Lord enable me to do this in Jesus name
- Lord, I accept Your invitation to come up higher around the throne, to stay in Your presence to behold Jesus, to see Him and believe
- Lord, touch my tongue today. Cleanse and transform me. Your word says that he that can bridle the tongue can bridle the whole body. Lord enable me to bridle my whole body
- Father remove the distractions in my life that can keep me away from Your presence
- Lord, may Your presence fill my life to bring peace, joy and comfort in Jesus name

Scriptures for further Prayers:

Ps 29:10, Psalms 27: 4 & 7

JUNE 16

REST UPON ME

Worship

Today's Scripture and Meditation

Isaiah 11:2. The Spirit of the LORD shall rest upon Him, The Spirit of wisdom and understanding, The Spirit of counsel and might, The Spirit of knowledge and of the fear of the LORD.

PRAYERS:

- Father, I thank You for Your Holy Spirit whom You gave to us to empower us on the journey of salvation
- Holy Spirit, I thank You for Your diverse gifts, differences of ministries, diversities of activities, for the edification and profit of the body of Christ.
- Spirit of the Living God, I ask that You rest upon me afresh today in the name of Jesus
- **Father, let the Spirit of God rest upon me:**
- to bring about new life within, to bring about restoration, to bring about wisdom, bring about capacity for judging rightly in matters relating to life and conduct
- to give me the road map of life
- That I will be able to execute His will and counsel on earth
- To bring wisdom that comes from above
- To bring peaceable wisdom to make life choices and to reach our destinies
- To bring wisdom that will cause me to be efficient and in control of all things and not lose control

- To bring might; that force, that dominion, that mastery, that potency, that efficiency that God already put within me and expects me to manifest in it
- To bring might, enabling me to run and not be weary. enabling me to walk in the might of the Lord, and enabling Your power to do all that I have been called to do on this earth in the name of Jesus, Amen
- To bring information and counsel, my heart will be instructed by the Spirit of the Lord and by the counsel of the Lord, that I may have direction in the name of Jesus, Amen
- To bring counsel to us in the journey of life, in the name of our Lord Jesus Christ, Amen
- I will not be moved by the goings-on   in the world; I will be confident in the Lord my God
- Let me hear the voice of the Lord behind me
- I will be quiet before You oh Lord that You might give me instructions in righteousness in the name of Jesus Christ, Amen
- Holy Spirit that raised Jesus Christ from death, come upon me and overshadow me for the rest of my life
- Dear Lord, Let me decrease while You increase in every department of my life
- I pray that I will not go to the grave with the gift and talents You bestowed on me but that I will manifest in it for the edification of the body of Christ and will make profit with it
- Thank You Heavenly Father, in Jesus mighty name I have prayed, Amen

Scriptures for further Prayers:

Isaiah 40:31. Matthew 25:14-30

JUNE 17

BE OF GOOD CHEER

Worship

Today's Scripture and Meditation

John 16:33 (RSV):
I have said this to you, that in me you may have peace. In the world you have tribulation; but be of good cheer, I have overcome the world."

PRAYERS:

- Oh Lord cause me to experience the peace that emanates from Your Manifold Presence.
- Oh Lord cause me to find You early that Your peace my abound in my life.
- My Father, cause my heart to be joyful in the face of tribulation.
- Give me the enabling power and ability to feel cheer amid mortal gloom and doom
- Give me courage that I may observe to do Your word.
- Enable me to be of good cheer, knowing that you will fight my cause.
- Enable me to be of good cheer, knowing that my tomorrow will be alright in Christ Jesus.
- Enable me to be of good cheer, knowing that I will not suffer eternal loss and damnation,
- Enable me to be of good cheer, knowing that Your thoughts towards me are good.
- I decree and declare that I have the peace of the Lord that supersedes all understanding.

- Oh Lord, cause my heart to be receptive to Your word and cause Your peace to fill my spirit.
    - Oh Lord stir my spirit within me to do right at all times that I may experience Your peace and security.
    - My father, cause me to find security and peace in every ramification of my life.
    - Let me have peace in You and in confidence that You have overcome the world.

Scriptures for further Prayers:

John 16:33, Psalm 4:8, Isaiah 32:17

JUNE 18

NO DOUBTING

Worship

Today's Scripture and Meditation

James 1:5-6: *If any of you lacks wisdom, let him ask of God, who gives to all liberally and without reproach, and it will be given to him. But let him ask in faith, with no doubting, for he who doubts is like a wave of the sea driven and tossed by the wind.*

PRAYERS:

- Father I thank You because You are a faithful God who does what He says.
- Father I know that wisdom does not come from men, books or advisers but from You so I ask for wisdom that I would know how to use the knowledge that You have given me.
- Father gives me wisdom according to Your excellent greatness; not according to my fitness to receive but according to Your generosity
- Enable me to constantly hear Your word that faith may rise and be strengthened within me.
- Father give me wisdom in Jesus name, Amen
- Father let me always find wisdom in the pages of the scripture
- Lack of faith shows no foundation and instability in our ways and so Lord I pray like the disciples prayed, that You will increase my faith in Jesus name, Amen!
- Father break though my doors of doubt and unbelief in Jesus Name, Amen!

- I know that everything is possible when I believe. Lord help my unbelief.
- I command fear that brings doubt, worry, discouragement to lose its grip over my life. Let every thought or image in my mind that brings fear be wiped out in Jesus name, Amen!
- Holy Spirit help me to be thoroughly persuaded that I will receive whatever I ask the Lord that I will not be like a wave of the sea in Jesus Name, Amen!
- Enable me to ask in faith that I might receive answers to my Prayers, in Jesus' Name, Amen!
- Through faith grant me rest, stability, and focus in Jesus Name, Amen!
- Thank You heavenly Father in Jesus Name, Amen

Scriptures for further Prayers:

Mark 9:23-24, Romans 10:17

JUNE 19

FIGHT TILL THE END

Worship

Today's Scripture and Meditation

2 Kings 13:15-19. And Elisha said to him, "Take a bow and some arrows." So, he took himself a bow and some arrows. 16 Then he said to the king of Israel, "Put your hand on the bow." So, he put his hand on it, and Elisha put his hands on the king's hands. 17 And he said, "Open the east window"; and he opened it. Then Elisha said, "Shoot"; and he shot. And he said, "The arrow of the Lord's deliverance and the arrow of deliverance from Syria; for you must strike the Syrians at Aphek till you have destroyed them." 18 Then he said, "Take the arrows"; so he took them. And he said to the king of Israel, "Strike the ground"; so he struck three times, and stopped. 19 And the man of God was angry with him, and said, "You should have struck five or six times; then you would have struck Syria till you had destroyed it! But now you will strike Syria only three times."

PRAYERS:

- Father, I thank You for You are the true God.
- Father enable me to be a true worshipper of a true God in spirit and in truth.
- Let the fear of God envelope me and give me the grace to honour Your servants.
- Enable me to live a life that will be so impactful that ungodly men will miss me when I am gone.
- Father no matter who has been the strength of my life and calling, let me always be acutely aware that the arrow of the Lord's deliverance is always present.

- ☐ Enable me to always act in faith in the knowledge that the Lord is with me
- ☐ Give me the grace to obey divine instructions to the fullest.
- ☐ Father Lord grant me discernment, to understand spiritual things and to follow through.
- ☐ Father let me not be content with small effort but to always seize the strategic moment for my victories.
- ☐ Help me to keep fighting in the battle against sin, in the attainment of Christian knowledge, in the attainment of faith, to do more for the kingdom of God.
- ☐ To keep fighting because the world, the flesh, and the devil will not stop their shooting.
- ☐ That I will fight the good fight of faith and complete my course.
- ☐ That I will not be weary of doing good.
- ☐ Give me boldness to step out in faith that affliction will not rise again.
- ☐ Thank You Father in Jesus' Name.

Scriptures for further Prayers

Galatians 5:17, 1 Corinthians 9:24, 2 Timothy 4:7

Revive, Rebuild and Restore

JUNE 20

PERFECT LAW OF LIBERTY

Worship

Today's Scripture and Meditation

James 1:25 *But he who looks into the perfect law of liberty and continues in it, and is not a forgetful hearer but a doer of the work, this one will be blessed in what he does.*

Prayers:

- Father thank You for Your word that brings all round liberty and sets free
- I pray that You give me grace to obey Your word in all things as obedience is the prerequisite for blessings.
- Help me to fulfil the conditions of blessings through obedience to You and to Your word.
- Hep me to do Your good will and continue to trust You.
- Enable me to continue to look into the perfect law of liberty and not be a forgetful hearer but a doer of the work.
- That I will not be overcome by doubt or fear but that my faith will arise as I continue to stay in Your word,
- Enable me to continue in sweet fellowship that I will sit at Your feet, and walk by Your side in the way.
- Enable me to continue to look into the perfect law of liberty.
- That I may do what You say and go where You send me in Jesus' Name!
- Thank You Father in Jesus' Name.

Scriptures for further Prayers:

Deuteronomy 28:1, 1 Corinthians 3:18

JUNE 21

HEARING HIS VOICE

Worship

Today's Scripture and Meditation

Psalm 85:8 *I will hear what God the Lord will speak, For He will speak peace To His people and to His saints.*

PRAYERS:

- Lord, I seek You today. I seek to hear Your voice, help me to desire more of Your presence that I might hear Your voice the more.
- Father enable me to settle down and not to be too busy to listen for Your voice.
- Lord enable me to stay focused and not be distracted by the cares of the day. I take authority over every distracting thought, take them captive to the obedience of Christ that I might be able to set my mind on You in Jesus Name, Amen!
- Father, that only Your Holy Spirit will speak to me now as I wait on You for wisdom, insight, and direction. And whatever You show I'll recognise Your voice and how You speak.
- Father You are the good shepherd and Your sheep hear your voice. Father, let me hear your voice continually and recognise it when I do in Jesus' Name.
- Enable me to willingly accept what You have for me so that I do not blank out Your voice and lack in guidance
- Father speak to me daily about all matters of life, direct my steps that I may not miss a step-in life.
- Thank You heavenly Father, I pray in Jesus name, Amen!

Scriptures for further Prayers:

2 Corinthians 10:5, Proverbs 16:9

JUNE 22

GOOD CONDUCT

Worship

Today's Scripture and Meditation

James 3:13-18. Who is wise and understanding among you? Let him show by good conduct that his works are done in the meekness of wisdom. 14 But if you have bitter envy and [a]self-seeking in your hearts, do not boast and lie against the truth. 15 This wisdom does not descend from above, but is earthly, sensual, demonic. 16 For where envy and self-seeking exist, confusion and every evil thing are there. 17 But the wisdom that is from above is first pure, then peaceable, gentle, willing to yield, full of mercy and good fruits, without partiality and without hypocrisy. 18 Now the fruit of righteousness is sown in peace by those who make peace.

PRAYERS:

- Father Lord, I have come to You Who are the only wise God.
- Enable me to be wise and full of understanding.
- Grant me grace to exhibit good conduct and work in the meekness of wisdom.
- That I will not live in bitter envy, selfishness and or be self-seeking in my heart.
- That I will not be a boaster and liar against the truth.
- That evil will not abound in my life or in my environment
- I pray for godly, heavenly wisdom and not the wisdom that comes from earthy, sensual and demonic ways.

- Lord Grant me wisdom from above which is pure, peaceable, gentle, full of mercy and good fruits.
- Lord purify my heart, let no jealousy or envy be found in in me.
- Let my love be perfect and without pretense towards all men.
- Father Lord please make us examples to the world, always bearing good fruits and impartial.
- Make me peace makers, carry Your presence everywhere Lord.

Scriptures for further Prayers:

Romans 12:9, Galatians 5:22-23

JUNE 23

DON'T BE CONCEITED

Worship:

Today's Scripture and Meditation

Isaiah 5:21

Woe to those who are wise in their own eyes, and shrewd in their own sight!

PRAYERS:

- Lord let me not be wise in my own eyes, deceiving myself. I submit everything about my life unto You; the hard things, the simple things, the easy and difficult things.
- I submit the challenges that I am facing, the things that are bothering me, the battles of my life, I submit them all. I put my trust in You and ask that You will take charge of them all in the name of Jesus, Amen.
- My wisdom has failed, my intellect has failed, my experience has failed, my abilities have failed, my pedigree has failed so, I submit all to Your wisdom, knowledge, ability and power!
- I acknowledge that You alone know all things and can do all things.
- Let the fear of the Lord fall upon me afresh that I might not partake in evil.
- It is possible for a man to do evil and not be conscious, let my eyes open to every evil that I do, whatever is against Your will, whatever is against Your plan, Lord, open my eyes, that there might be healing for my flesh, in the name of

the Lord Jesus, that there will be healing to my flesh and refreshment to my bones.

- Let me have that consciousness within me of who You are, of Your presence, to the extent that I will not do anything against Your will.
- Enable me to give attention to Your words, keeping them in my heart so that I will not sin against You but that it would be healing to my flesh and refreshment to my bones.
- By the Spirit of the Lord that raise Jesus from the dead, let healing manifest in my body and mind in Jesus' name, Amen.
- Thank You Heavenly Father, in Jesus mighty name I pray, Amen.

Scriptures for further Prayers

Proverbs 3:7-8, Psalm 119:11,

Revive, Rebuild and Restore

JUNE 24

DEALING WITH FOUNDATIONS

Worship

Today's Scripture and Meditation

Jeremiah 31:29-30. In those days they shall say no more, the fathers have eaten sour grapes, and the children's teeth are set on edge. But everyone shall die for his own iniquity [only]; every man who eats sour grapes – his [own] teeth shall be set on edge.

PRAYERS:

- ☐ Lord Jesus, I thank You for the finished work of calvary that redeems me from every entanglement with my past, my past generational activities and inheritances.
- ☐ You said to the children of Levi, that they will have no inheritance or any part among them, Father I reject every negative spiritual inheritance from my ancestors
- ☐ I will have no part in the generational sins, idolatry, curses, ungodly covenant and practices.
- ☐ I plead the blood of Jesus for mercy as I take generational repentance
- ☐ I ask for mercy and cleansing as regarding the sins of our generations past.
- ☐ Let the blood of Jesus touch our foundations, and cleanse it.
- ☐ I command every collective captivity, curse and satanic covenant be broken, let every association with every other god but the Almighty God be broken in Jesus Name.
- ☐ Let every negative family pattern be broken
- ☐ Every curse is broken for Christ has redeemed me from the curse of the law and there by no other curse stands.
- ☐ I will not be a victim of what I am ignorant of

- Only God-ordained purpose for my life shall manifest; every demonic yoke is broken, and I am set free whatever is blocking my harvest, is totally destroyed.
- Every tree planted in my life bearing undesirable fruit is uprooted
- I shall not inherit the sicknesses of my father and mother either genetically or spiritually.
- No more oppression, suppression, or possession by the enemy. I command strangers to come out of their closed places in my life.
- I pray for total divine cleansing and purification.
- It is a day of freedom; a new foundation has been laid by the blood of Jesus upon the Rock who is Christ in Jesus Name.
- I am set at liberty to worship God Almighty
- Thank You Father in Jesus name.

Scriptures for further Prayers:

Numbers 18:20, Galatians 3:13.

JUNE 25

REWARD OF UNBELIEF

Worship

Today's Scripture and Meditation

Joshua 5:6: For the children of Israel walked forty years in the wilderness, till all the people who were men of war, who came out of Egypt, were [a]consumed, because they did not obey the voice of the Lord – to whom the Lord swore that He would not show them the land which the Lord had sworn to their fathers that He would give us, "a land flowing with milk and honey."

PRAYERS:

- Thank You Oh God for every of Your promise to Your people which You always fulfil.
- Father forgive my unbelief and lack of trust, doubting You at the face of every obstacle or persecution.
- Father Lord I plead for mercy, every way I have sinned against You, every way I have not obeyed You completely, have mercy and forgive me.
- Oh God whatever wants to take me out from Your promises for my life, please Lord take it away.
- Father Lord please deliver me from evil that has come to me due disobedience to You, let every foot hold and legal ground of the enemy be destroyed.
- I pray that You will remember Your mercy in Your judgement Lord.
- My father, help me not to miss my blessings and Your fore-ordained place of rest.
- I declare that my joy and that of my family will not be cut

short in Jesus' Name.
- Father enable me to possess my possession,
- Give me an inheritance with You I declare that I and my generation are blessed in the Lord in Jesus' Name.

Scriptures for further Prayers:

Numbers 14:1-4, James 1:6-8

JUNE 26

BREAK UP YOUR FALLOW GROUND

Worship

Today's Scripture and Meditation

Jeremiah. 4:3-4a: *For thus says the Lord to the men of Judah and Jerusalem: "Break up your fallow ground, And do not sow among thorns. Circumcise yourselves to the Lord, And take away the foreskins of your hearts"*

PRAYERS:

- ⬜ Father I present my heart before You, let every fallow ground of my heart be broken
- ⬜ I return to You from a hardened condition. Let every area of my heart that has been fallow become cultivated again that every area that has laid dormant be broken up so that seeds of righteousness be sown in my life in Jesus name
- ⬜ I pray that every weed sown into my life because of inactivity be uprooted in Jesus mighty name
- ⬜ I repent of every resistance and rejection of the workings and plantings of God in my life
- ⬜ I repent of my carelessness, lukewarmness and hardness of heart. I ask for a restoration of fruitfulness in my life
- ⬜ Let everything that hinders growth in my life be eradicated let there be a bountiful harvest of the sowings of the Lord in my life in Jesus name
- ⬜ It's a season of humility, that I know nothing amongst men, except Christ and Him crucified

- ⬚ This is the season to crucify the flesh
- ⬚ I open up my heart to the Holy Spirit, I repent of every hardness of heart on any and every point in Jesus name
- ⬚ I repent of every presumption, pretence, and everything I have been hiding. I repent of every assumption, sin covered and hidden, I repent of every hardness of heart in Jesus name

Scriptures for further Prayers:

Romans 2, Romans 4

JUNE 27

ABOVE ALL

Worship

Today's Scripture and Meditation

Philippians 2:9-11. Therefore God also has highly exalted Him and given Him the name which is above every name, that at the name of Jesus every knee should bow, of those in heaven, and of those on earth, and of those under the earth, and that every tongue should confess that Jesus Christ is Lord, to the glory of God the Father.

PRAYERS:

- Father I worship You with my heart and voice today. Let Your name be glorified
- I declare that You are Lord. I proclaim You as Lord. I worship You as Lord.
- I magnify You as the Lord. You are the Lord over our lives.
- You are the Lord over every circumstances. You are the Lord over families.
- You are the Lord over our towns and cities. You are the Lord over nation. Because You are the Lord, every knee shall bow before You.
- Every knee bows. Every power bows. Every principality bows.
- Spiritual wickedness in high and low places bow, because You are Lord.
- You are the Lord of Lords. You are the Lord of host; The one that has never lost a battle before. You fight to win.
- You are the victorious Lord, I bow before You Lord in worship You.

- ▢ I'm in awe and in honour of You, our King. I bless Your holy name.
- ▢ All the kings of the earth must bow at Your feet   because You are our Lord Jesus Christ.
- ▢ Lord, I pray that every argument   and every lofty opinion raised against the knowledge of God in my life be destroyed
- ▢ Let the Spirit of God bring about new life within me
- ▢ Let the Spirit of God bring about restoration
- ▢ You are our Lord Jesus Christ, You are the Lord, Jesus Christ, You are Lord
- ▢ I give You the highest praise. Hallelujah to the reigning King.
- ▢ Blessed be Your name oh Lord, in Jesus name I have prayed, Amen.

Scriptures for further Prayers:

Philippians 2:9-10, Psalm 95:3

Revive, Rebuild and Restore

JUNE 28

REJOICE

Worship

Today's Scripture and Meditation

Philippians 4:4: *Rejoice in the Lord always. Again, I will say, rejoice!*

PRAYERS:

- I come before You rejoicing because Your word instructed me to rejoice. It doesn't matter what is going on around me, I rejoice!
- I rejoice in the Lord my God because He has cloth me with salvation.
- I rejoice in singing, shouting and, dancing!
- Job says "He will yet fill your mouth with laughing, And your lips with [f]rejoicing."
- I rejoice because You are my Saviour and Redeemer.
- I rejoice because You are my banner and I am victorious.
- I rejoice because You are my avenger.
- I rejoice because You exalt my horn and I rejoice in Your salvation.
- I rejoice because You cause me to be fruitful.
- I rejoice for Your peace that surpasses all understanding that You give me.
- I because You have delivered me out of the hand of the enemy.
- I rejoice because my chains are broken and victory is mine.
- I rejoice because I sought the Lord and He answered me.
- I rejoice because You give us the former and latter rain.

- I rejoice in the God of our salvation, what You are doing in my life
- I rejoice in times of trouble because You are the one that can help me.
- I rejoice in times of storms because You calm the storms.
- I rejoice in times of drought because You will lead me beside the still waters.
- I rejoice because I am blessed with Your presence.
- I rejoice because I bask in Your glory. I rejoice in the good things you have done in my life and the perfect gifts you have given
- I shall continue to rejoice all the days of my life.
- Thank You for causing me to rejoice, in Jesus name. Amen!

Scriptures for further Prayers

Psalm 126:2; Job 8:21, Psalm 107:29

Revive, Rebuild and Restore

JUNE 29

MAN OF WAR

Worship

Today's Scripture and Meditation

Acts 12:7-11: Now behold, an angel of the Lord stood by him, and a light shone in the prison; and he struck Peter on the side and raised him up, saying, "Arise quickly!" And his chains fell off his hands. ⁸ Then the angel said to him, "Gird Yourself and tie on Your sandals"; and so he did. And he said to him, "Put on Your garment and follow me." ⁹ So he went out and followed him and did not know that what was done by the angel was real, but thought he was seeing a vision. When they were past the first and the second guard posts, they came to the iron gate that leads to the city, which opened to them of its own accord; and they went out and went down one street, and immediately the angel departed from him. And when Peter had come to himself, he said, "Now I know for certain that the Lord has sent His angel and has delivered me from the hand of Herod and from all the expectation of the Jewish people."

Exodus 15:3. *The Lord is a man of war; the Lord is His name.*

PRAYERS:

- Father Lord, I thank You because You oh Lord hear the call of Your children, and You deliver them out of all their troubles.
- I pray that You will shine Your light into any darkness in my life in Jesus name, Amen.

- Lord wake me up to the reality of my freedom in Christ and enable me to arise and walk into my freedom.
- Today, Lord I ask for an angelic visitation, to break the bonds of Satan in every facet of my life.
- Thank You for Your garment of righteousness upon me, that grants me access before You. I am set free by the truth.
- Let every strong gate (spiritually) shut against me or any department of my life against the will of God, be opened in Jesus Name, Amen. I walk into total freedom in Jesus' Name, Amen!
- I can no longer be held back or down. I am no longer in prison, I am free from bondage. I am free from sickness, I am free from failure, I am free from stagnancy, I am free from backwardness and from everything that has held me down and back before now. I am free to serve God.
- I am set at liberty to continue to worship in Spirit and in truth. I am ready to carry the gospel far and wide!
- Blessed be Your Holy Name in Jesus Mighty Name, Amen.

Scriptures for further Prayers:

Psalms 34: 17, Galatians 5:1, John 8:36

JUNE 30

GRAIN OF WHEAT

Worship

Today's Scripture and Meditation

John 12:24-25. Truly, truly, I say to you, unless a grain of wheat falls into the earth and dies, it remains alone; but if it dies, it bears much fruit. 25 Whoever loves his life loses it, and whoever hates his life in this world will keep it for eternal life.

PRAYERS:

- Father, You are the author and source of my life and of my salvation.
- I thank You that You are my Shepherd, my Helper, my Redeemer and my Lord.
- You came to this earth for my salvation, died the horrible death on the cross that You might gain more brothers and sisters of which I am one. I am grateful for the finished work for calvary.
- You have called us to a life of death in the flesh that we will no longer live in sin; Father enable me to mortify my flesh.
- Enable me to live in the reality of the death I died in Christ as symbolized at baptism and to walk in the newness of life.
- Father, I pray that by the working of our Spirit in my life, sin will not reign in my mortal body and I will not obey its lust
- I will not present my body to be used for unrighteousness, I am alive to God and therefore dead to sin.
- I pray that You will enable me by Your Spirit to bear much fruit of the Spirit and also the fruit of souls into the Kingdom.

- ▢ I will not hold on to my old life of unrighteousness but for Christ's sake I surrender it that I might gain eternal
- ▢ I am a pilgrim on this earth. Therefore, I do not love life in this world or hold on to it. Rather, I look forward to my eternal home
- ▢ Thank You Heavenly Father in Jesus Name I pray Amen!

Scriptures for further Prayers

Romans 6:4-11

JULY 1

GIFTED IN WORKMANSHIP

Worship

Today's Scripture and Meditation

Exodus 31:1-5. 31: *Then the Lord spoke to Moses, saying: "See, I have called by name Bezalel the son of Uri, the son of Hur, of the tribe of Judah. And I have filled him with the Spirit of God, in wisdom, in understanding, in knowledge, and in all manner of workmanship, to design artistic works, to work in gold, in silver, in bronze, in cutting jewels for setting, in carving wood, and to work in all manner of workmanship.*

PRAYERS:

- Father Lord, we thank You, Lord we praise and magnify Your holy Name.
- There is none like You oh God, in heaven and on earth, for You are the one that has the master plan.
- From the foundations of the world, You have planned everything that is happening today and that will happen till eternity.
- Lord in the process of building an earthly sanctuary, Lord You called men and You filled men with gifts by Your Spirit.
- You filled them with wisdom, You filled them with ability, You filled them with understanding, and You filled them with intelligence, You fill them with knowledge and craftmanship.

- Lord to build an eternal sanctuary, but You said oh Lord that You we are building a spiritual house.
- Each and every one of us are part of this spiritual house, and we are a pof this eternal sanctuary.
- You said You have given gifts. Each and every one of us have gifts that the Almighty God has given.
- And not only that, we are gifts, but He has also given us gifts to perform what He has actually apportioned to us from the foundation of the world.
- Thank You Lord, for calling us to be living stones in the spiritual house that You are building.
- I arise by the power of the Spirit of God to begin to use the gift you have given for the building of your house.
- You have chosen the foolish things to confound the wise, show me how and give me wisdom to use the gift anointing you have placed upon my life.
- My gift and calling will not be in vain, have mercy on us Your children in theName of the Lord Jesus.
- Give me grace to use my gift on the journey of fulfilling purpose and profit with it
- I give you the right of way in the use of the gift you have endowed me according to Your will, strength, and ability. You are the sovereign God!
- I humble myself in your hands, give me grace and use me to beautify your house and edify the brethren!
- Thank You Heavenly Father, in Jesus mighty Name I pray, Amen.

Scriptures for further Prayers:

James 4:6, 1 Corinthians 1:27

JULY 2

CHRISTIAN PROSPERITY

Worship

Today's Scripture and Meditation

John 15:7-8: If you abide in Me, and My words abide in you, you will ask what you desire, and it shall be done for you. By this My Father is glorified, that you bear much fruit; so, you will be My disciples.

PRAYERS:

- Father I thank you because you are a good God
- I pray that by the power of the Holy Spirit, You will enable me to reorder my priority, that God will be first in my life.
- That Your Kingdom will be priority in my life and that Your people and the love for Your people uppermost in my heart.
- That Your work will be a priority for me and, that Your work will be first in my life and that my calling will be a priority, so my calling willbear fruits.
- Father enable me to abide in you and not stray away from your presence.
- Enable me to abide in your word. That I will speak your word, meditate on it day and night, observe to do according to all that is written in it. So that it will make my way prosperous, and then I will have good success.
- Let whatever I lay my hands unto to do or touch prosper without measure.

- Father please incline your ears to my words, hear my request and answer me in your mercy.
- Enable me to go out there to preach the gospel that I might win souls into Your kingdom.
- Holy Spirit help me for I cannot do anything without You, please help me to seek You and Your Kingdom first and everything can be added to me.
- Love is a difficult thing for human race, I submit to You, e n a b l e my love go beyond those of the Pharisees.
- Lord help me to love unconditionally, to love even those who do not fit into our mould.
- Anything that clashes with Your work, that very moment will become second priority.
- Give me the grace to study Your word daily and receive daily instructions the day.
- You said we should go out to preach the gospel and not worry for You will give us the word to say, father please equip me to share the gospel
- Give me the unction, the anointing and multiplied grace to go, to bear the Gospel and to Prosper in it.
- Thank You for the secrets You have revealed to me, that I should go, preach the Gospel, and bear Fruits, and I will prosper, and I will have my Prayers answered.
- Lord I surrender to You so that You will be able to perform Your work and Your will in my life.
- You are not man that you should lie or the son of man that You should repent; whatever you say you do and whatever you say, you make it good.
- You are a faithful God and I give You the highest praise, in Jesus mighty Name I have prayed, Amen!

Scriptures for further Prayers:

Psalm 2:8, Matthew 6:33, Numbers 23:19m

JULY 3

DIVINE SUPPORT

Worship

Today's Scripture and Meditation

Joshua 1:5. *"there shall not any man be able to stand before thee all the days of thy life: as I was with Moses, so I will be with thee: I will not fail thee, nor forsake thee."*

PRAYERS:

- Father I thank You because You desire us to do exploits for You.
- Thank You for You have already gone ahead of me.
- Father I pray that You will be with me all the days of my life as You were with the early Christians
- I pray that You fortify me that as I do Your work no one shall be able to stand before me.
- Father, put Your glory upon me and cause anyone that sees it to know that You are with me.
- Father put Your fear and dread upon me that every enemy will turn their back (and follow me) or from following me
- Give me grace to be strong and courageous, to step out in faith and do exploits for You.
- Enable me to know You more that I might be strong, and carry out great exploits for You.
- Father enable be to possess every place the soul of my feet steps upon for You.
- I take territories, nations, cities and streets for You.
- Let Your presence be tangible in my life, family and ministry.

Revive, Rebuild and Restore

- Thank You Father in Jesus Name.

Scriptures for further Prayers:

Exodus 23:27, Daniel 11:32

JULY 4

NO LIMITS

Worship

Today's Scripture and Meditation

Joshua 6:20 So the people shouted when the priests blew the trumpets. And it happened when the people heard the sound of the trumpet, and the people shouted with a great shout, that the wall fell down flat.

Hebrews 11:30 By faith the walls of Jericho fell down after they were encircled for seven days.

PRAYERS:

- ⏹ Thank You Lord because You cannot be limited in time and space. Nothing can withstand Your power.
- ⏹ Because I am in You, I cannot be limited, restrained, or pushed down.
- ⏹ Any limitation placed upon my life by myself or others not giving me freedom in any department of my life be broken.
- ⏹ Whosoever the Lord sets free is free indeed by the reason of the blood that was shed on the cross of Calvary, limitations are taken away from my life
- ⏹ Every limitation that is performing contrary to the will of God is broken. I begin to progress in the Name of the Lord Jesus, I begin to advance in the Name of the Lord Jesus, I am not a failure, I am a success, I will go higher in the Name of the Lord Jesus.
- ⏹ Father, I decree every embargo against my upliftment be destroyed

- ⬚ I break every sense and power of poverty, every physical disability, spiritual disability, mental disability over my life
- ⬚ In the name of the Lord Jesus, every restriction, every delay with the strength, power and Influence that may be a limiting factor in my life be destroyed.
- ⬚ Whatever it is that is affecting my potential and talent and preventing me from using my gift, destroyed.
- ⬚ I am made for greatness; I am catapulted for greatness because every limitation to greatness is broken, every wall of Jericho has fallen.
- ⬚ I will no longer run around in circles every cyclical issue is dealt with in the Name of the Lord Jesus
- ⬚ I receive the ability to advance; I received grace for achievements: from crawling to walking. From walking to running, from running to flying. I can no longer be held back in Jesus' Name.
- ⬚ The Lord has given me a possession and I possess it by faith!
- ⬚ Thank you heavenly Father in Jesus Name I have prayed. Amen!

Scriptures for further Prayers

John 8:36, Isaiah 10:27

JULY 5

THIS BOOK OF THE LAW

Worship

Today's Scripture and Meditation

Joshua 1:8: This Book of the Law shall not depart from your mouth, but you[a] shall meditate in it day and night, that you may observe to do according to all that is written in it. For then you will make your way prosperous, and then you will have good success.

PRAYERS:

- Thank you Lord, for Your word which is yea and amen, thank You for Your word gives us life.
- Grant me the grace to speak Your word into my life and that of others because Your word is Spirit and it is life.
- Oh Lord please take away every form of laziness in studying the scriptures.
- I break every yoke of laziness and procrastination in studying the word of God in Jesus Name.
- Give me grace to meditate on Your word thereby assimilating and imbibing it.
- Enable me to be a doer of Your word; observing to do all that is written.
- Help me to live by Your word that I may not be a hypocrite
- Let Your word cleanse me of spots, wrinkles and blemishes, that I may be presentable to the groom on the day of His appearing.
- Help me Lord to always minister Your word to people, help me to take Your message to the uttermost part of the world.

- I pray that You grant me the grace to obey Your word fully; help me not to go against what You say.
- Almighty God as I obey Your word, please grant me all round good.
- Thank You heavenly Father, in Jesus name.

Scriptures for further Prayers:

James 1:22:25, Ephesians 5:26-27

JULY 6

THE LORD WILL GIVE YOU REST

Worship

Today's Scripture and Meditation

Joshua 1:13-15: "Remember the word which Moses the servant of the Lord commanded you, saying, 'The Lord Your God is giving you rest and is giving you this land.' Your wives, your little ones, and your livestock shall remain in the land which Moses gave you on this side of the Jordan.

But you shall pass before your brethren armed, all your mighty men of valour, and help them, until the Lord has given your brethren rest, as He gave you, and they also have taken possession of the land which the Lord your God is giving them. Then you shall return to the land of your possession and enjoy it, which Moses the Lord's servant gave you on this side of the Jordan toward the sunrise."

PRAYERS:

- Father, I thank You for Your loving kindness
- Thank You that You call to me to one purpose, one mission and a time of unity, selflessness and sacrifice
- Lord, I thank You because You have raised people to intercede for me. Thank You for the knowledge that if one suffers   we all suffer and we only have rest when all have rest
- Father grant me the grace to stand in the gap where necessary, to fight in the night where required

- Grant me the grace to go out of my way, to cross the Jordan, in other to fight for the possession of our brethren
- Grant unto me the spirit of unity in the bond of peace that there will not be any schism in the body of Christ because of lack of unity and selfishness
- I bind the spirit of selfishness in the name of the Lord Jesus Christ, amen.
- Lord I ask oh God for the Spirit of God, the Spirit of unity, to fill my heart, to fill my life and overshadow us
- Holy Spirit of the living God enable us as this word says, to go ahead of our brethren hand in hand
- That the mighty men of valour in our camp will go ahead of the weak ones oh God in battle but fight to victory that all may have rest
- I banish every strive, every competition, every selfish attitude in the name of Jesus
- I ask oh Lord that everyone will be self-aware in the name of Jesus, amen
- That the matters of our brothers and sisters, will concern us in the name of our Lord Jesus, amen
- While I am still here on this side of eternity, take each and every one of us who have deemed it important to obey Your word for this season to charge up
- Let us all be built up in our inner minds, let us be built up physically, let us be built up in every department of my life
- As I am being built up in the Spirit oh God, please build up other areas of our lives in the name of the Lord Jesus Christ, amen.
- Thank You, heavenly Father, I praise You Lord, in Jesus mighty name I pray, amen

Scriptures for further Prayers:

Nehemiah 4: I4, Ephesians 4:3, Acts 2:42

Revive, Rebuild and Restore

JULY 7

BUILD UP YOURSELF

Worship

Today's Scripture and Meditation

Jude 1:14-20. (NKJV) Now Enoch, the seventh from Adam, prophesied about these men also, saying, "Behold, the Lord comes with ten thousands of His saints, to execute judgment on all, to convict all who are ungodly among them of all their ungodly deeds which they have committed in an ungodly way, and of all the harsh things which ungodly sinners have spoken against Him."

These are grumblers, complainers, walking according to their own lusts; and they mouth great swelling words, flattering people to gain advantage. But you, beloved, remember the words which were spoken before by the apostles of our Lord Jesus Christ: how they told you that there would be mockers in the last time who would walk according to their own ungodly lusts.

These are sensual persons, who cause divisions, not having the Spirit. But you, beloved, building yourselves up on your most holy faith, praying in the Holy Spirit

PRAYERS:

- Father Lord I am sensitized about the fact that You are coming back again with tens of thousands of Your saints who will judge with You.
- Lord, may I be a partaker   , among the tens of thousands of Your saints that will be coming back with You to rule the

nations and to execute judgement in the name of the Lord Jesus Christ, Amen

- Lord make me accountable to You in all I do that I am not be found among the grumblers, the complainers, and those walking according to their own lusts; those whose mouth has great swelling of words, those who flatters
- Holy Spirit I surrender to You for Your work of transformation in my life; I put aside the old man and put on the new man
- Lord, I will not partake among the mockers or scorners or those who cause divisions   , who do not have Your spirit, in the name of Jesus
- Looking inward, I come unto You to be built up today *(speak in tongues for a few minutes)* Build me up in my most Holy faith and keep me in the love of God, in the name of our Lord Jesus Christ, Amen
- Lord help me to walk in Your counsel and not in the counsel of the ungodly
- Enable me by the power of Your Spirit working in me to delight in the law of the Lord
- Enable me to stay in the place of prayer, the word and of Your Spirit.
- Help me to stay in that the word of God till it dwell in me richly and that Your spirit would breathe upon it in the name Jesus, Amen
- Give me the grace to have compassion and make a distinction to continue to love all men and be compassionate towards them to the effect of enabling their salvation
- Let our eyes be fixed on the goal to be found faithful on the day of Your appearing, on the day You shall come for us. blessed be Your name oh Lord
- I give You praise Lord, thank You Heavenly Father, in Jesus mighty name, Amen.

Scriptures for further Prayers:

1 Peter 2:5, Nehemiah 2:20,

Revive, Rebuild and Restore

JULY 8

WHAT MANNER OF SPIRIT

Worship

Today's Scripture and Meditation

Luke 9:54-56. And when His disciples James and John saw this, they said, "Lord, do You want us to command fire to come down from heaven and consume them, just as Elijah did?" But He turned and rebuked them, and said, "you do not know what manner of Spirit you are of. For the Son of Man did not come to destroy men's lives but to save them." And they went to another village.

PRAYERS:

- Father, I thank You for the gift of the Holy Spirit, who resides in me
- I thank You for You are powerful but gentle, You can consume by Your fire, yet You chose to exercise restraint
- I pray Lord that I will never be overzealous in wanting to fight for You, because You can fight for Yourself and do not need anyone to defend You
- The Spirit within me is a meek spirit, enable me to be meek, forbearing, patient, and slow to respond in anger; and to be in control in the face of insults or injuries
- The spirit within me is not a vengeful spirit father, please take away from me every attitude or tendency for vindictiveness and revenge
- Enable me to know the manner of Spirit that is within me experientially in Jesus name

- ☐ I submit my will to You. Teach me to remain silent and keep my emotions and temper under control.
- ☐ Grant me power over my appetites and indulgences; over-worry, overwork, overeat, overindulge, and every other that could literally run itself to death. That I might live a balanced life
- ☐ Holy Spirit, I submit to Your control, please produce a discipline that will help me to sustain a good physical condition, stay in good health, remain free from sin, and live a life that is moderate and balanced.

Scriptures for further Prayers:

Isaiah 53:7, Numbers 12:3, Isaiah 29:19

JULY 9

YOKE BROKEN

Worship

Today's Scripture and Meditation

Jeremiah 30:8-9. *'For it shall come to pass in that day,' says the Lord of hosts, 'That I will break his yoke from your neck, and will burst your bonds; Foreigners shall no longer enslave them. 9 But they shall serve the Lord their God, and David their king, whom I will raise up for them.*

PRAYERS:

- Father, I thank You because You have power over everything, in heaven on earth and under the earth.
- You are the Lord of hosts, the Captain of the heavenly armies, Who battles to win
- You are the great deliverer who breaks the bonds of the oppressor and suppressors
- I pray that You break the yoke of the oppressor off my neck by the power of the Spirit of God.
- I pray that every bond in my life is burst by the power of the Spirit of God.
- Lord, break the yoke of the enemy's burden and break the staff and the rod of the oppressor as in the day of Midian.
- Let every yoke of (mention any known yokes e.g. fear, frustration, anxiety, insecurity, religiosity, debt, sickness, stagnancy, failure, backwardness, poverty, low or insignificant achievements, mental breakdown) be destroyed.

- I pull down every stronghold erected against any department of my life.
- I destroy every yoke and burden of religion and legalism on my life.
- I reject every evil arrangement concerning my life and family and I receive the arrangement of God.
- I reject every evil direction or redirection concerning my life and family and I receive the direction of God.
- I break every yoke of hard labour with no results and command fruits for all my labour.
- Father Lord, I pray that you will build for me that my labour in the church of God, in family, in ministry, in business will not be in vain!
- I reverse any mandate given to any evil power to supervise my life.
- You came that I might have life in abundance; I receive into manifestation abundant life.
- Thank You God, I have Jesus. I am an overcomer because You walk with me. I will not fear because Your anointing will make the way!"

Scriptures for further Prayers

Isaiah 9:4, Psalm 127:1

Revive, Rebuild and Restore

JULY 10

NO EVIL WILL TOUCH YOU

Worship

Today's Scripture and Meditation

Job 5:19. *He will rescue you in six troubles; in seven nothing that is evil [for you] will touch you.*

PRAYERS:

- Father I thank You because You are a rescuer.
- Six is the number of imperfection and seven is the number of perfection
- Lord help me to hate the things that you hate; a pride look, lying tongues, hands that shed innocent blood, heart that manufactures wicked thoughts and plans, feet that are swift in running to evil, A false witness, and he who sows discord among his brethren. That I will not be a partaker in these things in Jesus name
- Lord I come in repentance of every unholy action of wicked, and negative thoughts of vengeance that I have had.
- Lord have mercy for every prideful look for everything we have is from You.
- We repent of every lying tongue hypocrisy gossiping backbiting untamed tongue
- Have mercy on us for using our tongue to discourage others.
- We repent of going to places where we should not be found as Christians

Revive, Rebuild and Restore

- Have mercy for bearing false witness and causing misunderstanding among brethren, causing strain with the brethren.
- Help us not to sow discord among the brethren. Forgive us.
- Six speaks of the evil work of Satan so we decree that evil work of satan in my life be destroyed in each of our lives in the Name of Jesus.

- Let the works of human and spiritual emotional enemies be destroyed, sickness and attack fiery darts be destroyed.
- Let failures stagnancy, non-achievement lack of progress, backwardness, retrogression be destroyed, in the Name of Jesus.
- A Hebrew slave would normally serve six years and in the seventh year, they are released totally set free; Lord I pray for deliverance from every form of slavery and bondage, from every work of darkness in the Name of Jesus!
- "In seven, nothing shall touch You", today marks an end of torment, attacks, famine in my life, I am redeemed from death. The wars and battle of my life has ended by the power of God, no destruction shall come upon me rather, I will laugh at destruction and anof the evildoers
- Lord I pray that you manifest in my life today and destroy every evil works of the enemy in Jesus Name.
- Deliver me from all manner of troubles in Jesus' Name. You are a faithful God, we honor You, thank You for Your word,

Scriptures for further Prayers:

Proverbs 6:16-19, 1 John 1:9, 1 John 3:8 & 15

Revive, Rebuild and Restore

JULY 11

NO KNOWLEDGE

Worship

Today's Scripture and Meditation

Prov. 29:18(NIV). *Where there is no revelation, people cast off restraint; but blessed is the one who heeds wisdom's instruction.*

PRAYERS:

- Thank you, Lord, for revealing Yourself to me regularly.
- Father, I want to know You more, show me more of Yourself, Your way, and Your act.
- Father, I ask that You grant to me the wisdom from Your word, make me wise.
- Let Your word be laid up in my heart and in my soul that it might be well with me
- Enable me to know Your word and that your word will dwell in me richly
- Help me Lord to receive Your word with meekness which is able to save my soul
- Enable me to obey every one of Your instructions, no matter how it sounds to me.
- That I will walk circumspectly according to Your rules and on Your terms.
- Enable me to walk in wisdom according to Your counsel in Jesus' Name.
- Father, please do not allow me to perish, grant unto me the knowledge of Your will.
- That I might be found among the wise blessed by You.
- Thank You Father in Jesus Name.

Scriptures for further Prayers

Deuteronomy 11:18, James 1:21

JULY 12

NOTHING IS IMPOSSIBLE

Worship

Today's Scripture and Meditation

Luke 1:37: *For nothing will be impossible with God."*

PRAYERS:

- Indeed, there is nothing too hard for You to do and there is nothing impossible for You to do because all power belongs to You.
- No circumstance or situation can defy Your power
- Father, I release the circumstances of my life into Your hands, because I am confident that You have a plan, and You are working out Your plan. You never fail and You are never late.
- You will not lose a battle and I will not suffer losses in the name of Jesus.
- Every long-standing problem (e.g., 38years by the pool of Bethsaida or 12 years issue of blood) in my life is resolved this season in Jesus' name, Amen!
- Every door shut against me, contrary to the will of God, be opened! Let the gates open, let heaven open above me in the name Jesus!
- I trust You Lord and my mind is stayed on You; I will not be derailed, distracted, diverted, or take a detour but I am kept in perfect peace by the Lord!

- My pain and sorrow are taken away, my sicknesses are taken away, any bondage is taken away, the bonds of the oppressor and suppressor is broken.
- My head shall not be bowed I shall not be put to shame in the name of the Lord Jesus Christ. Amen
- Lord do Your work in my life and circumstances, that all ears that hear it, will tingle in the Name of Jesus, Amen.
- *(Mention any impossible situation that may be present in your life or that of your loved ones)*
- Today my strength, faith, focus, is renewed in Jesus' name, Amen!
- I look to You the Author, the Finisher of my faith. I know that You never fail.

Scriptures for further Prayers:

Psalm 62:11

JULY 13

WHO SHALL I SEND?

Worship

Today's Scripture and Meditation

Isaiah 6:8 8 Also I heard the voice of the Lord, saying: "Whom shall I send, And who will go for Us?" Then I said, "Here am I! Send me."

PRAYERS:

- Father, I thank You because You called me in the first place to be Your child.
- Thank You for the blessing of being called by You, to serve before You and for working it out in me to be able to do so.
- I thank You because You have endowed me with all the resources I require to serve You, Father enable me to be available whenever You need me.
- Lord that my own plans and agenda will not be clashing with Your plans for my life.
- That I will use my time and resources for the Kingdom, that You will be my priority and not pursuing my own things.
- Lord I'm available to You, send me!
- Lord I'm available to You; my will I give to You, I'll do what You say to do, use me Lord, to show someone the way.
- My storage is empty, I have emptied out my cup, fill me up Lord, I am available to You.
- Use me to answer the cry of sinners, to wipe away tears, to be Your voice, to mend broken hearts.
- I am available to You Lord; use me for Your glory.
- Thank You heavenly Father in Jesus Name.

Further Praying Scriptures

2 Timothy 2: 20-21, 1 Samuel 3:9-10

JULY 14

BOOK OF REMEMBRANCE

Worship

Today's Scripture and Meditation

Malachi 3:16-18. Then those who feared the Lord spoke to one another, And the Lord listened and heard them; So a book of remembrance was written before Him. For those who fear the Lord. And who meditate on His name. "They shall be Mine," says the Lord of hosts, "On the day that I make them My jewels. And I will spare them. As a man spares his own son who serves him." Then you shall again discern. Between the righteous and the wicked, Between one who serves God. And one who does not serve Him.

PRAYERS:

- ⬚ Father Lord I thank and praise You that You always listen to and hear us
- ⬚ Thank You Lord, for acknowledging me as Yours, and that I am Your jewel and treasured possession
- ⬚ Thank You Lord, that a book of remembrance is written for me before You concerning my season, the things You have apportioned unto me to do, the things that You are doing in my life.
- ⬚ You are the Lord of host the captain of the army of heaven and the victorious Lord
- ⬚ I am grateful that I belong to You who never loses a battle
- ⬚ You are my Father and I am Your child, You will spare me as a father spares his son in the day of trouble
- ⬚ Lord spare me as You have said in Your word, spare all members of my family and our church, spare us oh Lord in Your mercy

- In war, in tribulation, in sickness, in drought, the plague, spare us oh God, spare me as a father spares his own child in the name of Jesus, Amen
- Lord, let the difference between the righteous and the wicked be discerned by the things You do in my life and through me
- Let it be a testimony for the world to see, that they will know that indeed our God lives and reigns in the name of the Lord Jesus, Amen
- Thank You Lord.

Scriptures for further Prayers:

John 14:18, Hebrews 13b

JULY 15

PEACE BE STILL

Worship

Today's Scripture and Meditation

Mark 4:39-41. Then He arose and rebuked the wind, and said to the sea, "Peace, be still!" And the wind ceased and there was a great calm. But He said to them, "Why are you so fearful? How is it that you have no faith?" And they feared exceedingly, and said to one another, "Who can this be, that even the wind and the sea obey Him!"

PRAYERS:

- Lord Jesus, I thank You because You have authority over the winds and the storms.
- I invite You into the boat of my life, take over and still the storms of battles in the name of Jesus.
- Only You can bring order out of this chaos. Take care of all those concerns that rise up around me like stormy waves
- Lord Jesus, at the sound of Your voice even the raging sea is hushed. Today, still my heart to experience Your perfect peace.
- Lord, thank that You can calm any storm; those around us and those within. Lord, speak to our storms, speak 'Peace Be Still'.
- Silence our emotions, dispel confusion and fear, quiet our souls, that we may clearly hear Your voice and be led by Your Spirit.
- Help me to walk in the Spirit and keep in step. Help me to be still and know You are God! Thank You Lord for the blessing of Your stillness and Your peace — thank You that You are the Prince of Peace. Lead me into Your safe harbour.

- ⏻ Lord Jesus, I pray that You arise and rebuke every wind and storm in my life
- ⏻ I pray in the name of Jesus that every fear loose Your hold, hold over me
- ⏻ The righteous are as bold as a lion and I have not been given the Spirit of fear, but of love, of power and a sound mind
- ⏻ I ask for the manifestation of the Spirit of God
- ⏻ Let every source of fear be dealt with in my life, I speak peace to every tumultuous situation
- ⏻ Let the answer and solution come, Let victory be established
- ⏻ Thank You Heavenly Father in Jesus name

Scriptures for further Prayers:

Proverbs 28:1b, 2 Timothy 1:7, Mark 4:36.

JULY 16

DEALING WITH FOUNDATIONS

Worship

Today's Scripture and Meditation

Jeremiah 31:29-30. In those days they shall say no more, the fathers have eaten sour grapes, and the children's teeth are set on edge. But everyone shall die for his own iniquity [only]; every man who eats sour grapes — his [own] teeth shall be set on edge.

PRAYERS:

- Lord Jesus, I thank You for the finished work of calvary that redeems me from every entanglement with my past, my past generational activities and inheritances.
- You said to the children of Levi, that they will have no inheritance or any part among them, Father I reject every negative spiritual inheritance from my ancestors
- I will have no part in the generational sins, idolatry, curses, ungodly covenant and practices.
- I plead the blood of Jesus for mercy as I take generational repentance
- I ask for mercy and cleansing as regarding the sins of our generations past.
- Let the blood of Jesus touch our foundations, and cleanse it.
- I command every collective captivity, curse and satanic covenant be broken, let every association with every other god but the Almighty God be broken in Jesus Name.
- Let every negative family pattern be broken
- Every curse is broken for Christ has redeemed me from the curse of the law and there by no other curse stands.

- ▢ I will not be a victim of what I am ignorant of
- ▢ Only God-ordained purpose for my life shall manifest; every demonic yoke is broken, and I am set free whatever is blocking my harvest, is totally destroyed.
- ▢ Every tree planted in my life bearing undesirable fruit is uprooted
- ▢ I shall not inherit the sicknesses of my father and mother either genetically or spiritually.
- ▢ No more oppression, suppression or possession by the enemy. I command strangers to come out of their closed places in my life.
- ▢ I pray for total divine cleansing and purification.
- ▢ It is a day of freedom; a new foundation has been laid by the blood of Jesus upon the Rock who is Christ in Jesus Name.
- ▢ I am set at liberty to worship God Almighty
- ▢ Thank You Father in Jesus name.▢

Scriptures for further Prayers

Numbers 18:20, Galatians 3:13.

JULY 17

AN OVERFLOW

Worship

Today's Scripture and Meditation

John 7: 37-39: *On the last day, that great day of the feast,
Jesus stood and cried out, saying, "If anyone thirsts, let
him come to Me and drink. He who believes in Me, as the
Scripture has said, out of his heart will flow rivers of
living water. But this He spoke concerning the Spirit,
whom those believing in Him would receive; for the Holy
Spirit was not yet given, because Jesus was not yet
glorified.*

PRAYERS:

- Father Lord I believe in You, You came and died. You were buried and resurrected for my sake
- Lord, I Thirst for You, I long to be filled by Your Spirit and to be in Your presence. My soul waits on You, Father, draw me close to You
- Brood over my life and let every area that manifest darkness receive light. Let there be more light in my soul
- Let there be order and orderliness, where there has been voidness. Let there be no emptiness in my life
- Fill me afresh Lord and fill me till it overflows
- Let there be a living and continually flowing fountain of the Holy Spirit in my life
- Lord open and display the hidden treasures of God in me

- Let there be an abundance of Your Spirit, and an overflow in my life
- Let the living water flow over my soul, Let the Holy Spirit take control
- Let the fountain that never grows dry, nor ceases, flow continually into me and through me
- Let there be an abundant outpouring of Your Spirit in my life, so much that out of my belly flow rivers of living water
- Take me to a new level of intimacy with You, where I will live in the overflow of Your Spirit
- Pour out Your Spirit upon me Lord; Let fresh grace, fresh unction, fresh anointing be released. Fill me afresh Lord
- I will seek You God to fill me with all joy and peace as I trust in Him that I may overflow onto others by the power of the Holy Spirit at work in me
- I want more of You; I am desperate for You because without You I am nothing and I am lost; Jesus! More of You Lord!
- Overshadow me Lord. Not my will but Yours in Jesus name

Scriptures for further Prayers

Isaiah 44:3-4; Joel 3:18. Genesis 1:1-3

JULY 18

THE ENABLING SPIRIT OF GOD

Worship

Today's Scripture and Meditation

John 14:16-17: *And I will ask the Father, and He will give you another Comforter (Counselor, Helper, Intercessor, Advocate, Strengthener, and Standby), that He may remain with you forever – 17 The Spirit of Truth, Whom the world cannot receive (welcome, take to its heart), because it does not see Him or know and recognize Him. But you know and recognize Him, for He lives with you [constantly] and will be in you.*

PRAYERS:

- Thank You Lord for sending Your Holy Spirit my comforter, Counselor, Helper, Intercessor, Advocate, Strengthener, and Standby!
- Thank You because You are not a temporary Help or temporary Fix but You will remain with me forever.
- Thank You because I am a house for the Holy Spirit Who dwells in my heart.
- Thank You for the spiritual gifts that You have brought into my life.
- I ask for the activation and the operation of these spiritual gifts that I might be used as a vessel of honour to edify Your body.
- You have been given as my comforter, father bring me deep inner comfort and healing
- Manifest Yourself as my counselor; direct my paths and grant me the understanding of the big picture always.

- Lord render help to me from Your throne; be my advocate against every accusation of the enemy
- I ask for Your strength to be made manifest in me; Stand by me always
- You empowered Peter to preach and he won five thousand souls in one day, Father empower me to preach the Gospel!
- You empowered David and he killed two strong animals; the lion and the bear, Lord empower me to deal with every strong enemy that come against me!
- You empowered powered Paul and handkerchiefs and aprons that had touched him were taken to the sick, and the diseases and evil spirits left them, Father empower me for signs and wonders.
- Thank You Father blessed be Your Name in Jesus Name!

Scriptures for further Prayers:

1 Corinthians 6:19, 1 Samuel 17:34-36, Acts 19:12,

JULY 19

HE COMMANDS NATURE

Worship

Today's Scripture and Meditation

Jeremiah 31: 33. Thus says the Lord who writes the songs for The Light by the day, for the moon and stars for a light by night with the stubs the sea and its way through.

PRAYERS:

⬜ Father, I thank You because You know all things and can do all things

⬜ I know that I can do nothing about my past, my present or even my future and that I have no power of my own but I take Your sacrifice into our future manifestly in the Name of Jesus.

⬜ You are the Lord of host who gives commands to all things created animate or inanimate.

⬜ You give directions to everything You created and they work according to Your plan and according to Your purpose, according to Your future destiny for me.

⬜ I pray that everything created will work together for my good in the Name of Jesus.

⬜ I am asking for ordinances and elements to work together for my good and for my in the name of Jesus.

- The light will not work against me neither will the moon and stars work against me. I will not be afflicted by seasonal problems in Jesus name.
- God said in the book Job, "have you commanded the morning"? Father today I command the morning, the beginning of a new day, the beginning of a new season I command my morning to align with the plan of God in the Name of the Lord Jesus Christ.
- Let every evil plan, every evil programming, be rejected by this day in the name of Jesus.
- Every element that has been assigned to stop me from entering my promised land, to stop me from fulfilling purpose, let every programming and planting of God manifest in my life
- My purpose in God will be established and grounded.
- I will enter my God-ordained future because the Lord will contend on my behalf for my future.
- I am walking into all that is written of me and I will prosper in it.
- Whatever is contending with me physically, spiritually, mentally, contending with me in my body and soul and spirit, the Lord contend with them in Jesus Name.
- The almighty God contends with them and will save me and my family in my present and my future.
- Enable me to sow in righteousness so that I will reap in righteousness today and in my future.
- I refuse to sow evil in the Name of Jesus.
- I will sow good with my hands, I will sow good with my feet, I will sow good with my voice, •   I will sow good with my heart.
- Lord Jesus, I put my trust in You God, as You have gone ahead of into my future timeline, lead me, guide me, protect me, comfort me, support me in the Name of Jesus.
- Thank You Father in Jesus Name.

Scriptures for further Prayers

Revive, Rebuild and Restore

Job 38:12, Exodus 14:28, Galatians 6:7b

JULY 20

WATCH AND PRAY

Worship

Today's Scripture and Meditation

Mark 14:38. *Watch and pray, lest you enter into temptation. The spirit indeed is willing, but the flesh is weak."*

PRAYERS:

- Thank You for You are a God Who empowers.
- Even though I live in this flesh, I am not of the flesh, I will not walk in the flesh, I choose to walk in the Spirit.
- Enable me to keep watch, to stand guard, to be sober, to be vigilant, not to be controlled by my feelings or emotions.
- Enable me not to fall into the trap of the enemy or become meat for the roaring lion.
- Enable me to be watchful while I work, worship and serve You; to hold in the other hand, the weapons of my warfare.
- Enable me to put on the whole armour of God; that I will not be engaged or be entangled with affairs of civilians because I am a soldier in the army of the Lord.
- Enable me to watch and pray so I will not fall into temptation.
- No destiny manipulation will prosper in my life and circumstances.

- Lord I surrender my emotions to You and my feelings, that my feelings will not run riot.
- That my emotions will not control me, but that I will be controlled by the Holy Spirit.
- Father, I pray, that You make it impossible for me to reposition myself outside Your will and outside Your divine positioning, in the Name of the Lord Jesus, Amen!
- Make it impossible for me to reposition myself outside Your will and outside Your wall.
- Lord I decree, no fiery dart of the enemy will touch me in the Name of the Lord Jesus, Amen.
- That I will live my life from that position where I am seated in heavenly places far above principalities and power.
- My faith will not fail and my trust in God will increase this year in the Name of the Lord Jesus.
- Let me be sensitive to the Spirit and not to the flesh in the Name of the Lord Jesus Christ.
- That I will not fall into the temptations that the enemy has set for me but I will stand as a solider of Christ.
- Help me to put my body under while I obey the Spirit; That I will win the battle of my soul, I will win the battle of life.
- Father Lord, I give You praise, help me every moment to recognize the new things that You are doing in my life.
- Blessed be Your Name oh God, in Jesus' mighty Name, I have prayed, Amen.

Scriptures for further Prayers:

Ephesians 2:6, Ephesians 6:11

Revive, Rebuild and Restore

JULY 21

I WILL SEEK GOD

Worship

Today's Scripture and Meditation

Job 5:8*: "But as for me, I would seek God, And to God I would commit my cause."*

PRAYERS:

- Lord I come to this altar daily and to call upon You and to meet with You.
- I come to You because I want to know You more, I call upon You because I want to experience You deeper.
- I come because I want more of You, I want to Love You more. I want to be transformed by You.
- I come daily because we want to take of You, we want to learn of You want and to receive from You.
- You said You love those who love You, that those who seek You diligently will find You, Father, let me find You today.
- Father I listen to You, I seek to follow after righteousness, I see You, I look to You the rock from whom I was hewed in Jesus Name, Amen!
- I come that You may touch my life, that You might touch my heart and soul and touch my body and touch everything that concerns me and make them good.
- I come Lord to have fellowship with You and hear from You, that I might not go blind in this world that I might not live without guidance, without instructions in this world.

- I am grateful for the privilege to come before You, knowing that You will answer.
- I am grateful that I am nor serving a dead God, You are a prayer answering God and You act on time.
- Father put me in that place of real and vibrant relationship with You in the Name of the Lord Jesus Christ.
- That my heart will beat in a rhythm with Your heart in the name of the Lord Jesus Christ.
- When You look down from heaven upon the children of men, to see if there are any who understand, who seek God, Lord may You find me worthy.
- I commit my cause into your hands because you never fail and you will lead me in the way that I should go.
- Lord that You might hear us in the name of the Lord Jesus, that You might grant unto us the things that we desire, in the Name of Jesus, Amen.
- You said You will grant unto us the desires of our heart, as we ask, oh God, answer us in the Name of Jesus, Amen (*Now add personal prayer points*)

Scriptures for further Prayers:

Psalm 14:2, Proverbs 8:17, Isaiah 51:1

JULY 22

DIE TO THE FLESH

Worship

Today's Scripture and Meditation

John 12:24 *Most assuredly, I say to you, unless a grain of wheat falls into the ground and dies, it remains alone; but if it dies, it produces much grain.*

PRAYERS:

- Father, I thank You for the work of the Spirit in my life to make me look more and more like the image of Christ.

- I surrender myself to You that You will work in me to be broken by Your spirit, that I will not resist this process.
- Let the voice of my flesh be silent, let my agenda and will be silenced.
- I give up my self-dependence to take up dependence on You in every area of life.
- I know that I cannot achieve this by myself so Lord, I come to You for divine help and surrender to You.
- Enable me to die to the world, that my flesh will not be in control that my own agenda will not rule, but that Your will be done, that Your counsel will stand and Your purpose established in my life in Jesus name.
- Let nothing of my former existence remain, let all old things pass away and let all things be new. Let me be with looks totally and extremely different in looks, expression and lifestyle.

- Let me truly die to sin, the flesh, the world and self and life break forth in the process, let my new identity in You be formed in Jesus name
- I surrender myself body, spirit and soul. Come and have Your way in my life.
- Direct my affairs Oh Lord I surrender to You, Holy Spirit, come and do a new work come and put the flesh and its appetite down, kill my own agenda and enforce your agenda.
- My agenda will be to do Your bidding, let my agenda by Your agenda, let my will be swallowed up in Your own will let the old man be buried.
- Whatever it is that is happening in my life, whatever my cross may I carry it and follow You no turning back, no retreat.
- I will not look backwards, whatever is going on in my life will not stop me from serving You, there is nothing of the old man remaining in me.
- Teach me to crucify the flesh and to put it under, that I might be ruled by the Spirit of God!
- Prune every unprofitable thing from my life that I will produce plenty of fruit.
- Break me, Lord that through me diffuses the fragrance of Your knowledge in every place.
- Let the Spirit of God change me into a different being not looking like the person I used to be That I will live in the newness I have in Jesus with a different identity and outlook on life in Jesus Name. Amen.

Scriptures for further Prayers

Romans 6:1-2, 2 Corinthians 5:17, Galatians 2:20, 2 Corinthians 2:14-15

Revive, Rebuild and Restore

JULY 23

SELF RIGHTEOUSNESS

Worship

Today's Scripture and Meditation

*Luke 18:9-14 Also He spoke this parable to some who trusted
in themselves that they were righteous, and despised
others: 10 "Two men went up to the temple to pray, one a
Pharisee and the other a tax collector. 11 The Pharisee
stood and prayed thus with himself, 'God, I thank You
that I am not like other men – extortioners, unjust,
adulterers, or even as this tax collector. 12 I fast twice a
week; I give tithes of all that I possess.' 13 And the tax
collector, standing afar off, would not so much as raise his
eyes to heaven, but beat his breast, saying, 'God, be
merciful to me a sinner!' 14 I tell you this man went
down to his house justified rather than the other; for
everyone who exalts himself will be [d]humbled, and he
who humbles himself will be exalted."*

PRAYERS:

- Lord, I thank you for your bloodshed for me
- Just as I am, though tossed about, with many a conflict,
many a doubt, fighting and fears within without, Oh, Lamb
of God, I come to you!
- Oh Lord, I repent from every known and unknown
disposition of pride in my life!
- Father, take every inherent spirit of pride away from me.
- Oh Lord, I repent from every sin of covetousness.
- Father, help me to make restitution of all that I have coveted

- ▢ Father, I repent from every spirit of self -righteousness and self-glorification
- ▢ Help me to live in the knowledge of the fact that I am forgiven by God, loved by God, changed by God, freed by God, provided for by God and made righteous by God, That I may not be conceited.
- ▢ Father, cause me to be completely sold out and dependent on You
- ▢ Father, all I am, all I will be, it's by Your grace and not by my power.
- ▢ Father, my righteousness is as a filthy rag, none of my efforts add to Your blessings in my life.
- ▢ Father, teach me to walk with You one day at a time
- ▢ Father, teach me to die daily and number my days.
- ▢ Thank You Father in Jesus' Name! Amen.

Scriptures for further Prayers

Psalm 90:12, 2 Corinthians 5:21

JULY 24

THE DANGER OF UNBELIEF

Worship

Today's Scripture and Meditation

Mark 6:5-6. Now, He could do no mighty work there, except that He laid His hands on a few sick people and healed them. 6 And He marveled because of their unbelief. Then He went about the villages in a circuit, teaching.

PRAYERS:

- Father Lord, I thank You because You are a miracle worker.
- I bring my heart before You that You might rid me of every doubt and unbelief that could hinder Your mighty work in my life in Jesus' Name.
- I ask for mercy for every time I have magnified situations and issues above You.
- Lord Jesus my advocate, You are the almighty God and there is nothing impossible with You.
- Let me be consumed by the LORD and not by my issues. I lay all matter at Your feet while I seek daily encounters with You.
- Lord I choose to take up my cross, and follow You, come what may. Enable me to deny myself as required by You.
- Have mercy on me for the times I have despised my pastors and other ministers of the gospel and have minimized and hindered the work that You purposed to do through them.
- I have looked at the packaging of ministers, forgetting the treasure within their earthen vessels, I have worked by sight, and have missed what I really needed for the season, Father forgive me.

- ⬛ Father I now understand that only the anointing I value and respect works for me, I choose to trust Your grace and anointing upon the ministers You have placed over me.
- ⬛ Your word says when we are united, the anointing will flow from their head, enable me to keep the unity of the Spirit in the bond of peace.
- ⬛ Father give me grace to submit to and obey everyone You have placed in authority over me.

- ⬛ I pull down theologies, philosophies, ideologies or theories working against the supernatural.
- ⬛ Father I ask for a mind shift, work in me and pulldown strongholds of ideology in my life.
- ⬛ Every scepticism towards church leaders be cast out of my mind.
- ⬛ Lord I surrender everything that has hindered the manifestation of Your work in me.
- ⬛ I submit to You Holy Spirit, walk in my heart, oh God, that I will manifest the fruit of the Spirit.
- ⬛ Uproot bitterness, strife, unholy competition. jealousy, and envy from my mind.
- ⬛ Take my love for You and the brethren to next level.
- ⬛ Thank You Father in Jesus Name.

Scriptures for further Prayers

Psalms 133, Acts 19:14-15, Galatians 5:22-23

JULY 25

MAKE ME YOUR MOUTHPIECE

Worship

Today's Scripture and Meditation

Jeremiah 15:19-21 Therefore, thus says the Lord: "If You return, I will restore You, and You shall stand before me. If You utter what is precious, and not what is worthless, you shall be as my mouth. They shall turn to you, but you shall not turn to them.

And I will make you to this people a fortified wall of bronze; they will fight against you, but they shall not prevail over you, for I am with you to save you and deliver you, declares the Lord. I will deliver you out of the hand of the wicked and redeem you from the grasp of the ruthless."

PRAYERS:

- Father thank You that You are the God of restoration. You are plenteous in mercy that is from everlasting to everlasting.
- The world has rejected You and Your way, we have strayed away from You, doing our own things, and living on our own terms.
- The families, streets, cities and nations are in shambles, but You are caring and reliable; Father I pray that You will return and restore, in Jesus' name, Amen.
- We stand before You in awe of You and in repentance. Let the words of my mouth be precious and acceptable before You.

- That I will not utter worthless words before You that I shall be used as Your mouthpiece on the earth.
- Father make me strong, immovable, unconquerable that I cannot be dragged down by anyone.
- Father deliver me from the hand of the enemy and redeem from the grip of the terrible.
- Father let there be a restoration of the years that the swarming locust has eaten. Let there be a restoration of the years that the crawling locust, the consuming locust, and the chewing locust have eaten.
- Let there be a restoration of all that the thief has stolen, killed, and destroyed.
- Let there be restoration of my ...... *(mention all You need restored)*
- I lift up my soul to You Lord let me not be ashamed in Jesus' Name, Amen.
- Thank You Father in Jesus' Name. Amen!

Scriptures for further Prayers:

Joel 2:25-27, Zephaniah 3:20

JULY 26

DIVINE SELECTION

Worship

Today's Scripture and Meditation

John 5:5-9. There was a certain man there who had suffered with a deep-seated and lingering disorder for thirty-eight years. 6 When Jesus noticed him lying there [helpless], knowing that he had already been a long time in that condition, He said to him, do you want to become well? [Are you really in earnest about getting well?] 7 The invalid answered, Sir, I have nobody when the water is moving to put me into the pool; but while I am trying to come [into it] myself, somebody else steps down ahead of me. 8 Jesus said to him, Get up! Pick up your bed (sleeping pad) and walk! 9 Instantly the man became well and recovered his strength and picked up his bed and walked. But that happened on the Sabbath.

PRAYERS:

- Thank You for remembering me and coming by to do me good.
- The Lord is walking through the crowd seeking whom to heal and bless. Let me be that man or woman.
- I receive healing for any deep-seated or lingering disorder that may be present in my life.
- I ask that You notice me and grant me help when I am helpless.
- I ask that You select me from the crowd for a blessing in Jesus Name.
- Let me be earnest regarding any of my desire and needs before You.

- ☐ I ask that heaven will focus on me, my family, my word and my ministry today.
- ☐ Lord let me not be waiting for the stirring of water when You are right there doing a new thing in my life.
- ☐ I cast down every Pharisee spirit standing in the way of healing.
- ☐ I will not lean on my sense, my knowledge, my understanding but that I will listen to Your word and act appropriately in Jesus Name.
- ☐ When I am down, You will cause me to arise from the bed of affliction, stagnancy, and failure.
- ☐ Let every sign of the issue be removed from my life
- ☐ I receive grace to receive. To begin to walk, to run, to begin to fly.
- ☐ I thank You Lord for in Jesus' Name we have prayed! Amen

Scriptures for further Prayers

Hebrews 12:2, Isaiah 43:19, Proverbs 3:5

JULY 27

FILTHY GARMENTS REMOVED

Worship

Today's Scripture and Meditation

Zechariah 3:1-5. *Then he showed me Joshua the high priest standing before the Angel of the Lord, and Satan[a] standing at his right hand to oppose him. 2 And the Lord said to Satan, "The Lord rebuke you, Satan! The Lord who has chosen Jerusalem rebuke you! Is this not a brand plucked from the fire?" 3 Now Joshua was clothed with filthy garments, and was standing before the Angel.4 Then He answered and spoke to those who stood before Him, saying, "Take away the filthy garments from him." And to him He said, "See, I have removed your iniquity from you, and I will clothe you with rich robes." 5 And I said, "Let them put a clean turban on his head." So, they put a clean turban on his head, and they put the clothes on him. And the Angel of the Lord stood by.*

PRAYERS:

- ☐ I am grateful You have accepted me just as I am. I do not have to impress You.
- ☐ Thank you for Your righteousness imputed for me that gives me access to Your presence.
- ☐ Father, I pray that whatever opposition that satan has against me be squashed by the blood of Jesus, the price that was paid for my redemption.
- ☐ Let every area of my life being opposed by the enemy be completely free from every opposition and oppression
- ☐ Father, I pray that any answers to my Prayers are delayed because the enemy is opposing be released.

- ⬚ Satan, the Lord rebuke you in my life, in my family, career, business, health, body spirit and soul, wellbeing .... *(Mention every area you need more freedom)*
- ⬚ Satan the Lord rebuke you in the place of my calling, assignment, vision and mission
- ⬚ Every accusation and legal ground for accusations is squashed, every certificate of debt is cancelled.
- ⬚ Every filthy garment is taken away, the blood of Jesus cleanses me, my iniquity and transgression is removed from me.
- ⬚ I manifest the righteousness of Jesus, a new turban of holiness is upon my head.
- ⬚ The power of besetting sins is destroyed, I am enabled and empowered, I receive grace to run the race and finish well.
- ⬚ I cast out of my life every guilt, timidity, I arise to fulfil my purpose.
- ⬚ The old mindset is exchanged for a new God-ordained and inspired mindset.
- ⬚ Lord, my confidence is in You, and I give You praise, I worship You
- ⬚ Thank you father, in Jesus name I pray. Amen!

Scriptures for further Prayers

1 John 1:7, Revelations 12:10b, Romans 4:6

JULY 28

GREAT IS YOUR FAITHFULNESS

Worship

Today's Scripture and Meditation

Psalm 100:5. For the Lord is good; His mercy is everlasting, And His truth endures to all generations.

PRAYERS:

- I bless You Oh God continually and Your praise shall continually be in my mouth.
- I honour You, my King. Thank You for Your faithfulness.
- Your faithfulness that goes from everlasting to everlasting.
- Your faithfulness that are new every morning, I worship You this morning.
- Great is the faithfulness of God, there is none like Him in heaven and on earth.
- You forgave my sins and granted me peace with the Father and with all men.
- You give me strength for today and hope for tomorrow.
- You spared me, oh God when the devil and evil men were working.
- You protected me from all harm. I am grateful that You have been my hiding place.
- You have been the rock that cleft me from generation to generation and from ages past.
- I am grateful that You are the Father that spares Your children and You have spared me.
- I am grateful that You called me a friend. I am grateful You adopted me and called me your own child,

- I am grateful for Your covenant loyalty and the covenant blessings that I enjoy.
- I will constantly speak Your praises and boast in You because You're faithful.
- You help the helpless, I worship You, You are husband to the widow and You are a great God,
- I prayed to You, and You answered me.
- Thank You for removing my shame. thank You that I am no longer ashamed or timid.
- No matter what my past looks like. No matter the things that I did or did not do,
- No matter what I went through, or did not go through, Lord no more shame in You, because You are our beautifier.
- I thank You because my face is not darkened. I thank You oh God because You listen to my Prayers
- Thank You for saving me from all troubles, and You answer my Prayers; faithful God.
- Thank You for Your love which I don't deserve yet You give, it is Your mercy that manifests.
- I am special because I am loved and cared for by the Almighty God not because I am good.
- I thank You for Your angels on guard in my life; I thank You for they surround and defend me.
- I thank You, because You have taken away my fears, and I am confident in You.
- Oh! the psalmist say God is good; I can testify Oh God, that indeed You are good.
- I am standing today because of Your faithfulness, I could have fallen, I could have wavered, I could have been dead.
- Despite all, I am still standing, left for the enemy, I would have been consumed,
- Left for the enemy I would be overrun, if not by Your mercies, I would have been consumed.
- Oh! but for Your grace and mercy. Blessed be Your name oh God!
- Be Thou exalted Oh God. Be Thou glorified, my Father. I honour You In Jesus Name, Amen!

Scriptures for further Prayers

Psalm 91:4, Psalm 34 Psalms 136:1

JULY 29

THANKSGIVING FOR DAILY BENEFIT

Worship

Today's Scripture and Meditation and Meditation

Psalm 103:1-2: *Bless the Lord, O my soul; And all that is within me, bless His holy name! Bless the Lord, O my soul, and forget not all His benefits.*

PRAYERS:

- Bless the Lord, O my soul; And all that is within me, bless His holy name!
- Bless the Lord, O my soul, and forget not all His benefits that He loads us with daily
- The benefit of Your covenant and all the covenant blessings; for healing my diseases and for physical health, psychological health and emotional health
- Thank You for provision, overflowing generosity, spiritual renewal, Your discipline, and Your comfort
- Thank You for victories in all battles for destroying the power of the enemy and preventing any deadly thing to harm me
- Father, I thank You for Your goodness and faithfulness in my life that endures through all generations
- Father, I thank You for answering my payers, granting my request and meeting my demands
- Thank You for Your grace and mercy, for life, for safety and security and for Your peace that surpasses all understanding

- ⬚ Father, I thank You for all the signs, wonders and miracles that You have worked in my life. You are the Lord of heaven and earth
- ⬚ I thank You for all Your miracles in my life. I will proclaim Your wonders tirelessly, for You alone deserve the glory
- ⬚ Lord, I am grateful for the benefit of a goodly heritage: the lines are fallen unto me in pleasant places; yea, I have a goodly heritage
- ⬚ Thank You for satisfying me with good things and for renewing my Youth like the eagle's
- ⬚ The benefit of Your covenant and all the covenant blessings; for healing my diseases and for health, for the provision of all my needs, for victories in all battles
- ⬚ Thank You for Your grace and mercy, for life, for safety and security
- ⬚ Thank You for overflowing joy even in difficult situations
- ⬚ Thank You Lord for being my refuge from the storm and shelter from the heat, my shield, my fortress, my strong tower and my hiding place
- ⬚ You are my strength and my shield; my heart trusts in You, and I am helped; therefore, my heart exalts You, and with my song I shall thank You
- ⬚ Thank You Father for Your goodness and mercy that follow me always
- ⬚ You are an amazing God!

Scriptures for further Prayers:

Psalm. 136:1, Psalm 23:6,

JULY 30

WARFARE

Worship

Today's Scripture and Meditation

Colossians 2:14 (AMP): *Having cancelled out the certificate of debt consisting of legal demands [which were in force] against us and which were hostile to us. And this certificate He has set aside and completely removed by nailing it to the cross.*

PRAYERS:

- ⬜ Thank You, Lord, for the finished work on the cross for my sake; taking out of the way and nailing every record of charges that was against me to the cross
- ⬜ I challenge every certificate of debt consisting of legal demands which were in force against me, and which were hostile to me with the blood of Jesus. According to the word of God, this certificate He has set aside and completely removed by nailing it to the cross
- ⬜ Every legal ground of the enemy in my life is broken and all accusations are destroyed in Jesus name.
- ⬜ Father disarm all rulers and authorities [those supernatural forces of evil operating against me] working against my faith in God. Make a public example of them, triumph over them in my life by the reason of the cross
- ⬜ I command all heads of gates and everlasting doors, preventing the presence and manifestation of God - the King of glory, in my life to be lifted. Let the King of glory come into my life

- I bind the strong man and dispossess him of any grounds or territory taken, and I command release, restoration and resurrection of all that the enemy has stolen, killed or destroyed
- Every stronghold of the enemy preventing a consistent Christian walk, prayer life and ministry, be pulled down in the powerful name of Jesus
- Let every clog in my spiritual wheel be flushed out by the blood of Jesus
- I frustrate the token of the liar and the deceiver and wise men; I bind every monitoring spirit and destroy every monitoring apparatus with which my life is been monitored in the spirit in Jesus name
- I connect with the covenant that I have with God in the blood of Jesus and claim the covenant blessings in Jesus name
- Blessed be Your name oh God, in Jesus mighty name I pray. Amen.

Scriptures for further Prayers

Psalms 24:7-10, Isaiah 44:25, John 10:10

JULY 31

VICTORY FROM THE CROSS

Worship

Today's Scripture and Meditation

Colossians 2:15 (AMP): *God disarmed the principalities and powers that were ranged against us and made a bold display and public example of them, in triumphing over them in Him and in it [the cross].*

PRAYERS:

- Lord, I thank You that You are a man of war, the captain of the host of heaven
- You already disarmed the principalities and powers that were arrayed against me. Thank You Lord because You already triumphed over them, and have won the victory, You won my freedom.
- By Your stripes, I am healed; by Your nail-pierced hands I am free.
- Every spiritual rural authority is disarmed in my life in the name of Jesus.
- Therefore, I pray to enforce all that has already been done on my behalf in Jesus Name, Amen!
- Every spiritual tyrant oppressing me, loose Your hold, influence and authority in Jesus Name, Amen.
- Every attack of the enemy against me, lose their power physically and spiritually in the Name of the Lord Jesus Christ. Amen.
- In the Name of Jesus Christ, every power and accusation against me is broken and destroyed.

- Every principality and powers ascribed against me and every department of my life, today the Lord makes a public display and example of them in the Name of the Lord Jesus. I have victory!
- Father, trouble the enemy of my soul, that his mission in my life be hindered in Jesus Name
- The Lord has put them to shame, they are disgraced publicly. Every works of darkness is disarmed in my life.
- I am totally delivered; physically, emotionally, financially, maritally, career wise. I receive all round deliverance in Jesus' name, Amen!

Scriptures for further Prayers:

Exodus 15:3, Exodus 14:24-25.

AUGUST 1

WITHOUT FAITH

Worship

Today's Scripture and Meditation

Hebrews 11:6. (AMPC) But without faith it is impossible to please and be satisfactory to Him. For whoever would come near to God must [necessarily] believe that God exists and that He is the rewarder of those who earnestly and diligently seek Him.

PRAYERS:

- ☐ I praise You Lord from the depth of my heart. I praise You with all that I have within me and bless Your holy Name.
- ☐ Lord I want to please You, therefore I pray like the disciples prayed, increase my faith
- ☐ Lord I want know You more, hear Your voice more, seek Your face more. and touch you more and experience You more
- ☐ I come to You with no doubt in my heart that You exist; all the other gods are the works of men but You are the self-existing true God.
- ☐ You are the rewarder of those that diligently seek You. Father let me receive reward for seeking You today as I seek.
- ☐ Lord, You have revealed your power over to the faint hearted.
- ☐ God, You revealed Your love, strength in the lives of Your people, so Lord I ask that You reveal Your strength in my life.
- ☐ Lord revealed Your covenant loyalty and faithfulness in my life.

Revive, Rebuild and Restore

- ⬜ I am a product of Your Almightiness, Lord revealed your ability and power Indeed!
- ⬜ You have done enough for me that I can put my faith in You.
- ⬜ I choose to put my faith in You even when You move and act in ways that do not make human sense.
- ⬜ Give me the mountain moving faith, so that Your will and purpose in and through me will be fulfilled.
- ⬜ I put my faith in You, I believe Your word, and I trust completely in You, Father reward me.
- ⬜ Let my life please and satisfy You, Continue to glorify Yourself in my life.
- ⬜ Thank you, Heavenly Father, blessed be Your name in Jesus Name.

Scriptures for further Prayers

Mark   11:23,   Luke   17:

AUGUST 2

FILTHY GARMENTS REMOVED

Worship

Today's Scripture and Meditation

Zechariah 3:1-5. Then he showed me Joshua the high priest standing before the Angel of the Lord, and Satan[a] standing at his right hand to oppose him. 2 And the Lord said to Satan, "The Lord rebuke you, Satan! The Lord who has chosen Jerusalem rebuke you! Is this not a brand plucked from the fire?" 3 Now Joshua was clothed with filthy garments, and was standing before the Angel.4 Then He answered and spoke to those who stood before Him, saying, "Take away the filthy garments from him." And to him He said, "See, I have removed your iniquity from you, and I will clothe you with rich robes." 5 And I said, "Let them put a clean turban on his head." So, they put a clean turban on his head, and they put the clothes on him. And the Angel of the Lord stood by.

PRAYERS:

- ⬚ I am grateful You have accepted me just as I am. I do not have to impress You.
- ⬚ Thank you for Your righteousness imputed for me that gives me access to Your presence.
- ⬚ Father, I pray that whatever opposition that satan has against me be squashed by the blood of Jesus, the price that was paid for my redemption.
- ⬚ Let every area of my life being opposed by the enemy be completely free from every opposition and oppression
- ⬚ Father, I pray that any answers to my Prayers are delayed because the enemy is opposing be released.

- ☐ Satan, the Lord rebuke you in my life, in my family, career, business, health, body spirit and soul, wellbeing …. *(Mention every area you need more freedom)*
- ☐ Satan the Lord rebuke you in the place of my calling, assignment, vision and mission
- ☐ Every accusation and legal ground for accusations is squashed, every certificate of debt is cancelled.
- ☐ Every filthy garment is taken away, the blood of Jesus cleanses me, my iniquity and transgression is removed from me.
- ☐ I manifest the righteousness of Jesus, a new turban of holiness is upon my head.
- ☐ The power of besetting sins is destroyed, I am enabled and empowered, I receive grace to run the race and finish well.
- ☐ I cast out of my life every guilt, timidity, I arise to fulfil my purpose.
- ☐ The old mindset is exchanged for a new God-ordained and inspired mindset.
- ☐ Lord confidence is in You, and I give You praise, I worship You
- ☐ Thank You, Father, in Jesus name I pray. Amen!

Scriptures for further Prayers

1 John 1:7, Revelations 12:10b, Romans 4:6

AUGUST 3

REHOBOTH

Worship

Today's Scripture and Meditation

Genesis 26:19-22: Also Isaac's servants dug in the valley, and found a well of running water there. But the herdsmen of Gerar quarreled with Isaac's herdsmen, saying, "The water is ours." So, he called the name of the well Esek, because they quarrelled with him.

Then they dug another well, and they quarrelled over that one also. So, he called its name Sitnah. And he moved from there and dug another well, and they did not quarrel over it. So, he called its name Rehoboth, because he said, "For now the Lord has made room for us, and we shall be fruitful in the land."

- Father Lord we bless You because You are interested in posterity and in generations.
- Thank you for those who have gone before us in the faith.
- The spiritual resources that sustained them is available to us today so Lord, I pray that we seek these resources with faith and commitment in Jesus Name.
- Our spiritual lives are sustained by the water of the word and by the power of the Holy Spirit, Father I pray that you grant me grace to continue to dig deep into Your word in Jesus Name.
- Father help me to honour the provision of our fathers in the faith by keeping the landmarks that have been placed.
- I tap into the wells of peace, of power, of grace, of wisdom, of transformation of the previous generations of Christians.

Revive, Rebuild and Restore

- Give me grace and the required faith, the work, and the commitment to dig the wells again
- Running water depicts the outpouring of you Spirit, I pray Lord that as I dig into your word, there will be a manifestation of the Spirit of God and that out my belly shall flow rivers if living water in Jesus' Name.
- Father I realise that there may be contention and opposition as I dig deeper but Lord I ask that you will make room for me. That you word will have its free course and be fruitful in my life in Jesus Name.
- Grant
- unto me the perseverance to keep on and focus despite oppositions and conspiracies
- I pray that my labour shall not be in vain. It is time to reap the harvest. Let every opposition and contention cease in Jesus Name.
- I speak fruitfulness in every area of my life in Jesus Name, Amen!
- We give You praise: we magnify Your holy Name in Jesus Name, Amen!

Scriptures for further Prayers:

Revelation   2:3,   Romans   5:3-4,   James   5:11

AUGUST 4

YOUR GIFT WILL MAKE A WAY

Worship

Today's Scripture and Meditation

Gen 41:14. *Then Pharaoh sent and called Joseph, and they brought him quickly out of the dungeon; and he shaved, changed his clothing, and came to Pharaoh.*

PRAYERS:

- Father Lord, I pray that You will grant me favour before You and cause me to seat with kings.
- Father, all by Yourself deliver me from every situation that poses as dungeon in our lives.
- Father enable me to continue to use my gifts and talents for You no matter the restraints.
- Let my gift not be dormant or buried but Lord let my gift make a way from me.
- Almighty God I pray that clean me from every spiritual and physical dirt, make me presentable before Your altar Lord.
- Mighty and everlasting Father please take away every garment of shame and cloth your children sometimes and cover us with Your glory.
- Lord, send your angels for my freedom. Let bondage be over and let my glory come
- Father, I pray that You single me out to be used by You oh Lord.
- Thank You Father, in Jesus name I pray. Amen

Scriptures for further Prayers:

Acts 12:7-9, 2 Timothy 1:6.

AUGUST 5

ARGUE YOUR CASE

Worship

Today's Scripture and Meditation

Isaiah 43:26(AMPC) Put Me in remembrance [remind Me of your merits]; let us plead and argue together. Set forth your case, that you may be justified (proved right).

PRAYERS:

- ☐ Father, I thank You because You are a just God. You do righteousness and Your ways are perfect.
- ☐ You are just and even to creatures that You created, Thank you Lord!
- ☐ You have asked me to put forward my merit, before You Lord, I am inadequate.
- ☐ There is nothing I do that You have not given me the strength and ability to do.
- ☐ There is nothing I do that is not by Your grace because without You I can do nothing.
- ☐ I therefore come before You seeking mercy, seeking Your grace, and appealing to Your generosity.

Revive, Rebuild and Restore

- ☐ I can only ask for Your faithfulness to be manifest in my life.
- ☐ Father, I pray that You will perform Your promises in my life.
- ☐ Father, I pray that You will fulfil Your promise that pertains to … *(Remember any promise that pertains to whatever circumstance you are praying about)* …. . in my life and that of my family, my work, my ministry in Jesus Name.
- ☐ Father fulfil Your promise in my life concerning today, tomorrow, and the future.
- ☐ Father, You have promised grace, goodness, mercy, salvation, healing, deliverance, breakthroughs, and every good gift. Father make Your promises good in my life in Jesus Name, Amen.
- ☐ Let what You say happen for me to see and to proclaim to all.
- ☐ Thank You Father in Jesus Name, Amen.

Scriptures for further Prayers

Jeremiah 1:12, Numbers 11:23

AUGUST 6

SEED TO THE SOWER

Worship

Today's Scripture and Meditation

Isaiah 55:10-11

> *"For as the rain comes down, and the snow from heaven, And do not return there, But water the earth, And make it bring forth and bud, That it may give seed to the sower, And bread to the eater, So shall My word be that goes forth from My mouth; It shall not return to Me [c]void, But it shall accomplish what I please, And it shall prosper in the thing for which I sent it"*

PRAYERS:

- Father I thank You that You gave Your word, and You continually speak to us.
- Thank You that once Your word is spoken, it does not return to You.
- I ask that You word will have its free course in my life.
- Lord, Your word has power, it never fails in its intended purpose. Father let there be a performance of Your word in my life
- No matter how Your word is presented, let it be performed in my life, let it succeed in what it is being sent. Amen
- As the rain and snow come down and do not return to heaven, let Your word be irreversible in my life
- Let your word which is imperishable and enduring bring about long-lasting effect in my life

- Let Your word and Your Spirit water my earth and cause it to bring forth and to bud.
- Let Your word be that seed that I may sow in the lives and hearts of men by the power of your Spirit.
- Let Your word be the Bread of life to many, that they may eat it and live.
- Let Your word continually prosper in all it is being used for in my life
- Let your word accomplish the whole counsel of God in my life in Jesus Name.

Scriptures for further Prayers

Hebrews 4:12, 1 Peter 1:23

AUGUST 7

DOUBLE HONOR

Worship

Today's Scripture and Meditation

Isaiah 61:7. instead of your shame you shall have double honour and instead of your confusion they shall rejoice in their portion therefore in their land they shall process double everlasting joy shall be theirs.

PRAYERS:

- Father, I thank You for You are the God of wisdom, I receive wisdom from You today.
- You are the God of knowledge: I receive knowledge from You.
- You are the owner of cattle upon a thousand hills, I receive wealth and riches and honour from you Lord!
- For every time of shame, I receive double honour as my portion and possess my possessions
- I receive dignity!
- Let the record book of Chronicles open; let God remember me today.
- Let my reward be highlighted. Let God raise helpers to honour me.
- According to the order of Mordecai I shall be rewarded where it matters most when it is a matter of life and death when there is need to spoil the plan and plots of the enemy in the Name of Jesus.
- The grace of God is upon me, and every plan of the enemy is spoilt and destroyed this season.

- ⬚ I will shine this season and when I call one, a multitude will answer in Jesus' Name.
- ⬚ I am clothed with strength and honour in Jesus name
- ⬚ The Lord will give men for me this season the Lord will give people for your life.
- ⬚ I humble myself that I might not refuse correction and end up missing my portion
- ⬚ Thank you for your love that spurs you into actions and expressions in my life
- ⬚ I receive the garment, the regalia that the king has already won as it carries authority.
- ⬚ I receive the authority of the king to make decrees and rule in my territory for Christ
- ⬚ Lord, I give You praise, I worship, and I bless Your holy Name in the Name of Jesus.

Scriptures for further Prayers

2 Chronicles 1:12, Esther 6:1 Proverbs 13:18

AUGUST 8

ENJOY THE WORKS OF YOUR HANDS

Worship

Today's Scripture and Meditation

Isaiah 65:22: They shall not build and another inhabit; They shall not plant and another eat; For as the days of a tree, so shall be the days of My people, And My elect shall long enjoy the work of their hands.

PRAYERS

- Thank You, Lord, for all Your promises from this scripture, thank You Lord.
- Father Lord please let it please You to make me Your chosen one.
- By the authority in the word of God, I pray that I will not build for another person to occupy,
- I declare that I shall build and inhabit; I will labour and enjoy the product of my work in Jesus' Name.
- I pray Lord that You cause me to enjoy the work of my hand because I am your elect
- Thank you for you predestined me for adoption as sons and to be conformed to the image of Christ
- Father watch over my labour and cause it to yield increase
- Father let my hand finish what you have helped me to start. That my mission will not be terminated
- Father I surrender to You to bring to completion the good

Revive, Rebuild and Restore

work You have started in me in Jesus name.

- Mighty God please cause our life to flourish in Jesus' name Amen!

Scriptures for further Prayers:

Philippians 1:6, Psalm 127:1-5.

AUGUST 9

COUNT IT ALL JOY

Worship

Today's Scripture and Meditation

James 1:2-4 *Count it all joy, my brothers, when you meet trials of various kinds, 3 for you know that the testing of your faith produces steadfastness. 4 And let steadfastness have its full effect, that you may be perfect and complete, lacking in nothing.*

PRAYERS:

- Father Lord, we thank You because You came to suffer and die for me.
- I thank You because no trial or temptation come to me but with Your knowledge.
- I thank You because You allow me to be tested for my growth in You and for my promotion.
- I ask for grace to look beyond the present pain and rejoice for every temptation that comes to me is an opportunity to fellowship with Your sufferings.
- Enable me to remain steadfast in You despite all pressures and no matter what I face in life.
- That I will consider the trials and pressures of this world as light afflictions which are outweighed by the glory that is to be revealed.
- Father I ask that steadfastness will be a watchword for the church that we may progress in our commission to disciple the nations.

- Build me up through the trials and temptations that I go through.
- That faith be produced in me as You see me through and that my love for You and steadfastness in You be resolute.
- Almighty God let steadfastness have its full effect in me that I may be perfect as You are perfect
- Father, I pray that all that I need to continue to serve You and not to miss it be granted unto me.
- Activate in me all that pertains to life and godliness that I may lack in nothing in Jesus' Name. Amen.

Scriptures for further Prayers:

2 Corinthians 4:17, 1 Corinthians 15:58

AUGUST 10

FAITH WITH WORKS

Worship

Today's Scripture and Meditation

James 2:14-17 What does it profit, my brethren, if someone says he has faith but does not have works? Can faith save him? 15 If a brother or sister is naked and destitute of daily food, 16 and one of you says to them, "Depart in peace, be warmed and filled," but you do not give them the things which are needed for the body, what does it profit? 17 Thus also faith by itself, if it does not have works, is dead.

PRAYERS:

▢   My father thank You for the salvation of my soul.

▢   Lord Jesus, thank you that you save me through washing of rebirth and renewal by the Holy Spirit

▢   That I will not neglect the practice of holiness and righteousness

▢   Help me grow in faith that it may be counted as righteousness for me

▢   Father enable me to add works to my faith that my faith will not be dead

▢   That I will not be insensitive to the practical needs of the brethren

▢   That I will be used to distribute to and meet the need of the household of faith

▢   That I will go past religion to being a disciple of Jesus Christ

- ▢ That I will be an extension of Your hand in our world as I help to feed the hungry, visit the sick and those in prison.
- ▢ Grant me the grace to prove my faith by feeding the hungry giving a drink to the thirsty receiving the stranger into my homes, clothing the naked caring for the sick and visiting the prisoners.
- ▢ Grant me the grace to prove my faith in Your word through obedience
- ▢ Lord Jesus, cause me to be the doer of Your word and not just the hearer.
- ▢ Thank You for the privilege of knowing You and being used of You in Jesus name.

Scriptures for further Prayers

Matthew 25:35, James 2:26

AUGUST 11

NO REJECTION

Worship

Today's Scripture and Meditation

Isaiah 53:3 *He is despised and rejected of men, a man of Sorrows and acquainted with grief, and we hid it as it is were our faces from him and despised and we did not esteemed him.*

PRAYERS:

- ⏃ Thank You Lord Jesus for the pain and suffering that You went through for my sake.
- ⏃ Thank You that You took the rejection and sorrow for my sake.
- ⏃ The enemy can no longer steal from me. He tries to steal purposes, to steal the confidence of the people of God, to steal self-esteem, to steal Your future.
- ⏃ I pray against the feeling of rejection today because You took it on my behalf; rejection by parents, rejection because of gender, rejection by in-laws, rejection from friendships and relationships, rejection due to loss of jobs, rejection by authority, rejection by brethren, rejection even in the church. Father erase the effect and pain of rejection in Jesus' Name.
- ⏃ I submit them at the cross of Jesus: every rejection I thought I had dealt with that is still informing my thinking and behaviour be dealt with by Your Spirit in Jesus' Name.
- ⏃ I destroy the very silent potent weapon of rejection in my life, It can no longer steal my potentials, achievements, destiny or purpose,

Revive, Rebuild and Restore

- ▢ I command every spirit of fear preventing you from being your best to get out of your life in the Name of Jesus.
- ▢ I address Your Spirit of fear and Your Spirit of rejection get out of the life of the people this morning.
- ▢ Every mark of hatred, every mark of disfavour, every mark of rejection, every mark of depression upon your life is wiped out in the Name of Jesus.
- ▢ I pray that the Balm in Gilead will bring total and complete emotional healing in the Name of Jesus.
- ▢ I command every spirit of rejection including self -rejections to come out of my life in Jesus' Name.
- ▢ We break every power of illness and disorders and apply the blood of Jesus in the Name of Jesus.
- ▢ Every spirit that tortures you in your mind telling you that you are not good enough, we bind and cast it out of your mind.
- ▢ Spirit of the Living God brings healing for discouragement or despair or dispute, for despondency, for shame for defeat, for hopelessness, for suicide, for disgust in the Name of Jesus.
- ▢ For rejection, bring healing and the confidence of the Lord; possess me, for, the righteous are as bold as a lion.
- ▢ Thank You heavenly Father, we praise You Lord, in Jesus mighty Name we pray. Amen!

Scriptures for further Prayers

Isaiah 53:3, Colossians 2:14, Exodus 2:11-15

AUGUST 12

DELIVERANCE AND RESTORATION

Worship

Today's Scripture and Meditation

Isa 59:1: *Behold, the Lord's hand is not shortened at all, that it cannot save, nor His ear dull with deafness, that it cannot hear.*

PRAYERS:

- Lord, I thank You because You are Almighty, powerful and magnificent God
- I thank You because You are my Saviour and the Redeemer of my soul
- You are the great defender and deliverer; Your everlasting arms are underneath me; I shall not fall, and I shall not fail
- I bring myself and all that pertains to me under the covering of the blood of Jesus as I take the battle to the gate of the enemy, and I declare my victory in Jesus name

- I pray that every area of my life will receive the light of God, deliverance, and salvation of the Lord
- Your hand is not too short to deliver, Father deliver me from every oppression and suppression of the enemy. I cry out to the Lord to deliver me
- When light shines in darkness, darkness cannot comprehend it; let the light of God shine in every facet of my life that darkness might go in Jesus name

527   *Revive, Rebuild and Restore*

- ☐ I pray that everything that preys upon me or has kept me captive will lose its hold upon my life today in Jesus name
- ☐ Let every chain, limitations, snares and cords of bondage in my life (physical and spiritual) be broken in Jesus name
- ☐ Let prison doors open that I might escape every oppression and suppression of the enemy in Jesus name
- ☐ Lord You were manifested to destroy the words of the enemy. I pray that every works of darkness in my life be destroyed in the powerful name of Jesus
- ☐ By the word of the Lord, I decree it is enough to the angel of death, it is enough, angel of sickness, it is enough, angel of mishap, it is enough, it is enough, today is the expiry date, end of trouble, it is enough, I receive peace of God in Jesus name
- ☐ I command every stranger in my life to come out of their closed places
- ☐ It is enough! That trouble is enough, that problem is enough, that sickness is enough, that failure is enough. You go no further in the name of Jesus, Amen.
- ☐ Let every other spirit other than the Spirit of God loose their hold upon my life. Every spirit of fear, spirit of doubt, spirit of worry, spirit of anxiety, spirit of unforgiveness, spirit of bitterness spirit of anger, spirit of failure and stagnancy, spirit of infirmity, all demonic spirits loose your hold in Jesus name
- ☐ Father restore all that the enemy has stolen, killed or destroyed in my life in Jesus name
- ☐ I recover all and I declare that all wasted time is redeemed today. Thank You Lord for You are my help and my deliverer.
- ☐ I appreciate You, in Jesus name. Amen.

Scriptures for further Prayers

Galatians 5:1, Deuteronomy 33:27, Isaiah 59:1, Psalms 127:6

AUGUST 13

DRAW NEAR

Worship

Today's Scripture and Meditation

James 4:8-10. Draw near to God and He will draw near to you. Cleanse your hands, you sinners; and purify your hearts, you double-minded. 9 Lament and mourn and weep! Let your laughter be turned to mourning and your joy to gloom. 10 Humble yourselves in the sight of the Lord, and He will lift you up.

PRAYERS:

- Father, I come to You humbly today knowing that I am a sinner in need of forgiveness
- If I say I have no sin, I am lying and the truth is not in me; this is what your word says
- I come before You Lord confessing my sins (mention all you can remember)
- Lord, I know that You are faithful and just and I come to You with a broken heart.
- I rid my heart of every sin in thoughts, words and action
- I rid my heart of every doubt, unbelief, double mindedness
- I repent of all sins and will no longer go back into it.
- Father, I draw near to You today and ask that You will draw near to me. Reveal more of Your person, Your kingdom and Your ways to me.
- I draw close that I might find cleansing at the cross.
- I draw near to You that I might become pure, that I might be able to think about eternal things.

- ⬦ I draw near in praise, in worship, in enjoying communion, in asking for counsel
- ⬦ I submit to You, I surrender to You. Help me to resist the devil.
- ⬦ Convict me by Your Spirit in godly sorrow and draw me close to You.
- ⬦ I humble myself before You because You resist the proud.
- ⬦ Father lift me like you lift up the humble.
- ⬦ Thank you father in Jesus name. Amen

Scriptures for further Prayers

Luke 18:10-14.

AUGUST 14

HIS KINGDOM FIRST

Worship

Today's Scripture and Meditation

Matthew 6:33 (NIV): *But seek first his kingdom and his righteousness, and all these things will be given to you as well.*

PRAYERS:

- Father, I thank You that I belong to Your kingdom grace and beauty
- I thank You that I am a citizen of Your kingdom
- My allegiance is to You and Your kingdom; My worship is unto You
- I pray Lord that my priorities will not be misplaced, help me to seek first Your kingdom, not my own wealth
- Father, let my priorities be based on spiritual values and not on worldly values, that I will prioritize my spiritual growth above growth in other areas
- Father teach me to work to expand Your kingdom, not my own. Help me to walk by Your word, not by my own selfishness.
- Let me not be complacent and content with what I have achieved, there are more mountains to climb and more grounds to conquer – help me to work in Your righteous cause
- Enable me to use whatever gift I have received to serve others, as faithful stewards of God's grace in its various forms.

- Enable me to make the decision to give cheerfully to God's righteous cause, the cause of the kingdom
- Enable me to prioritize the word, my personal fellowship with You and fellowship with other Christians above every other form of fellowship.
- Father enable me to see my daily life through the eyes of Your kingdom. Help me to seek Your kingdom in my heart, mind, and not to spend this life focused on myself
- Father enable to be a kingdom builder, let me not continue to control everything and everyone, including You
- As a labourer in God's vineyard, let my liberty be found in doing Your will in order that I will walk in the manner of Your calling for my life. Give me the strength, grace, and patience that I need to walk in true liberty in Christ
- I am available to You Lord, use me as You will in Your Kingdom in Jesus name

Scriptures for further Prayers

2 Peter 3:18, Hebrews 10:24-25, 2 Tim 3:16-17

Revive, Rebuild and Restore

AUGUST 15

I WILL GIVE YOU REST

Worship

Today's Scripture and Meditation

Matthew 11:28-31: Come to Me, all you who labour and are heavy laden, and I will give you rest. Take My yoke upon you and learn from Me, for I am [f]gentle and lowly in heart, and you will find rest for your souls. For My yoke is easy and My burden is light.

PRAYERS:

- Lord thank You for coming to this earth, dying on the cross for my sake. Thank You for rising from the dead and for the finished work of Calvary.
- You wiped my sins, and reconciled me to the Father. I am already healed and delivered by the blood of that You shed on the cross.
- Thank You for the cross. Through the cross I am forgiven, victorious, and delivered, forgiven, and transformed; It has been done already!
- I come to You, not to man, not to a doctrine, not to a ministry but to You Lord Jesus will I lay my burdens that I might find rest.
- I come to You because I need You as I am not self sufficient.
- I come to You that I might receive rest. I come to receive refreshment, ease, redemption, quietness for my soul and all-round rest.
- Let me follow the ancient landmark that I might cease from worries and find relief quietness for my soul.

- I come that I might cease from struggles, I know that manifestation of Your rest is not in the place of crying, anxiety or stress but that I might live by faith and receive grace to rest in You, in Your promises and in Your word.

- I enter Your rest and I will not fret; I will not put my faith in the things that I see because they are temporal but in things that are not seen which are eternal.
- I willingly take up your yoke which is easy and your burden which is light, give me a servant heart.
- I receive gentleness in my spirit that I might find rest for my soul.

- Holy Spirit help me and take me to that place of rest fully and completely, where I will experience peace like a river for my soul that I may receive your promises.
- In that place of rest, the healing manifests, the deliverance manifests and peace manifests, Prosperity manifests
- Let my eyes be single, looking unto You, he Author and Finisher of my faith, enable me to concentrate on You, I do not go to the right, or left.
- I chose to concentrate on You Lord, to receive of You, receive from You, to have faith in You and to live by faith for "the just shall live by faith"
- Let your living water flow over my soul, let the Holy spirit come and take control of every situation of my life.
- Lord, You said it is finished, hence all my struggles are finished, and I therefore find rest as I put my faith in you and grow in it.
- Thank You Father, be exalted oh God, in Jesus Name.

Scriptures for further Prayers:

2 Corinthians 4:18, Jeremiah 6:16, John 19:30

AUGUST 16

PROTECTED BY GOD

Worship

Today's Scripture and Meditation

Psalm 91:1-11

He who dwells in the secret place of the Most High, shall abide under the shadow of the Almighty. I will say of the Lord, "He is my refuge and my fortress; My God, in Him I will trust." Surely He shall deliver you from the snare of the [a]fowler And from the perilous pestilence. He shall cover you with His feathers, And under His wings you shall take refuge; His truth shall be your shield and buckler. You shall not be afraid of the terror by night, nor of the arrow that flies by day;

Nor of the pestilence that walks in darkness, nor of the destruction that lays waste at noonday. A thousand may fall at your side, and ten thousand at your right hand; But it shall not come near you. Only with your eyes shall you look and see the reward of the wicked.

Because you have made the Lord, who is my refuge, Even the Most High, your dwelling place, No evil shall befall you, nor shall any plague come near your dwelling; For He shall give His angels charge over you, to keep you in all your ways.

PRAYERS:

- Father I thank You for the place of Your presence.

- Enable me to dwell in Your secret place most high God, where no attack can penetrate, where no power of the enemy can reach me, where no foe can withstand, where we; can be covered, where we can be protected, that is where we want to stay.
- I will not leave the place of my divine positioning; I will not break the hedge in the Name of Jesus.
- You are my refuge, and You are my fortress in whom we trust, You are our shield, You are our cover, restrain me from going away from that cover, Let me not stray away or walk out on You.
- Let me walk in great nearness and very close to You,, so Your shadow will be cast on me.
- Enable me to be intimate with You so I can know the greatness of Your protection.
- I will not fear any terror, pestilence, or destruction because I am fortified by God and inaccessible by the enemy, no plagues shall come near my dwelling.
- Let me be ever guarded from destructive spiritual forces as I dwell in the secret place of the Most High.
- We will not fear any form of destruction and sudden death that surprise and lay waste at noonday.
- You are the great Protector and Helper, hence a thousand may fall at my side, and ten thousand at my right hand, but it shall not come near me.
- You said we are only going to be spectators to the reward of the wicked.
- I am inaccessible to the enemy, because I have made You my refuge, and the Most High, my dwelling place.
- I ask for angelic assignment to protect and to bear me in their hand that I will not dash my feet against the stone; that I will not be out on the day of accidents or mishaps.
- Give them charge to accompany, defend, and preserve me from the power and influence of evil spirits that they cannot prevail.
- That my dwelling place be attack-proof. My jobs, spouses, children, and grandchildren (if applicable) are bullet proof to the enemy.

- Let the enemy be turned back at the gate; because I am impenetrable and in accessible by the kingdom of darkness.
- No weapon formed against me shall prosper, and every tongue which rises against me in judgment I shall condemn in the Name of Jesus!
- I will not just be a survivor but a victor who trample the enemy under foot.
- Enable me to delight in You, spending time with You, listening to You, reading what You have written to us, speaking to You, thinking of You in unoccupied moments, adoring You, Speaking of You to others.
- Deliver me and answer me when I call., Thank You father in Jesus name, Amen

Scriptures for further Prayers:

1 John 4:18, Psalm 3:3, Luke 10:19

AUGUST 17

GRACE! GRACE!! TO IT

Worship

Today's Scripture and Meditation

Zechariah 4:7: *'Who are you, O great mountain? Before Zerubbabel you shall become a plain! And he shall bring forth the capstone with shouts of "Grace, grace to it!"'*

PRAYERS:

- Thank You for the authority given to me to speak to every mountain. So I command every mountain in my life to be removed and cast into the Sea, in the name of Jesus
- I command every health mountain, family mountain, marital mountain, financial mountain, ministry mountain *(mention as applies to You)* be removed from my life in the name of Jesus
- Let every mountain of opposition, be removed by the command of the Lord in the name of Jesus
- I contend with every mountain of delay, distraction, derailment, disappointment, discouragement, hindrances and command them: to be removed in the name of Jesus
- I speak to every mountain of debt, poverty, lack, sickness, hardship, bareness, sorrow, attack, *(mention as applies to You)* in my life, marriage and business, be removed and cast into the sea, in the name of Jesus
- I command every mountain of cyclical problems, repeated affliction, un-sustained progress in my life to become a plain now in the name of Jesus

- I pray for grace for completion, achievement and accomplishment of every assignment, project in Jesu name
- Grant unto me the anointing to stand and not to fall in the name of Jesus
- Grant me grace to know You more, anointing to serve You more and to go deeper with You
- I shout Grace! Grace!! Grace!!! With thanksgiving in my heart in Jesus mighty name, Amen.

Scriptures for further Prayers

Mark 11:23, Malachi.1:3, Isaiah.42:15, Job 28:9

AUGUST 18

ENDUED WITH POWER

Worship:

Today's Scripture and Meditation:

Luke 24:49: *Behold, I send the promise of my Father upon You; but tarry in the city of Jerusalem until you are endued with power from on high.*

PRAYERS:

- Father Lord, I thank You for the gift of the Holy Spirit whom You sent to us. Thank You for He empowers and equips us for the work of the kingdom.
- I am acutely aware that I cannot do the work You called me to do unless I am endued with power from on high, I ask that the Holy Spirit be poured out upon me afresh Jesus' Name.
- Father Help me to tarry in Your presence until the appointed time of Your visitation in Jesus Name, Amen!
- That I may not serve in my strength and according to the flesh.
- Father give me grace to overcome every distraction that is programmed to stop me from tarrying and help me to tarry in Your presence in Jesus Name, Amen.
- By faith I receive a fresh infilling of the Holy Spirit, I am endued with power to progress and to overcome all challenges in Jesus' Name, Amen.
- I am endued with power to progress and preach the gospel and be a witness for our Lord Jesus Christ in Jesus name, Amen.

- I am endued with power to heal the sick and cast out devils in Jesus name, Amen!
- I am endued with power to set the captives free and proclaim liberty to those who are bound in Jesus' Name, Amen!
- I am endued with power to live a life worthy of my Lord and Saviour Jesus Christ.
- I am endued with power to teach principalities and power the manifold wisdom of God and to show forth the praises of our God in Jesus name, Amen!
- Spirit of God come upon me afresh and release far greater unction and grace into my life in Jesus' Name, Amen!

Scriptures for further Prayers:

Acts 2:1, Mark 16:17-18, Acts 4:31

AUGUST 19

NO ATTACKS

Worship

Today's Scripture and Meditation

Zechariah 12:8-10 (AMPC). *In that day will the Lord guard and defend the inhabitants of Jerusalem, and he who is [spiritually] feeble and stumbles among them in that day [of persecution] shall become [strong and noble] like David; and the house of David [shall maintain its supremacy] like God, like the [a]Angel of the Lord Who is before them. 9 And it shall be in that day that I will make it My aim to destroy all the nations that come against Jerusalem. 10 And I will pour out upon the house of David and upon the inhabitants of Jerusalem the Spirit of grace or unmerited favor and supplication. And they shall look [earnestly] upon Me Whom they have pierced, and they shall mourn for Him as one mourns for his only son, and shall be in bitterness for Him as one who is in bitterness for his firstborn.*

PRAYERS:

- Thank You Lord for You are our defence, as the mountains surround Jerusalem so do You defend us.
- Father, you are   my physical and spiritual defence all round me and my family.
- Defend me when I have battles in my life. Defend me when I am weak and feeble.
- I ask that You strengthen me so that I am not overrun by the enemy and that I may not stumble

- ▢ I ask that You show Yourself strong amid those who do not know You, that they may surrender to You.
- ▢ Show You are strong, show You are big and show Your supremacy against every persecution or onslaught of the enemy.
- ▢ Let me not be physically or spiritually weak. I receive strength from above.
- ▢ Reveal in me that I am of superior stock, because of the Spirit of the Lord is in me. No weapon formed against me shall prosper and every tongue that rises up against me in judgement is condemned in Jesus Name.
- ▢ Whatever is coming against me is destroyed; Let destruction come upon everything that preys upon me.
- ▢ I command destruction on everything that does not bring glory to God in my life
- ▢ I pray that every satanic agenda and implantation be destroyed.
- ▢ Let every evil report about any area of my life be changed into a good report By the power of Your Spirit
- ▢ Take me back to the cross, take me back to where I first met You.
- ▢ Pour upon me the spirit of grace, unmerited favour and supplication   that I might pray more.
- ▢ I look earnestly to you that I might come closer to You, draw me nearer Lord to come deeper with You, I desire with you a closer walk.
- ▢ Thank You Father in Jesus Name. Amen!

Scriptures for further Prayers:

Isaiah 54:17, Psalm 105:37

AUGUST 20

FOLLOW ME

Worship

Today's Scripture and Meditation

John 12:26. *If anyone serves Me, let him follow Me; and where I am, there My servant will be also. If anyone serves Me, him My Father will honour.*

PRAYERS:

- Father, I bless You oh God for Your saving grace upon my life, thank You Jesus.
- Everlasting Father, I ask that You help us to constantly follow You without looking back.
- I thank You because You called me to follow You and gave me the grace to answer Your call.
- Lord I ask for grace to deny myself, discipline myself and to follow You.
- I cast down every fear and distraction in form of problems or satanic manipulations.
- I look unto Jesus the Author and the Finisher of my faith to receive grace to endure as I look forward to the rewards and glory that is to come.
- Enable me to follow You in step one day at a time.
- Almighty God please help me to always dwell in Your sweet presence, Lord please always abide with me.
- Mighty and everlasting Father, please grant me the grace to serve You in all diligence without hypocrite.

- That I might be where You are and receive honour from the Father.
- Almighty Father I look to You oh God! As I serve You both in secret and in open in Jesus' Name.

Scriptures for further Prayers:

Matthew 16:24, Hebrews 12:2

AUGUST 21

I WILL GATHER THEM

Worship

Today's Scripture and Meditation

Zephaniah 3:17-19: *The Lord Your God is in the midst of You, a Mighty One, a Saviour [Who saves]! He will rejoice over You with joy; He will rest [in silent satisfaction] and in His love He will be silent and make no mention [of past sins, or even recall them].*

He will exult over You with singing. I will gather those belonging to You [those Israelites in captivity] who yearn and grieve for the solemn assembly [and the festivals], on whom [their exile and inability to attend services at Jerusalem have brought derision and] the reproach of it is a burden. 19 Behold, at that time I will deal with all those who afflict You; I will save the limping [ones] and gather the outcasts and will make them a praise and a name in every land of their shame.

PRAYERS:

- Thank Lord because You are interested in me, thank You because You rejoice over me.
- Thank You for Your love towards us, for the forgiveness of sins, thank You for Your joy over us.
- I am grateful for Your presence in our midst, lives, hearts, family, houses, huts streets, towns and nation.

- I am grateful because You saved us for love, thank You for the love with which You love us, an unconditional love.
- Love that does not end, an ending and everlasting love, I worship You and I magnify Your Holy Name.
- Thank You Lord that as faulty as I am you rejoice over me with joy and are delighted to break into song with singing over me.
- I pray against the spirit of torment and guilt over past sins and present sin, I cast you out in Jesus' Name.
- Lord the knowledge of your love for me takes away my fear and strengthen my hands.
- Father Lord Let me not be absent from or neglect in the gathering together of the saints that I might not be reproached or burdened again for you are mighty in our midst.
- Father deal with every affliction in my life in Jesus' Name.
- Father encourage me when I am discouraged and defeat the enemy for my sake.
- Gather us your children together when we faint and are scattered for the praise and fame of your Name
- Let the zeal of your house consume us and that our fellowship with You and with one another is sustained. Thank You Father in Jesus name

Scriptures for further Prayers:

Romans 8:1, Hebrews 10:25

AUGUST 22

DIVINE SELECTION

Worship

Today's Scripture and Meditation

Judges 7:1-2: Then Jerubbaal, that is, Gideon, and all the people who were with him rose early and encamped beside the spring of Harod; and the camp of Midian was north of them by the hill of Moreh in the valley. The Lord said to Gideon, the people who are with You are too many for Me to give the Midianites into their hands, lest Israel boast about themselves against Me, saying, my own hand has delivered me.

PRAYERS:

- Father, thank You for choosing to fight for me and letting me know that it is not according to strength, power, ability, multitude but for God's glory.
- It is not by power or by might but by His spirit, without Him I can do nothing.
- I release every aspect of my life to You; my ministry, my child(ren), my marriage, my job, my business, my health, my wellbeing.
- In this scripture we see that little with God will do more., achieve more and conquer. Father I pray let my little achieve more and become plenty and enough to achieve the task.
- Let me not despise the days of little beginning but trust You to bring increase my way.
- Your battle strategy is always the winning strategy, the strategy to conquer, the strategy to overcome, enable me to

trust Your strategy even when it does not make human sense so my victory will be assured.

- Father I will not fear, be timid, or falter, my hope and faith is in You, so I cast down every fear; I will not claim comfort over sacrifice in Jesus' Name, Amen!
- Enable me to be watchful, alert, prepared and ready to go lest the enemy come upon me.
- Father let me be usable by You and let me be the one that is needed for Your work, to do of Your good pleasure.
- Lord let me be chosen for Your assignment and for victory in Jesus' name, Amen!
- Let my sacrifices and faithfulness be rewarded for the sake of the Kingdom.
- The King's business requires haste, help me not to be slothful in the work of the Kingdom.
- The hands that cannot work for God cannot be anointed, Lord take my hands and use for Your glory.
- Enable me to be dependable and chose me for Your work Lord.
- Let me not stop at the level of being capable, let me be watchful, prepared, and available.
- Lord, enable us to be the salt of the earth and the light of the world and make impact for You.
- Enable me to do it according to Your will in Jesus' Name, Amen.

Scriptures for further Prayers:

2 Timothy 2:3-4, John 15:16

AUGUST 23

I COME QUICKLY

Worship

Today's Scripture and Meditation

Matt 25: 11-13. *He who is unjust, let him be unjust still; he who is filthy, let him be filthy still; he who is righteous, let him be righteous still; he who is holy, let him be holy still."*

12 *"And behold, I am coming quickly, and My reward is with Me, to give to everyone according to his work. 13 I am the Alpha and the Omega, the Beginning and the End, the First and the Last."*

PRAYERS:

▢ Father, I thank You because You are a gracious God.

▢ I come today repenting of any injustice I may have been involved in knowingly and unknowingly.

▢ I reject anything that catches my attention more than God and has become an idol to me, whatever takes more time from me than the time I give You, I cast down and put in the background from today.

▢ I repent of every time I have caused pain or divisions because of what I have said or done.

▢ I repent of every form of pollution caused through gossiping, backstabbing, slandering, I may have partaken in, I ask that You will be merciful unto me and cleanse me from all unrighteousness.

- ☐ Lord help me to set my affection on things above and not lose out on Your coming like the five foolish virgins.
- ☐ Holy Spirit, help me not to be deceived, enable me to put to death everything that causes my members to sin, I put to death the flesh that causes me to sin, let there be a manifestation of the death of my flesh to the world in Jesus name
- ☐ I dethrone the flesh and refuse its promptings, desires, reactions and works.
- ☐ I cast down pride, arrogance, that I may not live in bitterness, I cast down every activity and power of the flesh.
- ☐ The flesh no longer has an influence on me. Today I am delivered from the rule of flesh, I will no longer be ruled by the flesh or by the quest for popularity, I belong to Jesus and I am dead to them, from today I set my affection on Jesus.
- ☐ Give me the zeal to serve you till the end out of a pure heart and not to lose my reward.
- ☐ Enable me to continue to be righteous and to be Holy that I might receive Your reward.
- ☐ Thank You Father in Jesus name I pray. Amen.

Scriptures for further Prayers

Ephesians 4:31, Colossians 3:2

AUGUST 24

WHAT IS HE HEARING FROM YOU?

Worship

Today's Scripture and Meditation

Numbers 14:28(AMP). Say to them, 'As I live,' says the LORD, 'just what you have spoken in My hearing I will most certainly do to you.

PRAYERS:

- Father I repent of times I have lived in unbelief and haven't trusted You to take me into Your promises.
- I repent of every time I have hardened my heart and have rebelled and have tested You despite seeing Your works and miracles in my life and that of others.
- I repent of when I have gone astray in my heart and did not acknowledge Your ways and I have not been mindful of Your wonders in my life.
- I repent of when I have despised Your gift and Your promises and have grumbled and complained.
- Father, enable me enter the place of rest and promise that You have for me by faith.
- I cast down every unbelief, self-reliance, and self-focus so I can enter Your rest and abundance.
- Today, I chose to speak Your that You might perform them in my life
- That I will show forth Your praises who have translated me from the kingdom of darkness into the Kingdom of light.
- That I will manifest as a son of God to teach all creation the manifold wisdom of God.

- ▢ That I am a vessel of honour and will be used of God to root out and pull down, to destroy and to overthrow, to build and to plant.
- ▢ That Your grace be sufficient for me.
- ▢ That You will supply my needs according to Your riches in glory, spiritual needs, physical needs, marital needs, family needs, ministerial need.
- ▢ That sickness will not reign in my mortal body but that by the stripes of Jesus I am healed.
- ▢ That I will not be under any oppression, suppression or bondage of the enemy
- ▢ That You will go ahead of me and make crooked ways straight and give to me the treasures and hidden riches of darkness. *(Mention all the scriptures that pertain to any facet of life that you want God to respond)*
- ▢ That I am victorious in every battle, and I overcome because you are with me always
- ▢ Father, please d to me all that I have spoken in your ears today.
- ▢ Thank You Lord, because you are a faithful God, in Jesus Name I have prayed.

Scriptures for further Prayers

Psalm 95:7b-11, Jeremiah 1:10

AUGUST 25

SPIRITUAL ASSIMILATION

Worship

Today's Scripture and Meditation

Joshua 5:9: *Then the Lord said to Joshua, "This day I have rolled away the reproach of Egypt from you." Therefore, the name of the place is called Gilgal to this day.*

PRAYERS:

- ☐ Father Lord, I thank You for Your word.
- ☐ I surrender to You and to Your work in my life. I yield to You
- ☐ Have mercy on us Lord, I bring our heart before You for purification
- ☐ You said You will circumcise our hearts; I bring our heart before You for circumcision
- ☐ Oh Lord, roll away every stone of Egypt, either physical or spiritual
- ☐ Roll away and destroy every assimilation to Egypt in the name of Jesus; Carve it out of our hearts oh God in the name of Jesus.
- ☐ Make a difference between Egypt and ourselves
- ☐ Father show me mercy and purify my heart completely for You. Amen
- ☐ Search me Oh God and help me to become bare before You that my heart shall be circumcised
- ☐ You said "I will roll away the reproach of Egypt from". Every form of spiritual assimilation to the Egypt in any way

in my life, May the Almighty God roll it away in the mighty name of Jesus. Amen

- ☐ Whether I am conscious or unconscious, the Lord will remove and destroy every spiritual assimilation to Egypt in our lives and will put a difference between us and the people of the world in the name of our Lord Jesus Christ. Amen
- ☐ I accept the painful process of submitting to God's will knowing that I will come out on the other side shinning for him, being a true worshiper
- ☐ The reproach of Egypt is all the stigma that was with Israel throughout their relationships with Egypt. I remove such representation in my life in Jesus name
- ☐ The Inner Stigma, that feeling of humiliation, reproach and self-reproach that came upon the children of Israel because of their bondage and oppression is removed in Jesus name
- ☐ Every inner humiliation and reproach that came upon me years ago which I do not even recognise, but is informing the way I relate to people, do things and relate with God – It is uprooted in Jesus name

Scriptures for further Prayers:

Malachi 3:16-17, Isaiah 54:4a, Jeremiah 4:4a

AUGUST 26

NO MORE LABOURING IN VAIN

Worship

Today's Scripture and Meditation

Judges 6:1-6: Then the children of Israel did evil in the sight of the Lord. So, the Lord delivered them into the hand of Midian for seven years, and the hand of Midian prevailed against Israel. Because of the Midianites, the children of Israel made for themselves the dens, the caves, and the strongholds which are in the mountains.

So it was, whenever Israel had sown, Midianites would come up; also, Amalekites and the people of the East would come up against them. Then they would encamp against them and destroy the produce of the earth as far as Gaza, and leave no sustenance for Israel, neither sheep nor ox nor donkey.

For they would come up with their livestock and their tents, coming in as numerous as locusts; both they and their camels were [a]without number; and they would enter the land to destroy it. 6 So Israel was greatly impoverished because of the Midianites, and the children of Israel cried out to the Lord.

PRAYERS:

- I thank You and bless Your Holy name with praise and adoration for You are God.
- I repent of my sins and ask for forgiveness for every way in which I have sinned against You.
- I ask Lord that I will not be delivered to the enemy for punishment in Jesus Name, Amen!
- I ask that every encampment and entrapment of the enemy around my life be dismantled in Jesus' Name, Amen!
- Let the enemy not be able to lay a hand on my sustenance.
- Let my harvest not be eaten up by the enemy.
- Let my harvest not be wasted or destroyed.
- Let poverty not be my portion in Jesus name, Amen!
- Father let there be a restoration of the years that the swarming locust has eaten, the crawling locust, the consuming locust, and the chewing locust have eaten.
- Let there be a restoration of all that the thief has stolen, killed, and destroyed.
- I shall not build, and another inhabit; I shall not plant, and another eat. From now on when I sow, I will be the one reaping the fruit of multiple harvest, will not labour in vain, When I build another will not inhabit, I will be the one inhabiting, I will not put forth trouble in the Name of the Lord Jesus Christ.
- I am your elect, Father, rebuke the devourer for my sake and let me enjoy the work of my hands for long.
- According to Your word, let all those who devour me be devoured; they shall go into captivity; let the plunderer become the plundered, and all who prey upon me, You Lord will make them a prey.
- Let strangers not be filled with my wealth, and my labours not go to the house of a foreigner.
- The enemy will not plunder me or plunder my goods in the name of the Lord Jesus Christ!

- From here on, every little effort will bring forth great results in the Name.

Scriptures for further Prayers:

Proverbs 5:10,, Isaiah 65:22, Malachi 3:10-11

AUGUST 27

THANKSGIVING YOU FOR VICTORIES

Worship

Today's Scripture and Meditation

Psalm 106:10 *He saved them from the hand of him who hated them, and redeemed them from the hand of the enemy.*

PRAYERS:

- I give You all the glory for all You have done in my life, for all that You are doing right now and for Your mighty power and acts.
- The God that delivered me in time of trouble and from the hand of the enemy and from his will, You did not allow the will of the enemy to prosper.
- I worship You oh my God, the One that blesses me in the day and night. I worship You because
- You, oh God, strengthen, sustain and uphold me, You lift up my head and has not allowed shame and reproach to be my portion.
- I worship the God that nullifies the plans and counsel of the enemy for He said, speak the word and it shall come to nought.
- I worship the Lord that cancels the evil speaking of men and the enemy, I worship the Lord that delivered me from the scourge of the tongue and did not allow me to be prey to the teeth of the enemy.

- I worship the Lord that sees, hears and answers me all the time, whose everlasting arms are beneath me, so I am not let down and have not fallen.
- I worship the God that vindicates me when lies are spoken against me when there was a conspiracy and opposition, You will never allow the will of man to come to pass, nor will you allow wickedness to prosper in my life,
- You never allow the agenda of those that arose against me due to jealousy, when there was envy and evil plot of the enemy You stood for me.
- Lord, I thank You because You are the Living God, the Life and Resurrection. You have proven Yourself time and time over, like the Resurrection.
- I worship You because You raised me up, from the miry clay, from the floor when I fell, when I was sick, bound, despaired, condemned, when there was a fight, an opposition, when I was relegated to the background when I was condemned and trampled upon, looked over, forgotten, the God that raises up His children, raised me up; I worship You
- I thank You because You broke my chains, You tore down lies, You kicked down doors, You dispersed shadows so You could save me, I give You praise and honour.
- I thank You because You have not allowed the enemy to triumph over me, You uphold me with Your integrity, I am always before Your face, I thank You because You wiped my tears by day and night when the world asked where is my God, You showed up and revealed Yourself as God, shut the mouth of the lion, quenched the fire, drained the flood, and obtained glory for Yourself.
- I thank You because you are my strength, You showed up in the day of my joy, in the day of my mourning and oppression, You set me free, You brought light in my darkness.
- I thank You because You are my king, Battle Fighter, You pushed down my enemies, You trampled upon them, You are trustworthy, You put to shame those who hate me for being Your child
- I praise Your holy Name, oh God of my salvation!

▢ Thank you Lord!

Scriptures for further Prayers

Job 6:23, Isaiah 26:3, Job 5:12, Jeremiah 20:13, Psalm 106:10

AUGUST 28

PRAISE THE LORD!

Worship

Today's Scripture and Meditation

Psalm 111:1-5. Praise the Lord! With all my heart I will thank the Lord in the assembly of his people.

2 How wonderful are the things the Lord does! All who are delighted with them want to understand them.

3 All he does is full of honor and majesty; his righteousness is eternal. 4 The Lord does not let us forget his wonderful actions; he is kind and merciful. 5 He provides food for those who honor him; he never forgets his covenant.

PRAYERS:

- ⊡ I praise You with all my heart and I thank You for Your wonderful works in my life.
- ⊡ I thank You because You are full of honour and majesty because Your righteousness is eternal.
- ⊡ I will bless the Lord at all times and Your praises will continually be in my mouth.
- ⊡ Lord accept my word of praise, appreciation, and thanksgiving, from the bottom of my heart.
- ⊡ You make all manner of provision and never forget Your covenant.
- ⊡ You are faithful and just in all You do, and You are dependable.
- ⊡ You set me free and give me Your covenant.

- That I will not be influenced by physical things or relegate the Spirit of God to the background.
- Give me the grace to be upright in every situation and challenges, temptations and trials. Help me to be faithful across the board.
- Lord be gracious to me, have compassion on me. Your compassion fails not, they are new every morning.
- Lord, I thank You for Your faithfulness, Your mercies that have sustained and carried me so far.
- Lord give me the grace to fear You. Let Your fear be entrenched in my heart in Jesus' Name! Amen!
- You will arise with healing in Your wings to heal me physically and spiritually when needed
- Lord who is gracious and merciful. Let Your mercy visit me,
- Give me the grace to remain in Your covenant, that I will not break the hedge, release into my life the grace to abide in Your grace.
- The heir is not different from a slave as long as he is a child. Lord give me the grace to grow in knowledge, wisdom and understanding.
- Father give me an understanding of Your word and my circumstances. Give me the grace to act correctly so I can take possession of the heritage You have for me.
- The works of His hands are true and just. You cannot be bribed.
- Lord help me to live in truth and in justice in every situation and circumstance.
- Father I pray for every virtue and blessing You have earmarked for me, let there be no miscarriage or diversion in Jesus' Name.
- Father let Your fear be properly and completely entrenched in my heart in everything I do. Give me the grace to obey commandments.
- Lord, I thank You for the opportunity to give You continual praise for what You have done in Jesus Name! Amen!

Revive, Rebuild and Restore

Scriptures for further Prayers

Psalm 122:1, Lamentations 3:22-23, Galatians 4:1

AUGUST 29

SPIRITUAL WARFARE

Worship

Today's Scripture and Meditation

Ephesian 6:12: *For our struggle is not against flesh and blood, but against the rulers, against the authorities, against the powers of this dark world and against the spiritual forces of evil in the heavenly realms.*

PRAYERS:

- Thank You Lord that You are the Lord of hosts, mighty in battle.
- Thank You that You are with us in the raging spiritual battle that we do wrestle in against principalities and so forth.
- It is a battle we cannot fight nor ignore but by Your power less I become a casualty of the war.
- I thank You because because captain of the army of heaven who fights and wins and have never lost a battle.
- Help me to always remember that the real battle is not with flesh and blood so as not to fight people but deal with the source of all evil.
- I submit to God, as I resist the devil and his cohorts in Jesus Name.
- I bring myself under the covering of the blood of Jesus as I address all personality of darkness arrayed against me or any department of my life in Jesus Name.
- For this purpose was the son of God manifested to destroy the works of Satan.

- Today by the power of the Spirit of God, I overthrow and neutralise the bullying and the beguiling force of the enemy against me in Jesus Name.
- I bind the strongman in charge of any of the activities in my life as I take plunder of everything that the enemy has stolen from me.
- I plead the blood of Jesus to neutralise every activities of darkness in my environment, every bewitchment, spells, jinx, divination,
- I cancel by the blood of Jesus sicknesses diseases, death, premature death, marriage destroying activities, childlessness, bareness, unfruitfulness.
- I pull down the stronghold of lies, deceit, failure, delay, stagnancy, no-achievement, strife, anger, pride, hypocrisy, jealousy/envy, disobedience, rebellion.
- I command that every form of insanity, anxiety, depression, fear, paranoia, doubt, unbelief to go!
- I plead the blood to dislodge and cleanse out every satanic deposits, implantation, demon engineered diseases.
- We destroy all the wiles, his devices, his deceit, his lies, his agenda his attacks. - we are more conquerors.
- Let every chain, fetters, spiritual prisons, enclosures, snare of the enemy, the rod of the oppressor, every suppression be broken in Jesus Name.
- Every legal ground that made us lawful captives are destroyed in Jesus Name.
- Every stranger in our body, mind, spirit we command to come out of your closed places for our bodies are temples Holy Ghost
- I speak thorough spiritual cleansing in the Name of Jesus.
- Thank You Father in Jesus Name.

Scriptures for further Prayers:

1 John 3:8b, Matthew 16:19, 2 Corinthians 10:4

AUGUST 30

ARMOUR OF GOD

Worship

Today's Scripture and Meditation

Ephesians 6:13-18: *Therefore, take up the whole armor of God, that You may be able to withstand in the evil day, and having done all, to stand. Stand therefore, having girded your waist with truth, having put on the breastplate of righteousness, and having shod your feet with the preparation of the gospel of peace;*

Above all, taking the shield of faith with which, you will be able to quench all the fiery darts of the wicked one. And take the helmet of salvation, and the sword of the Spirit, which is the word of God; praying always with all prayer and supplication in the Spirit, being watchful to this end with all perseverance and supplication for all the saints.

PRAYERS:

- Father Lord thank you that You constantly fight for, defend, shield and strengthen me.
- You never sleep, slumber or go in holidays, Your eyes are constantly watching over me
- Thank you for the finished work of Calvary that grants me access to the heavenly artillery
- Today I put on the whole armour of God to guard me against the attacks and wiles of the enemy.

Revive, Rebuild and Restore

- I choose a lifestyle of honesty and integrity as a belt of truth exposing the lies and deceit that I have unconsciously believed.
- I put on Your righteousness against all temptations, accusations, condemnation, and corruption that I might be shielded from all assaults against my heart and mind.
- I put the gospel of peace on my feet, choosing a life for the gospel and taking the light of the gospel wherever You send me. I walk in the liberty that Christ has given me overcoming the devil's wiles.
- I take up the shield of faith to quench all darts and threats of the enemy against my mind and thoughts.
- I put on the helmet of salvation that grants me access to the grace of our Lord Jesus Christ and all the benefits that flow from the cross.
- I take up the sword of the Spirit, the word of God, potent to pull down strongholds, and counter every snare of the enemy. It is alive, sharper than any two-edged sword impacting both the physical and spiritual realm.
- Lord, give me grace to put on Your whole armour whole heartedly and not as a mere routine and put on me the spirit of prayer and supplication.
- Holy Spirit, I pray for constant communion with You all through the day and night that I might have constant victory in Jesus Name, Amen.

Scriptures for further Prayers:

Psalm 121:4

AUGUST 31

DIVINE MARK

Worship

Today's Scripture and Meditation:

Exodus 12:7

And they shall take some of the blood and put it on the two doorposts and on the lintel of the houses where they eat it.

Exodus 12:13

Now the blood shall be a sign for You on the houses where You are. And when I see the blood, I will pass over You; and the plague shall not be on You to destroy You when I strike the land of Egypt.

PRAYERS:

- Father we thank You for the blood of Jesus that was shed for us on the cross of Calvary and its efficacy.
- I place the blood upon the doors, gates, and every opening of my life as a mark for exemption from all sicknesses, disease and all evil.
- Prophetically, I place the blood upon the doors, gates, and every opening of my house as a mark for exemption from all sicknesses, disease and all evil.
- By the blood of Jesus, a mark of exemption from evil and devourers, flood and ravages is placed upon my life. No weapon of the enemy formed against me shall prosper.

571   *Revive, Rebuild and Restore*

- By the reason of the blood of Jesus, no evil shall befall me, and no plague shall come near my dwelling place.
- You said, You will give Egypt for my ransom. I will give people in exchange for You and nations for Your life. Father in Jesus name, based on Your word, let there be a divine substitution for my life and family.
- I am the anointed of the Lord therefore, no harm will touch me according to your word which says "Touch not my anointed and do my prophets no harm."
- You said, oh lord that everyone who steps into the spiritual office of service to the Lord benefits from this.
- Lord let the heavens place a mark on me to preserve from evil and perilous times. Father restrain any evil from coming to me because of your mark upon my life in the Name of Jesus.
- Lord destroy everything that stands as Egypt in my life in Jesus Name.
- Thank Father in Jesus name, Amen!

Scriptures for further Prayers

Isaiah 43:3, Psalm 105:15, Ezekiel 9:6.

SEPTEMBER 1

POWER OVER NATURE

Worship

Today's Scripture and Meditation

Nahum 1:3b-5. *The Lord has His way in the whirlwind and in the storm, and the clouds are the dust of His feet. 4 He rebukes the sea and makes it dry, and dries up all the rivers. Bashan and Carmel wither, And the flower of Lebanon wilts. 5 The mountains quake before Him, the hills melt, And the earth heaves at His presence, Yes, the world and all who dwell in it.*

PRAYERS:

- ⬚ I worship You the almighty God, power belongs to You in all the earth.
- ⬚ You are the creator of all things and give them instructions regarding their purposes.
- ⬚ Your power is so great that it controls the mightiest forces known to man.
- ⬚ Even a huge whirlwind or storm is nothing to You Lord, because You have Your His way in them.
- ⬚ I pray that when I go through storms, You will quieten the storms of my life.
- ⬚ You are bigger than the clouds, You rebuke the sea, and they obey. You walked on the seas and suspended all the natural laws.
- ⬚ You dry up the rivers and You spring forth rivers.
- ⬚ The mountains quake before You, the hills melt and the earth heaves at His presence, yes, the world and all who dwell in it.

Revive, Rebuild and Restore

- ⬚ Nothing is impossible for You; nothing is beyond Your power.
- ⬚ I pray that You will reveal Your unmatched supernatural ability and power in my life
- ⬚ Reveal Your power over nature and create miracles in my life.
- ⬚ Lord Jesus, I ask for Your intervention in the midst of any problems. Bring solutions into my life that only You can provide.
- ⬚ Thank you because you are a faithful God, and you are eager to bless me.
- ⬚ I give you the highest praise in Jesus name I have Prayed

Scriptures for further Prayers

Gen 1:1-3

SEPTEMBER 2

WILL GOD FORGIVE ME?

Worship

Today's Scripture and Meditation

Matthew 6:14. For if you forgive other people when they sin against you, your heavenly father will also forgive you.

PRAYERS:

- Father I thank you because you forgave all my sins, iniquities and transgressions.

- Heavenly Father, I pray Lord that You grant me the grace and the will to forgive those who hurt me.

- Father Lord, please touch my heart and help me let go of every bitterness and pains.

- Almighty God, please help me to be truthful to everyone and make amends quickly where necessary.

- I pray that nothing will hinder me from coming before Your presence.

- Lord I humbly come to You for mercy, forgive me of every short coming.

- Lord please heal Your church from every grudge and divisions amongst us.

- Father Lord please in your mercy take away pride from our lives.

- I forgive all that have offended or hurt me that I may receive forgives from the father

- For your name's sake oh Lord please cleanse us from every unrighteousness

- Make me a dispenser of forgiveness and grace to others just as I have received from You

- Thank You Father, in Jesus name. Amen! name.

Scriptures for further Prayers
1 John 2:12, MK 11:25

SEPTEMBER 3

SPEAK THE WORD

Worship

Today's Scripture and Meditation

Matthew 8:6-10. saying, "Lord, my servant is lying at home paralyzed, dreadfully tormented." 7 And Jesus said to him, "I will come and heal him." 8 The centurion answered and said, "Lord, I am not worthy that You should come under my roof. But only speak a word, and my servant will be healed. 9 For I also am a man under authority, having soldiers under me. And I say to this one, 'Go,' and he goes; and to another, 'Come,' and he comes; and to my servant, 'Do this,' and he does it." 10 When Jesus heard it, He marveled, and said to those who followed, "Assuredly, I say to you, I have not found such great faith, not even in Israel!

PRAYERS:

- Father, I thank You because Your word is Yes and Amen. What you say is what You do!
- We are grateful that You are not limited by time or distance. You send Your word, and it brings about healing and deliverance.
- Thank You because Your word carries authority and power, and You do nothing outside your word.
- Just like the Centurion, I have faith in Your authority and capacity.

▢   I thank You for the potency of Your word. I repent of times I have not believed, meditated upon, spoken or applied Your word and have relegated Your word to the background.

▢   It is by Your word that I receive divine approval, enable me to be a worthy servant and an ambassador of You

▢   That I will be approved a workman that need not be ashamed that I might grow in leaps and bounds and be able to rightly divide the word of God.

▢   Enable me to grow in Your word so I am not stagnant in my walk and my faith is not stale. Enlighten my eyes of understanding that I might gain insight into your word and grow in the knowledge of you and Your word

▢   I receive everlasting life by your word. let me always take Your word as a source of life and stay and live in Your WORD, let Your word become real to me.

▢   Let my eyes of understanding be enlightened by Your word.

▢   Let Your word abide in me that I might be fruitful and receive answers to my prayer by Your word.

▢   Let Your word be health to my [flesh, and strength[b] to my bones.

▢   Be exalted oh God, be glorified. Hallelujah to Your Name, in Jesus mighty Name I have prayed. Amen.

Scriptures for further Prayers

Psalm 107:20, Ephesians 1:18, Proverbs 3:8, 2 Timothy 2:15

SEPTEMBER 4

TAKE UP YOUR CROSS

Worship

Today's Scripture and Meditation

Matthew 16:24. Then Jesus told his disciples, "If anyone would come after me, let him deny himself and take up his cross and follow me.

PRAYERS:

- Lord I thank You for You called me to follow You, I genuinely want to follow You till the end of time
- Lord I choose to deny myself, I surrender myself to Christ and determine to obey Your will, to be others-centred, and not self-oriented
- Enable me to obey the command of the Christian life to deny self
- I choose to take up my cross to follow You; I know that taking up my cross is a one-way trip, it is death to self-promotion and self-affirmation. Help me Spirit of God to deny myself and take up my cross
- Enable me to walk by the Spirit, so as not to gratify the desires of the flesh but to put my body under subjection
- In obedience to the whisperings and the promptings of the Holy Spirit that will lead us to righteousness
- I have been set free from sin, and having become slaves of God, I will continually bear fruit to holiness.
- I chose to deny myself of worldly pleasures; I choose to
- Bear the fruit of the Spirit and manifest the fruit of the Spirit
- Not give myself to the flesh

- Let no characteristics of the world be found in me in Jesus name I Pray

Scriptures for further Prayers:

Galatians 5:16, Romans 6:22

SEPTEMBER 5

PREACH THE GOSPEL

Worship

Today's Scripture and Meditation

Nahum 1:15. (AMPC). Behold! upon the mountains the feet of him who brings good tidings [telling of the Assyrian's death], who publishes peace! Celebrate your feasts, O Judah; perform your vows. For the wicked counsellor [the king of Assyria] shall no more come against you or pass through your land; he is utterly cut off.

PRAYERS:

- Father, I thank you that You chose the simple gospel of our Lord Jesus Christ to save all men
- Father enable me to go into the world and preach the gospel! Let the work of the Kingdom be a priority to me. All shall marvel at me and what you are doing in my life and through me.
- Enable me to partner with You for the salvation of the souls of men in evangelism and discipleship.
- Thank You for making our feet beautiful, for drawing men to Yourself, thank You for making us as You are on this earth.
- Let the beauty of the Lord manifest in my soul and character.
- Enable me to commit to publishing Your gospel of peace.
- Heaven rejoices when a soul is won into the Kingdom. Lord let me be a partaker in reaping the souls of men into the kingdom.
- Direct and connect me to those You have prepared to hear the gospel.

- ⬚ Give me the words to speak in sharing the Gospel and the opportunity to share.
- ⬚ Beautify my life with Your glory for the people of the world to see.
- ⬚ Father enable me to pay my vows and not make a foolish vow.
- ⬚ Father protect me from wicked counsellors that they don't come against me in Jesus' Name.
- ⬚ Thank You Father in Jesus Name.

Scriptures for further Prayers

1 Corinthians 15:2-4, Matthew 28:19-20

SEPTEMBER 6

I SPEAK LIFE

Worship

Today's Scripture and Meditation

Number 14:28. Tell them, As I live, says the Lord, what you have said in My hearing I will do to you:

PRAYERS:

- Father I thank You because you do listen when I speak.
- Thank You for the privilege of speaking into Your ears; I will not be silent or mute but I will speak in Your ears the desire of my heart and my needs unto You by day and by night I will present my case.
- Whatever I speak in Your ears, so shall You do unto me so I refuse to speak negatives, doubts unbelief, evil with my mouth
- I speak victories in the day of temptation that - no matter how it comes or where it leads I will overcome because You will not allow me to be tempted beyond that which I can take But You will make a way of escape.
- It is with the mouth that confession is made unto salvation, therefore, I confess that it is well with me on all sides.
- Death and life are in the power of the tongue; I chose to speak life and not death.
- That I will speak things that are true, noble, pure, lovely, good report, virtuous and praise-worthy.
- I speak life into my body, spirit and soul by the power of the Holy Spirit

Revive, Rebuild and Restore

- Thank you father, in Jesus name I pray. Amen

Scriptures for further Prayers:

1 Corinthians 10:13, Proverbs 18:21, Philippians 4:8

SEPTEMBER 7

ABOUT MY THOUGHTS

Worship

Today's Scripture and Meditation

Philippians 4:8: *Finally, brothers, whatever is true, whatever is honourable, whatever is just, whatever is pure, whatever is lovely, whatever is commendable, if there is any excellence, if there is anything worthy of praise, think about these things.*

PRAYERS:

- Father Lord I present my thoughts before You, I pray that You rid me from unhelpful, negative and ungodly thoughts
- Enable me to keep my heart with all diligence, for the spring of life flows from it
- Give me the ability to control my thoughts, that my mind might be stayed on You
- I will not be double minded and unstable, but my eyes will be single, looking unto You alone
- Help me to keep my thought continually fixed on all that is authentic and real, honourable and admirable, beautiful and respectful, pure and holy, merciful and kind
- I refuse to obey the law in my members waging war against the law of my mind which may cause me to sin against You or take me captive
- I destroy every argument and every lofty opinion raised against the knowledge of God in my life, and take every thought captive to obey Christ
- I fasten my thoughts on Your glorious word, praising You always.

- ☐ I chose to think about what I am thinking. Let the Holy Spirit change my way of thinking that I will think about whatever is true, honourable, just, pure, lovely, commendable, excellent, and that which is worthy of praise in Jesus name
- ☐ Let the meditation of my heart, be acceptable in Your sight, Oh Lord, my strength, and my redeemer

Scriptures for further Prayers

James 1:8, Romans 7:23, 2 Corinthians10

SEPTEMBER 8

DON'T ENVY SINNERS

Worship

Today's Scripture and Meditation

Proverbs 23:17-18

Do not let Your heart envy sinners, But be zealous for the fear of the LORD all the day;

For surely there is a hereafter, And your hope will not be cut off.

PRAYERS:

- Father, I thank You that you are dependable; You are an extraordinary strategist, and You are a just God.
- Your ways are not my ways, and my timing is not Your timing, give me grace to wait on You.
- Grant me the grace to be content with what You have already given me knowing that You are always there for me.
- Grant me a peaceful heart that I will not seek after what others seek and I will not desire what others have.
- That nothing would attract me to the lifestyle, possession and success of sinners.
- That You will wash my mind and heart of any iota of ungodly jealousy with the blood of your Son Jesus Christ.
- That the root of jealousy be uprooted from my heart and mind in Jesus Name
- Help me to find fulfilment in Your promises and not in the things of this world. In Jesus' Name, I believe and pray, Amen.

- ▢ Let me be confident in You and in what You have the ability to do in my life.
- ▢ Enable me to be zealous for the fear of the Lord and for the will of God, that my hope will not be cut off.
- ▢ Enable me to be zealous for the house of the Lord
- ▢ Thank You Father in Jesus Name. Amen!

Scriptures for further Prayers

James 3:16, Proverb 14:30

SEPTEMBER 9

WALKING IN GOD'S COUNSEL

Worship

Today's Scripture and Meditation

Psalms 1:1. (NKJV): *Blessed is the man who walks not in the counsel of the ungodly, Nor stands in the path of sinners, Nor sits in the seat of the scornful; But his delight is in the law of the Lord, And in His law he meditates day and night. He shall be like a tree Planted by the rivers of water, That brings forth its fruit in its season, Whose leaf also shall not wither; And whatever he does shall prosper.*

PRAYERS:

- Father Lord, I thank You for giving me life today
- Father, empower me to speak, study, mediate (day and night) and be obedient to Your Word so that I will prosper and have good success
- Lord Jesus, thank You for the finished work of Calvary that made it possible for Your righteousness to be imputed unto me and to be counted among the righteous
- I receive grace not to walk in the counsel of the ungodly, nor stands in the path of sinners, nor sits in the seat of the scornful
- I receive grace to live and conduct myself in a manner that is worthy of You; that every area of my life will be pleasing unto You
- Let the whole of my desire be to please You in all things: let the words of my mouth and the meditations of my heart and the actions that I take, be acceptable in Your sight, O Lord

- Enable me to grow into maturity of godliness in mind and character, let me reach the height of virtue and integrity, as even as You are perfect
- Father enable me to be alert and, on my guard, to stand firm in my faith and in my convictions respecting Your precepts and keeping Your sound doctrine
- Enable me to delight in Your word all the days of my life
- Father God, let me experience good success in every area of my life so that Your name will be glorified in me
- Your word says that righteous shall flourish like the evergreen palm tree, Father, enable me to be independent of circumstances but give me divine grace to live and thrive where all things else perish
- Enable me to grow big, strong, durable, beautiful, incorruptible and useful like the cedar of Lebanon
- Enable me to be planted, firmly rooted and prospering in the house of the Lord
- Enable me to prosper in all I do in the family, work, calling and ministry, and in every facet of my life in Jesus name
- Let me not be lacking in physical and spiritual supply because You are my source, let me not wither away in any department of my life but enable me to bring forth much for every of my labour in its season, and to prosper in all things I do.

Scriptures for further Prayers

Psalms 92:12-14, Joshua 1:8,

SEPTEMBER 10

NO PRETENSE IN LOVE

Worship

Today's Scripture and Meditation

Romans 12:9 *"Love should be shown without pretending. Hate evil and hold on to what is good."*

PRAYERS:

- Thank You because You are the God of love, thank You because Your love is unconditional.
- Enable me to love without pretense, let my love for all men be honest and real
- That my love would not just be mere politeness but deep and not superficial.
- That my love will run deeper than sentiments and emotions.
- That love will proceed from my heart and then further expressed in my actions.
- That I will do all things in love no matter who I am relating with.
- Enable me to hate every evil work, and to hold on to that which is good.
- That I will remain in love that I may remain in God and God will remain in me.

Scriptures for further Prayers:

1 Corinthians 16:14, 1 John 4:16

SEPTEMBER 11

BREAK THE YOKE

Worship

Today's Scripture and Meditation

Isaiah 10:27 It shall come to pass in that day that his burden will be taken away from Your shoulder, And his yoke from Your neck, And the yoke will be destroyed because of the anointing oil.

PRAYERS:

- Father I thank You for You are gracious and You are long suffering towards us. You do not leave us nor forsake us even when we deserve it, but You always bring comfort
- Father help me to always depend on an You and not look for help where there is no help because You are a dependable God
- Father help me to solve every problem I have put myself in while looking for help from man and preserve me in Jesus' Name, Amen!
- Father You have the power to put an end to anything that does not bring glory to Your name in my life so, have Your way lord and bring Your will to pass in my life in Jesus Name, Amen!
- I thank You because You will never leave Your people at the mercy of the enemy, and I trust You because You are in charge.
- Father, please take away every burden upon my shoulder by the reason of the anointing oil depicting You are the Source of my victory and freedom.

- Father break every yoke from my neck by Your anointing and burst my bonds asunder that I might be free indeed.
- Enable me to stand fast in the liberty by which Christ has made us free, and not be entangled again with a yoke of bondage in Jesus Name, Amen!
- Thank You Father in Jesus Name I pray, Amen!

Scriptures for further Prayers:

Jeremiah 2:20, Nahum 1:13, Galatians 5:1

SEPTEMBER 12

FEAR NOT

Worship

Today's Scripture and Meditation

Isaiah 41:10-15(AMPC) *Fear not [there is nothing to fear], for I am with you; do not look around you in terror and be dismayed, for I am your God. I will strengthen and harden you to difficulties, yes, I will help you; yes, I will hold you up and retain you with My [victorious] right hand of rightness and justice. Behold, all they who are enraged and inflamed against you shall be put to shame and confounded; they who strive against you shall be as nothing and shall perish.*

You shall seek those who contend with you but shall not find them; they who war against you shall be as nothing, as nothing at all. For I the Lord your God hold your right hand; I am the Lord, Who says to you, Fear not; I will help you! Fear not, you worm Jacob, You men of Israel! I will help you, says the Lord; your Redeemer is the Holy One of Israel. Behold, I will make you to be a new, sharp, threshing instrument which has teeth; you shall thresh the mountains and beat them small, and shall make the hills like chaff.

PRAYERS:

- Thank You for You are my help that I receive every moment.
- I acknowledge that You have all power over all.
- Thank You for the Your presence in my life that gives me courage. I am not moved by what I see because You are with me.
- I will not be afraid, I cannot be dismayed.

- I will not look around in terror, no evil shall befall us or plague near my dwelling in the Name of the Lord Jesus Christ!
- Father uphold and retain me with Your victorious right hand of my righteousness and justice. I receive divine help, assistance, and breakthrough from You!
- Put to shame all that are enraged and are contending physically and spiritually against my life, my purpose, my calling that they be no more.
- I shall be established in righteousness and conformity to the way of God.
- I shall be far away from every oppression and disruption and every terror.
- No evil or terror shall come near our dwelling in the Name of the Lord Jesus Christ!
- I shall not fear because the Almighty God is on my side and the Lord of host who never loses any battle is fighting on my side!
- It does not matter the evidence I see around me right now I am victorious in Jesus' Name, Amen!
- The everlasting arm of the Lord is holding me up, so I shall not be moved, dislocated, or dislodged or let down.
- Nothing will be pulling and pushing me down, the Almighty is fighting and winning battles for my sake; I will not doubt, or despair nor weep for the enemy.
- I arise in the place of victory where God has placed me. I have overcome, I have won the battle.
- Oh Lord help! Redeem me from everything plaguing me. Manifest Your redemption in every department of our lives.
- Thank You for a season of turning us into immovable and unshakable people that You can use as instruments in Your house.
- We surrender to You and yield to Your hands. Make me into a new instrument to thrash and make the hills as small.
- To dismantle the enemy, make me an instrument of honour and war in our generation. Use us for Your glory.
- I do not fear to work for You because You are not like the rulers of the world.

- I praise You for the things You want to do in our lives. I will not fear but wait on You.
- Do a work that none can reverse in Jesus' Name Amen!

Scriptures for further Prayers:

Psalm 91:9-19, Isaiah 54:14

SEPTEMBER 13

SEEKING HIM WITH MY HEART

Worship

Today's Scripture and Meditation

Jeremiah 29:13: *And you will seek Me and find Me, when you search for Me with all your heart.*

PRAYERS:

- My Saviour and Redeemer, early in the morning do I seek Your face
- I turn my heart unto You. Oh Lord, that I might discover You in my every day of my life
- Father, I thank You that You know me, You know my reins, You know my thoughts, You hear me when I speak, and You see my actions. Lord, I want to know You more
- That I may know You Lord, let me know the extent of Your love, kindness, mercy, and grace
- I seek to know what You have intended me to be and to know what I should be doing
- I seek to be guided by You. Lord direct my steps one step at a time - always closer to You
- Lord fill me with Your light and life, Your grace and mercy, Your love and power.
- Let my hearts draw near to You today. I seek You with all my heart because I know that my desires are found and fulfilled in You.
- Enable me to serve You with wholehearted devotion and with a willing mind, for You search every heart and understand every motive behind the thoughts.

- ⬚ I say yes to Your call, Your bidding, Your will, Your purpose, Your whole counsel. Oh Lord reveal Yourself to me today as we seek Your face, Lord
- ⬚ Without You my life loses its zeal, and my doing loses its meaning and purpose
- ⬚ Help me to know Your voice and respond when You call; fill my life with seeking and knowing You more
- ⬚ Father Let me hear You when You speak, for You will speak peace to me, let me not turn back to folly
- ⬚ As I call to You, Lord answer me, and tell me great and hidden things that I had have not known

Scriptures for further Prayers

Psalm 85:8, 1 Chronicles 28:9

SEPTEMBER 14

SEEK THE LORD

Worship

Today's Scripture and Meditation

Zephaniah 2:3 (NLT): Seek the Lord, all who are humble, and follow his commands. Seek to do what is right and to live humbly. Perhaps even yet the Lord will protect you - protect you from his anger on that day of destruction.

PRAYERS:

- ⍰ I worship and adore You. I am awestruck by who You are. You are light and life, grace and mercy, just and right, and filled with love and power
- ⍰ I seek Your face, let my heart draw near to You. You said we should seek You first and this is all I want to do Lord. I seek You with all our hearts because I know that my desires are found in and will be fulfilled in You
- ⍰ As the deer pants for the water brooks so I pant after You Lord. I thirst for You and want to be filled by You
- ⍰ I surrender all to You and give everything to You just to know You more, Lord. You desire a relationship and so I say, Yes Lord!
- ⍰ Reveal Yourself to me afresh. As I seek Your face. Let me find You
- ⍰ I need to know You personally, face-to-face as Moses did - the real You, not some image I already picture I have had in my mind
- ⍰ I want to do more than lip service to You, I want to know, love and obey You

Revive, Rebuild and Restore

- Father Lord, I pray that pride and vanity will not get in the way of Your kingdom being built in my life. That I will not think of myself more highly than I should. I pray You will grant me humility. I pray that Your gifts in my life will be used to bring glory to You, not myself
- Father, I ask that You put eternity into my heart, that I would be heavenly minded. Let me live my life with more purpose and on a mission with You
- Lord, let me see this earth as a temporary abode and let my heart be at home in You alone
- Father help me to be humble, patient, and gentle. Grant me strength to bear with others and to love unconditionally. Help me to obey Your commands and do what is right before You

Scriptures for further Prayers

Romans12:3-7, James 4:14, Ephesians 4:1-3

Revive, Rebuild and Restore

SEPTEMBER 15

GOD IS MY REFUGE

Worship

Today's Scripture and Meditation

Nahum 1:7: The LORD is good, a strong refuge when trouble comes. He is close to those who trust in him

PRAYERS:

- Lord, You are good, You are kind, You are strong and powerful. I cannot praise You enough, I owe You my life
- You are the defender of the weak and the one that protects us
- I just want to say You are my shield, my strength, my portion, deliverer, my shelter, strong tower, My very present help in time of need
- Let me know You as my refuge in this troubled world, the nations are troubled, the towns and cities are troubled, the church is troubled, the families are troubled, individuals are troubled. Father be my refuge in these days of trouble in Jesus name
- Lord Let me know Your closeness, let us know the warmth of Your embrace, let me know the warmth of Your presence
- Enable me to dwell in Your secret place and abide under the shadow of Your covering
- Enable me to fully and perfectly trust in You, that I will not panic, that I will not be fearful and that I will not despair

Revive, Rebuild and Restore

- My life is hidden in Christ and Christ in God, nothing can touch me physically, spiritually, emotionally
- I trust in You Lord, draw me close to You, no one else can do what You do for me
- Thank You for being my Lord, thank You for being a consuming fire
- Thank You for being our protector
- Blessed be Your name oh God, Hallelujah to Your name, in Jesus mighty name I have prayed, Amen

Scriptures for further Prayers:

Jeremiah 17:7, Psalm 46:1, Psalm 91:4, 9

SEPTEMBER 16

IDENTITY

Worship

Today's Scripture and Meditation

Numbers 13:30-33. Then Caleb quieted the people before Moses, and said, "Let us go up at once and take possession, for I am well able to overcome it."

But the men who had gone up with him said, "I am not able to go up against the people, for they are stronger than we." And they gave the children of Israel a bad report of the land which they had spied out, saying, "The land through which I have gone as spies is a land that devours its inhabitants, and all the people whom I saw in it are men of great stature. There I saw the giants (the descendants of Anak came from the giants); and We were like grasshoppers in our own sight, and so We were in their sight."

PRAYERS:

- Father, I thank You that You made me unique in Your image; fearfully and wonderfully made. Thank You that You adopted me into Your family, and I am Your child
- Father let me know You as a loving father and grow in understanding of this reality in my heart
- Let me continually have the assurance of Your love and care in my heart so that I might fulfil Your will, my calling and purpose in life without fear.

- My identity is in You and in the finished work of Calvary, I chose to see myself as You see me; not as man sees me or the system has placed on me
- Father unlock my heart that I may fully understand my identity in You. That I might not be swayed by the destructive lies of the enemy
- Father let every stronghold of images of my past informing my identity and causing unbelief and doubt about the love of God and His faithfulness to His promises be pulled down
- I arise to take possession of all that God has given to me for I am well able to overcome.
- I am loved by God, I belong to God, I am chosen by God, and I am forgiven by God. I have an eternal purpose and I have an inheritance in Christ
- Let the language and values and customs and expectations of this world increasingly feel foreign to us
- Thank You for my Identity in You, in Jesus glorious name

Scriptures for further Prayers:

Ephesians 1:8, Colossians 1:12, 1John 3:1

SEPTEMBER 17

LOOK UPON ME WITH MERCY

Worship

Today's Scripture and Meditation:

Psalm 119:132 *Look upon me, and be merciful unto me, as You use to do unto those that love Your name.*

PRAYERS:

- Heavenly Father, I thank You Lord Jesus, in Jesus mighty Name I pray.
- Looking to Christ is the way of salvation but when You look upon me with mercy, it is a great blessing.
- Thank You because You have a custom, a pattern of looking toward those who love Your name. Father give attention to me today in Jesus name, Amen.
- Your custom of showing mercy on those who love Your name is a solid ground for trusting You and coming boldly before You in prayer. Halleluyah!
- Lord I love Your name, Your person, Your character, Your glory, be merciful unto me and order my steps in Your word!
- Father have mercy on me because I love Your name, let mercy manifest in my life; I activate the covenant of mercy in my life. Amen!
- Whenever I have sinned against You or come short of Your glory Lord, show Your abundant mercy.
- Grant mercy in place of judgment in the Name of Jesus. Let mercy open those doors in the Name of Jesus.

Revive, Rebuild and Restore

- Let the doors that look like they will not open, be opened today by the reason of Your mercy, let those doors open in miraculous ways in the name of Jesus.
- Lord, give me liberty in loving and serving you in Jesus Name

Scriptures for further Prayers

Exodus 20:6, Numbers 14:18

SEPTEMBER 18

FACE TO FACE WITH GOD

Worship

Today's Scripture and Meditation

Numbers 12:6-8: *Hear now My words: If there is a prophet among you, I, the Lord, make Myself known to him in a vision; I speak to him in a dream. Not so with My servant Moses. He is faithful in all My house.*

I speak with him face to face, even plainly, and not in dark sayings; And he sees the form of the Lord. Why then are you not afraid, To speak against My servants?"

PRAYERS:

- Father Lord, I thank You that You do not leave us blind. You said in Your word that You will do nothing without revealing Your plan to Your servant the prophets.
- Thank You for calling me Your servant and ordaining me as Your mouthpiece
- Thank You for not leaving us to be without a vision or without a dream
- Father Lord, I thank You for showing what is good and what You require of me in Your word
- Teach me Lord, not to forget Your blessings that You have shown me no matter what trials await me tomorrow
- Lord, help me cling to You as my anchor. Help me remember Your steadfast love for me and faithfulness to me in all things in Jesus Name, Amen

Revive, Rebuild and Restore

- Father help me to be faithful in all Your house; help me to be faithful in love, giving, in ministry, in service, in holiness, and in relationship
- Father, please help me to faithfully serve You and care for other people. Do not let me practice eye-service
- Father show me how best I can serve You, and how to offer an acceptable sacrifice unto You. I choose to honour You always
- Father help me to serve You without ulterior motives, let me be sincere with my gifts, and let my service come from a pure heart
- Let my sacrifices of thanksgiving be acceptable unto You, and enable me to offer consistent services to You, so that I can be qualified to receive Your reward
- Open the eyes of my heart Lord, I want to see You
- Father, I desire intimacy with You. Lord draw me close to You. I want to hear Your voice so that You may speak to me plainly and not in dark sayings
- Give me grace not to speak against Your servants and those in authority over me but that I will believe in You and also believe in Your prophets so that I may prosper in all Your ways

Scriptures for further Prayers

Amos 3:7, 2 Chronicles 20:20b, 1 Corinthians 1:27a

SEPTEMBER 19

THE SECRET OF THE LORD

Worship

Today's Scripture and Meditation

> *Psalm 25:12-15. Who is the man that fears the Lord? Him shall He teach in the way He chooses. He himself shall dwell in prosperity, And his descendants shall inherit the earth. The secret of the Lord is with those who fear Him, And He will show them His covenant. My eyes are ever toward the Lord, For He shall pluck my feet out of the net.*

PRAYERS:

- Father, I worship before You in the splendour of His Holiness, I stand in awe of You, You are the Almighty God!
- I stand in awe of Your majesty, power, wisdom, justice and mercy, I see You in Your glory and I humble myself before You.
- I approach the throne of grace today with this reverent fear that I might worship in truth and spirit
- Lord let Your referent fear come upon me afresh in the name of the Lord Jesus Christ, Amen.
- God of heaven, I choose to fear the Lord that I might apply my heart to wisdom
- Enable me to walk circumspectly, walking in the fear of the Lord
- That I will walk the path of the fear of the Lord, in all things oh God, I do, I will fear the Lord

- In the thought I allow to linger in our heart and mind, I will fear the Lord in them, in the name of the Lord Jesus Christ, Amen.
- Reveal Your secrets to me Lord for I fear You
- My eyes are turned towards You oh God, this morning
- I choose oh God to put away whatever it is that has stood as a god in my life
- Lord, I choose to serve You in spirit and in truth; Lord teach me the way You have chosen, let me dwell in prosperity, let my generation present and to come to inherit the earth and let Your secret be with me, oh Lor
- Lord show me Your covenant and release into my life the covenant rights and blessings
- Father pluck my feet out of the net, pluck my feet out of every trap of the enemy and out of everything the enemy has planted
- I bow before You to acknowledge You as Lord and Saviour of my life, I praise You for Your might, Your sovereignty, Your power, Your strength, Your mercy, and Your justice. I stand in awe of You, surrendering my heart to You and I put You first in my life in Jesus name.

Scriptures for further Prayers:

Joshua 24: 14, Psalm 33:8, Proverbs 9:10

SEPTEMBER 20

ARE YOU RUNNING WISELY?

Worship

Today's Scripture and Meditation

Matt 25:1-13. Then the kingdom of heaven shall be likened to ten virgins who took their lamps and went out to meet the Bridegroom. 2 Now five of them were wise, and five were foolish. 3 Those who were foolish took their lamps and took no oil with them, 4 but the wise took oil in their vessels with their lamps. 5 But while the bridegroom was delayed, they all slumbered and slept.

6 "And at midnight a cry was heard: 'Behold, the bridegroom [a]is coming; go out to meet him!' 7 Then all those virgins arose and trimmed their lamps. 8 And the foolish said to the wise, 'Give us some of your oil, for our lamps are going out.' 9 But the wise answered, saying, 'No, lest there should not be enough for us and you; but go rather to those who sell, and buy for yourselves.' 10 And while they went to buy, the bridegroom came, and those who were ready went in with him to the wedding; and the door was shut.

11 "Afterward the other virgins came also, saying, 'Lord, Lord, open to us!' 12 But he answered and said, 'Assuredly, I say to you, I do not know you.'13 "Watch therefore, for you know neither the day nor the hour [b]in which the Son of Man is coming.

PRAYERS:

- Father Lord, I honour You because You are my Lord and the Bridegroom of the church.
- Father, I am grateful that You have not left me here forever but You are coming back for me.
- Father let me be ready for Your coming, that I will not be a hypocrite, appearing to be ready while I am not.
- Give me oil in my lamp, keep me burning till the end of the day.
- I open my heart only to Your Spirit, the Holy Spirit that raised Jesus from the dead, I give You the right to influence my life and circumstances, I give You the right of way, the only One to influence my heart and spirit, I give you unrestricted access.
- Oil gives lights when it is burned in a lamp; When the Holy Spirit is present, there is light, Father let your light shine in me and through me in Jesus Name.
- Oil warms when it is used as fuel for a flame; Holy Spirit of God be my fuel, let me feel the warmth of your love and bring comfort in times of need.
- Oil adorns when applied as a perfume; –Holy Spirit of God, I pray that You will adorn me and make me a fragrance of Your knowledge in every place.
- Oil heals– Holy Spirit of God please bring healing and restoration into my life and through me to others in Jesus Name.
- Oil polishes when used to shine metal; Holy Spirit please wipe away grime from my life and smoothen out all my rough edges.
- Father, let me be constantly filled with the Spirit that I will not run out of oil on the day of Your appearing in Jesus Name.
- That I might not be weak, defeated and lethargic in my spiritual life.
- Father let nothing or no one take or catch my attention more than You.
- Let me not miss the marriage supper of the lamb, let the door not be shut against me.

▪ The price for failing to be ready is severe, Father, let me not be rejected but I will be known of You in the day of Your appearing.

Scriptures for further Prayers

2 Corinthians 2:14, Luke 10:34, Ephesians 5:18

SEPTEMBER 21

WISE MEN

Worship

Today's Scripture and Meditation

Matthew 2:1-2. *Now after Jesus was born in Bethlehem of Judea in the days of Herod the king, behold, [a]wise men from the East came to Jerusalem, 2 saying, "Where is He who has been born King of the Jews? For we have seen His Star in the East and have come to worship Him."*

PRAYERS:

- Father Lord, I thank and praise You because You know all things and You are wiser than all.
- I thank You because from the foundations of the world You have written the days of my life and have ordained me for my calling and assignment.
- I pray that no wise man would be able to read my star and know the details of my life.
- That no wise man will give the enemy information to use against me.
- Lord, I pray that You will deal with monitoring spirits and those monitoring me to cause harm or delay my purpose in God.
- I pray that the enemy will not have an in-road into my life.
- I take refuge in the rock of ages, Lord, arise and scatter every operation of monitoring spirits.
- I pray and cast down every evil altar, every monitoring spirit within our houses get out in the Name of the Lord Jesus!
- Monitoring spirits of my health, marriage, success, education of my children, be destroyed!

- ▢ Let every object used to monitor my life in the dark be shattered.
- ▢ Through the blood of Jesus let every divination, enchantment, jinx and bewitchment me be made null and void.
- ▢ Le all Information gathered against me be useless and let the wisdom of the wise men be turned into foolishness.
- ▢ I command a stop to every informed work of darkness, I receive total deliverance and liberty to serve You all my life.
- ▢ Thank you Lord for answering my Prayers for in Jesus Name I have prayed. Amen!

Scriptures for further Prayers

Isaiah 44:25b, Exodus 33:22

Revive, Rebuild and Restore

SEPTEMBER 22

FOLLOW ME

Worship

Today's Scripture and Meditation

Matthew 4:19. And he saith unto them, follow me, and I will make you fishers of men.

PRAYERS:

- Thank You, Lord, for calling me Your own, thank You Jesus.
- You said to deny myself take up my cross and follow You, Father I pray that You will enable me to deny myself of all the pleasures of this world, of fame, ambition and vision to take up Yours.
- Father enable me to take my relationship with You as a priority over other relationships with family, friends, etc.
- Oh Lord I choose to answer to Your call, I choose to follow You.
- Help me to carry my cross, ignoring everything and concentrating on You and my life in You.
- Lord I yield to You, use me to win souls to Your Kingdom.
- Almighty God I ask of Your help that my life will draw men to You.
- I ask for the grace to follow You till the end in the mighty
- Thank you father, in Jesus name I pray. Amen

Scriptures for further Prayers:

Matthew 10:37, Matt 28:18-20

SEPTEMBER 23

SPIRITUAL BLINDNESS

Worship

Today's Scripture and Meditation

Numbers 22:31-34(NIV). Then the Lord opened Balaam's eyes, and he saw the angel of the Lord standing in the road with his sword drawn. So, he bowed low and fell facedown.32 The angel of the Lord asked him, "Why have you beaten your donkey these three times? I have come here to oppose you because your path is a reckless one before me. [a] 33 The donkey saw me and turned away from me these three times. If it had not turned away, I would certainly have killed you by now, but I would have spared it."

34 Balaam said to the angel of the Lord, "I have sinned. I did not realize you were standing in the road to oppose me. Now if you are displeased, I will go back."

PRAYERS:

- ▢ Oh Lord, I pray that when I have sinned against You, when I have gone on my own way, please forgive me Lord.
- ▢ Lord, show me mercy, please forgive all my wrongs doings
- ▢ Father Lord, please heal me of every spiritual blindness
- ▢ Grant me eyes to see into the supernatural, through visions, dreams, etc
- ▢ Open my eyes to see You and enable me to sense Your presence

Revive, Rebuild and Restore

- ⯈ Open my eyes to see that
- ⯈ Father, please draw me back from every wrong step I am about to take no matter how right it seems in my own eyes.
- ⯈ Deliver me oh lord from every reckless path.
- ⯈ Let my senses not be dulled but let me be sensitive to the Spirit of God
- ⯈ Let me not be conceited or proud or assume that I know
- ⯈ Let me keep short accounts with you, daily examining that I am still in the faith
- ⯈ Oh Lord in Your mercy please spare my life and forgive me.
- ⯈ Thank You Father in Jesus Name.

Scriptures for further Prayers

Genesis 28: 12-17, 2 Kings 6:17

SEPTEMBER 24

BROKEN WALLS

Worship

Today's Scripture and Meditation

Proverbs 25:28

A man without self-control is like a city broken into and left without walls.

PRAYERS:

- Lord, that I will not be without self-control, let me not be left without defence like a city that's broken into.
- Lord that our lives oh God, will not be left in danger in the Name of the Lord Jesus Christ. Amen.
- That harm would not come to us, that the enemy would not be able to kill, steal, or destroy and that peace and prosperity will be our portion, in the Name of the Lord Jesus Christ!
- Self-control helps us to control and check our wills and regulates our conduct. Let me not be swayed by my appetites in Jesus name
- Lord enable me to be self-controlled that I will be kept from evil and danger!
- I will not be left vulnerable, defenceless, without protection, or without security.
- I will not self-indulge or self-destruct in the Name of the Lord Jesus!
- Holy Spirit I give You the right of way to interrupt and invade my life. I pray that you work in me to bear fruits.

- Fill my life with Your presence, instructions and enablement in the Name of the Lord Jesus Christ! Amen
- Lord, enable me to cultivate an intimacy with You that spiritual fruits might be born in me.
- I will not run aimlessly in the Name of Jesus! I will not be boxing like those who are beating the air in the Name of the Lord Jesus Christ!
- Grant unto me this virtue to be able to control my appetites or keep my appetite in check. Oh God, in the Name of the Lord Jesus Amen!
- Father I pray that You break the power of every addiction in my life in the name of Jesus!
- Father break the power of common addictions like addiction to television, food, alcohol, sex, pornography, spending, drugs including prescribed medications, gambling, grumbling and complaining, quarrelling, internet games, laziness and slothfulness, loafing, oversleeping, etc in Jesus' name, Amen!
- I bring myself to Your secret place and under Your cover, let my walls not be broken in Jesus Name, Amen!

Scriptures for further Prayers

2 Samuel 11:1-4, 2 Kings 5:20-23

SEPTEMBER 25

HEALING IN HIS WINGS

Worship:

Today's Scripture and Meditation:

Malachi 4:2-4.

> *But to You who fear My name The Sun of Righteousness shall arise with healing in His wings; And You shall go out and grow fat like stall-fed calves.[3] You shall trample the wicked, for they shall be ashes under the soles of your feet On the day that I do this," Says the Lord of hosts.*

PRAYERS:

- Heavenly Father I thank You for moments like this when I can express my deep gratitude for Your protection and preservation of my life.
- I give You the glory and honour due to Your name; for where would I be if You were not with me?
- You are the sun of righteousness that brings healing in Your wings, let Your healing infuse our lives, removing the negative impact of sin.
- Father, enable me to enjoy Your freedom and liberty as obtained on the cross, to grow strong and prosperous in You and to enjoy all round victory.
- Father, send Your word to heal me and deliver me from any destruction, let Your word bring healing, health, and deliverance to my body in order to rescue me from destruction.

621   *Revive, Rebuild and Restore*

- According to Your word, "Heal me, Lord, and I will be healed; save me and I will be saved, for You are the one I praise."
- I declare Your word this morning that "by the stripes of Jesus I am healed."
- Let power flow from Your presence into my life to bring healing. I receive grace to receive my healing and command my body to receive healing in Jesus' name, Amen.

Scriptures for further Prayers

Luke 6:19, Psalms 107:20, Jeremiah 17:14.

SEPTEMBER 26

THANKING GOD FOR DELIVERANCES

Worship

Today's Scripture and Meditation

Psalm 124:1-8, *"If it had not been the Lord who was on our side,"*

Let Israel now say – 2 "If it had not been the Lord who was on our side, when men rose up against us, 3 Then they would have swallowed us alive, when their wrath was kindled against us;

4 Then the waters would have overwhelmed us, The stream would have [a]gone over our soul;

5 Then the swollen waters would have [b]gone over our soul."6 Blessed be the Lord,

Who has not given us as prey to their teeth. 7 Our soul has escaped as a bird from the snare of the [c]fowlers; The snare is broken, and we have escaped. 8 Our help is in the Name of the Lord, Who made heaven and earth.

PRAYERS:

- Father God I thank You for Your deliverance and protection
- Thank God for delivering me from the hand of the enemy, and not allowing him to consume me.

- Thank you for not giving me as prey to the teeth of the enemy, so that I can worship You,
- I bless You for being there when men rose up against me; you did not allow them to swallow me alive.
- You have not allowed the waters of life to overflow me
- Your will not allow the fire burn me or its flame to scorch me
- Thank the Lord, because my soul has escaped, as a bird from the snare of the fowler,
- I thank the Lord because this snare is broken, and we have escaped.
- I thank the Lord because He is my helper.
- I bless His holy Name, I worship and adore You for Your great deliverance in my life and family.
- Thank You for You have preserved and kept me alive,
- Thank You for You have strengthened me in the day of battle, and You have already given me
- victories on all sides.
- I thank the Lord because He is my deliverer,
- Lord for You delivered me from evil speaking.
- Oh God for You delivered me from the wickedness of man, from every crime, gun crime, knife crime, thieves, robbers, kidnappers and terrorism.
- You delivered from terrible diseases. (if applicable)
- You have delivered me oh God from all manner of disabilities, and its effect
- Thank You for turning trouble into triumph.
- Thank you for you broke bondages, fetters you broke the gates of brass and iron gates
- You broke the everlasting doors, You lifted me up and You came through for me.
- I thank You oh God and submit my life to You all the days of my life because You have the ability to keep it.
- Father enable me to serve only You, to worship, only You, to adore only You by the power of your Spirit all the days of my life
- Oh God, I worship You, I adore you, I magnify Your holy Name.
- Thank You heavenly Father.

▢   Blessed be Your Name oh God, hallelujah to Your Name. In Jesus mighty Name.

Scriptures for further Prayers

Luke 1:74-75, Isaiah 43:2

SEPTEMBER 27

TAKE OFF THE CHARIOT'S WHEEL

Worship

Today's Scripture and Meditation

Exodus 12:5-7; 24-25. *Now it was told the king of Egypt that the people had fled, and the heart of Pharaoh and his servants was turned against the people; and they said, "Why have we done this, that we have let Israel go from serving us?" 6 So he made ready his chariot and took his people with him. 7 Also, he took six hundred choice chariots, and all the chariots of Egypt with captains over every one of them.* ....

24 Now it came to pass, in the morning watch, that the LORD looked down upon the army of the Egyptians through the pillar of fire and cloud, and He troubled the army of the Egyptians. 25 And He took off their chariot wheels, so that they drove them with difficulty; and the Egyptians said, "Let us flee from the face of Israel, for the LORD fights for them against the Egyptians."

PRAYERS:

- Father I thank you for your power to save and to deliver
- I pray that whatever is contending against freedom, advancement, redirection, worshipping of God in my life be confounded, silenced, and destroyed in Jesus name
- Every gathering together of the enemy in armour, in weapon, in strategy, in systems, in church against my children, be scattered.in the physical and/or spiritual.

- Father make a complete end to every affliction of the past that it will not rise again
- Let me not be afraid but rather look unto God my helper in all circumstances
- Lord, slow down the advancement of the enemy against me
- Let the enemy be afraid and flee before me because of my God
- Father give me total victory that I will no longer see the enemy I see today ever again
- Thank you father, in Jesus name. Amen

Scriptures for further Prayers:

Isaiah 8:9-10, Nahum 1:9

SEPTEMBER 28

PRAISE AND ACKNOWLEDGE HIM

Worship

Today's Scripture and Meditation

Psalm 136:1: *Oh, give thanks to the Lord, for He is good! For His mercy endures forever.*

PRAYERS:

- Father Lord, You are worthy. I will declare Your name to My brethren; in the midst of the assembly I will praise You.
- Oh, give thanks to the Lord, for He is good! For His mercy endures forever. Who can utter the mighty acts of the Lord? Who can declare all His praise?
- For you are the almighty God, great God among other gods.
- I am grateful that You do not lie, or You are not a wicked God. I know that we do not seek You in vain.
- Thank You for releasing Your presence into my life daily, and for revealing Your glory.
- Thank You for the word that You have open unto me giving me understanding.
- You said will proclaim Your name through me, though I am frail, You will put Your power nme
- Father put Your name upon me and put Your power in me to perform signs and wonders before You.
- I am so undeserving of Your mercy, grace and power yet You pour Your power upon me because You use the foolish things to confound the wise.

- Lord release the fullness of joy into my life, reveal Your goodness Your mercy and let me see Your glory.
- Let Your presence go before me and give me rest, Let me not walk according to the wisdom of men, but according to Your power.
- Oh Lord I receive Your power and presence in an unusual measure.
- I receive Your rest, I receive rest in my family, I receive rest in my ministry. I receive rest in the work of my hands, I receive rest for my family.
- Lord lead me into all truth, I receive Your secrets that You are releasing unto me and, I receive Your goodness that You have released.
- That I will not receive the grace of God in vain.
- Lord, let them manifest for the Glory of Your Name, such that the whole world will know that Your presence is with me.
- That those that despise me will see the Almighty God and is presence upon my life.
- Give me grace to walk in Your presence, let me not do anything that will grieve the Holy Spirit of God.
- Father Lord, we praise You, we worship You, we magnify Your holy Name.
- Lord, continue to glorify Yourself in my life and continue to keep me in that place of humility, Lord that I will never go out of my r place of divine positioning.
- Blessed be Your name oh God, in Jesus' Name we have prayed

Further Praying Scriptures.

Psalm 106:2, Psalm 22:22

SEPTEMBER 29

WHEN GOD FIGHTS

Worship

Today's Scripture and Meditation

Exodus 14:21: *Then Moses stretched out his hand over the sea; and the Lord caused the sea to go back by a strong east wind all that night, and made the sea into dry land, and the waters were divided. So the children of Israel went into the midst of the sea on the dry ground, and the waters were a wall to them on their right hand and on their left. And the Egyptians pursued and went after them into the midst of the sea, all Pharaoh's horses, his chariots, and his horsemen*

Now it came to pass, in the morning watch, that the Lord looked down upon the army of the Egyptians through the pillar of fire and cloud, and He troubled the army of the Egyptians. And He took off their chariot wheels, so that they drove them with difficulty; and the Egyptians said, "Let us flee from the face of Israel, for the Lord fights for them against the Egyptians."

PRAYERS:

- Father Lord, I worship You today as the Almighty God Who fights our battle, our victorious Lord!
- You are jealous for Your children and can do anything to save and protect them.
- I worship You God because You are great in power, great in mercy

Revive, Rebuild and Restore

- You are great in glory and great in battle. You always win, the victorious God today I turn over the battles of my life to You.
- Father I ask that You stop the advancement of anything that pursues me physically and spiritually, bodily or in my soul and spirit in Jesus' Name, Amen!
- Father God I pray that You will miraculously work and fight on my behalf against the enemy.
- That You will trouble the cohorts of the enemy and anything that stands for Egypt in my life.
- I receive freedom from every unrelenting, aggressive pursuer and every long-standing issue in the Name of Jesus.
- Grant me grace to cross to the other side of the sea, no delay, no stopping, and no stagnancy in Jesus Name, Amen!
- Father I pray that whatever I need to do to connect to the manifestation of my miracles and breakthrough to manifest please reveal to me and instruct me in Jesus Name, Amen.
- As Pharaoh never troubled Israel after this incident, let this season be the season of final victory over every area of my life where there is oppression or no sustained freedom and breakthrough in Jesus Name, Amen,
- Today I walk on dry land, the water shall not overflow me because You are with me.
- Lord as You are working in my life this season let me know and recognize it.
- Though the pressure of my trial is almost unbearable, let me see that the "Egyptian" is dead and that this is the dawn of joy!
- Let the enemy of my salvation, my purpose in You, my wellbeing, my family, my health, my ministries, my business be drowned in Jesus Name, Amen.
- The yoke that burdens, and the rod of the oppressor is shattered in my life.
- That the Egyptians I see in my life today, I will see them no more again in the mighty Name of Jesus, I am free indeed.
- Thank You Heavenly Father, In Jesus name I have prayed. Amen.

Scriptures for further Prayers:

Isaiah 43:2, Isaiah 9:4

SEPTEMBER 30

IT IS ENOUGH

Worship

Today's Scripture and Meditation

Ezekiel 21:27: I will overturn, overturn, overturn, it: and it shall be no more, until he come whose right it is; and I will give it him.

PRAYERS:

- Father Lord, I thank You because you have all power in heaven, on earth and under the earth.
- I pray for forgiveness for every door I have opened to the enemy due to our own fault and ask for forgiveness in Jesus Name.
- Father draw the sword against every enemy if mu=y soul and defeat them on my behalf.
- I humble myself before you that you might lift me up
- Let your blood with which I was purchased avail for me and speak better things in Jesus name
- I command a stop to every plague, calamity, attacks and every destruction, every evil in Jesus Name.
- Father let the enemy relent of all evil against me in Jesus Name.
- I pray for the mark of the blood to be activated upon my life such that when any angel of destruction passes, he shall see the blood and shall pass over me in Jesus name.
- Let every diabolic activities against be overturned, let every enchantment and divination against me be nullified

Revive, Rebuild and Restore

- I pray that you will overturn, overturn, until it is no more and give me my portion.
- Thank You Father in Jesus Name.

Scriptures for further Prayers

Hebrews 12:24, Numbers 23:23.

OCTOBER 1

TRIALS BUILD CHARACTER

Worship

Today's Scripture and Meditation

Romans 5:2-6 (AMP) Through Him we also have access by faith into this [remarkable state of] grace in which we [firmly and safely and securely] stand. Let us rejoice in our [a]hope and the confident assurance of [experiencing and enjoying] the glory of [our great] God [the manifestation of His excellence and power]. 3 And not only this, but [with joy] let us exult in our sufferings and rejoice in our hardships, knowing that hardship (distress, pressure, trouble) produces patient endurance; 4 and endurance, proven character (spiritual maturity); and proven character, hope and confident assurance [of eternal salvation]. 5 Such hope [in God's promises] never disappoints us, because God's love has been abundantly poured out within our hearts through the Holy Spirit who was given to us.

6 While we were still helpless [powerless to provide for our salvation], at the right time Christ died [as a substitute] for the ungodly.

PRAYERS:

- Lord, I thank You for the access that I have to the Father through Christ, I rejoice for I have access into Your manifest presence.
- Let me be safely and firmly secured in my faith
- I rejoice in Your hope and I have a confident hope that Your glory will manifest in my life.

- Father let me experience the full manifestation of Your excellence, power and splendour.

Revive, Rebuild and Restore

- ⏹ Let me glory in persecution knowing that there is a crown of glory awaiting me.
- ⏹ Let my experiences work out patience, endurance, proven character, spiritual maturity; and proven and confident assurance of eternal salvation in me.
- ⏹ Father make me a better version of myself, shape my character, my integrity, and my all.
- ⏹ Lord Jesus, pour Your love abundantly upon me through Your Holy Spirit.
- ⏹ Lord Jesus, help my helplessness.
- ⏹ My father do not let the death of Christ be in vain over my life.
- ⏹ Lord Jesus, secure me portions, thank You heavenly father in Jesus name, Amen!
- ⏹ I thank you that hope in God's promises never disappoints me
- ⏹ Thank you that Your love has been abundantly poured out within our hearts through the Holy Spirit

Scriptures for further Prayers

James 1:12, 1 Corinthians 9:25, Philippians 4:1

OCTOBER 2

OPEN THE EYES OF MY HEART

Worship

Today's Scripture and Meditation

Ephesians 1:17-18 *that the god of our Lord Jesus Christ, the father of glory may give to you wisdom and revelation in the knowledge of Him. The eyes of your understanding being enlightened that you may know what is the hope of His calling what are the riches of his glory, of his inheritance according to the workings of his mighty power.*

PRAYERS:

- Father Lord I worship You, I magnify You, I give You the highest praise, I honour You.
- Father, according to Your word, I pray that You will give unto me the wisdom and revelation to know You.
- Grant unto me the fear of the Lord which is the beginning of wisdom and to live my life in the light of the true meaning of it.
- Grant unto me the required wisdom that we will not just make me a religious person but make me Christlike and take me into a deep relationship with You.
- Open the eyes of my understanding that I may know You and know how to engage You in a deeper manner.
- Grant unto me divine insights into Your word, Your kingdom and Your person.
- I love You and want an intimate relationship with You.
- Let me know you more; both your acts and your ways
- Let the revelation of the hope of my calling be burst on my sight.

- Open my eyes oh God that I will not go into error or be deceived but that I will do your bidding.
- Open the eyes of my heart that I may see You take me to level, where I have never been before.
- Open the eyes of our understanding that we may continue to work Your part that we will not miss our steps in God,
- Open the eyes of our understanding that I may know how to live and run this race according to Your will.
- When You opened Isaiah's eyes, His fear of You deepened, He saw and he realized his low estate as a man with unclean lips, Father open my eyes to see myself that I may seek You more.
- This is the cry of my heart today in Jesus Name
- Lord, I thank You Lord Blessed be Your mighty Name, in Jesus' Name I have prayed. Amen.

Scriptures for further Prayers

Proverbs 9:10, 2 Kings 2:9,11-12, Genesis 21:19, Acts 9:3-5

OCTOBER 3

HONOUR YOUR LEADERS

Worship

Today's Scripture and Meditation

Numbers 12:6-8. Hear now My words: If there is a prophet among you, I, the Lord, make Myself known to him in a vision; I speak to him in a dream. Not so with My servant Moses. He is faithful in all My house. I speak with him face to face, even plainly, and not in dark sayings; And he sees the form of the Lord. Why then were you not afraid, To speak against My servants?"

PRAYERS:

- ☐ Father, I give You thanks and praise for Your unending love even when I do not deserve it
- ☐ I repent of the times I have doubted Your word in the mouth of Your servants and have dishonoured and disobeyed them
- ☐ When I have not acknowledged Your grace and anointing upon their lives nor have regarded them as Your representatives and have grieved Your Spirit, Lord, I repent
- ☐ I ask for a time of refreshing in Your presence
- ☐ I recognise that You have degrees of revelation that You give to Your prophets; some in visions, some in dreams and others face to face plainly
- ☐ Father give me grace not to use the messenger as my yardstick of Your grace and anointing

- ⯀ Give me the grace to be discerning in dealing with Your servants that I may not sin against You
- ⯀ I believe in You Lord and so will I be established; I ask for help in believing Your prophets so that I shall prosper.
- ⯀ You have chosen to use the foolish things to confound the wise and good things come in simple packages; let me quit being childish to You so that I can focus on the race and run it in fear and trembling
- ⯀ In the name of Jesus, I rebuke every work of darkness that has come into my life because of the way I have treated Your servants in the past
- ⯀ Father let there be a manifestation of that which You have proposed for my life in the name of Jesus
- ⯀ Let Your plans begin to manifest in my life. Blessed be Your holy name in Jesus name, Amen

Scriptures for further Prayers:

2 Chronicles 20:20b, 1 Corinthians 1:27a.

OCTOBER 4

BE BLAMELESS

Worship

Today's Scripture and Meditation

Philippians 1:9-10. (AMPC): And this I pray: that your love may abound yet more and more and extend to its fullest development in knowledge and all keen insight [that your love may [d]display itself in greater depth of acquaintance and more comprehensive discernment],

So that you may surely learn to sense what is vital, and approve and prize what is excellent and of real value [recognizing the highest and the best, and distinguishing the moral differences], and that you may be untainted and pure and unerring and blameless [so that with hearts sincere and certain and unsullied, you may approach] the day of Christ [not stumbling nor causing others to stumble].

PRAYERS:

- Father I thank You that You reveal more and more of yourself to me daily.
- Father I can never love too much, let my love abound more and more, extending to full development in knowledge in Jesus Name.
- Let my love not be blind but have knowledge and discernment so that I will be able to approve the things that are excellent.

Revive, Rebuild and Restore

- Lord grant me deep insight and revelation of Your person, Your ways and Your will in Jesus Name.
- That I will learn to discern what is vital and of real value that I may remain pure and unerring and blameless in Jesus Name.
- Enable me to be sincere and without offence approving the things that are excellent till the day of Your appearing.
- That I will not stumble or cause others to stumble as the day approaches in Jesus Name.
- Thank You Father in Jesus Name.

Scriptures for further Prayers:

Ephesians 1:18, Luke 6:39

OCTOBER 5

FORGIVENESS

Worship

Today's Scripture and Meditation

Psalm 32:1. *Blessed is the one whose transgressions are forgiven, whose sins are covered.*

PRAYERS:

- Father Lord, we thank You for the blood that washed us clean.

- I confess my sins to You this today (list any sins you are aware of)

- I pray that you will forgive me and cleanse me from all unrighteousness

- Almighty God please help me break down the walls that separates between me and anyone due to transgression and unforgiveness.

- Every wall that the devil has put to cause hatred in the church I break you down in the mighty Name of Jesus.

- Father Lord please teach me to love and tolerate all men as Christ would.

- Father, please help me to become our brother's keepers. Give me the burden to look after people and help to uplift others.

- Father, please help me to take heed so I don't fall even while helping each other to stand.

- Almighty God I need Your help, please help me love care for the brethren and look beyond their faults

- Let my love cover a multitude of sin that I might enable many on the journey of salvation

- Thank You father in Jesus name I have prayed. Amen!

Scriptures for further Prayers:

Galatians 6:1, Proverbs 17:9

OCTOBER 6

FAVOUR SURROUNDS YOU

Worship

Today's Scripture and Meditation

Psalm 5:12. For You, O Lord, will bless the righteous; With favor You will surround him as with a shield.

PRAYERS:

- ⬜ Lord, I thank You for your favour that surrounds me
- ⬜ No matter my history I have received the grace of God and the favour of the Lord is upon me
- ⬜ I confess that favour of the Lord surrounds me like a shield, as I continue to seek the Lord.
- ⬜ The favour of the Lord will speak for me today and I receive rest on every side and in every circumstance
- ⬜ The Lord has distinguished between me and the rest of the people on the face of the earth because I fear the Lord; I am favoured by Him
- ⬜ Because I am favoured by the Lord, I have favour in the eyes of all men; whosoever sets eyes on me or my name will favour me.
- ⬜ Favour is my portion no matter when I started; early in the morning or in the third hour or in the sixth hour or in the ninth hour or the eleventh Hour, His favour is mine.
- ⬜ I receive the same wages because favour has found me in the Name of Jesus.
- ⬜ I have full results, full lifting and full promotions because I have found You this morning.

Revive, Rebuild and Restore

- ▫ I receive unquantifiable undeserved favour from the Lord as His child.
- ▫ Favour lifts me up and nothing can limit me or stop me.
- ▫ I begin to ride in the wings of favour in the Name Jesus.

Scriptures for further Prayers

Matthew 20:1-9, Mark 7:24-30

OCTOBER 7

YOUR WORK MERIT

Worship

Today's Scripture and Meditation

Revelations 22:12: *Behold, I am coming soon, and I shall bring My wages and rewards with Me, to repay and render to each one just what his own actions and his own work merit*

PRAYERS:

- Father I thank You because You are a faithful God, You never owe any man and You are a rewarder.
- I come to You with confidence in the atonement and finished work of Calvary.
- Lord Jesus, my heart desire that you (Maranatha) come now. Come, as the world keeps degenerating and disintegrating the more.
- The more I know You, the more I want to know You and the more I desire Your return.
- Enable me to watch and be wide awake and not sleep. Let me be alert, cautious, and on guard. Let me be sober, calm, collected, and circumspect as I wait in Jesus' Name, Amen!
- I will not be caught sleeping or unawares because I belong to the day, help me to be sober and to put on the breastplate of faith, love and the helmet the hope of salvation.
- May Your coming not catch me unprepared, and lacking oil in my lamp rather enable me to always and have extra oil

- Let me be heavenly focused that my mind will be set on things above and not things here on earth.
- Enable me to deprive myself of every evil desire and impulse power in my members that I might not be found wanting on the day of Your appearing
- Father enable me to work for my reward while I am still here on this side of eternity, Thank you heavenly father in Jesus' Name Amen!

Scriptures for further Prayers:

1 Thessalonians 5:6-9, Colossians 3:2-5, 2 Corinthians 3:12

OCTOBER 8

JOY FROM THE LORD

Worship

Today's Scripture and Meditation

Romans 15:13: *May the God of hope fill You with all joy and peace as You trust in him, so that You may overflow with hope by the power of the Holy Spirit.*

PRAYERS:

- ⬚ My Father, You created me out of joy. When You made me, You said that I am perfect. You made me live a prosperous life, full of happiness and peace
- ⬚ You said the prospect of the righteous is joy, I stand in the righteousness imputed for me and ask that You fill my heart with Your unending joy
- ⬚ Father give me fullness of joy unending that comes from staying long in Your presence
- ⬚ Father, I have set You always before me; because You are at my right hand, I shall not be shaken by any storm
- ⬚ Father, I pray that You fill me with the overwhelming joy of the Lord, which the world cannot give. When I am afflicted, let me know the joy that comes in the morning
- ⬚ Father, fill my heart with Your abiding joy so that I may rejoice in life's circumstances, knowing that the testing of my faith brings perseverance

- Lord help me to find joy, peace and rest within Your plan for my life
- Father renew in me the sense of joy daily and let the eternal Spirit of the Father dwell in my soul and body, filling every corner of my heart with light and grace
- Nothing in this world would ever bring me joy but You, Lord, give me Your own joy that is unending
- For the LORD is great and highly praised; He is feared above all gods. For all the gods of peoples are idols, but the LORD made the heavens. Splendour and majesty are before him; strength and joy are in his place
- I declare that the joy of the Lord is my strength always

Scriptures for further Prayers:

Proverbs 10:28, James 1:2-3, Nehemiah 8:10

Revive, Rebuild and Restore

OCTOBER 9

I WILL RETURN TO ZION

Worship

Today's Scripture and Meditation

Zechariah 8: 3

"Thus says the LORD: 'I will return to Zion, And dwell in the midst of Jerusalem. Jerusalem shall be called the City of Truth, The Mountain of the LORD of hosts, The Holy Mountain.'

PRAYERS:

- Father, I thank You for grace and strength, thank You for empowerment by Your Spirit
- Thank You for Your presence and all that happens in Your presence.
- Lord, I pray for Your manifest presence in my life in a more tangible way.
- I ask that I will be changed and transformed by Your presence.
- That your presence be real and tangible in my life, to be transformed into a place of truth and holiness.
- Let my life be transformed into the same image of Christ from glory to glory by the Spirit of the Lord.
- I want to worship only You; Father take me deeper into intimacy with You.
- Teach me to acclaim You, as I walk in the light of your presence, O Lord"

Revive, Rebuild and Restore

- ⊡ Give me joy in Your presence and make the path of life known to me, fill me with joy in Your presence, grant me eternal pleasures at Your right hand"
- ⊡ I want to dwell in Your house and gaze on Your beauty. I want to seek Your face.
- ⊡ To seek You in Your temple. Hear my voice when I call, O LORD in Jesus' Name, Amen.

Scriptures for further Prayers

Psalm 16:11, Psalm 89:15, Psalm 27:4, 7

OCTOBER 10

DO NOT FEAR

Worship

Today's Scripture and Meditation

2 Timothy 1:7. *For God has not given us a spirit of fear, but of power and of love and of a sound mind.*

PRAYERS:

- Thank You Lord for adopting me into Your family. I have not received the spirit of bondage to fear; I am a child of the Most High God and my confidence is in You
- Father I turn over my fears unto You because fear has torment and cripples, I have received the spirit of adoption
- I turn over all circumstances that causes me to fear unto You the Almighty and powerful God
- I take authority over every works of the enemy that causes me to fear
- I cast out fear from my life in Jesus name.

- the Fear of death
- the Fear of failure
- the Fear of lack and poverty
- the Fear of losses, etc. and every phobia. I can no longer be held in bondage

- When light shines in darkness, darkness cannot comprehend it, I am Your ark that carries Your presence; I am a child of light

653   *Revive, Rebuild and Restore*

- ▢ I speak light into every darkness and every false evidence appearing real in Jesus name
- ▢ Lord, Holy Spirit of the living God I ask for a fresh filling in the name of the Jesus, amen
- ▢ Thank You, Heavenly Father, in Jesus mighty name amen.

Scriptures for further Prayers:

Romans 8:15, John 1:5

OCTOBER 11

THE BLOOD OF THE LAMB

Worship

Today's Scripture and Meditation

Exodus 12:21-23. *Then Moses called for all the elders of Israel and said to them, "Pick out and take lambs for yourselves according to your families and kill the Passover lamb.* [22] *And you shall take a bunch of hyssop, dip it in the blood that is in the basin, and strike the lintel and the two doorposts with the blood that is in the basin. And none of you shall go out of the door of his house until morning.* [23] *For the LORD will pass through to strike the Egyptians; and when He sees the blood on the* [a]*lintel and on the two doorposts, the LORD will pass over the door and not allow the destroyer to come into your houses to strike you.*

PRAYERS:

- Father, I thank You for Your divine covering. Thank You for Your protection
- I thank You for going to calvary's cross as our Passover lamb.
- Thank You for the blood that You shed for me, that is a token of the covenant we have with the Father.

- Father enable me to shut to the door to the enemy and grant him no access to my life in Jesus Name.
- Father let me not open the door of my life to enemy attacks through sins in thoughts, in words and in actions.
- When I have opened the door to the enemy to operate in my life through anger, Father, let the door in Jesus Name.

- Let me not be involved in the pollution of the members of my body through sins committed with the tongue.
- By the reason of the shed blood on the cross of calvary for my sake, Lord, prevent the destroyer from coming into the house.
- Lord, rebuke the devourer for my sake and open the doors of heaven onto me.
- I pray that every hole that the enemy made into my purse or finances be sealed with the blood of Jesus Christ.
- Every draining pipe to my resources is sealed, in the Name of the Lord Jesus.
- I will gather and will no longer scatter, my resources will begin to grow, in the Name of the Lord Jesus.
- I will no longer go round in circles, by the power of the Holy Ghost!
- I will not be under the oppression, suppression or attack of the enemy because the blood of Jesus speaks for me.
- I will not lose members of my family and I shall not die but live to declare the work of the Lord in Jesus name. Amen!

Scriptures for further Prayers

Malachi 3:10, Ephesians 4:29

Revive, Rebuild and Restore

OCTOBER 12

IT IS I

Worship

Today's Scripture and Meditation

John 6:16-21: Now when evening came, His disciples went down to the sea, got into the boat, and went over the sea toward Capernaum. And it was already dark, and Jesus had not come to them. Then the sea arose because a great wind was blowing.

So when they had rowed about [c]three or four miles, they saw Jesus walking on the sea and drawing near the boat; and they were afraid. But He said to them, "It is I; do not be afraid." Then they willingly received Him into the boat, and immediately the boat was at the land where they were going.

PRAYERS:

- Father I thank you for you are the creator of the whole universe who gave instructions to everything made and is still in control of them all.
- I realise that when you are not in the boat there is stormy and turbulent weather, therefore, I invite you into my boat.
- I invite you into my life, my family, my ministry, my work and every aspect of my life.
- You always walk towards us when we are in trouble. You never leave us nor forsake us.
- Father come and intervene in my life by Your divine visitation and create hope to fill the space occupied by hopelessness in Jesus' Name.

- Father I willingly surrender to you because you never force yourself on us, takeover Lord, I put my trust in You.
- I do struggle when I try to do things by my own strength, come into my life and situation and make it perfect.
- My heart is before you Lord, let your presence bring joy and peace and not fear into me because I am the righteousness of God in Christ Jesus.
- Lord let me always know that you are there, let me know that it is you with me.
- 'Immediately Jesus entered they landed at shore'. Father as you enter my boat today, let fear go, let solution come, let a miracle be activated.
- As I cry out in my time of distress and trouble hear me hear me, save me, heal me, deliver me Lord, in Jesus Name.
- Let peace come, let calmness come in every area of life in Jesus Name.
- The wind slowed them down until Jesus came. Father I pray that you will deal with every time wasters and things that slow me down in life and salvation journey in Jesus Name.
- Every appointment with delay is terminated, every agent of delay removed and every appointment with the devourer is terminated.
- Everything that is being wasted in my life is restored: resources, talents, health, family, etc.
- Whatever has been programmed to manifest in the future against my progress and maturity in life and in God be destroyed in Jesus Name.
- Father move supernaturally in my life that the past and the future will meet in the arena of the present time to redeem the time for me in Jesus Name.
- Jesus suspended law of gravity, law of floatation to walk on water to them. Father I pray that you suspend any natural laws to bless me with your presence and your benefits in Jesus' Name.
- Father fill my body, my soul and my spirit with your awesome presence
- Thank You Heavenly Father in Jesus Name.

Scriptures for further Prayers:

Psalm107:19-20, Jeremiah 31:35.

OCTOBER 13

THY KINGDOM COME

Worship

Today's Scripture and Meditation

Matthew 6:10: *Your kingdom come. Your will be done on earth as it is in heaven*

PRAYERS:

- Father I thank You because You are Lord over everything. You are Lord over everyone, You are Lord over everything made, animate or inanimate. Everything must answer to Your command.
- Lord I pray Your kingdom come! Let Your kingdom come in my life. Amen!
- Let Your kingdom come in our families, our cities and in our nations!
- Establish Your rulership in our lives, let Your rulership be established in our families, our circumstances, our streets, in our nations.
- Your word says You are the One that rules and reigns in the affair of men; rule in my affairs oh Lord, I submit all to You.
- Lord I commit to You alone, I will serve You alone all the days of my life.
- It is Your Spirit alone, that Spirit that raised Jesus from death, that I submit to and will have influence over my body, spirit, and soul.
- Holy Spirit I submit to You this season; Let Your kingdom come in my life.

Revive, Rebuild and Restore

- I know that my plan may not fit into Your plan so, I submit my plans to You, Lord have Your way in my life and let Your will be done.
- I commit to seeking first the kingdom of God and His righteousness.
- Lord, I choose to seek You first and seek Your kingdom first, I set my eyes on You, I set my mind on seeking Your kingdom.
- I am acutely aware that without You, I can do nothing. So, Lord Help me to seek You as priority.
- Holy Spirit enable me to seek the kingdom of God first. In reality, and not just in words, that I may encounter You deeper.
- Enable me to apply my heart to wisdom, to seeking You in the real sense of it. Thank you Lord! I bless You. In Jesus name I pray, Amen.

Scriptures for further Prayers:

Matthew 6:33, Matthew 10:38-39

OCTOBER 14

MY INTERCESSOR

Worship

Today's Scripture and Meditation

Rom 8:26-27. Likewise the Spirit also helps in our weaknesses. For I do not know what I should pray for as I ought, but the Spirit Himself makes intercession for us with groanings which cannot be uttered. Now He who searches the hearts knows what the mind of the Spirit is, because He makes intercession for the saints according to the will of God.

PRAYERS:

- Father Lord, I thank You that You didn't leave us without help
- Thank You for giving me the gift of the Holy Spirit, You gave me a helper, the Holy Spirit, to teach me all things, and bring to my remembrance all things that You have said
- Spirit of God, You search all things, even the depths of God. And You reveal the things of God to us that we will not walk blindly
- Reveal the Father to me that I may know Him, as that Spirit that raised Jesus from the dead and quickens our mortal bodies
- Reveal Your divine ability to heal and to deliver by quickening my mortal body to strengthen, to give life and to heal

- Lord help my weaknesses will enable me not to stay down but to rise up each time
- Reveal Your ability to teach so I will not be ignorant, or be a novice.
- Reveal the depth of God to me that I will not stay shallow
- Reveal Your ability to transform and empower me in those areas where I struggle
- Lord help me when I don't know what to pray, help me in the place of intercession
- Holy Spirit of God, please make intercessions for me according to the will of God in Jesus name I pray. Amen

Scriptures for further Prayers:

John 14:26, I Corinthians. 6:10, Romans 8:11

OCTOBER 15

ALWAYS WATCHING

Worship

Today's Scripture and Meditation

Psalm 121:4-8. *Behold, He who keeps Israel will neither slumber nor sleep. The Lord is your keeper; the Lord is your shade on your right hand [the side not carrying a shield]. The sun shall not smite you by day, nor the moon by night. The Lord will keep you from all evil; He will keep your life. The Lord will keep your going out and your coming in from this time forth and forevermore.*

PRAYERS:

- ⬚ Father Lord, I thank you that I am reminded and assured daily that You are a constant and consistent God.
- ⬚ It gives me the confidence to know that You do not sleep, slumber, go on holidays, you are always watching over me.
- ⬚ It gives me the confidence to know that You are always on Your throne, You cannot be dethroned or impeached, You are always on the throne.
- ⬚ And You who keep us never sleep, nor slumber.
  You're always on duty. You're always on alert.
- ⬚ You are my keeper, Your watchful eye is always open, looking with love and care upon Your people.
- ⬚ Just as You were the pillar of cloud by the day as You led Israel in the wilderness, You are my shade and my Shadow where I hide.
- ⬚ Just as You were the pillar of fire by the night as You led Israel in the wilderness, You are my light and my guide in the way.

- Preserve me Lord, that nothing either of the day or night can harm me as You are keeping guard.
- You are my covering against every calamity, my shade against the visible perils of the day as well as the hidden perils of the night.
- Father preserve me from all evil that rages in our current world, let all evil be averted from me.
- Father preserve my soul from the dominion of sin, the infection of error, the crush of despondency, the puffing up of pride.
- Keep me from the world, the flesh and the devil; keep me for holier and greater things that give You pleasure.
- Keep me in the love of God; keep me for the eternal Kingdom and glory.
- Thank You Father Lord in Jesus Name, I pray. Amen!

Scriptures for further Prayers

Psalm 118:17, Colossians 2:14, Isaiah 4:6, Psalm 25:4. Psalm 91:1

Revive, Rebuild and Restore

OCTOBER 16

A TABLE BEFORE ME

Worship

Today's Scripture and Meditation:

Psalm 23:5a*: You prepare a table before me in the presence of my enemies....*

PRAYERS:

- Father God, I thank You because You are a good Shepherd, my Protector, my Daily Provider, my Peace, my Resting Place, You are my Guide through every circumstance, You are a faithful God.
- Thank You for the table of provision set before me. You have set a table before me in the presence of my enemies. Even in the presence of danger, You bless me with Your provision and goodness. Thank You for Your benevolence to provide and Your power to protect. Where I am in the Valley or on the mountain, it does not matter to you as you are always there.
- Even though the enemy is at the door, there is no panic, no confusion, no haste, because in You, I have peace.
- Lord I receive from the varieties prepared for me at the table, I receive all manner of provisions (physical, emotional, financial, marital, ministerial, family), I receive grace, victories in all battles, I receive peace. I receive security, safety, I receive deliverance.
- Lord I receive goodly and godly friendships, covenant friendships, in the family, in the workplace and in the

kingdom. I receive success, achievements, marriages, fruit of the womb *(please receive from this table what you need)*

- With joy shall I draw from the well of salvation, all that pertain to life and godliness. I can no longer lack or want for anything, I cannot be despised, mocked, or oppressed. I have all I need to fulfil God's will

- You have set a table before me in the presence of my enemies, You have magnified me before the people. In their presence I am victorious, in their presence I achieve greatness, in their presence I am prosperous, in their presence I am fulfilling my purpose in God.

- The enemy is present to see the blessings of God but can do nothing about it.

- Thank You Jesus, Thank You Lord for Your endless love and grace.

- Thank You for Your invitation to be honoured guests in Your eternal home with a permanent place at Your banquet table. Thank You for Your everlasting love in Jesus name, Amen.

Scriptures for further Prayers:

Isaiah 12:3, Philippians 4:19

OCTOBER 17

SATISFY WITH YOUR MERCY

Worship:

Today's Scripture and Meditation:

Psalm 90:14.

O satisfy us in the morning with Your mercy; that we may rejoice and be glad all our days.

PRAYERS:

- Lord this morning, I receive mercy, before the throne of grace in the Name of Jesus.
- There is no condemnation, no judgement, no affliction, no to works of darkness against me because of Your mercy.
- Father I understand that satisfaction is not rooted in money, fame, romance, pleasure, or success but in Your mercy, faithfulness, covenant goodness to Your people, I pray that You will satisfy me with Your mercy in Jesus Name!
- Look upon me with mercy as You normally do to the those who love Your Name.
- Let my heart be secured with Your gladness that comes from the experience of Your love.
- Let rejoicing that is rooted in your mercy ring through my life in Jesus' Name!
- Lord, enable me to have consistent fellowship with You that I may have joy and gladness ever more.

Scriptures for further Prayers

Revive, Rebuild and Restore

Psalm 119:132, Psalm 6:9

OCTOBER 18

I THIRST FOR YOU

Worship

Today's Scripture and Meditation

Psalm 42:1-2: *As the deer pants for streams of water, so my soul pants for You, my God. My soul thirsts for God, for the living God, When can I go and meet with God?*

PRAYERS:

- ☐ Dear Father, You are my God and I earnestly seek You; my soul thirsts for You; my flesh faints for You
- ☐ I come to You to drink from the well of water springing up to eternal. You said You will pour out water on the thirsty; Lord pour out Your Spirit on me
- ☐ You said You will satisfy the thirsty soul that comes to You to drink, Lord I come that You may satisfy my soul and my lips will be full of Your praise
- ☐ I come thirsty to You, Lord, to take the water of life without cost
- ☐ As a deer pants for flowing streams, so pants my soul for You, Oh God
- ☐ Lord, may I continually thirst for Your presence, just as the deer requires daily water to survive. Father, may I see my daily need for You. Father, I want to be in Your presence and experience You in all I do
- ☐ You said whoever believes in You shall never thirst, Lord, I believe in You, fill me up
- ☐ As I seek You today, Lord, let me find You, let me drink from the spiritual "Rock" today who is Christ Jesus

- ☐ David said, one thing have I asked of the Lord, that will I seek after: that I may dwell in the house of the Lord all the days of my life, to gaze upon the beauty of the Lord and to inquire in his temple. Lord, this is my desire also; enable me to continuously seek after You
- ☐ Father send Your light and Your truth; let them lead me; let them bring me to Your holy hill and to Your dwelling, then I will go to the altar of God, to God my exceeding joy
- ☐ Lord I have looked upon You in the sanctuary, to see Your power and glory, for Your steadfast love is better than life, my lips will praise You
- ☐ Your presence is more than life, lead me always into the fullness of Your presence daily

Scriptures for further Prayers:

Psalm 63:1, Psalm 27:4, 1 Corinthians 10:4

OCTOBER 19

KEEP ME IN YOUR PRESENCE

Worship

Today's Scripture and Meditation

Psalms 51:10-12: *Create in me a clean heart, O God, and renew a right, persevering, and steadfast spirit within me. Do not cast me away from Your presence, And do not take Your Holy Spirit from me. Restore to me the joy of Your salvation and make me willing to obey You all the days of my life.*

PRAYERS:

- Father Lord, have mercy on me, because of Your unfailing love. Because of Your great compassion, blot out the stain of my sins; wash me clean from my guilt in Jesus name

- Purify me from my sins, and I will be clean; wash me, and I will be whiter than snow. Oh Lord, give me back my joy again; You have broken me — now let me rejoice

- Create in me a clean heart, O God. Renew a loyal spirit within me. The sacrifice You desire is a broken spirit. You will not reject a broken and repentant heart, O God

- Father Lord, in Your mercy, do not banish me from Your presence, and don't take Your Holy Spirit from me

- Your presence is more than life to me, without Your presence I am nothing and will be lost in this world, it is with Your Spirit I am sealed, and He is the surety for my redemption, do not take Your Spirit from me Lord

- ☐ I am desperate for You lord, Your presence is the air I breathe, I am desperate to bask in Your presence and be a carrier of Your presence Lord
- ☐ Draw me close to You Lord, Let me experience You deeper in Jesus name
- ☐ My acceptable sacrifice to You is a broken spirit; a heartbroken down with sorrow for sin and a contrite heart, humble and thoroughly penitent.
- ☐ Lord, I thank You for You are the God of my salvation. Thank You for the freshness of Your presence. I long for a pure heart. I desire a heart that will produce the fruit of the Spirit and be a blessing to those around me.
- ☐ Father, renew my spirit, revive my soul and restore to me the joy of Your salvation. Renew my zeal and passion for You. Grant me a willing spirit
- ☐ Father keep me safeguarded from the enemy, that I will not be overpowered by temptation but teach me to overcome that I will be able to teach others also
- ☐ Deliver me from my guilt and renew my thoughts so that I might not fall prey to the accuser of the brethren
- ☐ Grant me the grace to obey You willingly all the days of my life in Jesus name. Amen

Scriptures for further Prayers:

Psalm 27:8, Psalm 140:1, Psalms I39:7. Psalm 91:17

OCTOBER 20

BUILDING ON SAND?

Worship

Today's Scripture and Meditation

Matthew 7:26-27. *"But everyone who hears these sayings of Mine, and does not do them, will be like a foolish man who built his house on the sand: [27] and the rain descended, the floods came, and the winds blew and beat on that house; and it fell. And great was its fall."*

PRAYERS:

- ⬜ Father, I thank You for Your Word that is Yes and Amen.
- ⬜ Your word is true and will accomplish the purpose for which it's been sent.
- ⬜ Help me not to despise or disrespect Your word but to expect the performance of your word.
- ⬜ Let me be a doer of the word, not just a hearer deceiving myself.
- ⬜ Let my house not be built on sand that I might not suffer a tragedy of dismal collapse.
- ⬜ Grant me the understanding that the blessing is to the doer and not to the hearer or the reader.
- ⬜ Give me the grace to be willing and obedient, that I will eat the fruit and best of the land.
- ⬜ Give me the grace to study Your word, meditate on it, confess it and, above all, obey Your word
- ⬜ I realize that everything I require or desire is in Your word, let Your word give me life
- ⬜ I pray that Your Spirit will breathe upon Your word for the performance of Your word in my life.

- ▢ I will not despise, neglect or disrespect Your word.
- ▢ I know that You watch over Your Word to perform it.
- ▢ Enable me to hide Your word in my heart and be grounded in it so that when the rain falls and the floods come, when the wind blows, I will not fall
- ▢ That I might not be tossed to and fro like a reed and become unstable in my ways
- ▢ Let me not be swayed by every wind of doctrine and philosophies and theories of me.
- ▢ May the word of the Lord bring the creation of opportunities and creative miracles in our midst.
- ▢ Let Your word have its full course in my life, let there be a performance of everything You have said concerning me.
- ▢ Grant me insight and Revelations that I might be a recipient of Your blessings and promises
- ▢ Blessed be Your Name in the Name of Jesus Amen.

Scriptures for further Prayers

James 1:23, Isaiah 1:19, Jeremiah 15:16, Psalm 119:50,

OCTOBER 21

NEW ORDER

Worship

Today's Scripture and Meditation

Matthew 9:16 − 17 (GNT): "No one patches up an old coat with a piece of new cloth, for the new patch will shrink and make an even bigger hole in the coat. ¹⁷ Nor does anyone pour new wine into used wineskins, for the skins will burst, the wine will pour out, and the skins will be ruined. Instead, new wine is poured into fresh wineskins, and both will keep in good condition."

PRAYERS:

- Father Lord thank You because You are always doing new things.
- Let me not be ignorant when You are doing new things but that I shall know it and partake in it.
- Father I pray for guidance and instruction by Your Spirit that I will not be misdirected.
- Enable me to move from religion to a relationship with You.
- Thank You for fulfilling the law and for the new covenant that we have with the Father through the blood of Jesus.
- Thank You that I have brothers and sisters in Christ across nations, colour, race and status.
- Enable me to understand the new covenant.
- Oh Lord help me to separate wheat from shaft and help me not to be careless with Your word.
- Oh Lord help me not to be ignorant and insensitive to the leading of Your Spirit.
- Lord Jesus, teach me to be selfless but to prefer others

- Enable me to accept and run with the new things You are doing in this end time
- Oh Lord, teach me to walk in Your precepts.
- Lord Jesus, cause me to remain relevant to Your scheme.
- Oh Lord, may I not entangle myself with the wrong sect or group
- Thank You Father in Jesus name I pray. Amen!

Scriptures for further Prayers:

Ephesians 2:16

OCTOBER 22

TEST THE SPIRIT

Worship:

Today's Scripture and Meditation:

Proverbs 16:1-2. *The plans of the hearts belong to man. But the answer of the tongue is from the Lord. All the ways of a man are pure in his own eyes. But the Lord weighs the spirit.*

PRAYERS:

- I bless You Lord because You know all things and can do all things.
- I am made in Your image, so I have the ability to plan and prepare.
- Lord I pray that You inspire and lead me as I plan, so that my plans will succeed. I give over to you, all my planning and plans and I ask that Your will be done.
- Lord examine my motives and cause Your own counsel to stand.
- You see the heart, Lord look at the plans made in humility and those made in pride and sift through them as You establish Your own counsel in my life
- Lord beyond my preparations and plan, give wisdom a voice and let me receive an answer from Your tongue.
- Grant unto me Your own answer; grant unto me Your own plan, grant unto me Your own counsel.
- Father reveal every aspect of my life where I have missed it, every aspect of my life that seems pure in my own eyes but not acceptable to You.
- Let my judgements be according to Your own judgment.

- I commit my walks into Your hands, I commit my plans into Your hands, Lord that You may establish it, according to Your will, plan and purpose in the Name of the Lord Jesus Christ, Amen.
- You made everything. Please take charge of everything and grant unto me the answer to everything I ask of in the Name of the Lord Jesus Christ.
- Weigh my spirit, weigh our motives. Let me be constantly conscious of my motives, let me be constantly conscious of my spirit and the spirit behind all I do.
- I acknowledge You in all my ways, direct my path and make my ways straight, in Jesus name, Amen.

Scriptures for further Prayers

Genesis 1:27, Proverbs 3:5-7,

OCTOBER 23

GOD'S TRAINING

Worship

Today's Scripture and Meditation

Psalm 118:18(NIV). *The Lord has chastened me severely, but he has not given me over to death.*

PRAYERS:

- ⬚ Father, I thank you because I am Your child, and I am loved by You.
- ⬚ I am grateful that I am not a bastard, You chastise only the ones You love.
- ⬚ I am sorry for all I have done wrong and ask for forgiveness.
- ⬚ Thank You, Lord, for not judging me according to my sins.
- ⬚ Thank You for not giving me over to the enemy or to death.
- ⬚ I do not despise your chastening, rather, I surrender to Your training and corrective purpose.
- ⬚ Chasten me that my soul will not be lost but be received by You
- ⬚ Lord Jesus, You endured the Father's purposeful suffering for my sake.
- ⬚ Open unto me the gates of righteousness that I may not sin against You.
- ⬚ Thank You for not giving me over to death blessed be Your Name in Jesus Name.

Revive, Rebuild and Restore

Scriptures for further Prayers

Hebrews 12:6, Job 5:1

OCTOBER 24

SANCTIFICATION

Worship

Today's Scripture and Meditation

Psalms 51:5-9: *Behold, I was brought forth in iniquity, and in sin my mother conceived me. Behold, You desire truth in the inward parts, and in the hidden part You will make me to know wisdom. Purify me with hyssop, and I shall be clean [ceremonially]; wash me, and I shall [in reality] be whiter than snow. Hide Your face from my sins and blot out all my guilt and iniquities.*

PRAYERS:

▢ Dear Father, I thank You for saving me. Thank You for separating me from the world, for calling me to Yourself for justification, for declaring me righteous by faith

▢ I turn to You now for continuous cleansing of my mind and my thoughts that I might not be conformed to this world but be transformed by the renewing of my mind

▢ Let sin not reign in my heart and do not let me fall away from Your steadfast mercy but guard my heart oh God

▢ I was born with the sinful nature from Adam. Therefore, I am predisposed to a life of sin and do sin. Father forgive me and uproot the sinful nature in me that I might live in the power of Your Spirit above sin

⊡ Father, You had predestined me to conform into the image of Your Son, so I submit completely to the workings of the Holy Spirit in my life to change and transform me progressively from glory to glory through the word

⊡ Deliver me, oh Lord from the law of sin and death that I see manifesting in my body

⊡ Cleanse me by the water of Your word so that I can depart from unrighteousness to embrace righteousness by the power of Your Holy Spirit

⊡ Help me to seek You as my first priority in life and let my relationship with You be the most important thing in my life

⊡ Restrain me from living according to the dictates of the flesh so that I will not mind the things of the flesh, but I will be after the things of the Spirit.

⊡ Lord, I do not want to be carnally minded. I will not yield my members as instruments of unrighteousness, but I will be spiritually minded walking in the liberty which I have received in Christ Jesus

⊡ I rededicate myself to You wholly. I surrender my will to Your will. I give You total control of my life. You are my Lord and my Redeemer, the Holy one of Israel

⊡ Thank You Lord!

Scriptures for further Prayers:

Romans 8:2, Romans 8:28-9, Ephesians 5:26

OCTOBER 25

SECOND TOUCH

Worship

Today's Scripture and Meditation

Mark 8:22-25. Then He came to Bethsaida; and they brought a blind man to Him, and begged Him to touch him. 23 So He took the blind man by the hand and led him out of the town. And when He had spit on his eyes and put His hands on him, He asked him if he saw anything. 24 And he looked up and said, "I see men like trees, walking." 25 Then He put His hands on his eyes again and made him look up. And he was restored and saw everyone clearly.

PRAYERS:

- Father I thank You for the ministry of the Holy Spirit in my life and Your progressive work of enlightenment of my soul.
- I pray Lord that after seeing the light, I will not go back into darkness.
- I will pray that after seeing the light, my vision will not become blurred in Jesus' Name
- I pray for every area where there are shadows and patches in my life to be lightened up.
- Release Your grace and mercy so I can experience the gospel truth and look forward to the glory to come.
- Open the eyes of my understanding. Lift me up and lead me to that place to be alone with You.
- Let me go deeper than crowd led devotion to but not in personal devotion. (this should be rephrased)

Revive, Rebuild and Restore

- ⬚ Let me receive grace and anointing from the place of constant fellowship with You that I will not be presumptuous.
- ⬚ Take me to that quiet place from the noise around. Guide me so I will lean on our own understanding.
- ⬚ Take me in the way I do not know, that I will not be misled, so on the day of Your appearing, I will not be ashamed.
- ⬚ I surrender and separate myself to You that You will not become just a routine or religion.
- ⬚ Oh Lord take me out of unfruitful work of darkness.
- ⬚ I receive the eye salve of the Word to get the manifestation of Your POWER!
- ⬚ Put Your hands upon us as You did to the blind man so he received complete eyesight and insight.
- ⬚ I receive a new and another touch to see You early.
- ⬚ Let the battles of my life be completed. Touch me a second time. I receive a second divine touch.
- ⬚ Father Lord, touch me a second time, I receive a fresh touch. Increase my faith so I can see clearly.
- ⬚ Do a higher work of grace. For anyone requiring healing receive a 2nd touch for complete total healing for mind body ministry.
- ⬚ I receive clear understanding so You no longer see men as trees.
- ⬚ All the days of my life we will praise and serve You, in Jesus Name we have prayed. Amen!

Scriptures for further Prayers

Psalm 32:8, 2 Corinthians 6:14, John 19:30, Mark 9:24, Philippians 3:10

OCTOBER 26

UPROOTING

Worship

Today's Scripture and Meditation

Matthew 15:13. *But He answered and said, "Every plant which My heavenly Father has not planted will be uprooted.*

PRAYERS:

- Father, I thank you that You are the giver of good gifts and a planter of good things; you do not plant evil.
- I thank You that the planting of the Lord always grow and blossom and will grow in me
- I repent of the time of slumber when the enemy came in and planted tares.
- Father, I pray that anything that You have not planted in my life is uprooted
- Let every false doctrine and idea, anxiety, fear, sorrow depression planted in my mind and subconscious be uprooted.
- Let every lethargy, slothfulness, sadness, etc planted in my spirit be uprooted.
- Let every darkness, sickness, disease, planted in my body be uprooted
- Let there not be a return of the enemy's planting, and work in my life
- Let every physical plant of the enemy on my life be uprooted; every growth, every sickness *(mention how it applies to you)*
- Bring total restoration to my body, spirit and soul.

▢ Lord, I ask that You begin to sow for me and sow in me, make me a seed of highest quality and Your planting in the world in Jesus Name.

Scriptures for further Prayers

Matthew 15:13, Matthew 13:25, Jeremiah 2:21

OCTOBER 27

HOLINESS

Worship

Today's Scripture and Meditation

1 *Peter 1:16:* *Because it is written, "Be holy, for I am holy."*

PRAYERS:

- Thank You Lord Jesus, we praise You Lord, I adore You, Holy God Holy! Holy!
- Lord I come before You by the blood of Jesus, the blood of cleansing, that I may obtain mercy before the throne of grace.
- I confess of all sins wilful and against one another, against the body of Christ, and anything, against organization thinking no one will know, every sin against one another is against You, against our spouses, children, parents, families, acquaintances etc.
- Lord I ask that You help me to do that which You are asking of us this morning. I receive grace to live a holy life, blameless and without blemish in the Name of Jesus!
- Help me to be holy in conduct and in all godliness.
- I put down the old man and put my body under subjection. I silence the flesh in our lives in the Name of Jesus, Amen!
- Sanctify me oh God uproot the Adamic nature from our hearts.
- I pour out myself for cleansing by the blood of Jesus that I will be a holy vessel that is usable by You, and be a useful vessel in Your Kingdom in the Name of the Lord Jesus!

- I receive the ability to be holy, let Your presence flood my life, that no darkness will remain.
- Let me live a holy life that I might be free of every oppression, and be filled with fullness of joy.
- I ask oh God, the grace to be holy so that we will be permanent carriers of Your presence.
- Let Your presence be with me, enable me to live a holy life so that I can make it to Your kingdom at last in Jesus Name, I pray, Amen.
- Thank You Heavenly Father, blessed be Your Name oh God. Amen.

Scriptures for further Prayers:

Isaiah 6:3, Habakkuk 1:13 - Peter 3:11

OCTOBER 28

MY CUP RUNS OVER

Worship

Today's Scripture and Meditation:

Psalm 23:5b: *You anoint my head with oil; my cup overflows*

PRAYERS:

- Thank You Lord for anointing my head with oil. Thank You for making me glad.
- Father thank You for being my Shepherd.
- You have anointed my head with oil, for protection, for deliverance and for breakthrough
- You have anointed my head with oil that the yoke may be broken in Name of the Lord Jesus Christ, Amen.
- Thanks for filling my cup of joy from your presence.
- Thank You for refreshing my heart and soul even in face of the immediate threat of the enemies. Being in Your presence rejuvenates me, it gives me the strength to face all the challenges and pressures of life. My enemies could snarl and roar all they want, but in the shelter of Your presence, I would feast and be refreshed.
- With my head anointed with oil, I am protected from every enemy infestation in Jesus Name, Amen.
- Your anointing protects me against any charge. You are for me; I am confident that no one can be against me
- Your anointing separates me unto God and nothing can separate me from your love; no trouble or hardship or persecution or famine or nakedness or danger or sword. Neither death nor life; neither height nor depth, nor

anything else in all creation, shall separate me from the love of Christ.

- You are for me, I am more than conquerors in all these things
- Thank You for Your love, I delight in the comfort of Your presence, protection, and care. Like David, I can say, "You anoint my head with oil" because Jesus Christ fills me with joy overflow, and His joy is the strength of my life, I have joy unspeakable today and always in Jesus name. Amen.
- Today is a day of joy; Glory be to God! Amen!

Scriptures for further Prayers:

Romans 8:31–39, Psalm 16:11

OCTOBER 29

THE NEW COVENANT

Worship

Today's Scripture and Meditation

Hebrews 12:24 To Jesus the Mediator of the new covenant, and to the blood of sprinkling that speaks better things than that of Abel

PRAYERS:

- I come before the throne of grace by the blood of Jesus, to obtain mercy and to find grace.
- I come before You by the blood sprinkled.
- We plead the blood of Jesus, for a cleansing and for a purging in the Name of Jesus.
- We plead the blood of Jesus that nothing will stand between me and my God as I pray.
- Cleanse my heart and my soul from any demonic deposits, ancestral and generational issues.
- Cleanse my mind and memory by the power in the blood of Jesus!
- Cleanse my body of every disease and demonic implants, every physical and spiritual marks.
- I place a demand of the blood of Jesus to cleanse and wipe out traditional satanic marks, evil identities and evil family patterns.
- I plead the blood of Jesus to silence every voice speaking from any negative inheritance into my life.
- Every clog in the wheel of my spiritual growth be

dislodged so I can manifest in Your growth.

- Every cyclic illness at a particular time of the year is dealt with.
- Every power of cyclic illness that comes with different seasons and times of the day is broken.
- Every element created by God will work for my good for I am a child of God.
- I plead the blood of Jesus to flush out anything not planted by God in my life.
- I pray that daily as I live my lives will be a pleasant aroma to God.
- Let the blood of sprinkling speak mercy, grace, peace, joy, healing and deliverance into my life.
- Let the blood of sprinkling speak growth in grace, in love, in consecration and in the knowledge of Christ
- Our lives will be a sweet fragrance in our communities so we will be true ambassadors of You, true witnesses of the Lord. That our lives will be impactful in a positive way in Jesus' Name! Amen!
- I ask that the blood of Jesus will speak for me!
- Thank You Father, in Jesus name I pray. Amen

Scriptures for further Prayers:

Hebrews 8:15, Jeremiah 31:31, Hebrews 9:15

OCTOBER 30

THE SON'S PURPOSE

Worship

Today's Scripture and Meditation

1 John 3:8: For this purpose the Son of God was manifested, that He might destroy the works of the devil.

PRAYERS:

- Lord, I thank for manifesting Your love towards us by sending Your only begotten Son into the world, that we might live through Him.
- Thank You Lord for the purpose for which You came. To retrieve dominion handed by man to the devil and to destroy his works.
- I pray to enforce what You have done this morning. That every works of the devil against my soul be destroyed in Jesus Name, Amen.
- Every works of the devil against my knowledge of God, my prayer life, my growth in the Lord, my advancement in the things of the kingdom, my calling and my assignment in the kingdom; be cast down and be destroyed in Jesus' Name, Amen.
- Every imagination, philosophy, ideology and idea, theory, reasoning, argument, outlook, lofty thing, system, every thinking, viewpoint, wisdom, tenet, doctrine, intellect and attitude in my mind that works to prevent the deep knowledge of God in my life be destroyed in Jesus Name, Amen.

Revive, Rebuild and Restore

- Father Lord, I pray that You destroy every unhelpful thought pattern, emotions, and memories, I command every one of my thoughts and purpose into the obedience of Christ. Let my will be swallowed up by Your will in Jesus name, Amen.
- I destroyed every works of the devil that has manifested as sicknesses, diseases and affliction in the Name of Jesus be destroyed. The word of God says that by His stripes I am healed and so I command healing to my body by the word of God in Jesus name, Amen.
- Thank You Lord that You came that we might live through You. We give You the highest praise in Jesus name, Amen.

Scriptures for further Prayers:

2 Corinthians 10:5, 1 Peter 2:24, 1 John 4:9

OCTOBER 31

I WILL NOT BE A PREY

Worship

Today's Scripture and Meditation

Isaiah 49:24-26. *Can plunder be retrieved from a giant, prisoners of war gotten back from a tyrant? But God says, "Even if a giant grips the plunder and a tyrant holds my people prisoner, I'm the one who's on your side, defending your cause, rescuing your children.*
And your enemies, crazed and desperate, will turn on themselves, killing each other in a frenzy of self-destruction. Then everyone will know that I, God, have saved you – I, the Mighty One of Jacob."

PRAYERS:

- Thank You oh Lord for the things that You already began to do in my life
- Thank You Lord for the things You are doing right now
- Father I thank You that You are on my side, defending my cause, and the giant grip of the plunder is loosed.
- I pray for retrieval of every plunder that the enemy has taken in any department of Your life
- I pray that You contend with all that contend with me physically and spiritually
- The "snare of the fowler" is broken and I have escaped in the name of Jesus
- The attack of the enemy is made ineffective, null and void of no effect in the name of the Lord Jesus Christ
- I am rescued from anything and everything that the Father has not put in my life

- Whatever is not according to the plan, purpose and counsel of in my life is destroyed in the name of Jesus
- Whatever has plagued me in the past is destroyed
- There is confusion and self-destruction in the camp of the enemy. Any sickness or disease   in my body will self-destruct until it vanishes   from my body in Jesus name.
- The Almighty God is defending my cause, and the enemy is destroyed
- I receive deliverance, I receive it into physical manifestation. Father I thank You that You have not left us as orphans. Thank You for You have not forsaken us
- I receive strength and courage and I am not afraid for the Lord goes with me and will never leave me nor forsake me.
- The Lord Almighty has arisen on my behalf in the name of Jesus Christ. Amen
- I have seen and known the goodness of the Lord and all that see me   shall know it.
- I give You praise Lord, I worship and I adore You blessed be Your name

Scriptures for further Prayers:

Psalm 124:7, Isaiah 8:9-10, Deuteronomy. 31:6

NOVEMBER 1

BREAKTHROUGH

Worship

Today's Scripture and Meditation

Psalm 24 :7-10. *lift up your heads o ye gates and be lifted up everlasting doors and the king of glory shall come in! Who is the King of glory? the Lord strong and Mighty, the Lord mighty in battle! Lift up your heads o ye Gates, lift up Your head ye everlasting doors and the king of glory shall come in! Who is the King of glory? The Lord of hosts.*

PRAYERS:

- Thank You Lord for You are the King of glory, mighty in battle, Lord of host
- I command by the word of the Lord, lift up your heads o ye gates and be ye lifted up ye everlasting doors and let the King of glory come in.
- I invite the King of glory, the Lord of hosts, the mighty God to come into every difficult situation of my life and by His special grace.
- You have collected the keys of hell and of gates and disarmed principalities and power making for a public shew of the cohorts of satan.
- Let every difficult situation, every strong issue in my life begin to resolve and be totally dealt with; I begin to get results.
- I command every head of gates and everlasting doors be lifted!
- When the King of glory moves, fire goes before Him to

destroy His enemies, I pray that all the enemies of my purpose be burnt! Be it sickness, lack, demons, in Jesus Name.

- Father break in pieces any ancient and everlasting gates in my life
- That the king of glory might come into every facet of my life to bring life in Jesus name
- Oh! that men will praise the Lord for His goodness and for His mercies and wonderful works to the children of men for He has broken the gates of brass and cut the bars of iron asunder.
- I worship You, thank You for everlasting doors that has been lifted, and mountains that have melted.
- Blessed be Your name in Jesus name. Amen!

Scriptures for further Prayers:

Colossians 2:15, Psalm 97:3-5, Ephesians 1:20-22

NOVEMBER 2

EXPECTATIONS NOT COME SHORT

Worship

Today's Scripture and Meditation

Proverbs 23:18. *For surely there is an end; and thine expectation shall not be cut off.*

PRAYERS:

- Father I thank You for Your word that says that my expectations will not be cut short.
- Father I pray that You will grant be grace to fully obey You and not be presumptuous; that I might not suffer defeat or disappointment
- I pray that I will not fail or suffer loss in that day when I am expecting success
- Enable me to trust in You implicitly that I might not put my trust in man, systems, organizations, or governments
- I hold on to Your word today and ask that You grant my expectations to be fulfilled in Jesus Name.
- Father I pray that my expectations be based on Your will and not on assumptions but on Your approval.
- That my expectations will not be based on my senses, and I will not walk by sight.
- That my expectations will not be based on my connections or relationships but on Your word.
- That my expectations will not be based on ideas from fellow Christians but from the Holy Spirit in Jesus Name.

- I pray for divine guidance even in the area of my expectations that I will not suffer disappointments and discouragements.
- I take refuge in You and ask that You will take notice of me.
- I trust You Lord because You are trustworthy, dependable and You never fail.
- Thank You Lord because You are always there for me.
- Blessed be Your Name in Jesus Name. Amen!

Scriptures for further Prayers:

Deuteronomy 1:42-44, Jeremiah 17:5

NOVEMBER 3

ON MY BEHALF

Worship

Today's Scripture and Meditation

Psalm 127:1-2. Unless the Lord build a house, they labour in vain who build it, unless the Lord guides the city the Watchmen stays awake in vain. It is vain for you to rise up early to sit up late to eat the bread of sorrow for so he give the Beloved sound sleep.

PRAYERS:

- Father Lord, I praise You because You are the builder, You are the husbandman.
- I ask that in this current timeline you build my life, You will build everything that concerns me and I will not be derailed, I will not be distracted in the Name of Jesus.
- That I will seek help from You because You are my helper and from no other.
- Some trust in chariots, others in horses but I trust in the Name of the Lord my God!
- I understand that it is not of him who wills, nor of him who runs, but of God who shows mercy, so I plead for mercy Lord.
- I pray that my labour in the spiritual, in the physical, will not be in vain
- That I will not eat the bread of sorrow, every grief of labour loss in my life is destroyed.
- Everywhere there is poverty in spirit and the physical is rejuvenated.
- Let every cause of poverty sorrow or labour loss be addressed by the blood of Jesus for correction. Everything

Revive, Rebuild and Restore

that places a liability in my life is destroyed in the Name of Jesus.

- Let there be a re-alignment and correction of every seed I have sown, every work I have done, every sacrifice I have made that has gone unrewarded
- Isaac sowed in the land in the same year he reaped a hundredfold. Father let me enter into the season of results and harvest.
- Whatever I sow I shall reap a hundredfold in this timeline I begin to prosper physically, spiritually in every facet in the name of Jesus.
- Grant me the grace to continue to sow and not be weary.
- My seed will not fail and for my plantings, for my sacrifice, I receive a harvest.
- I repent of every of my mistakes, every slothfulness, nonchalant attitude, refusal to do and say the right things, lack of self-control
- Thank You Lord Jesus! Let Your Kingdom come in my life in Jesus Name. Amen!

Scriptures for further Prayers

Genesis 26:12, Galatians 6:9, Isaiah 58:10b

NOVEMBER 4

I WILL WATCH MY MOUTH

Worship

Today's Scripture and Meditation

Psalm 141:3. Set a guard, O Lord, over my mouth; Keep watch over the door of my lips.

PRAYERS:

- Thank You Lord for Your loving kindness in my life
- Your word says anyone that does not offend in word is a perfect man and he is able to bridle the whole body
- Father let me be excellent in speech. Let my words be seasoned with salt to minister grace to the hearers
- Let my words be full of grace, that which is good to the use of edifying,
- Lord set a watch over the door of my lips, that the words of my mouth will please You
- The mouth speaks the abundance of the heart; let the words of my mouth and the meditation of my heart be acceptable and pleasing unto You
- Oh Lord, set a watch at my mouth oh God, that I may know when to speak and when to be quiet
- Let no corrupt communication proceed out of my mouth, that it would not be a source of defilement to me
- Enable me to bridle my tongue so that I can bridle my whole body and put it in subjection to the Holy Spirit

Scriptures for further Prayers:

Matthew 15:18, Colossians 4:6, James 3:2, Ephesians 4:29

NOVEMBER 5

SIGNS FOLLOWING

Worship

Today's Scripture and Meditation

Mark 16: 17-18: *And these signs will follow those who believe: In My name they will cast out demons; they will speak with new tongues; they will take up serpents; and if they drink anything deadly, it will by no means hurt them; they will lay hands on the sick, and they will recover."*

PRAYERS:

- Thank You for Your power working in me
- Thank You for the gift of the grace of God given unto me by the effectual working of his power
- Thank You for the exceeding greatness of Your power towards us who believe, according to the working of his mighty power
- Thank You for the authority and power You have given me to trample upon serpents and scorpions
- You have given me physical, spiritual and mental strength and ability over all the power that the enemy possesses; and that nothing shall in any way harm me. I declare that I shall not be intimidated, I shall not be moved, and I am fortified by the Lord
- I receive grace to manifest the signs and wonders by the power of God
- I commit to going and doing everything in Your name

Revive, Rebuild and Restore

- I will not entangle myself with the affairs of this world, but I will mind the business of my Father bringing glory to His name
- Enable me to focus on that which You have apportioned to me that I may be fruitful in them all
- Father enable me to abide in You and for Your words to abide me so that I will receive all that I ask and desire in Jesus name
- Anoint my lips Lord such that when I pray for sick, oppressed, suppressed, the bound, and the afflicted, they will receive healing and freedom
- Let me bear much fruit; that my Father be glorified in my life and through me that I may be Your faithful disciples
- Lord I receive a fresh fire and fresh in-filling to launch out to do the miraculous
- Thank You Father in Jesus name

Scriptures for further Prayers:

Luke 10:19, John 15:7-8

NOVEMBER 6

WHICH SOIL?

Worship

Today's Scripture and Meditation

Matthew 13:18-23. *"Therefore, hear the parable of the sower: 19 When anyone hears the word of the kingdom, and does not understand it, then the wicked one comes and snatches away what was sown in his heart. This is he who received seed by the wayside. 20 But he who received the seed on stony places, this is he who hears the word and immediately receives it with joy; 21 yet he has no root in himself but endures only for a while. For when tribulation or persecution arises because of the word, immediately he stumbles. 22 Now he who received seed among the thorns is he who hears the word, and the cares of this world and the deceitfulness of riches choke the word, and he becomes unfruitful. 23 But he who received seed on the good ground is he who hears the word and understands it, who indeed bears fruit and produces: some a hundredfold, some sixty, some thirty."*

PRAYERS:

- ⏺ Father I thank You because Your word is powerful and potent to change and transform lives.
- ⏺ I pray that You teach me how to relate to Your word and that You will prepare my heart by Your Spirit to receive Your word accurately.
- ⏺ Let Your word find root in my heart and have its free course in my life
- ⏺ Let me hear Your word with understanding, let the t truth be imparted on my heart.

- Let the word not be hindered due to my life's past experiences that may have imparted my frame of reference.
- Let my mind not be blinded but Lord, enlighten my mind
- Let my response to the word not just be euphoria or short lived. Grant me depth and growth by Your word.
- Let me remember Your word in the day of tribulation and persecution and not fall away.
- Let my heart not be hardened against Your word but let my response to Your word be to observe to do it
- Let my heart not be fertile to every form of information been disseminated in the world through media and social media.
- Let my heart be fertile to receive Your word and imbibe it so I may grow and bear fruits thereby.
- Let the cares of this world and the deceitfulness of riches will not choke the word in my heart
- Let my heart be a good ground for Your word to be planted in, so that it will respond rightly to the word and bear fruit in Jesus Name.
- Enable me to hear Your word and increase in learning, understanding and wisdom that I may live in reverent fear all my life
- Let Your word accomplish the purpose for which it is being sent in my life
- Thank you Father for Your word in Jesus Name. Amen

Scriptures for further Prayers

2 Corinthians 4:3-4, Proverbs 1:5, Exodus 31:3

Revive, Rebuild and Restore

NOVEMBER 7

ZEALOUS FOR GOD

Worship

Today's Scripture and Meditation

Numbers 25:12-13: Therefore say, 'Behold, I give to him My covenant of peace; and it shall be to him and his descendants after him a covenant of an everlasting priesthood, because he was zealous for his God, and made atonement for the children of Israel.'

PRAYERS:

- Thank You Lord for You are the one that works in us to will and to do of Your good pleasure.
- Thank you for the privilege I have to serve You and to serve before You.
- The word of God says it is not of him the wills or runs but God that shows mercy. Thank You for showing me mercy and calling me to serve You.
- Lord I ask for the zeal the anointing to serve You acceptably in Jesus Name.
- Let me be zealous for Your righteousness's and Your righteous causes.
- That I will not stand for what my friends or family stand for but what You stand for and approve of.
- That I will not follow the crowd but give me grace to standalone with You in Jesus Name.
- Give me grace to be passionate about the things that You are passionate about.

- That I will live in obedience and be noticed by You as a person after God's heart.
- Father let there be a manifestation of the everlasting covenant of peace in my life and family.
- That we will experience peace like a river, peace that surpasses all understanding in Jesus Name. Thank You Father in Jesus Name.

Scriptures for further Prayers:

Romans 9:16, 1 Samuel 13:14

NOVEMBER 8

REACHING FORWARD

Worship

Today's scripture

Philippians 3:13-14: *Brethren, I do not count myself to have apprehended; but one thing I do, forgetting those things which are behind and reaching forward to those things which are ahead, I press toward the goal for the prize of the upward call of God in Christ Jesus.*

PRAYERS:

- Thank You, Lord, for the work You are doing in my life to build me up and to grow my understanding and knowledge of You
- Thank You because You chose to build me up during this season
- Thank You for enlightening my eyes daily and pouring more of Yourself into my life and keeping me in tune with Your Spirit
- I ask for more direct and unhindered communication and fellowship with You, Lord
- I am grateful for the work of transformation in my life: spirit, body and soul
- I thank You for how far You have led me, Your gifts and calling in my life and the exploits You have used me to do
- Like Paul said, I do not count myself to have apprehended as there are more grounds to conquer, more battles to win. More souls to win, greater heights to reach
- Give me grace to focus on the things that are ahead and to put behind me the failures of the past because You are a

God of never-ending chances in Jesus name. Give me the grace to focus on the things that are ahead and to put behind me the successes of the past because there are more exploits to do

- Father enable me to reach forward to those things that You have apportioned to me in the future. Setting my mind on things above not on things beneath
- There is a price of the upward calling of God, Father enable me to press towards this goal that I might achieve it in Jesus name
- Father enable me to rid myself of my former identity so that I can align myself with and walk in my new identity in You
- I pray that I will not dwell on the past but look forward to the brand-new things You are doing in my life
- Father take away every distraction and diversion in my journey that I may run with focus
- I honour You Lord and give You the highest praise in Jesus name I have prayed, Amen.

Scriptures for further Prayers:

Isaiah 43:18, Hebrews 11:1, Colossians 3:2

NOVEMBER 9

ACKNOWLEDGE HIM IN ALL YOUR WAYS

Worship

Today's scripture and Meditation

Proverbs 3:5-8 Trust in the Lord with all your heart And lean not on your own understanding; 6 In all your ways acknowledge Him, And He shall [b]direct your paths. 7 Do not be wise in your own eyes; Fear the Lord and depart from evil. 8 It will be health to your [c]flesh, And strength[d] to your bones.

PRAYERS:

- Father Lord, I am grateful that You are my God and that You are the sovereign God. You know all things and can do all things.
- Lord, come with open hearts before You and I surrender all to You and to Your ways; I submit to Your will and counsel and will not do evil
- Let my heart be continuously before You and always tender before You
- Give me a heart of flesh oh God; a heart that You can reach, a heart that You can change and mould
- I will no longer want to depend on my own wisdom and intelligence which are limited.
- I will not depend on my emotions which are unstable and cannot be trusted and I will not depend on, human traditions which are selfish, self-serving and self-centred and or on how I deem fit.

- Lord I acknowledge the fact that without You I can do nothing. I put all my ways before You as I acknowledge that You are the only wise God.
- I ask that You direct my path and order my steps in family, career, in ministry everywhere I go
- Give me direction that I may not miss my way, that I will not be diverted, derailed or distracted in the journey of life. I put all my trust in You, O God of my salvation.
- Uphold me with Your righteous hand that I will not be deceived by the enemy, and I will not do evil
- You never make mistakes, You are never late, and You do not sleep nor slumber, Lord I submit to Your wise counsel at every junction, I depend on You for everything that pertains to life and godliness
- Give me the strength to depend on You at all times
- I put my hands in Yours, Lord, take me safely to shore in Jesus name.
- I choose to do it Your way now, I acknowledge my total dependence on You at this moment. All that I have is Yours and they all belong to You.
- All my rights of ownership are Yours because You have purchased me for great price. Guide me into Your plan and purpose
- You are all I need, and You are the one I desire. I am under Your leadership. I chose to live by faith, sustain me Lord
- I depend on You for my very life, for my Christian walk, for my family, for my calling and ministry, for my business and career.
- Thank You, that Christ is the source and supply of my life and that without Him I can do nothing. May I live in total dependence upon Him in thought word and deed, so that today may be a fruitful and truly blessed day.
- Thank You that You know how to manage my life perfectly. I give it over to You that I may be blessed because of You.
- Thank You, father, In Jesus name, amen.

Scriptures for further Prayers

John 15:5b, 2 Peter 1:3, 1 Corinthians 6:20

NOVEMBER 10

HUMILITY AND HONOUR

Worship

Today's Scripture and Meditation:

Proverbs 18:12b. *But humility comes before honour.*

PRAYERS:

- Lord Your word is calling me to deeper humility.
- No one comes to You with pride in their hearts. It will be foolishness, as it is in the life of men.
- I do not come like the Pharisees, but I come to You like the publicans as I am not better than anyone.
- I come before You in humility; knowing that without You I can do nothing and know nothing. that in myself, I have no strength, I have no ability, I will faint, I will fail, and I will falter.
- And so, I come before You, bringing my heart before You, that you will deepen my humility, this season, deepen my humility, this season.
- Father, let pride not overcome me, look into every aspect of my life. Look into my perspectives.
- Look into the way I handle things, investigate the way I handle my relationships, look into the way I handle Your work.
- Look into the way I handle the things that You have given to us as possessions and instruct me in the way I should go.
- You said humility comes before honour, Lord humble me, so I might receive honour.

- That I will know that whatever I have, I have received and that You have apportioned to everyone as You want.
- Let me be acutely aware that it is not by power nor by might, but by the Spirit of the Lord.
- Let it be according to Your will, and by the power of Your Spirit.
- Lord, I thank You for how You have given me a portion in Your kingdom, teach me how to handle that which You have given to me.
- Let me not be presumptuous that I may not be proud.
- Lord enable me to be humble before You and before all men in the name of the Lord Jesus, Amen

Scriptures for further Prayers

Luke 18:9-14

NOVEMBER 11

FREEDOM IN CHRIST

Worship

Today's Scripture and Meditation

Galatians 5:1: *"It is for freedom that Christ has set us free. Stand firm, then, and do not let yourselves be burdened again by a yoke of slavery."*

PRAYERS:

- Thank You Lord for calling us to freedom, for where the Spirit of the Lord is, there is freedom.
- Thank You for the freedom that I received by knowing the truth.
- Thank you that the whole journey to the cross was about my freedom.
- I ask for grace to stand firm and live like one who has been set free
- That I will not take up yokes and burdens of the enemy.
- That I will not be possessed by any form of bondage to fear.
- Father, I pray that sin will not have dominion over me.
- That every snare of the enemy on my life be broken and I have escape as a bird to freedom.
- That I have been released from a lifetime of bondage that came through the fear of death.

Scriptures for further Prayers:

Psalm 124:7, Hebrew 2:15, Romans 8:15

NOVEMBER 12

ALONE WITH GOD

Worship

Today's Scripture and Meditation

Mark 1:35 " *In the early morning, while it was still dark, Jesus got up, left the house, and went away to a secluded place, and was praying there.*"

PRAYERS:

- Father enable me to fellowship with You and to pray early in the morning.
- Enable me to have daily time alone with You.

- That I will meet my creator first before I meet or face the world.
- That I will meet my creator first before I meet the devil and his agents in my daily activities.
- That I will meet God before I meet the circumstances of life every day.
- That I will talk to God before I talk to many people.
- That I will fellowship with God before I fellowship with other people.
- That I will hear news from heaven before I hear breaking news on earth.
- That I will sit before God before I sit before people.
- That I will kneel down before God before I kneel down before men.
- That I will honour God before I honour people.

Revive, Rebuild and Restore

- ☐ Enable me to seek for Your plan for the day; I come to You this morning with a humble heart to meet with You, to hear You speak words of affirmation, assurance, and wisdom over my heart as I prepare to go into my day.
- ☐ I come to draw strength for my spirit, soul and body, I seek encouragement, peace and rest from You.
- ☐ I ask that You will meet me in a very real and present way today.
- ☐ Father reveal Your heart to me and strengthen my faith. Grant me the instruction and strategy for this day that I might not beat about the bush or make mistakes.
- ☐ I am here to be filled by Your Spirit once again. I receive life and its abounding fullness of joy from Your presence.
- ☐ I receive a word for today, guidance and direction.
- ☐ By the power of the Spirit of God, I command this day, to bring peace, sound mind, goodness, success, progress, into my life.
- ☐ I command this day to refuse and reject sickness, failure, struggles, evil and evil attracts, mishaps and accidents.
- ☐ I decree blessings for this day and command the day to bring its goodness and increase.
- ☐ I receive grace to do the will of God and to excel in all I lay my hands unto in Jesus' Name. Amen!

Scriptures for further Prayers

Proverbs 3:5-7, Acts 13:52

Revive, Rebuild and Restore

NOVEMBER 13

LOVING GOD

Worship

Today's Scripture and Meditation

Matthew 22:37(NKJV): *Jesus said to him, "you shall love the Lord your God with all your heart, with all your soul, and with all your mind."*

PRAYERS:

- ☐ Father Lord, I thank You because You first loved me which was revealed on the cross when Jesus Christ died for my sins
- ☐ Thank You for Your love for mankind; love so undeserved yet unfailing: You loves me despite my weaknesses with an unconditional love
- ☐ Thank You for the gift of salvation and the blessings of the covenant
- ☐ Father place in my heart a desire to please You and fill my mind with thoughts of Your Love
- ☐ Let the demonstration of my love result in the glorification of Your name. Let my love be selfless, impartial, truthful, and fruitful!
- ☐ May I love You with all my heart, Let no other occupy Your place in my life
- ☐ Let loving You become the galvanizing power for how I feel about You. Let loving You inspires my thoughts about You and stimulate my desire for You
- ☐ Let Loving You motivate my every decision and empower my life.

- ⏹ Enable me to love You with an exclusive love that shuns all others
- ⏹ Let me love You in my understanding so that You will always be in my thoughts and that I will love You above all things
- ⏹ That my hearts be set only on what delights Your heart, my minds anchored only to Your word as the final authority, my soul be satisfied only with what pleases You and my strength spent on what serves You alone
- ⏹ Let my love for You be deep, abiding, surpassing my love for all others and for life, that I may take up my cross and follow You, that I may be worthy of You
- ⏹ Let my love for God surpass my love for things in this world that I will not trade away eternity for little pleasure on earth
- ⏹ Let my love be revealed in how I keep Your word, my obedience them because I belong to You
- ⏹ Father let my love for You not deplete in the day of trial, that I might not give up but that my love will endure
- ⏹ Let me love You with the strength that only the Holy Spirit provides

Scriptures for further Prayers

Matthew 6: 24, Matthew 10:37-39, 1John 2:15

NOVEMBER 14

YOUR FACE I SEEK

Worship

Today's Scripture and Meditation

Psalms 27:8-9: When You said, "Seek My face," My heart said to You, "Your face, Lord, I will seek". Do not hide Your face from me; Do not turn Your servant away in anger; You have been my help; Do not leave me nor forsake me, O God of my salvation.

PRAYERS:

- Father Lord, I thank You for Your faithfulness and Your commitment to me
- I am grateful for salvation, for the strength, for the help, the deliverance, I am grateful that You are my protector, You hide me in Your pavilion in the secret place of Your tabernacle
- You lift up of my head, above all my enemies. I realise that my enemies are anything that stands in the way of salvation and purpose, be it sickness, stagnancy, etc. My head is lifted for this I am grateful
- I will praise and worship You all the days of my life
- I am confident that You will answer me with mercy when I call upon You; Your face Lord I seek this day, do not hide Your face from me
- You are my help, You will never leave me nor forsake me
- When all forsake me Father stand by me, Father take care of me
- Teach me Your ways Lord it is the desire of my heart

Revive, Rebuild and Restore

- Father deliver me and lead me on   the smooth path because of my enemies
- I am amazed at Your calling and embraced by Your mercy Lord. I live to serve and worship You.
- Let there be a manifestation of the required strength, required help, required deliverances, required salvation in me
- I receive strength and help (physical and spiritual) from the presence of the Lord

Scriptures for further Prayers:

Jeremiah 29:13, Zephaniah 2:3

Revive, Rebuild and Restore

NOVEMBER 15

HE HUSHED THE STORM

Worship:

Today's Scripture and Meditation:

Psalm 107:29-30.

He made the storm be still, and the waves of the sea were hushed. Then You will be glad that the waters are quiet, and I will bring you to Your desired haven.

PRAYERS:

- Thank You Lord, for Your goodness and mercy in my life. I proclaim that indeed by Your mercy You redeemed me from the hand of the enemy; Your mercy endures forever!
- You are the King over the storms, and You give command to the storms.
- I turn over any storm that I might be experiencing in my life this moment unto You because You give the storm its command!
- Father I pray that You will still every family storm, relationship storm, health storm, financial storm, business storm, work storm, ministry storm, storms in the city, storm in the nation every area of life in the Name of the Lord Jesus Christ Amen!
- Father, please bring stillness to the storms of my life in the Name of the Lord Jesus Christ.

- I pray that I will not throw away or jettison the treasure that You have given to me, and planted in me, because of the storms.
- Lord, enable me to hold on and hold steadfastly to You despite any storm that may rise.
- I pray for peace where anxiety, worry and depression are arising in my mind and ask for Your peace that surpasses all understanding to guard my mind and heart today. Amen!

Scriptures for further Prayers

Mark 4:39, Jonah 1:4-9

NOVEMBER 16

MOUNTAINS MELT LIKE WAX

Worship

Today's Scripture and Meditation

Psalm 97:1-6(NKJV): *The Lord reigns; Let the earth rejoice; Let the multitude of isles be glad! Clouds and darkness surround Him; Righteousness and justice are the foundation of His throne. A fire goes before Him, And burns up His enemies round about.*

His lightnings light the world; The earth sees and trembles. The mountains melt like wax at the presence of the Lord, At the presence of the Lord of the whole earth. The heavens declare His righteousness, And all the peoples see His glory.

PRAYERS:

- Lord You reign on high over all the earth, and You reign in heaven. You reign over thrones and dominions, over principalities and power, rulers and spiritual hosts. You are in control of everything
- You reign in majesty, in righteousness and justice
- Father let the enemy tremble like water boiling over a hot fire. Come and reveal your power to your enemies and make them tremble at your presence!
- Lord come down and make Your name known to Your adversaries in my life in the name of the Lord Jesus Christ, Amen
- My enemies are nothing, standing in the way of God's will and purpose in my life; I pray that You will deliver me from the hand of my enemies that I might serve You

without fear, in holiness and righteousness before You all the days of my life
- Let every mountain in any department of my life melt at Your presence
- Let every sickness, disease, satanic bondage, lack, failure, stagnancy (if applicable) be destroyed in the name of Jesus name
- Every oppression, suppression ad possession of the enemy in my life be broken in Jesus name. Amen
- At Your presence let the enemy turn their backs and take to flight in my life
- Lord begin to do wonderful, mighty and awesome things in the life that none shall be able to stand before me because of Your presence in my life Let the world know that indeed God is with me
- I pray commanding everything that stands like a mountain in my life to melt like wax at Your presence
- Thank You Father for Your righteousness and justice, for Your miracles and deliverances in Jesus name, Amen

Scriptures for further Prayers

Isaiah 64:2, Luke 1:74-75, Exodus 23:27

NOVEMBER 17

GOD IS FOR US

Worship

Today's Scripture and Meditation

Romans 8:31 What then shall we say to these things? If God is for us, who can be against us? 32 He who did not spare His own Son, but delivered Him up for us all, how shall He not with Him also freely give us all things? 33 Who shall bring a charge against God's elect? It is God who justifies. 34 Who is he who condemns? It is Christ who died, and furthermore is also risen, who is even at the right hand of God, who also makes intercession for us. 35 Who shall separate us from the love of Christ? Shall tribulation, or distress, or persecution, or famine, or nakedness, or peril, or sword? 36 As it is written: "For Your sake we are killed all day long; We are accounted as sheep for the slaughter." 37 Yet in all these things we are more than conquerors through Him who loved us.

PRAYERS:

- Father I thank You because You are my Defender, my Protector and the victorious Lord

- Thank You for the ultimate price that You gave for my sake not sparing Your own Son, but You delivered Him up for me and for us all.

- For this I am assure that You will not withhold any good thing from me.

- I am assured that nothing and no one can stand against me; You will deal with them all.

- I am grateful that no charge and no accusation can be brought against me because You have justified me.

- I overcome the accuser by the blood of the Lamb and the word of my testimony.

- I am grateful that I cannot be condemned because You died, You rose from the dead and You are now seated at the right hand of God, making intercessions for me.

- I am convinced that without any doubt, nothing can separate me from the love of God neither tribulation, or distress, or persecution, or famine, or nakedness, or peril, or sword.

- In all things I am more than conquerors through Christ Who loves me in Jesus' Name.

- Thank You heavenly Father in Jesus' Name.

Scriptures for further Prayers:

John 3:16, 1 John 1-2

NOVEMBER 18

BY THE SPIRIT

Worship

Today's Scripture and Meditation

Zechariah 4:6-9

*So, he answered and said to me: "This is the word of
the LORD to Zerubbabel: 'Not by might nor by power, but by My
Spirit,' says the LORD of hosts.*

PRAYERS:

- Father, I thank You for the power of Your Spirit in my life.
- I thank You Lord that when You call Your children, You also give us assignments.
- When You give an assignment, You do the work by the power of Your Spirit.
- Thank You that I am equipped to carry out Your work in my life, not through my own might or my own cleverness or intelligence – but through Your Spirit Who lives in me.
- Father I pray that You will carry out Your plans, which You alone have purposed.
- Father enable me to live by faith in God to trust Your Word and to believe all that You have told us.
- I am Your workmanship… a spiritual temple of God, that is being built together by His Holy(word).
- I am being built up by the work of the indwelling Spirit of God.
- I surrender myself in Your hands that You will build me brick by brick, line by line, precept upon precept.

- Father teach me to trust You enough to leave my life in Your hands.
- Father teach me to rest in You not exerting energy, strength or might.
- Father enable me live my life knowing that I cannot be built by my strength or intelligence but by dependence on you
- Take over my call assignment and perform it by Your own power and ability.
- Build by your power, all that you have ordained be to achieve for you Lord.
- That I may finish my course and not fall, be weary or falter but that I will finish my course.
- Thank You Father in Jesus Name. Amen!

Scriptures for further Prayers

2 Timothy 4:7, 1 Peter 2:5

NOVEMBER 19

ZEALOUSNESS

Worship

Today's Scripture and Meditation

Zechariah 8:2-3: *"Thus says the Lord of hosts: 'I am zealous for Zion with great zeal; With great fervour I am zealous for her.' Thus says the Lord: 'I will return to Zion, And dwell in the midst of Jerusalem. Jerusalem shall be called the City of Truth, The Mountain of the Lord of hosts, The Holy Mountain.'*

PRAYERS:

- Father Lord, You are Lord of host, the Captain of the army of heaven
- When You fight a battle You fight to win. You have never lost a battle, I ask that You will fight the battles of my life in the family, in the relationships and the places of work, in Your church, in our individual lives. Fight for us concerning our bodies, soul and spirit.
- Thank You for Your zealousness for Zion with great zeal, with great fervour, for Your graciousness are manifesting in my life.
- Father, You said You will return to Zion. Oh Lord, let me be transformed by Your presence; return to me – Your Zion so that You will dwell in the midst of my life
- Oh Lord manifest Your power, and Your presence. Dwell in the midst of us, Lord dwell in my life, Lord dwell in my family, Lord dwell in our churches, Lord dwell in our towns and cities, Lord dwell in our nations, where I reside and where I am from.

- Lord, let the manifestation of Your presence, be real, be tangible, be seen by all that encounter us or engages us, in the name of the Lord Jesus Christ
- That all may see and all may know the God I serve.
- Lord Manifest Your   presence that I may encounter and find You today, a place where Your presence manifests exist. A place where problems are solved.
- A place oh God, where issues are resolved, a place oh God where vows are broken, a place oh God where healing takes   place.
- Holy Spirit breakout, Lord of host breakout, Let the things that can only manifest in Your presence to manifest in our lives to Your glory
- That all may know that God is not dead. That all may know that God is the one that has power in heaven, on earth and under the earth, in the name of the Lord Jesus Christ, Amen.
- According to the order of Phinehas in the name of Jesus, I receive grace for zealousness that I will not even love my life in this world but begin to experience the blessing of the covenant of peace in every department of my life.
- I put down self and fear, I receive grace to step out for the Lord. I receive grace to be zealous for the Lord and I receive the empowerment by the Spirit of God.
- I cast down every lukewarmness, every laziness, every slothfulness, every fear, every complacency, every lackadaisical attitude. I cast it down in the name of Jesus.
- I destroy the power and the influence of every peer pressure causing me to slow down in the works of the Lord.
- Let the peace of God manifest in the lives of my family and that of my generations forever
- Your peace will be the portion of my family, wherever I go, wherever I am, all the days of my life, in the name of the Lord Jesus, Amen
- May the Spirit of the fear of the Lord rest   upon me afresh today

735   *Revive, Rebuild and Restore*

- Blessed be Your name, oh God, we receive the manifestation of the covenant of peace, in our hearts in our lives, in our families, in our circumstances, in our situations, in our bodies, in our spirits and in our souls.

Scriptures for further Prayers:

2 Corinthians 3:18, Proverbs 23:17-18, Numbers 25:11-13

NOVEMBER 20

A BLESSED MAN

Worship

Today's Scripture and Meditation

Psalm 1:1. *Blessed is the man, who walks not in the counsel of the wicked, nor stands in the way of sinners, nor sits in the seat of scoffers;*

PRAYERS:

- Father enable me to be right with You walking according to Your word and in Your counsel.
- Grant unto me the mind of Christ that I will be different in the way I think.
- That I will not act by bad counsel so I will not do evil deeds; and I will not abandon myself to evil doings.
- That I will not give in to the ideologies and philosophies of the world.
- Enable me to be discerning enough to know when each counsel is godly or ungodly, to know when the counsel is my own mind or conscience, my own heart,.
- Grant me self -control that I may not behave the way the world behaves, react and live their lives.
- Father be with me at every stage of my walk with You. Connect me with those that belong to You that will bring godly counsel to me.
- Enable me to take the narrow gate and walk through it for wide is the gate and broad is the way that leads to destruction.
- Show me the path of life; enable me to stay in Your

presence always.

- Enable me to be proud of following You, despite evil abounding in the world., despite sin and evil being the acceptable order of the day.

- I have decided to follow You Lord; no turning back, no retreat but by Your grace, I will continue to proclaim Your goodness and good news on the mountain top.

- Thank You heavenly Father in Jesus' Name.

Scriptures for further Prayers:

Matthew 7:13, Psalm 16a

NOVEMBER 21

MEDITATE ON THE WORD

Worship

Today's Scripture and Meditation

Psalm 119:14-16 *I'll meditate on Your precepts and contemplate on Your way, I would Delight myself in Your status, I will not forget Your word.*

PRAYERS:

- As a new born baby, I desire the milk of Your word that I may grow thereby.
- Father enable me to study, meditate on Your precepts, that I will continue on Your way,
- That You will constantly remind me of Your word, and I delight myself in Your word.
- I know that You will do nothing without Your word, that no door will open, no sickness healed, no deliverances.
- I open up my mind into the word of God and ask that You give me insight and understanding.
- Grant me understanding line by line precept upon precept.
- Lord enable me to turn to Your word in times of trouble in the Name of the Lord Jesus.
- let Your word take priority in my scheme of things and be priority in my life,
- Let Your word come to me that I will eat it that it and be joyful and rejoicing in my heart.
- Let my heart not be hard or shallow ground or full of the

cares of this world.

- God, we command every strong, shallow and thorny ground, let my heart be broken up and prepared for Your word to be sewn upon.
- Let Your world take root in my heart so that I will stand in time of tribulation and persecution and not stumble Name
- Lord enable me to grow in understanding and knowledge of You.
- Let Your word cleans us, let Your word heal us, let Your word deliver us.
- Grant unto me good success and cause me to prosper by Your word
- You sent Your word and You healed them, and You deliver them, send Your word of healing and deliverance.
- Let the word of God avail for me and deliver victories in the Name of Jesus. Amen!

Scriptures for further Prayers:

Psalm 119:14-16, Jeremiah 15:16, Matthew 13:1-10

NOVEMBER 22

THE LORD IS MY SHEPHERD

Worship

Today's Scripture and Meditation

Psalm 23:1-3AMPC)

The Lord is my Shepherd [to feed, guide, and shield me], I shall not lack. 2 He makes me lie down in [fresh, tender] green pastures; He leads me beside the still and restful waters.

3 He refreshes and restores my life (myself); He leads me in the paths of righteousness [uprightness and right standing with Him – not for my earning it, but] for His Name's sake.

PRAYERS:

- Thank You Lord for You are my faithful and responsible shepherd. I will not lack!
- Father feed, shield   and guide me so that I will not miss my way and I will not be left vulnerable
- Lead me to lie down in green pastures, the place of abundance.
- Lead me to the still and restful waters, let every storm cease in my life   and enable me to drink from your Word and Spirit.
- Restore and refresh me that I will not be weary, or faint.
- I receive freshness for my spirit and refuse every staleness

- ▢ Enable me to catch my breath and find rest, send me in the right direction.
- ▢ Manifest Yourself as my shepherd; speak to me and enable me to hear You.
- ▢ Give me grace of discernment to hear You..
- ▢ Let me know You as shepherd though I know You as healer and deliverer.
- ▢ Let me seek guidance from You so I will have peace in the time of storm.
- ▢ Because You are the Shepherd of my soul, I will not be drawn to perdition and sin, or be ashamed on the day of Your appearing.
- ▢ Prevent me from straying away but enable me to stay together with the rest of the sheep.
- ▢ Let me not be left at the mercy of scavengers or killed by the wolves.
- ▢ Destroy the power of strife and complacency and everything the enemy wants to use against me.
- ▢ Let me experience Your presence with me tangibly, let me know You are our SHEPHERD.
- ▢ Restore my soul. Manifest your sure protection in my life
- ▢ Because You are with me, I will fear no evil.
- ▢ Father leads me in the paths of uprightness and right standing with You as I cannot earn it.
- ▢ Thank You Lord, in Jesus name. Amen

Scriptures for further Prayers

Matthew 7:15, John 10:27

NOVEMBER 23

DEALING WITH THE FLESH

Worship

Today's Scripture and Meditation

Romans 6:19: *I speak in human terms because of the weakness of Your flesh. For just as You presented Your members as slaves of uncleanness, and of lawlessness leading to more lawlessness, so now present Your members as slaves of righteousness for holiness.*

PRAYERS:

- Father Lord, I thank You for saving my soul. Thank You for the daily work of the Holy Spirit to transform me

- I pray You enable me to live according to the Spirit, so that my mind will not be set on the things of the flesh, but on the things of the Spirit

- Heavenly Father, Let me not be estranged from You who created me and saved me by dying on the cross to pay the price for my sins

- Lord, help me when I am covered with a worldly and fleshly shroud that has caused me to wander from You and redirect me when I wander and pull away from You

- Deliver me from worldly thoughts, mindset actions, reactions, behaviours and lifestyles that doesn't glorify You

- ⬚ Search me Lord and examine my heart and my attitudes. May I keep my old fleshly self and the old sinful nature nailed to the cross of Christ, and learn to walk in spirit and truth more and more

- ⬚ Draw me back and close to You, whenever my fleshly desires cause me to leave my first Love, the Lord Jesus Christ

- ⬚ Deliver me from this fleshly   mindset that has swamped the heart which belongs to Christ, from whom I gained such joy and peace

- ⬚ Lord, I am not of the world and so I cannot have confidence in the flesh. Help me with Your loving spirit

- ⬚ Thank You for setting me free from slavery to sin, and having become a child of God, enable me to bear fruits in holiness and righteousness

- ⬚ I yield my members to You in obedience to You, to Your word, to the whisperings and the promptings of the Holy Spirit who will lead me to righteousness

- ⬚ I submit my body, spirit and soul unto You. Let the flesh be silenced and not gratified in my life but let the Spirit take authority of my life

- ⬚ I submit my will and my every plan, my agenda, my dreams, my aspirations, and ambitions let them be overtaken by Your will, plan and purpose

- ⬚ Let my mind be set on the things of God and not the things of the flesh. Let me not be carnally minded but spiritually minded that I may have life and peace

- ⬚ Lord transform my heart, ideas and perspectives let my heart be malleable, changeable, transformable and instructible by Your Spirit

- ⬚ Enable me to sow to the Spirit and not to the flesh so I do not reap corruption

- ⬚ Let me not be taken over by temptation, enable me to always see and take the way of escape which You have provided for me in Jesus name

- ⬚ Enable me to walk in the Spirit and live by the Spirit; that I will not be a people led or flesh led but rather -

Spirit led. Holy Spirit have Your way in my life. Thank You, Lord, in Jesus name. Amen!

Scriptures for further Prayers

Romans 8:5, Romans 6:22, Galatians 6:8, 1 Corinthians 10:13

NOVEMBER 24

HEAVENLY MINDS

Worship

Today's Scripture and Meditation

Romans 8:5: *For those who live according to the flesh set their minds on the things of the flesh, but those who live according to the Spirit, the things of the Spirit.*

PRAYERS:

- ▢ Heavenly Father, I repent and pray that You forgive me in any way I'm being so far away from You in my heart or estranged from the God who created me and the Saviour Who died on the cross to pay the price for my sins
- ▢ If there is any way that I have been covered with a worldly and fleshly shroud which has caused me to wander so far away from You, Lord refresh and renew me
- ▢ Let me not live according to the flesh. Let me not become more like the world in my thoughts, actions, reactions, and behaviour
- ▢ Let me not wander and be pulled away from You. Forgive me for any fleshly desires and thoughts
- ▢ Deliver me I pray, from a life so embroiled and return to me the joy of my Salvation. Deliver me from fleshly mindset that has swamped the heart of Christ, from whom I gained such joy and peace
- ▢ Let my heart not be set on things of the flesh that are corruptible but on things of the Spirit that are incorruptible

Revive, Rebuild and Restore

▪ Lord Jesus, I take possession of my mind by the power of Your Spirit, and I pray that You sanctify it with Your word, which is true

▪ I pray that I will not be conformed to this world but transformed by the renewal of my mind through Your word

▪ Enable me to puff my old self with its desires and to be renewed in the spirit of my mind unto a mindset f true righteousness and holiness

▪ Enable me to set my mind on things above not on things that are on the earth

Scriptures for further Prayers

John 17:17, Romans 12:2, Colossians 3:2

NOVEMBER 25

BUILD MY WALLS

Worship

Today's Scripture and Meditation

Nehemiah 1:3: *And they said to me, "The remnant there in the province who had survived the exile is in great trouble and shame. The wall of Jerusalem is broken down, and its gates are destroyed by fire."*

PRAYERS:

- Father I thank You for Your power manifested in my life at each turn. Thank You for Your deliverance from the hand of the enemy.
- Thank you that I have not only survived but I am victorious in the Name of the Lord Jesus Christ
- You are the strong tower and I bring myself under Your covering
- I rebuke the spirit of fear, worry, anxiety, and I cast you out of my life
- I have not been given the spirit of bondage again to fear, but I have received the Spirit of adoption by whom I cry out, "Abba, Father."
- The Bible says, my body is a temple of the Holy Ghost and since Light and darkness cannot cohabit, therefore fear and torment have no place in my life in Jesus Name, Amen!
- I command every form of darkness in my life (fear, anxiety, depression, etc.) to go in the Name of Jesus, Amen.

- I present the blood of Jesus as a payment of every debt owed and I command every bondage be broken in the Name of the Lord Jesus Christ.
- The scripture says, "The walls are broken, and the gates are destroyed by fire". I pray in the Name of Jesus that, every wall that has been broken causing distress and vulnerability in my life to be repaired and sealed off in Jesus name, Amen!
- You are my refuge and fortress, My God in whom I trust, build a wall of protection round about me, keep me under Your shadow in Jesus name, Amen
- Thank You Father in Jesus name, Amen!

Scriptures for further Prayers:

Romans 8:15, John 1:5. Proverb 18:10

NOVEMBER 26

O LORD HEAL ME

Worship

Today's Scripture and Meditation

Psalm 6:2 -5. Have mercy on me, O Lord, for I am weak; O Lord, heal me, for my bones are troubled. 3 My soul also is greatly troubled; But You, O Lord — how long? 4 Return, O Lord, deliver me! Oh, save me for Your mercies' sake! 5 For in death there is no remembrance of You; In the grave who will give You thanks?

PRAYERS:

- Thank You Lord for being a gracious and merciful God.
- I know that God is not a liar. I know that I am not perfect, I will even commit sins that I am not aware of, so Lord I confess every sin I have committed in thoughts, in words and in actions (*e.g. vengeful talks, unforgiveness, slander, backbiting, sins of discrimination and intolerance*) and I ask for Your forgiveness.
- Father God, I come before You, asking for mercy over all my sins, sins of prayerlessness, not studying the word, nonchalance towards the need of brethren and the church we belong to, the sin of slothfulness and action I have taken against one another, decisions and actions taken against the progress of God's work, killing other people's spirit, ministries, joy, job morals, wishing others are dead because of their offence to us, discouraging others, conspiring to impede other people's relationship with God or morals in a negative way *(please delete as applicable and add others not written)*

Revive, Rebuild and Restore

- Father have mercy on me for every way I have affected or impacted the lives of others in a negative way.
- I plead for mercy for scheming, absenting ourselves from the work of God, playing politics in church, absenting ourselves from Your service and making the work of the ministry difficult.
- You said in Your word that You forgive all our sins and heal all our diseases.
- Father forgive all my sins that you may heal me of all my sicknesses and diseases.
- Let your healing virtue flow from my head to the tip of my toes.
- Lord, You sent Your word and healed us from all their diseases.
- Let Your word be healing to my body, Holy Spirit heal me, my family and friends, completely by Your word.
- According to your word, the chastisement of my peace was upon Him and by Your stripe we are healed. I ask for the performance of this word in my life
- He Who raised Jesus will quicken your body through the Spirit that dwells in you; I pray to heal to my mortal body.
- I pray for restoration of my mind from every disease of the soul and mind (known and unknown) I declare complete healing from depression, anxiety, stress, S.A.D, sadness, Phobias, paranoia, OCD, and other challenges of the mind the Name of Jesus.
- I pray for the restoration of my health, The gates of healing are open I walk through it and, enter in.
- By Your mercy Lord save me, I shall not die but live to declare the work of the Lord in the land of the living in Jesus' Name.
- The Psalmist says; Bless the LORD, O my soul, and forget not all His benefits. Thank You for all the benefits bestowed upon me; the forgiveness of sins, healing of diseases, redemption from the pit and crowning me with love and compassion. I am indeed grateful
- Blessed be Your Name oh God, Hallelujah!

751   *Revive, Rebuild and Restore*

Scriptures for further Prayers

Psalm 103:2-4, 1 John 1:7-10, 1 Samuel 12:23, Isaiah 53:5b

Revive, Rebuild and Restore

NOVEMBER 27

THANKSGIVING FOR FUTURE

Worship

Today's Scripture and Meditation

Psalm 26:7 *That I may proclaim with the voice of thanksgiving, and tell of all Your wondrous works.*

PRAYERS:

- I come before the Lord with thanksgiving in my heart.
- I want to thank You in words. I want to thank You in songs, with musical instruments, with a dance offering.
- I thank You Lord for You are a great God, and You are the King, above other gods. I thank You for Your unfailing love.
- I thank you because You're the one that sits upon the throne; the only God.
- I give thanks to You for Your wonderful deeds, I give thanks for all that You do and all the benefits that He daily loads us with.
- You are the Good Shepherd, I thank You for Your everlasting arms will always be underneath me.
- Blessed be God for hearing my cries for mercy and helping me – now and in the future.
- You are my eternal strength and my shield, and my heart trusts in You. You are a stronghold of salvation for Your people.
- I thank You for Your salvation and for richly blessing Your inheritance.

- I want to thank the Lord for the difficult and the easy things, for the problems and the awaited answers and solutions.
- I thank the Lord for the things that have not happened yet, that I am waiting for from You.
- For all the things you have started, and yet to complete, thank You Lord for the completion.
- I thank the Lord ahead of time, for everything in my life, that needs divine intervention and visitation.
- I thank You because You are the One that rules in our lives. I thank You because Your will oh God concerning us will come to pass.
- Thank You that You will be our rock and our hiding place till the end.
- I thank You because Your thought towards me are thoughts of good and not of evil to bring us to an expected end.
- I thank You for good health and a sound mind till the end of my days.
- Thank You for the solutions You have for me when life happens.
- Thank You for provision for all my family's needs and we shall nor lack any good thing.
- I thank You for the doors You will open according to Your will if and when they close.
- I thank You oh God because You are the Great Physician and so, every healing that I am waiting for will manifest.
- Thank You for victory in all my life's battles for You are the victorious Lord.
- I thank You because You are the great Deliverer, that will break through all gates of brass and cut asunder the bars of iron before me.
- I thank You oh God for every deliverance that I require. I thank You oh God for every door that I need to open because you have gone ahead of me
- I thank You God for every provision and every multiplication you are bringing in my future

- I thank You God for that way that You are making in my future and for all the things that You have started to do in my life which I am confident You will complete.
- I thank You because You are in control of the life of every member of my family, please order all our steps. That none will walk away from You and all will serve You till the rest of their lives.
- I bless Your holy Name. Hallelujah to Your name, in Jesus mighty Name, we have given thanks. Amen.

Scriptures for further Prayers

Philippians 1:6, Ephesians 1:11-14, Isaiah 45:2

NOVEMBER 28

THANKSGIVING FOR PROTECTION

Worship

Today's Scripture and Meditation

Psalm 92:1-2 *It is good to give thanks to the Lord, and just sing praises to His name. To declare His lovingkindness in the morning, and his faithfulness in the night.*

PRAYERS:

- I thank You Lord and praise You for Your loving kindness and Your faithfulness.
- Thank You for Your commitment to me, Thank you for keeping me under you shadow.
- Thank You for being my refuge and my fortress; My God, in Him I will trust."
- Thank the Lord for protection, for safety, and for Your covering.
- Father, surpass my expectations and all that hear it will know that I serve a living God
- Thank You for Your deliverance from the traps of the enemy and the perilous pestilence that we have just been through.
- Thank You for safety and security under your wings. For averting the arrow that flies by day,

the pestilence that walks in darkness, and the destruction that lays waste at noonday.

- ⬚ Thank you for Your power to preserve. Many have fallen left and right but I bless You that it has not come near me.
- ⬚ Thank You for keeping at bay, all harm, all evil, all plagues.
- ⬚ Thank You for Your angels that bear me up and that watch over and guard me.
- ⬚ Thank You for power over the enemy and every of his power to tread upon and trample underfoot.
- ⬚ Thank You because You lift me up, You answer when I call, and You stay with me through every trouble.
- ⬚ Father, I thank You oh God from the depths of my heart, I thank you.
- ⬚ Please accept our feeble thanks oh God, in the Name of Jesus.
- ⬚ Blessed be Your name oh God, in Jesus mighty Name we have prayed. Amen.

Scriptures for further Prayers

Psalm 91:1-16, Luke 10:19

Revive, Rebuild and Restore

NOVEMBER 29

BATTLE FOR CHILDREN IN THE FAMILY

Worship

Today's Scripture and Meditation

Isaiah 54:13-14. *All your children shall be taught by the Lord, And great shall be the peace of your children.*
14 In righteousness you shall be established; You shall be far from oppression, for you shall not fear; And from terror, for it shall not come near you.

PRAYERS:

- Father, I thank You that children are gifts and rewards from You. You have also given us the responsibility to partner with You that Your plan and purpose for their lives be fulfilled.
- Father, I give all the children in our family over to You that You will teach them by Your Spirit,
- Give them good success and peace that passes all understanding, so they are not intimidated or overwhelmed.
- Lord, I pray for wisdom to function effectively at all levels to be released to the children in my family.
- Lord, I banish every fear and grant them favour to speak of lifting up while others are speaking of casting down.
- Let Your mercy and grace help them not to be stranded. Restore their hope.
- Lord give them hope. Give them vision, Your vision to see things like You do

- ⬧ Give them the grace to wait upon You patiently and expectantly, knowing You will make a way for them.
- ⬧ Let my children know that help comes only from God and let them know what to do when they need help.
- ⬧ Lord, we speak complete deliverance from everything plaguing children nowadays: depression, anxiety, (name the ones in your family…)
- ⬧ Lord help them to seek counsel from You and not rely on their intellect because the arm of flesh always fails
- ⬧ Lord, please help our children to shun every lure to be in the camp of the ungodly. Establish them in You so they will not seek strange fire.
- ⬧ Keep them solidly on the Rock of Ages. Help them to walk in obedience to godly principles.
- ⬧ Lord help them not to associate with the ungodly or fools. They will not be in ungodly relationships that will bring reproach to the Lord
- ⬧ Lord let them associate with those who will sharpen their iron and not be unequally yoked with unbelievers or ungodly friends.
- ⬧ Help them not to compromise their faith but to stand for you.
- ⬧ I pray for the children in my family who have been lured, pushed out of their faith to be restored and helped by Your Spirit.
- ⬧ Let my children not hear the voice of strangers but Yours alone in Jesus' Name! Amen!
- ⬧ Father equip me to guide them on life's journey and enable me to be a role model for them in Jesus' Name! Amen

Scriptures for further Prayers

Proverbs 3:5-6. Proverbs 13:2, Proverbs 9:10

NOVEMBER 30

BURN UP THE ENEMIES

Worship

Today's Scripture and Meditation

Isaiah 10:17. The LORD, the Light of Israel, will be a fire; the Holy One will be a flame. He will devour the thorns and briers with fire, burning up the enemy in a single night.

PRAYERS:

- ⬚ Lord, I thank You because You are our Lord, You are our light. You said You will be a fire and a flame to devour the thorns and the briers, burning up the enemies in a single night
- ⬚ Lord look on me, look into my life, look into my family and begin to burn and devour the thorns and the briers with fire
- ⬚ Devour everything that You have not planted in my life, and family, in every department   of our lives
- ⬚ Father, I ask, that You begin to burn and devour everything in every church represented, that You have not planted or grown in our churches
- ⬚ In the name of Jesus, I am asking Lord, that You look on me and begin to devour every thorn   and every brier   in the work of my hands
- ⬚ Lord, that You begin to burn every thorn   and every brier   in my body, spirit and soul, and in my relationship with You
- ⬚ Lord, burn every unfruitful and unproductive thing in my life. Deal with everything in my life the prevents

fruitfulness, growth, enlargement, advancement, increase and that prevent us from being built up in You, burn with Your fire tonight

▢ Everything that You have not planted, in our walk with You and in our relationship with You, everything that You have not planted, burn it oh God in one night in the name of our Lord Jesus Christ, Amen

▢ Burn up the glory of the enemy in our lives, that the enemy will not have glory in our lives and the enemy will not retain any glory for themselves, in the name of our Lord Jesus Christ, Amen

▢ Lord, burn up every work of darkness in my life, devour them that they are no more, in a single night

▢ Father let there be complete freedom and deliverance and liberty to serve You and to live a life that is worthy of You in the name of Jesus, Amen

▢ You are Lord and You do miraculous things, there is nothing that You cannot do, Thank You for Your deliverance today in Jesus name

Scriptures for further Prayers:

Matthew 15:13, Psalm 97:3

DECEMBER 1

SPIRIT FALL ON ME

Worship

Today's Scripture and Meditation

Acts 11:15. And as I began to speak, the Holy Spirit fell upon them, as upon us at the beginning.

PRAYERS:

- ⊡ I thank You Lord for giving me Your Holy Spirit to partner with me on the journey of salvation.
- ⊡ Holy Spirit I pray for fresh fire upon me today.
- ⊡ Let fresh fire fall upon me afresh; I pray for fresh grace and unction in the Name of Jesus.
- ⊡ I pray for fire to charge up, as on the day of Pentecost let there be fire of the Holy Ghost.
- ⊡ Release fire for charging up and replenishing lost virtues.
- ⊡ Let Your fire consume the dross, burn unhindered in me.
- ⊡ Grant unto me grace to receive the fire.
- ⊡ Holy Spirit, do a new work, let there be progressive measure of Your fire in me, let it burn upon the altar of my heart.
- ⊡ Give me grace, every morning to provide the firewood; for the fire and let it burn upon my heart.
- ⊡ Grant me grace every morning to provide fuel on fresh wood that the fire will not go out but will continue to burn.
- ⊡ Father ignite the fire upon my altar, let it be a perpetual fire.

- Holy Spirit flood my heart with Your presence like never before.

- This is what I long for, Your presence.

- Help us never to be absent before Your altar let my fire burn, bigger than before.

- That I may continue to burn for You and proclaiming Your good news to all.

- Enable me to go out as Your ambassador, remove anything that will douse my fire.

- Hallelujah! to Your Holy Name, in the Name of Jesus we have prayed, Amen!

Scriptures for further Prayers:

Leviticus 6:12, Acts 2:24

DECEMBER 2

IF YOU LOVE ME

Worship

Today's Scripture and Meditation

John 14:15. *"If you love Me, keep My commandments.*

PRAYERS:

- Thank You, Lord, for Your love towards me and my family.
- Help me oh Lord, to love as You would do, I cannot love without Your grace.
- Enable me to spend time with You so I might understand You and understand Your ways better.
- Forgive me Lord, when I am repeatedly falling short of perfection in my relationship with You and I'm imperfectly obedient at times in some areas of my life.
- Help me to obey Your commandments because they are not burdensome.
- Lord, please put the love for Your word and love for all that concerns You in me.
- Father You rank first in honours, power, authority, and glory, enable me to put You first.
- Give me grace to delight in Your word and profit from it.
- Enable me to obey Your commandments as a proof of my love for You.
- Father, please help me to go the extra mile for You no matter what others say.
- Your greatest commandment is love, enable me to love You

with all my heart, soul and mind.

- Help me to love my neighbour as myself and even to love my enemies as You have commanded.
- Father enable me walk in all Your ways, obeying Your commands, holding firmly to You, and serving You with all my heart and all my soul.
- Help me to live a life that is worthy of You and pleasing to You in all things.
- Thank You Father in Jesus' Name.

Scriptures for further Prayers:

Proverbs 8:17, Ecclesiastes 12:13, Joshua 22:5

Revive, Rebuild and Restore

DECEMBER 3

NO CONSPIRACY

Worship

Today's Scripture and Meditation

Isaiah 41:11-13 *"Behold, all those who were incensed against you shall be ashamed and disgraced; They shall be as nothing, and those who strive with you shall perish. 12 You shall seek them and not find them. Those who contended with you. Those who war against you shall be as nothing, As a nonexistent thing. 13 For I, the Lord your God, will hold your right hand, saying to you, 'Fear not, I will help you."*

PRAYERS:

- Thank you, Lord Jesus, because You care for me; You contend with any enemy and give victories.
- Father come and do a thing, all those that hear it, their ears will tingle.
- I stand still to see the salvation; come and fight your battle, give me victory.
- Your word says, "Weeping may endure for a night, but joy comes in the morning". Make an end to weeping, sorrow, depression, sadness, worry, etc in my life.
- Let this be my season of joy, let this be my morning of joy in Jesus Name.
- Let there be a scattering of every physical and spiritual conspiracy. Let there be an end to the activities of the enemy in my life in Jesus' Name.
- All incensed against me shall be confounded, all that compete against me, my family, my work, my relationship

with God, my ministry, they shall perish, their agenda and scheming shall perish, their words shall turn against them, they shall be put to shame.

▢   Let all that were incensed against me, my family, my work, my relationship with God, my ministry be it a system, a group, a person, physical or spiritual be ashamed and disgraced.

▢   Let them come to nothing so that they do not accomplish their enterprise.

▢   Whether it is a situation in the family, city, workplace, ministry, marriage, we decree according to the word of God, It is enough!

▢   The work of the enemy: the stealing, the killing, and the destruction of the enemy, it is enough.

▢   I address the personality of the enemy carrying out destruction, "it is enough", stay your hand, (…name the situation …) e.g., that sickness: heart condition, cancer, COVID, diabetes, ulcer, barrenness, it is enough! Nerve condition, digestive, and respiratory condition; it is enough! That reproductive system situation, conspiracy in your workplace, it is enough! That conspiracy against you, be broken! Siege against you is over.

▢   Every scheming against any department of my life is nullified in Jesus' Name.

▢   Lord God help me; that I will not be disgraced. I have set My face like a flint, I will not be ashamed. Lord obtain glory in my life and in every circumstance.

▢   I give You praise in Jesus' Name we have prayed, Amen.

Scriptures for further prayers

1 Samuel 3:11, Isaiah 50:7, Psalms 2:1-2

DECEMBER 4

DON'T GRIEVE GOD

Worship

Today's Scripture and Meditation

Ephesians 4:30 (MSG):

Don't grieve God. Don't break his heart. His Holy Spirit, moving and breathing in you, is the most intimate part of your life, making you fit for himself. Don't take such a gift for granted.

PRAYERS:

- Father I thank You for Your Holy Spirit.
- Oh Lord help me not to grieve Your Holy Spirit.
- Holy Spirit of God, breathe on me. I am in need of the breadth of God
- Holy Spirit move in every area of my life, take over all that concerns me.
- Lord Jesus, help me not to take You for granted.
- Holy Spirit let me experience Your Manifold Presence.
- Holy Spirit of God, be real to me, that I may know You and recognize Your voice
- Lord Jesus, as the deer pants after the waters, let me burn for You.
- Oh Lord, increase my appetite for a deeper and intimate relationship with You.
- Thank you father for access to You through Your spirit, in Jesus name I pray. Amen!

Scriptures for further Prayers:

Job 33:4, Exodus 33:4

DECEMBER 5

UNDEFILED IN THE WAY

Worship

Today's Scripture and Meditation

Psalm 119:1-2. *Blessed are the undefiled in the way who walk in the law of the Lord, blessed are those who keep his testimonies who seek him with their whole heart*

PRAYERS:

- Lord, I thank You because You want to share Your blessedness with us hence You sent Your son to die for us on the cross
- Enable me to live my life in conformity to Your standards in other to be content and flow in Your everlasting joy
- Enable me to live a pure life as revealed beyond my conscience but in Your word
- Enable me to make practical progress in Christian life doing something for my master so I might experience Your blessedness
- Enable me to search the scripture, get a firm grip of it and heartily embrace it to be a doer of Your word
- Enable me to Study and be eager, doing my utmost to present myself to God approved (tested by trial), a workman who has no cause to be ashamed, correctly analysing and accurately dividing [rightly handling and skilfully teaching] the Word of Truth.
- Enable me to know, love, respect God's word and live out Your precepts

☐ Lord, I love to seek You with my whole heart in prayer, worship, fasting, serving, enable me to seek You through Your word, that I will not be misdirected

☐ I pray that in seeking You, my heart will not be divided but that my heart be broken before You and that You will manifest Your heart to my heart and that I may comprehend You by affection and not by intelligence

☐ Thank You for You said that if I seek You, I will find You, let me find You today in Jesus name. Amen

Scriptures for further Prayers:

Psalm 25:4-5, Psalm 86:11, 2 Tim 2:24

DECEMBER 6

THE ENEMY THREATENED

Worship

Today's Scripture and Meditation

Joshua 2:8-11: Before the men lay down, she came up to them on the roof and said to the men, "I know that the LORD has given you the land, and that the fear of you has fallen upon us, and that all the inhabitants of the land melt away before you.

For we have heard how the LORD dried up the water of the Red Sea before you when you came out of Egypt, and what you did to the two kings of the Amorites who were beyond the Jordan, to Sihon and Og, whom You devoted to destruction. And as soon as we heard it, our hearts melted, and there was no spirit left in any man because of you, for the LORD your God, he is God in the heavens above and on the earth beneath.

PRAYERS:

- Father I pray that You will let all around me recognise You and Your presence in my life.
- Father do mighty things in my life, do miracles that will cause any ears that hear it to tingle.
- Let everyone that sees me, meets me, have contact with me, whoever comes to me and wherever I go, that hear about or reads about me will recognise God in me and will know that there is nothing they can do to me or about me.
- Reveal Yourself as my God to both friend and foe, reveal Yourself so that I will be not touched or harmed.

- Father reveal my divine inheritance to my enemy and cause them to fear and to give up.
- Let my enemies recognise Your blessings and the manifestation of Your promises in my life.
- Let Your glory be revealed in my life.
- Let fear fall upon my enemies, let them melt, lose courage, lose the motivation to fight.
- Lord, let them fade away. I command every of my enemy to fade away.
- Let the heart of the enemy melt within them by the miracles of God in my life.
- Let the enemies hear of Your miracles and victories in my life and tremble.
- Let everything and everyone that stands in my way of receiving and possessing my Promised Land fade away, so that I may be a terror to the kingdom of darkness and its works.
- Father, destroy everything that blocks my visions, everything that keeps me in bondage of slavery to, sin, addiction, hard labour; anything that introduces me to idolatry and pride, that wants to snuff out life before I manifest my purpose in Jesus Name, Amen!
- That all may know that You are my God, and that the LORD my God, is the God in the heavens above and on the earth beneath in Jesus' Name, Amen.

Scriptures for further Prayers:

Psalm 105:14-15, Exodus 23:27

DECEMBER 7

GOD LAUGHS

Worship

Today's Scripture and Meditation

Psalms 2:4-5: He who sits in the heavens laughs; the Lord holds them in derision. Then He will speak to them in his wrath, and terrify them in his fury

PRAYERS:

- Father Lord, I thank You that You are the God of justice, and You have all power.
- You look at how man plots and You are not afraid, confused, trembling or depressed about the opposition of man. But You laugh at it.
- You are the one who occupies the throne; it is the throne of heaven with authority over all creation.
- Your laughter means comfort, might of holiness, strength of love - Father speak a word of warning to the enemy, bring vindication and be compassionate towards me.
- Father hold in derision all the proud boastings and violence of such as seek to prevent Your accomplishment of Your will in my life in Jesus' name, Amen.
- Let all who have opposed You in my life and have opposed Your will and Your kingdom in my life be frustrated.
- Let the counsel of the enemy come to nothing and let no word spoken by the enemy stand.
- Let the token of the liars and let the devices of the crafty and the will of the enemy be frustrated.

Revive, Rebuild and Restore

Scriptures for further Prayers:

Psalm 135:14, Isaiah 44:25, Job 5:12

DECEMBER 8

TOTAL SURRENDER

Worship

Today's Scripture and Meditation

Romans 12:1-2. (NKJV): *I beseech you therefore, brethren, by the mercies of God, that you present your bodies a living sacrifice, holy, acceptable to God, which is Your reasonable service. And do not be conformed to this world, but be transformed by the renewing of Your mind, that You may prove what is that good and acceptable and perfect will of God.*

PRAYERS:

- Father Lord, I thank You for the matchless gift of salvation that You have given to me by grace, through faith
- I present my body to You a living sacrifice. I surrender to You completely laying my life on the altar as a response to Your love for me. It's my spiritual act of worship to You
- Let my life be my spiritual act of worship, let it be holy and acceptable to You
- Transform me as a person by renewing my mind by Your Spirit, so that I think the way You want me to think about everything, especially about You and about Your will
- May my will be consumed by Your will. Enable me to recognise Your will, and discover as I seek to do it, that it truly is good, acceptable and perfect.
- I pray that my life will not be conformed to the world that in the days of difficulties, my mind will not be deflected from You

- Father enable me to keep Christ on my mind and in my view, and that I will become increasingly aware of the promptings of the Holy Spirit in my life,
- Father, please transform my life daily, enable me to delight and dwell in Your word and renew my mind
- Help me to prove what Your will for my life is, so that I may apply myself to do those things that are good, acceptable and perfect in Your sight
- I thank You for the continuous work of the Holy Spirit in my life to change me to the image of Christ
- All to Jesus, I surrender; All to You I freely give, I will ever love and trust You and in Your presence, I will live daily in name of Jesus. Amen

Scriptures for further Prayers:

Mark 14:35-36, Luke 9:23-24

DECEMBER 9

GO INTO THE WORLD

Worship

Today's Scripture and Meditation

Mark 16:15: *And He said to them, "Go into all the world and preach the gospel to every creature.*

Matthew 28:19: *Go therefore and make disciples of all the nations, baptizing them in the name of the Father and of the Son and of the Holy Spirit*

PRAYERS:

- Father I thank You for the privilege of being given the commission to go into the world to preach the gospel
- Thank You for Your backing authority that guides us and empowers us in Your and that Your message would continue to the world through us.
- Help us/me to partake in making disciples and not just converts from all works of life, all races no matter their status in life
- Thank You for the assurance of Your presence to the ends of the earth, father grant me grace to make disciples through teachings, friendships, and ministry in Jesus name, Amen.
- Father give me passion for souls, and boldness as well as what to say. As I go, please convict souls, and bring them to Your saving grace
- Let there be signs and wonders and miracles following me so that the world will believe in Jesus name, Amen

- Let demons be cast out enable us to speak with new tongues, let the sick be healed
- Make us immune to physical and spiritual poisons; re-enact the signs of the early church
- Father enable me to be ready for Your appearing. Let me be without spots wrinkles, blemishes.
- Let me not be ashamed, let me be counted worthy to be a partaker of Your kingdom at last
- Give me the heavenly vision and let me run this race acceptably and according to Your rules to win the price.
- Thank You Heavenly Father in Jesus name. Amen

Scriptures for further Prayers:

1 Corinthians 3:9, Mark 16:17-18

DECEMBER 10

PRAY FOR THE CHURCH

Worship

Today's Scripture and Meditation

Matthew 18:20 *For where two or three are gathered together in My name, there am I in the midst of them.*

PRAYERS:

- Heavenly Father, I magnify and glorify Your name, I give You all the praise and honour You deserve.
- I know that where two or more are gathered in Your name, You are with us,
- Oh Lord be with us as we gather in our church and the body of Christ universal, let us know Your presence as we gather.
- Let there be a manifestation of Your presence and power.
- Enable us to be of one mind. one vision and one mission to propagate the gospel.
- Glorify God, even the Father of our Lord Jesus Christ.
- Enable us to find unity with each other, to work together to deliver Your word to the world.
- That we will endeavour to keep the unity in the body of Christ in peace.
- Enable us to be a blessing to one another, as we strive to be more like Jesus: kind, caring, compassionate, loving, giving, forgiving and humble.
- Enable us to put away lying, speak the truth with one

another: for we are members one of another.

- Help us as we work together to build Your empire, not ours, that we will the light and salt in this world, Enable us to be examples of the Christian and Christian role models to the people around us.
- Let the people of the world see You and Your love within us, so that they would want to know You more and more.
- Grant us the patience to work together and lets us all live together as a family.
- You wanted us to be one, so Lord help us to be one.
- Let us work together with understanding and compassion in our hearts.
- Let us not be rude or arrogant towards one another, as we light the way to your heavenly Kingdom.
- Enable us to take up the great commission preaching the gospel and making disciples of all nations.
- Thank You for the privilege of being in Your family. Thank You Father in Jesus Name.

Scriptures for further Prayers:

Ephesians 3:4, Ephesians 4:25, 31-32, Romans 15:5-6

DECEMBER 11

THE END TIMES

Worship

Today's Scripture and Meditation

Matthew 24:6-14: *You will hear of wars and rumours of wars, but see to it that you are not alarmed. Such things must happen, but the end is still to come. Nation will rise against nation, and kingdom against kingdom. There will be famines and earthquakes in various places. All these are the beginning of birth pains. Then you will be handed over to be persecuted and put to death, and you will be hated by all nations because of me. At that time many will turn away from the faith and will betray and hate each other, and many false prophets will appear and deceive many people. Because of the increase of wickedness, the love of most will grow cold, but the one who stands firm to the end will be saved. And this gospel of the kingdom will be preached in the whole world as a testimony to all nations, and then the end will come.*

PRAYERS:

- Father, I acknowledge that all the signs are there that Your coming is near
- We are persecuted and hard pressed, but we seek solace and strength from You
- Thank You Father for Your warnings regarding the signs of the end times so we are not ignorant and we are not disappointed, disillusioned, or fallen away
- We have begun to experience the "birth pains" in our world, yet we know that the time is yet to come, Father help us to focus in a world full of all manner of distractions

- In the midst of chaos, when nothing makes sense - Lord help us to find comfort in scriptures and not be caught unawares
- As the world continues to take delight in attacking our faith, values and beliefs, as they strip Your name from everything and remove the scriptures from everywhere, give me the courage to proclaim Your name louder than ever before
- Father give me discernment to discern falsehood. That I will be able to see beyond the faces of men and be alert to the false teachers and prophets
- As wickedness increases, let me not faint and let my love not grow cold
- Father strengthen me according to Your might that I will not fall away. Enable me to stand firm to the end so that I will be ultimately saved.
- Father use me to continue to proclaim the gospel of Jesus Christ that I might be a witness for You. Thank You Father in Jesus name. Amen
- I submit myself to You Lord that You will do whatever You need to do and change in my life, whichever way or format and in every department of my life so that I would not miss the rapture and Your coming, do so and have Your way, oh God, in our lives
- Apostle Paul said lest I be a cast away after having preached the gospel; Father let me not be a castaway after preaching the gospel and after parading myself as Christians in this world
- Let us not be ashamed but let me hear the trumpet on that day and let me be partakers in Your kingdom. Thank You, heavenly Father
- Let my love for You not grow cold, let Your grace be sufficient for me
- I will not yield oh God to the enticement of the enemy in the name of the Lord Jesus Christ. Amen. Oh Lord, have Your way
-

Scriptures for further Prayers:

Romans 15:5-6, Acts 20:29, 2 Corinthian 3:12, 1 Corinthians 9:27

DECEMBER 12

LOVE DOESN'T HURT

Worship

Today's Scripture and Meditation

Romans 13:10(AMPC) *love does no wrong to one's neighbour [it never hurts anybody]. Therefore. love meets all the requirements and is the fulfilling of the law.*

PRAYERS:

- Father I praise You because You are love and You are the God of life.
- Thank You, Jesus, for always loving me even when I was yet a sinner, thank You Lord.
- Oh God I ask that You put in me a love for my neighbors, help me to love my neighbor as myself.
- Help me oh God to restrain from offending others, and to forgive when there is an offence.
- Grant me that love that will help me be kind to others.
- Father Lord please help Your church to love each other, help us Lord.
- That I will not be vindictive or vengeful because love does not hurt another person
- That my love will surpass that of the Pharisees who only loved those who loved them.
- That I will love my enemies as You commanded
- We pray oh God that Your love will reigns all over the world.

Revive, Rebuild and Restore

▢   Lord, please give me a deeper understanding of what brotherly love is so that I will know not to hurt others.

▢   Be Thou glorified our Father, in Jesus Name, I have prayed, Amen!

Scriptures for further Prayers:

1 Corinthians 12: 4-8, Matthew 5:20

DECEMBER 13

STAND STILL

Worship

Today's Scripture and Meditation

2 Chronicles 20:17

You shall not need to fight in this battle; take your positions, stand still, and see the deliverance of the Lord [Who is] with you, O Judah and Jerusalem. Fear not nor be dismayed. Tomorrow go out against them, for the Lord is with you.

PRAYERS:

- Father I praise You because You are mighty in battle,
- I pray that You will take over the battles of my life be it physical or spiritual.
- Enable to take the position of trust in You, belief in You not doubtful, wavering or fearful.
- Enable me to stand still knowing that my Father is the Lord of Host.
- Father help me to depend on You solely.
- I surrender all my battles unto You the Lord of Host
- Oh Lord cause me to know my place in the battles of life.
- Lord make an end to my battles, fearfulness, storms and as I wait to see Your salvation.
- Lord put Your fear and dread upon the enemy, that they may take to flight at the sight of me
- Lod make the enemy to self destruct as you fight my battles and give me victory

- You are fearful in praises; Lord enable me to stay in the place of pray, praise and worship
- Oh Lord, open my eyes to see and behold Your wondrous work in my life that I might receive hope
- Oh Lord, help teach me to completely hearken to thy word even when it does not make sense to my five senses.
- Oh Lord help me to act on Your every command especially when my flesh says otherwise.
- My Father quicken my mortal body, my spirit and my soul to take my rightful place in You.
- Thank You Father, in Jesus name I pray. Amen

Scriptures for further Prayers:

Psalm 46:10, James 1:6-8

DECEMBER 14

NO MORE EGYPTIANS

Worship

Today's Scripture and Meditation

Exodus 14:13-14: *And Moses said to the people "do not be afraid, stand still and see the salvation of the Lord which He will accomplish for you today, for the Egyptians who you see today, you shall see them again, no more forever. The Lord will fight for You, and You shall hold Your peace.*

PRAYERS:

- Father Lord, we thank You for today and honour You because You are the Almighty God.
- You are the victorious Lord; You are mighty in battle, You are fearful in praises, You are glorious in holiness.
- Thank You for the confidence we have in You because You do mighty things, You do glorious things, You do terrible things in righteousness. You are the Lord of Host that fights all battles to win.
- Thank You for Your word that admonishes me not to be afraid or fear
- I turn all our fears, all our worries or anxieties unto You because You never fail or disappoint.
- I cast out every fear. every anxiety, every torment, I chose to believe Your word to stand still.
- I stand still, so I can see Your salvation. I enter (into) Your rest oh God, so I can see You.
- I enter Your rest, so I can see You working on my behalf, in the Name of the Lord Jesus Christ.

- I choose to go forward by faith, it is my time to advance in the Name of the Lord Jesus Christ.
- Father fight all my personal battles, family battles, financial battles, work battles, enemy battles on my behalf.
- Let every enemy of Your will, plan and purpose for my life be destroyed in Jesus' name, Amen.
- Let me see Your salvation manifested! Thank You Father in Jesus' Name, Amen!

Scriptures for further Prayers:

Exodus 14:27-31, 2 Chronicles 20:17

DECEMBER 15

STAND FAST

Worship

Today's Scripture and Meditation

Galatians 5:1. Stand fast therefore in the liberty by which Christ has made us free, and do not be entangled again with a yoke of bondage.

PRAYERS:

- Thank You for the sacrifice You made on the cross of calvary for us all.
- Lord I stand in the place of authority, the reason of Your blood shed for us, and I receive total freedom from sin, freedom from sickness, and anything that poses as a challenge to me.
- It was for freedom that Christ died, so, I declare freedom for every department of my life from the oppression and suppression of the enemy.
- By the word of the Lord, I pray to deforce every handwriting and requirements that was against me, which was contrary to me, they have been taken out of the way and nailed it to the cross, therefore, I am free from them all.
- I command that every evidence of bondage be wiped out by the power in the blood of Jesus.
- I declare that by the blood of Jesus, I am free to live and free to serve You Lord; no more chains holding me.
- Oh Lord enable me to walk circumspectly and not to be entangled in whatever that can enslave me again.
- Enable me to guard my life and not to be entangled with

Revive, Rebuild and Restore

the yoke of bondage.

- I receive the grace to remain in the liberty that Christ has brought for us and never to be enslaved in Jesus Name. Amen!

Scriptures for further Prayers:

Colossians 2:14, John 8:36

DECEMBER 16

LOVE GOD

Worship

Today's Scripture and Meditation

Matthew 22: 37. Jesus said to them (and he said to us this morning) you shall love the Lord your God with all your heart with all your soul and with all your mind.

PRAYERS:

- Father Lord, I thank You because You love me so much and You demonstrated this by sending Your son to come to this earth to die for my sake.
- I love You Lord because You first loved me.
- Help me to sacrificially love You, to sacrificially provide what is needed in Your kingdom a way and manner that You can receive it.
- I give my life to You Lord body, spirit and your soul.
- I choose to trust You with all my heart I choose to believe You when You speaks and to believe completely in Your word even in the face of contrary physical evidence.
- I choose to take You at Your word so You can perform them in my life
- Father Lord, I pray that in every area of my life that I have taken my heart back and I'm running my life according to how I deemed fit, have mercy Lord and deliver me.
- Help me to love You with my heart, my emotions, my intellect that I will respond to all matters as You would respond, responding to things the way God will respond.

Revive, Rebuild and Restore

- ⍰ Let my soul be completely converted by the word of God and my life consumed in God's will.
- ⍰ Lord help me to fully love you with my soul with my intellect with my consciousness with my conscience
- ⍰ Lord I pray, that you will enable me to love You with my mind as it is what you require, enable me to love you with my imagination, not as a daydreamer, help me to love You with my memory, that I will perceive things with the mind and in the ability of God that I will not perceive things through a negative mindset.
- ⍰ Lord that I will not be seeing things through the lens of my personal fears, will not be judged through my self - consciousness. I speak peace over my hyperactive mind in Jesus name
- ⍰ Let my mind receive divine order, let me have the mind of Christ that I will reason like Jesus does.
- ⍰ Bless my memories with the testimonies and acts of God and let the blood of Jesus erase every bad memory, every destruction, and every damage in my memory.
- ⍰ Let the blood of Jesus erase every memory that has served as a weapon in the hands of the enemy to keep me from loving God as I should.
- ⍰ Let all fears be taken away in the Name of Jesus whatever will cause me not to engage with God this new season be removed.
- ⍰ Whatever constitutes a limiting factor in my life or memory is taken out in the Name of Jesus.
- ⍰ I receive the complete l freedom of the mind and my channels are cleared and let my reception from God not be cloudy anymore in the Name of Jesus.
- ⍰ Grant me the grace to put off the old, grace to put off the corruption of the old mind be renewed in my mind this moment in the Name of Jesus.
- ⍰ I receive grace to put on the new mind in the Name of our Lord Jesus and to obey you in all things
- ⍰ I choose to love You with my heart, with my mind and with my spirit and soul, renew my mind oh God.
- ⍰ I give you full access to my spirit, mind and soul. Spirit Of the Living God, I open my heart to you.

▢ Do a factory reset of our minds Lord that I might indeed love You today and for the rest of my life. Thank You Father in Jesus name. Amen.

Scriptures for further Prayers

Matthew 22:37, Proverbs 4:20-23, Ephesians 4:22-24

DECEMBER 17

REST ON EVERY SIDE

Worship

Today's Scripture and Meditation

1 Chronicles 22:18. *"Is not the Lord your God with you? And has He not given you rest on every side?*

PRAYER:

- ☐ Father, I thank You because you have given me rest.
- ☐ My expectations shall not be cut off. Lord do great and mighty things in my life.
- ☐ And all that hear it shall know that I serve a living God who does not forget His people.
- ☐ I shall not be afraid; I shall not be put to shame because the Lord is the lifter of my head.
- ☐ Father I seek You with all my heart, please fight for me and give me victory and peace on every side.
- ☐ Lord, please reward my diligence. When I call You, Lord answer me. Lord show me Your righteous arm.
- ☐ Lord show mercy to me and my children and my generations as You have spoken in Your word.
- ☐ Lord give me rest from all my battles.
- ☐ Lord give me rest from every sickness, every depression, every suppression, every oppression, every bondage, every sorrow, every fear, every anxiety, every struggle, every pressure, every difficulty, every violence.
- ☐ Lord give me rest on all sides. Lord open doors on to me, that I do not expect. And Lord keep them open.

- ☐ Lord rewrite my story. Lord rewrite my history. "I am bringing pleasure out of this earthen clay."
- ☐ Lord pour Yourself into me. Lord beautify me, that I might be a blessing in the earth.
- ☐ "This day, I have poured out greater grace upon you." Hallelujah!
- ☐ Lord do great things. I have chosen the foolish things. I have chosen the weak things.
- ☐ I am raising you an apostolic generation. And you shall break ground and establish my counsel in these last days.
- ☐ Lord greatly contend with those who contend with me, and none shall be able to stand before me.
- ☐ I am the LORD says the Spirit of the Lord to us this morning. Amen!

Scriptures for further Prayers

Joshua 21:44, Exodus 7:16

Revive, Rebuild and Restore

DECEMBER 18

LOVE

Worship

Today's Scripture and Meditation

1 Corinthians 13:4-5. "*Love is patient, love is kind, it isn't jealous, it doesn't brag, it isn't arrogant, it isn't rude, it doesn't seek its own advantage, it isn't irritable, it doesn't keep a record of complaints.*"

PRAYERS:

- Father God, You are love and whosoever does not love does not know You.

- Lord give me exceeding grace to love, that I will not just be a religious person in the church who do not know You.

- Your word says love is the greatest. Father Lord, I pray that You will teach me how to love unconditionally.

- Spirit of God work in me to destroy any fruit of the flesh remaining in me and bear fruit of love with its manifestation in me.

- Lord, I pray that You will baptize me with Your Holy Spirit and power afresh with the Spirit of love that quickens and assists in living as God wants, give to me in the Name of Jesus.

- Let love be in the foundation of all I do, let love reign in my heart and give me the grace to overlook the wrongdoings of others, to shun every negative thing that people do to me in the Name of Jesus.

- Father Lord, I pray that You will help me to love people genuinely, regardless of their religious beliefs, doctrine, tribe or language, that You will help me to look beyond all the things that separate us.

• Lord, I pray for the grace to be kind to other people, give me the grace to treat people with kindness and humility.

Scriptures for further Prayers:

Galatians 5:19-23, 1 John 4:8

DECEMBER 19

AN EXCELLENT SPIRIT

Worship

Today's Scripture and Meditation

Daniel 5:11-12. There is a man in Your kingdom in whom is the Spirit of the Holy God. And in the days of Your father, light and understanding and wisdom, like the wisdom of the gods, were found in him; In as much as an excellent spirit, knowledge, understanding, interpreting dreams, solving riddles, and explaining enigmas were found in this Daniel, whom the king named Belteshazzar, now let Daniel be called, and he will give the interpretation."

PRAYERS:

- Father I thank You for giving me Your presence.
- Grant me an excellent spirit: knowledge, understanding, interpreting dreams, solving riddles, and explaining enigmas were found in this Daniel, whom the king named Belteshazzar, Now let it be said of me that an excellent spirit, knowledge, understanding, the gifts of the spirit operate in me.
- Father let Your presence be with me and enable me to engage with Your presence and be fully aware that I may fully live and walk in the Spirit, who is my inheritance.
- Holy Spirit will come upon me, and the power of the Highest will overshadow me.
- Let Your presence manifest in my life and go with me wherever I go and give me rest.
- I love to be in Your presence Lord fill me afresh with Your spirit and overflow in my soul.

Revive, Rebuild and Restore

- In Your presence I am being built up.,
- In Your presence I receive grace to overcome fleshly immaturity and be transformed.
- In Your presence I will receive comfort, instruction, direction, revelation of You and of my call and purpose, hope is ignited in my soul when You manifest Your presence.
- In Your presence faith arises and mountains melt like wax.
- In Your presence there is safety and security. There is fullness of joy.
- In Your presence, demons tremble, darkness vanishes. Healing, deliverance, emancipation takes place
- I pray that every sickness, disease, oppression, suppression, possession of the enemy be destroyed. We command every chain, fetters, padlocks prisons, cords of bondage to break.
- Nothing good exists outside Your presence; I seek Your presence Lord, You are the only one I need.
- As I stay in Your presence, deliver and rescue me from hidden traps, shield me from deadly hazards.
- Anything that stands in the way of me fulfilling my purposes is an enemy- let all my enemies be destroyed in Your presence.
- Father release gifts into my life that will bless this generation in Jesus name
- Thank You Father for hearing and answering me in Jesus' Name, Amen

Scriptures for further Prayers:

Exodus 33:14, Luke 1:35

DECEMBER 20

LET MY LIFE PLEASE YOU

Worship

Today's Scripture and Meditation

Psalm 37:23-25(NIV) *The Lord guides us in the way we should go and protects those who please him. 24 If they fall, they will not stay down, because the Lord will help them up. 25 I am old now; I have lived a long time, but I have never seen good people abandoned by the Lord or their children begging for food.*

PRAYERS:

- Father in Your mercy, may You delight in me, I pray Lord that my life will please You.
- Father guide and protect me in the way I should go and protect me like You normally do to those who please You, may I worship You in all I do.
- Father let my life please You, that You may delight in me.
- Raise me up when I fall, keep my step firm and help me.
- Father, I ask that You uphold me with the right hand of your righteousness, help me Lord!
- You're the God who takes care of Your own, father please take care of all that concerns me and mine.
- You never abandon Your children or neglect their needs, Lord let Your presence with me be tangible.
- Father supply my needs according to Your riches in glory by Christ Jesus.
- Thank You Father that You are eager to be gracious to me

Revive, Rebuild and Restore

▢   You have proved to be faithful in all Your ways, father let Your faithfulness in my life be seen by all men.

▢   Thank You for how You father me in Jesus Name! Amen!

Scriptures for further Prayers

Philippians 4:19, Proverbs 24:16a

DECEMBER 21

GOD IS GOOD

Worship

Today's Scripture and Meditation

Nahum 1:7(AMPC) The Lord is good, a Strength and Stronghold in the day of trouble; He knows (recognizes, has knowledge of, and understands) those who take refuge and trust in Him.

PRAYERS:

- Father I bless you because you are good in Your very being; it is Your very nature to be good
- I bless you because You are good independently, You do not need help to be good
- I worship You because you are eternally and unchangeably good.
- Lord You are all Your acts of grace and in all Your plans and purposes for my life.
- I trust You Lord; let me see Your goodness and find protection in You: my stronghold
- I thank You that You are in control of everything and there is an end to all our griefs
- I am grateful that you know me not only in identification but also in relationship
- Father You know my Prayers and tears, You knows my wishes; father please grant them all in Jesus name
- Father You know I am not what I want to be, and what I do desire to be; father enable me in Jesus name

Revive, Rebuild and Restore

- You know my aspirations, my sighs, my groans, my secret longings father intervene in Jesus name
- You know my own chastening of spirit when I fail, Lord empower me in Jesus name.
- You know all about me; You have been with you when I thought I was alone.
- You Know the secrets of my heart that I could not even decipher, Lord I trust you and I take refuge in You
- My life is safe in Your hands, so I leave it with You
- Thank You father, in Jesus name. Amen

Scriptures for further Prayers:

2 Samuel 22:3, Psalm 5:11

DECEMBER 22

KEEP THE FIRE BURNING

Worship

Today's Scripture and Meditation

Leviticus **6:12** *"And the fire upon the altar shall be kept burning on it; it shall not be allowed to go out. The priest shall burn wood on it every morning and lay the burnt offering in order upon it and he shall burn on it the fat of the peace offerings.*

PRAYERS:

- Father Lord, I thank You because You are a God that loves relationships, You made us because You desire fellowship with us.
- Father, I pray that you will take me deeper into the place of intimacy that I will not become mechanical in my relationship with You.
- Thank You for igniting Your fire in me, I know it's my responsibility to keep it burning. I ask You Lord for grace to keep the fire burning.
- I pray that Your fire in me will be on the increase daily and be the pattern of my lifestyle until You return.
- It is my responsibility to put fresh wood daily, Father enable me to attend to my altar daily.
- Give me the grace to put fresh wood upon that fire to have a fresh word from You daily.
- Father draw me closer unto You on a daily basis.
- I surrender to You and give myself completely to You God.
- I make a decisive dedication of my body and present all my members and faculties to You as a living sacrifice.

Revive, Rebuild and Restore

- Let the sacrifice of my life be holy and consecrated unto You.
- Let my sacrifice be well-pleasing unto You and accept this as my service unto You *and* spiritual worship of You.
- Father I, surrender and submit my entire life unto You. Without You, I am nobody.
- I pray for Fresh Fire upon the altar of my heart.
- Spirit of the Living God, fall afresh on me. Break me! melt me! mould me! fill me Spirit of the Living God, fall afresh on me!
- Spirit of the living God, baptize and fall upon me afresh! Fresh fire, I pray upon the altar of my heart fresh fire. Do it again Lord!
- Holy Ghost fire fall on me! Fresh fire fall on me!
- Consume all that hinders your work in my life and Clear every blockage that hinders my fellowship with You!
- Fall on me to enable, energize, empower, heal, consume all that hinders anointing, fresh grace, and unction.
- Thank you father in Jesus name. Amen

Scriptures for further Prayers

Romans 12:1, Matthew 5:15

DECEMBER 23

SET YOUR HEART ON THE PILGRIMAGE

Worship

Today's Scripture and Meditation

Psalm 84:5-7: *Blessed is the man whose strength is in You, whose heart is set on pilgrimage. As they pass through the Valley of Baca, they make it a spring; The rain also covers it with pools. They go from strength to strength; Each one appears before God in Zion.*

PRAYERS:

- Father I thank You for setting my feet on the path of salvation.
- Thank You for going ahead to prepare mansions for us. This world is not my home, I am just passing through.
- I receive grace to continually have the heavenly vision looking forward to the time of Your appearing to take me home.
- Father I cannot rely on my own strength or the strength of the world as I will faint, but I draw strength from You for my life's journey. My heart is set on this pilgrimage as I know that this world is not my home.
- I am accurately aware that this world is not my home and that I am passing through.
- We do not rely on self or the world for strength, but considers ourselves visitors, travellers, pilgrims in this world. Our strength and treasures are in the world to come.
- The zeal of the house of the Lord has consumed me, even as I delight in it, I am not of this world.

- Let me find strength in You: Let me enjoy Your sweetness and find strength in You.
- Give me wisdom and enable me to come before You in Zion that I might go from strength to strength
- When I pass through the the the Valley of Baca (weeping, drought and dryness) let it be transformed into a spring, covered with rain and pools of water.
- Deal with every difficulty and trouble today, refresh us by the streams of divine grace, release a fountain of comfort.
- While the world goes from strength to weakness, let me go from strength to strength, from one degree of grace to another, gaining divine virtue through every step. Let my relationship with God become richer and richer, sweeter, and sweeter.
- Give me an unending supply of strength for the journey, even in difficult seasons.
- Let me grow stronger as the days go by.
- Enable me to wait on You so that I will not faint or be weary, I receive refreshing, renewal, strength, grace to sustain and to stay on the journey.
- As I appear before God in Zion this morning, Oh Lord of host hear and answer my prayer in Jesus Name, Amen!

Scriptures for further Prayers:

Psalm 69:9, Job 22:29, Isaiah 40:31

DECEMBER 24

EXAMINE YOURSELF

Worship

Today's Scripture and Meditation

2 Corinthians 13:5-7. 5 *Examine yourselves as to whether you are in the faith. Test yourselves. Do you not know yourselves, that Jesus Christ is in you? — unless indeed you are disqualified. 6 But I trust that you will know that we are not disqualified. 7 Now I pray to God that you do no evil, not that we should appear approved, but that you should do what is Honorable, though we may seem disqualified.*

PRAYERS:

- Father thank You for the assurance of my salvation and grace to endure attacks that come in this area.
- I submit myself in the hand of the Holy Spirit for scrutiny and examination fixing my eyes on Christ.
- I ask that You reveal anything in me that grieves the Holy Spirit; give me grace that it might be put away and cleansed in Your precious blood.
- Father enable me to be tender hearted. Take the hardness away from my heart and the shadows from my life, to bring total freedom.
- Enable me to live in the consciousness of the fact that Christ is in me that I might be not be disqualified.
- Lord, let me not be presumptuous or complacent.
- Enable me to go all the way with You and never chasing after the world that I might not be disqualified.
- I pray that I will never do evil that I may be approved by

God.

▫   I pray that You will enable me to discipline my body, so I am not disqualified.

▫   I pray that I will do what is honorable always in Jesus Name. Amen

▫   Thank You Father, in Jesus' Name I have prayed. Amen!

Scriptures for further Prayers:

Ephesians 4:3, 1 Corinthians 9:27

DECEMBER 25

GOD'S DESIRE

Worship

Today's Scripture and Meditation

1 Timothy 2:4 who desires all men to be saved and to come to the knowledge of the truth.

PRAYERS:

- Thank You Lord because Your plan for the entire world is to be saved.
- I pray that the covering with which the enemy has blinded the eyes of men so that they do not see the light of the gospel of Christ be removed!
- Lord let Your Spirit brood over the lives of men in this nation to bring about light in their lives.
- Reveal the convicting power of the Holy spirit in our generation.
- Father Lord please let my friends and family members encounter You and receive salvation
- Father, grant me the grace to go out to preach the gospel so that souls can be saved into Your Kingdom.
- Father let the spiritual eyes of people be open to the truth that they might come to Your saving grace and knowledge.
- May I carry Your gospel to the ends of the earth and may You win souls into the kingdom Through me
- Thank You Father in Jesus Name.

Revive, Rebuild and Restore

Scriptures for further Prayers:

2 Corinthians 4:4

DECEMBER 26

HEALINGS FOR THE BODY

Worship

Today's Scripture and Meditation

Romans 8:11: *But if the Spirit of him that raised up Jesus from the dead dwell in you, he that raised up Christ from the dead shall also quicken your mortal bodies by his Spirit that dwelleth in you.*

PRAYERS:

- Father, I thank You that You sent Your Son Jesus to die for me on the cross of Calvary. Your word says that the chastisement for our peace was upon Him and by His stripes we are healed. I stand on Your word today, to claim my healing in Jesus name
- In the word, we see that the people all looked to You and power came out of You and healed them all, as I look to You this day for all manner of healing, Lord let Your power flow into my body, soul and spirit to heal me
- Lord, You sent Your word, healed them, and delivered them from their destructions, let Your word bring healing and health to my flesh and rescue me from destruction
- According to Your word, "Heal me, Lord, and I will be healed; save me and I will be saved, for You are the one I praise."

Revive, Rebuild and Restore

- ⬚ Bless my water and my bread let nothing I eat, or drink bring sickness or diseases to my body but let them bring healing and health to my body in Jesus name
- ⬚ According to Your word, Father take sickness away from me and my family in Jesus name
- ⬚ Every plant not planted by my heavenly Father will be uprooted, every planting, deposits, sicknesses, etc in my body be uprooted, only the plantings of the lord will germinate and grow in my life in Jesus name
- ⬚ Let the Sun of righteousness rise with healing in His wings to bring healing into my life
- ⬚ Let the Spirit of God who raised Jesus from the dead and dwells in me quicken and give life to my mortal body that I will live and not die and be in health in Jesus name
- ⬚ Father restore health to me and heal me of any wounds (body and mind) that all may go well with me
- ⬚ Thank You for answering my Prayers in Jesus name. Amen

Scriptures for further Prayers

Luke 6:19, Psalms 107:20, Jeremiah 17:14, Exodus 23:25

Revive, Rebuild and Restore

DECEMBER 27

RESTORATION OF GOD'S PEOPLE

Worship

Today's Scripture and Meditation

Zechariah 10:5-7: *And they shall be like mighty men treading down their enemies in the mire of the streets in the battle, and they shall fight because the Lord is with them, and the [oppressor's] riders on horses shall be confounded and put to shame. And I will strengthen the house of Judah and I will save the house of Joseph [Ephraim]. I will bring them back and cause them to dwell securely, for I have mercy, loving-kindness, and compassion for them. They shall be as though I had not cast them off, for I am the Lord their God, and I will hear them.*
Then Ephraim [the ten tribes] shall become like a mighty warrior, and their hearts shall rejoice as through wine; yes, their children shall see it and rejoice; their hearts shall feel great delight and glory triumphantly in the Lord!

PRAYERS:

- Thank You Lord for Your mercy towards me to save and deliver me
- Strengthen me to be like a mighty man treading down their enemies in the streets in the battle that I might be victorious in every battle
- Let everything that oppresses me be confounded and put to shame
- Father, I am mighty because You are with me, by Your power, I shall thread down the enemies

- ⬜ Father inspire me with the courage to subdue the enemy and cause me to triumphant in You
- ⬜ I have victory over every oppression and the enemy is confounded and defeated
- ⬜ Thank You for Your restoration, for security, mercy, loving-kindness and compassion
- ⬜ Thank You for every provision made for me, enable me to draw on Your resources for strength
- ⬜ Your word says, "Finally, my brethren, be strong in the Lord and in the power of His might". Father enable me to be invigorated and strengthened with all power according to the might of Your glory
- ⬜ Lord hear me when I call and let me find You when I seek You
- ⬜ Grant me the opportunity to use Your strength that You have made available to me
- ⬜ Lord, cause me to dwell securely and have mercy, loving-kindness, and compassion towards me
- ⬜ Lord bring me out from my labours, and strengthen me so that I will be able to perform the works of my hands excellently
- ⬜ That there may be gladness and rejoicing in my house for victory obtained; let every sense of defeat and weakness that may linger in me will be replaced with gladness

Scriptures for further Prayers

Ephesians 6:10, Romans 8:37, 1 John 5:4

DECEMBER 28

ACCORDING TO PLAN

Worship

Today's Scripture and Meditation

Psalm 40:7-8: Then I said, "Behold, I come; In the scroll of the book, it is written of me. I delight to do Your will, O my God, And Your law is within my heart."

PRAYERS:

- Father Lord I thank You that You have a plan and a purpose for my life and my days are already written before You.
- You chose me from the foundations of the world to save me and make me blameless before You.
- Lord I delight to do Your will.
- Enable me to walk the path set for me and to run the race set before me.
- Enable me to keep Your commandments and judgements
- I know that sometimes, Your plans for my life may not be comfortable. Sometimes, Your plans for my life may not be the plan that I want but I choose to accept Your own plan.
- Your plans for my life may not be the plan that I want to follow, it may not be attractive I choose to submit to You.
- Enable me to drop the known for the unknown that is according to Your own will and to take that step into Your next level, says the Lord!

- Lord I pray You will make it impossible for me to step out of what You have written of me from the foundations of the world in the Name of the Lord Jesus Christ, Amen!
- Oh Lord make it impossible for me oh God, to step out of Your plan, or Your purpose for my life even for a minute in the Name of the Lord Jesus Christ, Amen!
- I will not begin to do my own thing because it looks and it sounds familiar, it looks, and it sounds spiritual or religious.
- But Lord, I will do what You have apportioned to me.
- What You have ordained to me from the foundations of the world that is what I submit to this morning oh God, in the Name of Jesus!
- I submit to what You have ordained unto me, what You have purposed for me, what You have written about me from the foundation of the world oh God, in the Name of the Lord Jesus Christ, Amen!
- Even when it is uncomfortable, and out of my comfort zone. Enable me to delight in your will and to obey
- Even when it is new, it is uncharted, even when it is unknown to me, oh Lord I am willing to go in the Name of Jesus Amen!
- Enable me to walk worthy of You fully pleasing You in every good work in Jesus' name, Amen
- That I will serve before You all the days of my life in Jesus Name, Amen!

Scriptures for further Prayers:

Jeremiah 29:11, 1 Kings 2:3, Luke 1:

DECEMBER 29

KINGS AND PRIESTS

Worship

Today's Scripture and Meditation

Revelation 1:5-6. *and from Jesus Christ, the faithful witness, the firstborn from the dead, and the ruler over the kings of the earth. To Him who loved us and washed us from our sins in His own blood, 6 and has made us [c]kings and priests to His God and Father, to Him be glory and dominion forever and ever. Amen.*

PRAYERS:

- ☐ Lord, I worship You as the King who sits upon the throne and rules and reigns in the affairs of men. The earth is Yours and the fullness thereof.
- ☐ Thank You Jesus that You are the Faithful Witness and can be relied upon. Your faithfulness to the Father and to us Your people.
- ☐ I thank You because You are pre-eminent among all those who are or will be resurrected, being the firstborn among many brethren.
- ☐ Looking at the cross I am secured in Your love which is not touched by any circumstance or situation.
- ☐ Thank you for Your blood that cleanses me from all sins. I as if I have sinned in any way that you will forgive me my sins and cleanse me from all unrighteousness.
- ☐ Today I take responsibility to live a life that is worthy of God and is pleasing to Him

- Thank You for making us Kings and Priests; a priest to offer sacrifices to You and a King to take authority over darkness.
- Asa priest, today I offer You praise and thanks for You are God, the only true and immortal God.
- I ascribe greatness to the You, our God and King
- You are the King of kings, You are above all kings, You are above all powers, above all rulers above all government, above all nature, above all created things, above all knowledge, above all wisdom and I worship you Lord.
- As a king, I make decrees that the counsel of God will stand, His purpose will be established in my life, I will fulfil God's plan for my life and my calling, no weapon formed against me shall prosper, every tongue that shall rise against me in judgement is condemned.
- To You be glory and dominion forever and ever. Amen.

Scriptures for further Prayers

Romans 8:29, Colossians 1:10

Revive, Rebuild and Restore

DECEMBER 30

A FORTIFIED BRONZE WALL

Worship

Today's Scripture and Meditation

Jeremiah 15:20-21. And I will make you to this people a fortified bronze wall; And they will fight against you, but they shall not prevail against you; For I am with you to save you and deliver you," says the Lord. 21 *"I will deliver you from the hand of the wicked, and I will redeem you from the grip of the terrible."*

PRAYERS:

- Thank You Lord that You are my deliverer, my refuge, my fortress my strong tower.
- According to Your word do I pray that You will deliver me out of the hands of the wicked.
- Restore me from the palms of the terrible and ruthless tyrant, from the enemy that is bigger than I, that he will not prevail over my life ..
- Father, I thank You because nothing and no one is bigger than You or can defile your power.
- I come to You with all the simple and all the complicated issues that You will step in and solve and resolve them for me
- Jehoshaphat said, "we have no power against these multitudes, but our eyes are on You". Lord my eyes are on You to fight all the battles in my life (marital, physical, spiritual, financial etc). Do battle, fight my fight and give me victory. Break the staff of the wicked and sceptre of the tyrant ruler and the face of the authority, Redeem me from the hand of the terrible

Revive, Rebuild and Restore

- Father, break their authority and their seat. Break the arms of the wicked that oppose me, my family etc. for you are the STRONGER ONE
- Break the power of the enemy that all that he has plundered be restored in Jesus name
- I take back all that the enemy has stolen from me, no more stagnancy, I receive restoration for every department of my life.
- Bring total deliverance and restoration in every department of my life
- Thank You heavenly Father in Jesus Name. Amen!!

Scriptures for further Prayers

Psalms 24:9, Isaiah 14:5, Luke11:22

DECEMBER 31

THANKSGIVING FOR HIS GOODNESS

Worship

Today's Scripture and Meditation

Psalms 100:4-5: *Enter into His gates with thanksgiving, And into His courts with praise. Be thankful to Him and bless His name. 5 For the Lord is good; His mercy is everlasting, And His truth endures to all generations.*

PRAYERS:

- My Father and my God, I enter into Your gates with thanksgiving in my heart and into Your courts with praises on my lips

- I thank and bless Your Holy Name because You are good; Your mercy is from everlasting to everlasting extending to all generations

- You are the Almighty God and there is none like You. Your glory fills the heavens! I will praise Your Name forever, for You have all wisdom and power

- You are the self-existing God, the creator of all things. You are our help and our shield. Our hearts rejoice in You, and we trust in Your holy Name. Father

- You have performed many wonders for me. Your plans for me are good

- The all-knowing God; power belongs to You, to give wisdom to the wise and to give knowledge to those who have understanding.

Revive, Rebuild and Restore

- You are the only God, and You have no equal! If we tried to recite all Your wonderful deeds, we would never come to an end
- Thank You for Your unfailing love in the morning and Your faithfulness in the evening
- Thank You for the privilege of a new beginning. Thank You for all You have done in my life including those I do not know about. I praise You for Your faithfulness and covenant loyalty to me. I praise You Jesus
- Thank You for keeping Your covenant with me throughout the years
- Father God, I give You thanks and praise for Your amazing gift of salvation and for keeping me in the faith thus far
- Father, I thank You for sending Your only begotten son Jesus Christ to this world to die for me for the forgiveness of my sins
- Thank You for enlightening my heart to say "yes" to You when You called me to be Your child
- Thank You for revealing Yourself to me as the way, the truth and the life, the one who has the name through which all are saved
- You have the name above all names; at Your name every knee bows, and all confess that Jesus is Lord to the glory of God the Father
- I appreciate You for translating me from the kingdom of darkness to the kingdom of Your dear Son: the kingdom of light
- I thank You for Your deliverance from the hand of the enemy that I may serve You without fear, being set apart and made righteous before You all my days
- I surrender all to You, take my life and let it be as You have ordained it to be from the foundation of the world.
- Thank You Jesus - my Saviour, my Master and my Lord

Scriptures for further Prayers:

I Thessalonians 5:18, John 3:16, Psalms 107:1-2

Revive, Rebuild and Restore

ABOUT THE AUTHOR

Toyin Taiwo is the Senior Pastor of Grace Chapel Chesterfield, a growing multicultural church in the town of Chesterfield UK. She is a sound teacher of the Word. Through her cutting-edge revelations and divine instructions in admonishing others to apply simple biblical principles, the lives of many have been impacted Her pastoral heart has empowered her commitment to this sacrificial call upon her life and makes her to intercede for people, cities, and nations.

She is passionate about bringing the Grace of God unto everyone, reaching and making disciples of all mankind with the Good News of Jesus Christ, regardless of race, social or economic status. Toyin is committed to changing the world one person at a time and to seeing "the church" (Christ's Body) grow and produce true Christians that will light up the world by exceptional Christian living.

Toyin is well known as an international public speaker in conferences, seminars and leadership trainings all over Europe and North America. Through her prophetic declarations across the nations, lives have been changed and transformed by the power of God. She is married to Debo Taiwo, and they are blessed with children.

OTHER BOOKS

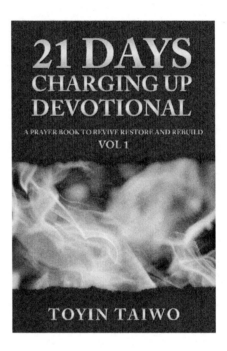

This book is an anointed manual with the capacity of reviving any Christian who is in a dry place or wants to go to the next level in intimacy with Christ in 21 days. It can be used for personal daily Prayers, in groups or in retreats.

"I woke up one beautiful Friday summer morning of July 2019 and noticed a sharp pain in my chest; just under the bust on both sides and I was severely breathless. Based on the amount of pain I was in; I knew I needed to see a GP urgently.

This book is a record of what I experienced physically, emotionally and spiritually and what I learnt during the six months of medical investigations, while I prayed and hoped for healing."

Alive By Grace was written to build up our faith in the healing power of God, so that we can lay claim to our divine healing which was concluded over 2000 years ago on the cross of Calvary

You can order these books from toyintaiwo.org or from Amazon.

Printed in Great Britain
by Amazon

21652281R00444